L'Entrée dans la Vallée de Lauterbrunnen vers le Staubbach et la Joungfrau.
Souvenirs des Costumes des XXII Cantons de la Suisse.

The world's largest collection of visual travel guides

SWITZERLAND

Updated by Erika Schumacher
Managing Editor: Dorothy Stannard

Editorial Director: Brian Bell

INSIGHT GUIDES
SWITZERLAND

CONTACTING THE EDITORS: Although every effort is made to provide accurate information in this publication, we live in a fast-changing world and would appreciate it if readers would call our attention to any errors or outdated information that may occur by writing to us at Apa Publications,
P.O. Box 7910, London SE1 1WE, England.
Fax: (44) 20-7403-0290.
e-mail: insight@apaguide.demon.co.uk.

First Edition 1993
Third Edition 2000

Distributed in the United States by
Langenscheidt Publishers Inc.
46–35 54th Road, Maspeth, NY 11378
Fax: (718) 784 -0640

Distributed in Canada by
Prologue Inc.
1650 Lionel Bertrand Blvd., Boisbriand
Québec, Canada J7H 1N7
Tel: (450) 434-0306. Fax: (450) 434-2627

Distributed in the UK & Ireland by
GeoCenter International Ltd
The Viables Centre, Harrow Way
Basingstoke, Hampshire RG22 4BJ
Fax: (44) 1256-817988

Distributed in Australia & New Zealand by
Hema Maps Pty. Ltd
24 Allgas Street, Slacks Creek 4127
Brisbane, Australia
Tel: (61) 7 3290 0322. Fax: (61) 7 3290 0478

Worldwide distribution enquiries:
APA Publications GmbH & Co. Verlag KG
(Singapore branch)
38 Joo Koon Road, Singapore 628990
Tel: (65) 8651600. Fax: (65) 8616438

Printed in Singapore by
Insight Print Services (Pte) Ltd
38 Joo Koon Road, Singapore 628990
Fax: (65) 8616438

This guidebook combines the interests and enthusiasms of two of the world's best known information providers: Insight Guides, whose range of titles has set the standard for visual travel guides since 1970, and Discovery Channel, the world's premier source of nonfiction television programming.

The editors of Insight Guides provide both practical advice and general understanding about a destination's history, culture, institutions and people. Discovery Channel and its Web site, www.discovery.com, help millions of viewers explore their world from the comfort of their own home and also encourage them to explore it firsthand.

In order to produce an authoritative and insightful guide to Switzerland, Apa Publications combined the skills of both its Munich and London editorial offices but decided to let the Swiss themselves do most of the talking. As project editor of the original book, Apa appointed **Marianne Flüeler-Grauwiler**, a journalist from Zurich running her own picture archive, Punktum. Her late husband, **Niklaus Flüeler**, was at that time scientific editor of the Zurich-based *Weltwoche*, and as editor of a varied assortment of publications on the country, she was able to assemble a team of expert authors. Her own written contributions were the chapters on bears, cows and Winterthur, and she invited her husband to provide chapters on Switzerland's sunny south, the Ticino, and Inner Switzerland, the geographical and historical heart of the country.

Flüeler-Grauwiler

Carter

For the English edition, Apa enlisted **Rowlinson Carter**, a journalist and television reporter whose narrative flair with the complexities of European history has enlivened many Insight Guides. Carter believes that history is not just about dates and events but is a story about people – their glory, bravery, villainy, vanity, lechery and greed. Swiss history *boring*? Not the way Carter tells it.

Carter also contributed a number of features, ranging from the Cresta Run to the Red Cross. For his introductory analysis of Swiss myths, he is indebted to the analysis by **Dieter Forte** in the German edition of this book. **Jost auf der Maur**, a native of St Gallen in the east of Switzerland, describes in the Places section of this book his city of residence, Basel. He is so fond of the city that he chose to remain there while commuting daily to his job on the editorial of the *Weltwoche* in Zurich.

Schwander

The journalist and publisher **Fridolin Leuzinger** also lives in Basel. Leuzinger was born in Glarus and has lived for many years in the Jura, which made him the ideal person to write on the Jura, the Foot of the Jura, and the little-known canton of Glarus.

The international banking centre of Zurich, Switzerland's largest city, is described by local man **Markus Mäder**. Since completing his studies in German and history, he has made his living from writing. He has spent time in India and China and has been awarded the Zurich Journalist Prize.

Heller

Andreas Heller, another *Weltwoche* man, was responsible for revealing the attractions of his own native lands, the highly varied region of Eastern Switzerland. The feature about the monastery town of St Gallen was supplied by the art historian **Klaus Speich**.

Very important for the Swiss and their identity are the cantons from which they hail. This attachment to hearth and home is no more pronounced than among the people of the Grisons, for whom the nicest thing about Zurich is Friday evening, when they can take the train back to their valleys. Certainly this holds true for **Margrit Sprecher**, who was born and raised in the town of Chur and claims to have relatives in all 150 valleys of the region. In this book, she describes her homeland in detail, as only a local could.

Sprecher

Just as proud of their roots and traditions are the people of the Valais. This region, full of of spellbinding mountains including the world-famous Matterhorn and Monte Rosa, is described by local man **Luzius Theler**, deputy editor of the local newspaper, the *Walliser Boten* (*Valais Messenger*).

Raphael Sennhauser describes the region around Lucerne in the chapter *The Reuss and the Aare*, and looks at the city of Berne before ascending to the legendary heights of the Bernese Oberland to take in the breathtaking scenery of the Jungfrau and the Eiger.

Marcel Schwander is something of a Swiss institution. He worked for more than 20 years in Lausanne as the Western Switzerland correspondent to the Zurich daily *Tages-Anzeiger*. In the course of his career, he has made a particular name for himself as *the* mediator between the different linguistic and cultural regions of the country and his writing has brought him a number of awards. In these pages he describes the delights of Western Switzerland and Geneva and its surroundings.

Insight Guide: Switzerland maintains the same high standard of photography for which this series has become renowned. Many of the pictures in the book are the work of photographers of the calibre of **Emanuel Ammon**, **Michael von Graffenried**, **Walter Imber** and **Alberto Venzago**. Other well-known Swiss photographers provided specialist material on themes such as mountains, churches, castles and palaces. Further contributions came from the Swiss Tourist Office and the Punktum Archives.

Thanks are due to the Swiss Tourist Office for providing material for the original Travel Tips, which was translated into English by **Susan Sting**. The Places section was translated by **David Ingram** and **Susan Bollans** under the supervision of **Tony Halliday.** This latest English edition, coordinated in Apa's London office by **Clare Griffiths**, has been updated by **Erika Schumacher**, who lives in Berne. Schumacher specialises in European tourism and culture and is the author of several travel guides to Switzerland.

CONTENTS

History

Features

Places

Preceding pages: an early souvenir: costumes from the twelve cantons; doorway in the Ardex Engeden region; Château Aigle; the mighty Matterhorn.

CONTENTS

Maps

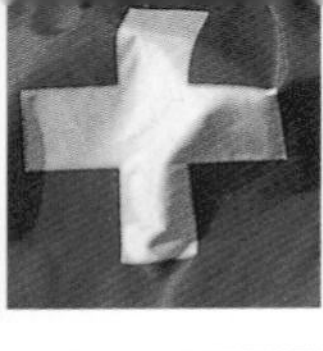

TRAVEL TIPS

Getting Acquainted

Planning the Trip

Practical Tips

Getting Around

Where to Stay

Where to Eat

Attractions

Sports

Shopping

Language

Further Reading

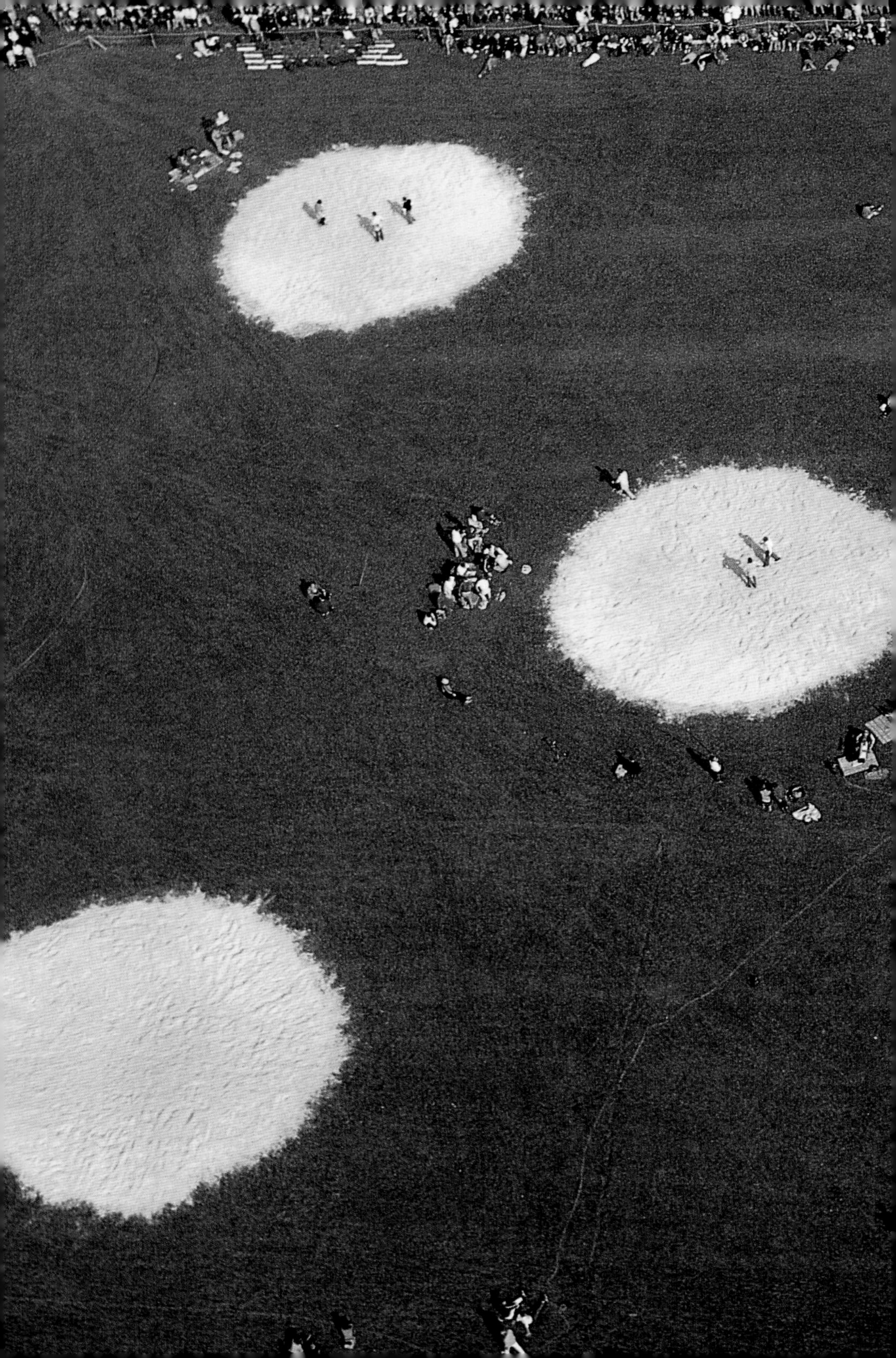

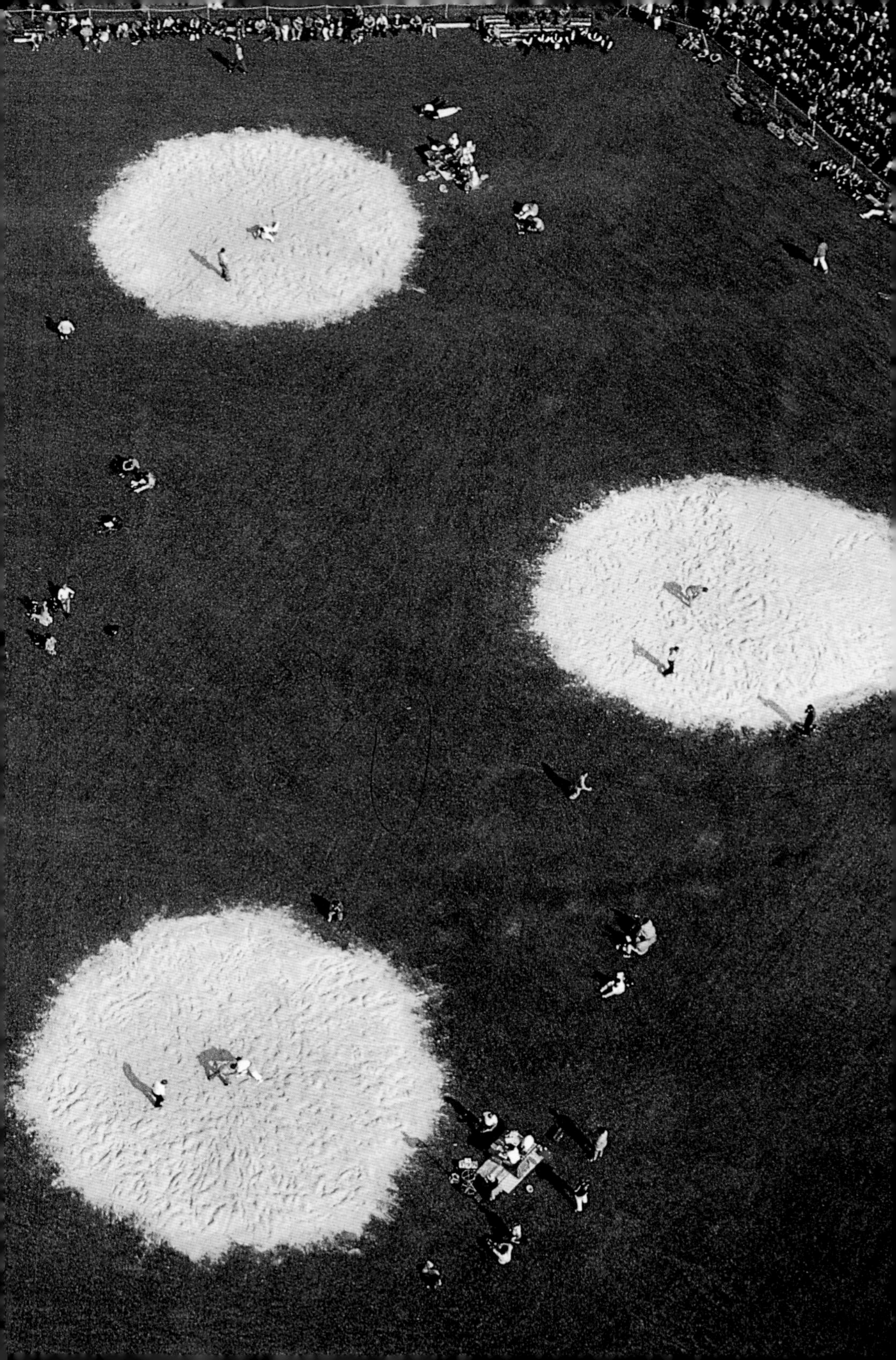

The popular image of Switzerland is so riddled with myth that books which propose to set the record straight hardly know where to begin. Most famously it has had to live with the dialogue of Orson Welles in *The Third Man*, to the effect that the whole product of Swiss civilisation was the cuckoo clock. Studying that civilisation another Englishman, an academic and a passionate Swissophile, confessed that he began to question whether Switzerland could or even should exist. The home of William Tell and the Gnomes of Zurich has no natural frontiers, no common language, culture or religion.

It has been a popular holiday destination since 1863 when Thomas Cook organised a package tour from Britain, the first in the history of the trade. Byron's *Prisoner of Chillon* and Conan Doyle's climactic struggle between Sherlock Holmes and Professor Moriarty at the Reichenbach Falls helped romanticise the mountainous country, as did Johanna Spyri with her popular Heidi stories, and Anita Brookner's *Hotel du Lac*. But visitors have not always been kind. Ernest Hemingway found the streets so clean he expressed a desire to foul them. F. Scott Fitzgerald maintained it was a country where very few things begin but many things end. Many famous people have passed through. But it is also unkind to say nothing begins here: the psychiatrist Karl Jung and the painter Paul Klee are among influential 20th-century Swiss.

The popular picture of bankers and milkmaids, chocolate and watches, ski resorts and yodelling is hard to reconcile even with the origins of Switzerland's name. It was the invention of the Habsburgs, who gave their motley collection of southern neighbours the name of their most pugnacious and troublesome members, the Schwyz. This played on on the German word for "sweat", implying a people not too fussy about personal hygiene.

A nation of mercenaries: The "peace-loving" Swiss were, up to about 150 years ago, almost constantly at war with themselves or others. Most of the foreign warfare had no bearing on Switzerland at all. Its men were the foremost mercenaries of the age, and for five centuries there was hardly a war in Europe in which Swiss troops were not to be found taking an enthusiastic part. The foreign wars which did impinge on Swiss territory were not to do with outsiders such as the land-hungry Habsburgs trying to detach tasty morsels, but the results of the attempts made to prevent the Swiss Confederation from breaking up simply of its own volition.

Preceding pages: alpine horn blowers; high flyer; cheese-maker; flagging cyclists; wrestling contest. Left, at the heart of Europe. Above, 19th-century view.

It suited Switzerland's powerful neighbours to have an adjacent neutral state – one border they didn't have to worry about and, *in extremis*, a convenient bolt-hole. Napoleon was the notable exception. He wanted to get his hands on Swiss gold to pay for his imperial ambitions and to hold the strategic mountain passes, but he also thought he could impose some order on the anarchy. He established the Helvetic Republic in 1798 with a constitution, the first Switzerland ever had, which sought to create a central government, uniform weights and measures, and so on. Six times between 1798 and 1803 he changed the constitution to accommodate Swiss peculiarities he had not anticipated. Then, after a final fling with his "Act of Mediation", he gave up.

The domestic squabbles included outright civil war, with mountain cantons fighting the lowlands on one occasion, peasant uprisings, and religious disputes of the type common in the heat of the Reformation. These were predictable causes. To Geneva, in contrast, belongs the distinction of civil unrest over whether it ought to have a theatre.

Somehow, the Swiss managed to pull themselves back from the brink of utter disaster. Religious conflict, for example, was restrained by comparison with the wars

which tore the rest of Europe apart. The things which did not happen in Switzerland were instrumental in making the country what it is. Nationalists of the 19th century advocated language ties as a prime criterion in setting the frontiers of modern Europe. The Swiss ignored this, as they did the various other arguments trotted out to promote nationalism. They also spurned the idea that centralised government was rational and desirable or that a monarch, a professional army or a grandiose capital was necessary.

Switzerland was in 1848 the most democratic state in Europe, yet it was not until 1971 that women were given the vote at national level. Even then it was too revolutionary a step for one particular canton, which continued to do without women voters for some years afterwards. The object, it was said, was not to deny women the right of self-determination but to prevent the dilution of the male "sabre", the symbol of the right to vote at the annual assemblies which in some cantons exercise direct power over local affairs. The women in question took this bit of political science to the supreme court where, with due reference to the federal constitution, they won the right to vote in 1990.

I spy troublemakers: The paragon of democracy took another bad knock in recent years when what everyone already knew was publicly revealed: at one time or another many Swiss people, either as part of their job or voluntarily, had spied on their fellow citizens and passed on details of activities which were considered to be less than exemplary to the police. All the information went into the secret files the government had been keeping since the war on hundreds of thousands of citizens and foreigners. It didn't much matter, those responsible protested. So much information had been collected, and so much of it was spurious, that it had never been properly processed.

"The Swiss believe," says one of them, "that they are rational and realistic. They are not. They will take pains to define a principle, immediately think of a dozen exceptions to the rule, then say it's better to use common sense. In other words, they believe in the principle of no principles.

"The attitude of a Swiss to Switzerland is opposition to a country he basically approves of. By opposing anything and everything, he remains neutral. If you mention to someone who lives in Basel that you think it is a pleasant place in which to live, he will give you a list of what's wrong with it. If you say you don't like Basel, you'll get a list of all its good points."

The English academic who was temporarily unsettled by doubts about whether Switzerland ought to exist eventually concluded that by the sheer scale of its accumulated improbabilities – a magnet for myths – the country stands as a monumental challenge to comfortable clichés.

Left, double protection. Right, the game of Jass.

CANTONES XIII OHRT der EIDGENOSSSCHAFT 1 ZURICH 2 BERN 3 LUCERN 4 URI 5 SCHWEIZ 6 UNDE
GALLEN ABT
N STATT 3 PUNDTEN 4 WALLIS 5 MULHAUSEN 6 BIEL 7 NEUBURG NEUFCHATEL 8 GENFF GENEVE 9 BISCHOFF BASEL
FREYE AMPTER
IN THAL
BADEN
ESCHALENS 4 ORBE 5 GRANSON
1 BELLINZONA 2 RIVIERA 3 VALLEBREGNIA PALENSERTHAL
GASTER CASTRA
NOUVELLE CARTE
DE LA
SUISSE
Divisées en ses
TREIZE CANTONS
A AMSTERDAM
VIER OSTERR
BOURGOGNE
BAILLADE DE GEX
LEMANUS LACUS LAC DE GENEVE
SAVOYE
MILANE

ZUG 8 GLARUS 9 BASEL 10 FREIBURG 11 SOLOTHURN 12 SCHAFFHAUSEN 13 APPENZELL. CONFOEDERATI ZUGEWANDTE OHRT

ensibus, Subsylvanis, Tugiensibus, Glaronensibus, qui VII Cantones veteres, VII alte Ohrt vulgo vocantur, parent 1 THURGEU, adscitis in criminalibus Bernensibus, Friburgensibus, et Solodorensibus 2 SARGANS

risdiction agnoscunt Præfecturæ Transalpinæ 1 LAUIS LUGANO 2 LUGGARUS LOCARNO 3 MENDRIS 4 MEINTHAL Bernensium et Friburgensium Dominio subsunt 1 MURTEN 2 SCHWARZENBURG

sunt 1 RAPERSCHWEIL 2 ENGELBERG 3 GERSAU. AMSTELODAMI Apud JOANNEM COVENS, et CORNELIUM MORTIER, Geographos.

Joh. Witt

During the unusually severe winter of 1853 the level of Zurich lake fell to an unprecedented level, exposing a considerable expanse of sticky mud around the shoreline. Enterprising residents realised that shoring up the perimeter would provide a windfall of free land, and with that they got busy with spade and shovel.

The eager opportunists of Obermeilen, a village about 12 miles from Zurich, found their digging impeded by what appeared to be a forest of wooden props just beneath the surface. Someone had the sense to summon the distinguished Dr Ferdinand Keller from Zurich and he, probably with the ancient Greek historian Herodotus in mind, was able to proclaim the discovery of one of the vital missing links in Switzerland's prehistory. The props, he concluded, were evidence of an ancient Celtic tribe who built their houses on stilts over water.

Tools found among the props were made of stone and bone rather than metal, indicating a date earlier than the Bronze Age, which is generally put at about 1500 BC onwards. Traces of human presence in Switzerland of course go back much farther. A fragment of jaw found in the Jura has been identified as belonging to a woman who lived about 50,000 years ago; a more complete skull from Neuchâtel is that of a young Cro-Magnon adult of about 12,000 BC. Caves which housed prehistoric troglodytes have been found near Geneva, Villeneuve and Thayngen. The special significance of the submerged props near Obermeilen was as evidence of people who constructed their homes, and quite elaborate ones at that.

Hundreds of similar aquatic villages, some with as many as 40,000 piles driven into the mud, have subsequently been discovered in lakes, rivers and swamps. A glimpse of life in such villages is provided by Herodotus, albeit at a rather later date: "The houses of these lake-dwellers are actually in the water, and stand on platforms supported on long piles and approached from the land by a single narrow bridge... Every man drives in three piles for each wife he marries – and they all have a great many wives. Each member of the tribe has his own hut on one of the platforms, with a trap-door opening on to the water underneath. To prevent their babies from tumbling in, they tie a string to their feet."

The village Herodotus saw was in Macedonia. The Swiss lake-dwellers, like the troglodytes before them and the so-called Beaker people afterwards, remain shrouded in prehistory. The transition to recorded history begins with Roman literature of the 1st century BC. The lake-dwellers had by then been replaced by other Celts and a branch of the Etruscans, the Rhaeti. The Helvetii were the most powerful of the Celtic tribes and lived between Lakes Constance and Geneva, in the Alps and on the Jura. By 58 BC, however, pressure from German tribes had persuaded them to destroy the 12 towns and 400 villages they occupied and to migrate en masse to Gaul. With their bridges burnt behind them, 368,000 men, women and chil-

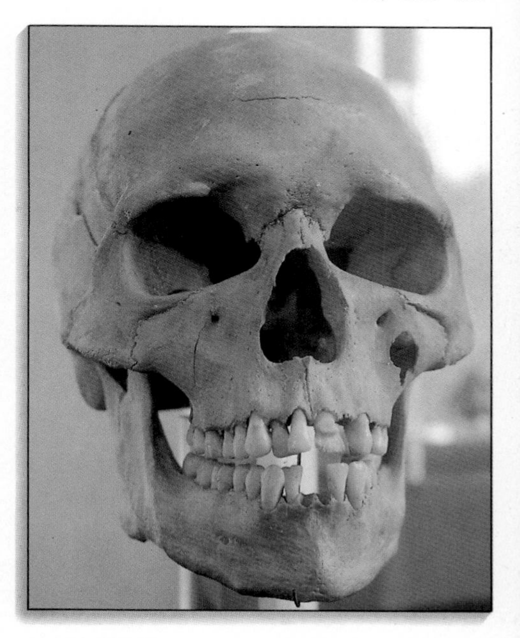

Preceding pages: map of of the Swiss Confederation when it had 13 members. Left, the Celt as romanticised in painting, an image used on the Swiss two-franc, one-franc and 50-rappen coins. Above, a 12,000-year-old skull from the Jura.

dren assembled in Geneva on 28 March 58 BC for the exodus, only to find their exit across the Rhone barred.

The barrier was Julius Caesar and his army, then embarking on his conquest of Gaul. Caesar's main concern was that the troublesome German tribes would fill the vacuum left behind by the Helvetii's departure and pose an intolerable threat to the borders of the new Roman province. The emigrants managed to slip past the Roman cordon but they were pursued and caught at Bibracte, near the modern town of Autun in Burgundy.

In his *Commentaries on the Gallic Wars*, Caesar pays tribute to the fighting spirit of

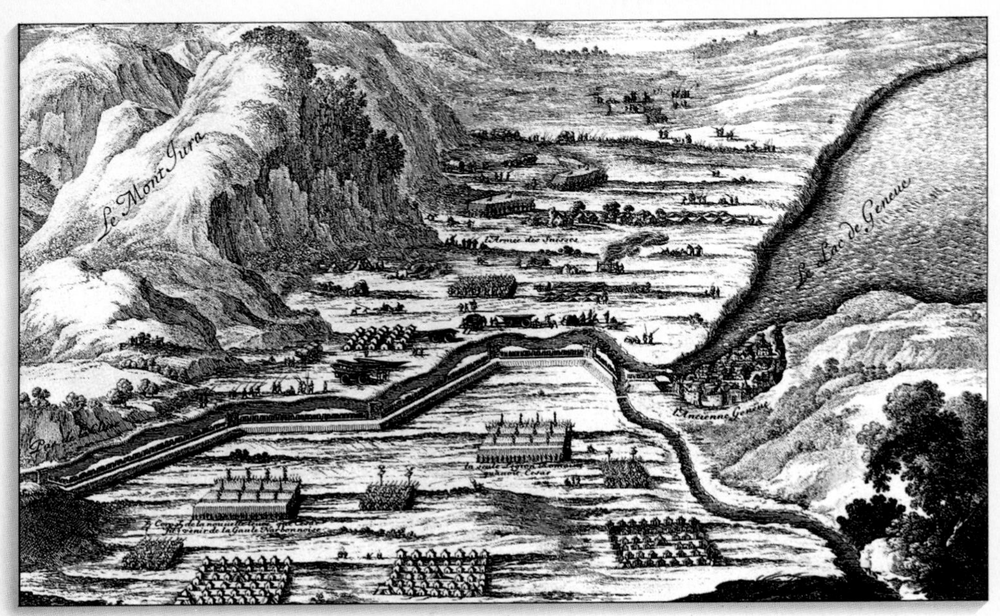

the Helvetii, whose last stand was behind a makeshift barricade of ox-carts. Their resistance held out from 1 p.m. until sunset, but the outcome against the drilled legions was inevitable and they were obliged to return whence they had come, albeit with the promise of Roman protection in future and a large measure of self-government in what became known as Helvetia.

The Etruscan Rhaeti refused to succumb to Rome for another 40 years, and one of the more colourful accounts of their resistance has Rhaeti women, frustrated by their lack of weapons, hurling their sucking children at the conquerors "through sheer exasperation". Like the Helvetii, however, the Rhaeti reached a *modus vivendi* with the Romans, and the Romansch language still spoken in Graubünden is a combination of Roman Latin and the Tuscan dialect of the Rhaeti.

As the Swiss province lay between Italy and the Roman defensive lines along the Rhine and Danube, the Romans fortified the key mountain passes and applied all their road-building skills to the territory. Switzerland is much richer in Roman remains than is popularly supposed. Baden (literally "bathing"), a well-known spa near Zurich, was described by Tacitus in his day as "a place which during long years of peace had grown to be a city, much frequented on account of the attraction of its salubrious waters." The greatest Roman city, though, was Aventicum, the modern Avenches, where a complex of splendid palaces, temples and triumphal arches was enclosed by a wall some 7 km (4 miles) in circumference.

Roman ruins bear testimony to the empire buckling under the pressure of the Germanic tribes at the turn of the 5th century. The Alemanni crossed the Rhine and the Jura to take possession of northern Switzerland, the Burgundians seized the south. Secure in the mountain fastnesses of Graubünden, the Rhaeti alone escaped almost untouched, whereas what is now Ticino was driven closer to Italy, sharing that country's fate under the Ostrogoths and Lombards until well into the Middle Ages. Relatively little is known about this transition, but the foundations were clearly laid for the German-French-Romansch-Italian components of modern Switzerland.

The mutual hostility of Alemanni and Burgundians was tempered by the common threat of the Franks under Clovis, but to no avail. The Franks were routed in 469; the Burgundians in 534 at Autun, where the Romans had turned back their Celtic predecessors. The Burgundian King Sigismund was ignominiously dumped in a well together with his family. The whole of modern Switzerland, Ticino excepted, was again united in subjugation to a single power, its future bound up with the varying vicissitudes of the Merovingian, Carolingian and Frankish rulers for centuries to come.

Clovis had sworn that if blessed with victory over the Alemanni he would convert to Christianity, and he was duly baptised on Christmas Day, 496. As the champion of orthodox Christianity, he was as opposed to the heretical Arian Christians as he was to heathens. The Burgundians were numbered among the former, the Alemanni among the latter, so one way or the other the history of Switzerland from the Merovingian kings to Charlemagne's coronation as Holy Roman Emperor in 800 was closely bound to the religious upheavals of the age.

According to tradition, Christianity first put in an appearance in Roman Helvetia in the person of Mauritius, the commander of a Christian legion posted there from Egypt. He fell victim to a purge of Christians by the Emperor Maximian and was executed at a place whose name was later changed to St Maurice to honour his martyrdom. In any case, it seems that Switzerland had a bishop, either Theodor or Theodul, as early as 381, In general, however, this was a false dawn for the new religion and over the course of a couple of centuries the remnants seem to have been infused with a good deal of heresy.

Band of Irish monks: The task of reasserting orthodoxy in Switzerland fell, curiously, to a caravan of tattooed, long-haired Irish monks who set out in 610 under the leadership of St Columba, armed with stout sticks and with a spare pair of boots slung round their necks. They followed the course of the Limmat River past Zurich to the lakeside village of Tuggen. "This place pleased them," says a chronicle of 771, "but not the evil ways of the dwellers. Cruelty and mischief ruled in their midst, and they were given over unto heathen superstitions." These included toasting their gods with beer. Gall, Columba's zealous assistant, threw the images of the local gods and the drinking vessels into the lake, whereupon the enraged Alemanni drove them away.

The monks transferred their attention to Pregentia (Bregenz), which they were advised was a hotbed of heathen practices. Gall found this to be true and again smashed the local gods, this time dumping the pieces in Lake Constance. "Then did a part of the people confess their sins and believed, but the others went away in anger and filled with wrath." Ordered out of the country for his actions, Columba led his band of monks across the Alps into Italy, but the fiery Gall was too unwell to travel and stayed behind in the forest east of Arbon. In 614 he founded the famous monastery which bears his name.

The monastery of St Gallen was later taken over by the Benedictine order and flourished between the 8th and 10th centu-

Left, the Battle of Bribacte; Caesar and the Helvetii near Geneva. Above, Clovis I.

ries as one of the greatest seats of learning in Europe. It produced the three famous Notkers: Notker the Stammerer, a composer of music; Notker the Physician, a genuine pioneer of modern medicine; and Notker the Thick-Lipped, one of the first to write prose in German. The monastery also produced the five Ekkeharts, one of whom was tainted by allegations of improper conduct with one of his pupils, the "beautiful but eccentric" dowager Duchess of Alemannia.

Alemannia, which had so doggedly resisted Christianity, became the seat of other great monasteries: Rheinau, founded in 724 by the Visigoth Pirminius, Pfäfers and Einsiedeln. Each of these monasteries established a network of parish churches which accelerated the complete conversion of Switzerland, effected a revolution in agriculture and cleared huge expanses of forest.

Fountain of intellectual life: As the Merovingian kingdom collapsed under the weight of its crimes and incapacity, it split into what were known as Austrasia and Neustria, in effect the same Burgundian-Alemannic dichotomy which existed in microcosm in Switzerland. Eventually the two halves were reunited as the Kingdom of the Franks under Charles, later Charlemagne, in 771. The future Holy Roman Emperor, crowned by Pope Hadrian in 800, endeared himself to the Swiss by spending what seemed to be a flatteringly disproportionate amount of his time in their little corner of empire. Zurich still likes to think of Charlemagne as the "fountain" of its intellectual life.

Under Charlemagne's administration, Switzerland was divided into shires, from which many of the present canton names are derived. Notker the Stammerer, whom we have already met as a monk at the St Gallen monastery, wrote a gushing life of Charlemagne which glorified the contributory role played by an Alemanni hero, Eishere the Giant. He fought at the emperor's side against the Avars, mowing down the enemy "like grass" and at one point stringing on his lance "some six or eight pygmy toads of Bohemians as if they were larks, carrying them hither and thither, not knowing what they were squawking about."

Another story is told of a bell which Charlemagne placed outside his Swiss residence so anyone who had a grievance could ring it for an imperial audience. One day, the bell rang repeatedly while he was having dinner with his queen but the servants did nothing about it. "I am sure there is some poor man you don't wish me to see," said the emperor, rising from the table. He found hanging on to the bell rope a large snake. Coiling in greeting, the snake led the way to a clump of nettles where a toad had usurped its nest and was sitting on its eggs. The emperor ordered the toad to be killed and quartered. The servants at dinner the next day scattered when the same snake entered the hall. It scaled the table to slither across and deposit in Charlemagne's goblet a beautiful jewel. It then withdrew, bowing graciously to the royal couple. The moral of this story does not now leap off the page, but the tale is quoted as evidence of mutual affection between Charlemagne and his Swiss subjects.

Conflict with the pope: The role of Holy Roman Emperor put Charlemagne almost on a level with the Pope, who, however, exceeded the secular power of ordinary kings by virtue of vast papal estates and wealth. The papacy and the imperial throne were, in short, closely-matched rivals for the leadership of the western world. As long as Charlemagne and Pope Hadrian remained on fairly friendly terms, conflict did not materialise, but the danger signs were evident in Switzerland. Clerical land barons were not inclined to take their orders from the secular counts. They insisted on a legal immunity which made them answerable only to the imperial crown. An ambiguous chain of command spelt potential trouble.

The threat was realised soon after Charlemagne's death in 814. His heir, Ludwig the Pious, was barely able to contain four rebellious sons, and on his death the empire was carved up among the three survivors: Lothar, Ludwig the German and Charles the Bald. The division, ratified by the Treaty of Verdun in 834, split Switzerland along the old lines. The Teutonic Alemanni joined the other subjects of Ludwig the German, the Romanised Burgundians those of Lothar.

The figure of the beloved Queen Bertha of Burgundy emerges in serene contrast to the tumultuous intrigue on both sides of the fence. She is represented in popular tradition as riding benignly among her people, dispensing sensible advice and forever spinning from her distaff. When once she rewarded a young shepherdess for conscientiously spinning away while keeping an eye on her flock, her ladies-in-waiting appeared en masse before her, all of them spinning in the hope that they, too, would be given presents. "My ladies," said the wise Bertha, "you come too late. The young peasant girl came first, and like Jacob, she has taken away my blessing."

The discovery of a sarcophagus containing a woman's bones in the Abbey at Payerne in 1817 caused considerable excitement because Bertha's unrelenting goodness had maintained a loyal band of admirers down the ages. The bones were proclaimed as hers, and a wooden contraption was assumed to be her saddle, especially as it had a hole which would have held the beloved distaff. Unhappily, archaeologists subsequently established that the wood was not old enough to have belonged to Bertha nor did it constitute a saddle. It was, in fact, a late-medieval instrument of torture.

The Kingdom of Burgundy, of which the Swiss "Kingdom of Transjurane" was but a small portion, eventually succumbed to the sheer incompetence of its successive kings and in 1032 it was swallowed up by Conrad II of Germany after the battle of Morat. Swiss Alemannia fared little better. Two attempts to revive an independent Duchy of Alemannia failed, so that the two principal parts of Switzerland fell under the sway of the German empire. Ticino, in the south, was wrapped up in Italian affairs, while the three

Far left, Lombard cross from the 7th century. Left, Carolingian monastery of Müstair (800). Above, Charlemagne, the Holy Roman Emperor.

so-called Forest Cantons of Switzerland were considered too remote to be of interest.

During the 12th and 13th centuries, practically the whole of Switzerland was under the supreme rule of the German kings and emperors, but beneath that was a typical patchwork of feudalism which produced four great families, each of whom attempted to wrest Switzerland for itself. All failed utterly, although two of them, the Savoys and Habsburgs, ended up elsewhere with a kingdom (Italy) and a dynastic empire (Austria-Hungary) apiece.

The first of these ambitious houses, the Zähringers, showed its hand in the almighty 11th-century struggle between Henry IV – both King of Germany and Holy Roman Emperor – and Pope Gregory VII. Even the remotest Swiss Alpine valleys took sides, and when the dust settled the Hohenstaufen family emerged as the shaky holders of the Duchy of Alemannia while the Zähringers had created a power-base in the town and estates of Zurich, one which they used as a springboard to become the masters of almost all of modern Switzerland by 1127. The system of defence with which the Zähringers attempted to consolidate their hold had a profound effect on the future shape of the country. They fortified a number of strategic villages and converted them into cities with chartered privileges. A small settlement on the banks of the Sarine became Fribourg, others grew into Burgdorf, Morat and Thun. The centre of the defensive line between Fribourg and Burgdorf necessitated a strong-point which became Berne.

The derivation of the name Berne subsequently gave rise to considerable conjecture. A 15th-century chronicler, Justinger, said that the city's founder, Berchthold V, decided to name it after the next animal caught in the oak forest on the site. The beast in question was a bear (Bär), hence Berne. This story at least ties in with the bear represented on the city's coat-of-arms, but it seems more likely that "Bern" was simply the German rendition of the Italian "Verona", a city which had formerly been a Zähringer possession.

A further 100 or more fledgling towns were founded in the following century, and it was reckoned that a traveller in the Lowlands passed a town gate every 20 km (13 miles) or so. Not all survived, but the successful ones steadily attained a measure of independence which they were ready to defend against any aggressor. As they were seldom strong enough to do so alone, they sought alliances with kindred communities or powerful princes, and Switzerland began to resemble a scaled-down version of the Greek city-states. The urban population remained relatively modest: by the end of the Middle Ages, Basle had between 9,000 and 12,000 inhabitants; Geneva, Zurich, Berne, Lausanne and Fribourg about 5,000 each.

Inspiring sermons: The founding of future cities aside, 12th-century Switzerland was marked by the passions aroused by the French-led second crusade. The Swiss were drawn in by the stirring sermons of a French Cistercian monk, Bernard de Clairvaux. "Your land is fertile," he told them, "and the world is filled with the reputation of your valour. Ye soldiers of Christ, arise and hurl down the enemies of the Cross!" To settle any doubts about the nobility of the cause,

Bernard is reputed to have performed a few exemplary miracles, restoring sight to the blind, putting cripples back on their feet, and so on. "*Kyrie eleison*, the saints are with us," the congregation roared. The French-speaking Swiss took up the cause more exuberantly than the German; nevertheless a procession of princes, nobles, knights and lesser beings set off on the long tramp to Palestine, many of them never to return.

Berchtold V's death in 1218 without issue was the recipe for a scramble among a crowd of relatives who, in their eagerness, seem to have been out-manoeuvred by the Counts of Kyburg, a family of uncertain origins whose castle stands near Winterthur. Both Count Hartmann the Elder and his nephew, Hartmann the Younger, also died without issue, however, and possession of the estates became a trial of strength between two formidable rivals, the Savoys and Habsburgs.

Thomas of Savoy had established a foothold for his still-obscure family on the northern shore of Lake Geneva. His son, Peter, continued these efforts first by an advantageous marriage with the heiress of Faucigny and then by the blatant intimidation of lesser neighbours. His horizons were considerably broadened by the marriage of his niece Eleanor, to Henry III of England and "he also became intimately associated with that country", so much so that on a visit to London he was created Duke of Richmond and his brother, Boniface, was made Archbishop of Canterbury.

Peter divided his time between collecting feudal estates, ending up as master of the Lower Rhône Valley and Vaud, and acting as a sort of adviser to the English crown. His services were clearly valued in England because Henry III gave him a plot of land in London on which to build a palace. The plot was on the Strand; it is still something of a landmark, the site of the Savoy Hotel.

Peter may have spent rather too much time in England. Count Rudolf of Habsburg took advantage of his absence to march on Vaud and was already encamped at Chillon before Peter could muster his forces. Leaving his army at Villeneuve, Peter personally went out to survey the opposition. He returned to his camp in high spirits. "What news?" his men asked. "Good news," he replied, "for if God be with us and you behave like men, the enemy is ours." At which, the *Chronicle of Savoy* records, "they all cried with one accord, 'Sir, you have but to command'." Peter led his men on the encampment with none of the customary blowing of trumpets. They achieved total surprise, the enemy being overwhelmed while "half awake and half asleep". Some 80 nobles were taken prisoner and conducted to the castle of Chillon; in the spirit of the chivalric age, however, they were treated on arrival to a splendid banquet.

Peter did not have long to relish his vic-

Left, fortified cave dwellings of Wichenstein in canton St Gallen dating from 12th/13th century. Above, a Swiss knight in battle.

tory. He died a few months later (in 1268) on his way home from a trip to Italy. His achievements were squandered by the gross incompetence of his brother, Philip. The family property in England passed to Queen Eleanor, although not the palace, the site of the future hotel. It went as an endowment to a hospice already riding on a reputation as the provider of life-saving brandy carried by dogs on the Great St Bernard Pass.

The future of Switzerland hung in the balance and the territory might easily have disintegrated into literally hundreds of pieces. Added to all the independently-minded new towns were scores of princelings not knowing which way to turn during the deadlock over the succession to the Kingdom of Germany and the Holy Roman Empire, which then amounted to almost the same thing. The powerful church estates, recognising no temporal authority within the country, were torn between loyalty to the semi-divine imperial crown and the papacy.

Thrust to greatness: Pope Gregory's ultimatum to the German princes was that if they could not agree among themselves on a new emperor he would impose one. Their response was to submit the name of a supposed nonentity whom they could keep under their thumb. The nominee was Count Rudolf of Habsburg, then 55 years of age. He could number among his accomplishments "great slaughter" of forces loyal to troublesome bishops, a stirring battle (at Zurich's behest) against the unsavoury Count of Regensburg, and the capture of a few castles. In the Terrible Times, however, that made him a rather ordinary German princeling and not necessarily imperial material. The electors may have been further deceived by his appearance. He was amazingly tall and as thin as a rake. His tiny head, completely bald, was thrown out of balance by a nose so large that if he turned sideways while riding along a narrow track, so it was said, it blocked riders coming the other way. His complexion was pale, his expression grave, and he tended to wear peasant dress rather than royal regalia. This was the man destined to become, rather unfairly, the pantomime villain of Swiss history, the arch-enemy of William Tell.

Rudolf had inherited some Swiss estates and was actually besieging the Bishop of Basel over a long-standing dispute when a messenger arrived in the middle of the night with the news that he had been elected to the imperial throne. Rudolf, roused from his tent, thought the messenger must be joking. "It would be farthest from my thoughts to joke with you, mightiest of all lords," the messenger replied solemnly.

Newly crowned, Rudolf set about laying the foundations of the great Habsburg dynasty. His aims in Switzerland were first to cut Philip of Savoy down to size and then to acquire as much land as he could, especially from the abbeys. The abbots of St Gallen were forced to cede land and farms; the monastery of Murbach, then in financial difficulties, was made to surrender Lucerne. Any estate whose ownership was in doubt went straight into the Habsburg bag. Rudolf's gobbling up of Switzerland is considered the catalyst of Swiss political history. All that had gone before – the Helvetian era, the Roman occupation, the Alemannian and Burgundian settlements, the supremacy of the Franks, the incorporation into the German Empire and the rise of the independent nobles – served merely as a prologue.

"There is no period in all history so generally misunderstood as that which marks the origin of the Swiss Confederation," says a Swiss historian, "principally on account of the false versions which unscrupulous chroniclers have handed down to us.

In fact, so great is this want of records, and so confusing are the traditions, that the dawn of Swiss history is probably doomed to remain shrouded in a certain amount of obscurity."

The setting for these contentious events is the three so-called Forest Cantons – Unterwalden, Schwyz and Uri – on Lake Lucerne, north of the Alps. These have barely been mentioned in this history so far because they existed as a world apart from other cantons, an idyllic spot which has traditionally tested the lyrical powers of poets and patriots. The lyricism does not stop with the scenery. "Sinewy, robust, quick, shrewd, (the inhabitants) are persevering, fearless, bold, and self-reliant; they are yet simple in their habits, artless in manner, pious... Ever exposed to danger, their struggles with nature for the supply of their daily wants have increased their strength of body, brought out their mettle, and quickened their natural intelligence." Such a man was William Tell – if there ever was a William Tell.

A 15th-century theory about the origins of the people of the Forest Cantons started the confusion about what really happened. It postulated that they were Swedes, a startling thought which proved to have no sounder basis than the similarity between the Latin names given to the inhabitants of Schwyz and of Sweden, Schwidones and Schwedones. Although the theory was later discredited, it seems that the people concerned quite liked the idea of Viking links.

It is not now questioned that they were actually Alemanni. What distinguished them from the rest of the nation was that in their remote station they had escaped rigorous feudalism. Since time immemorial the valleys of Uri and Schwyz had enjoyed virtual self-government under popular assemblies – *Markgenossenschaft* – which ran contrary to the structured tiers of feudalism.

The Forest Cantons were not entirely divorced from feudalism, however, because their ultimate "ownership" was passed around in the manner of the times. Louis the German, whom we have previously met as one of Charlemagne's grandsons, gave a large part of Uri, for example, to the Abbey of Our Lady at Zurich, which he founded for his daughters almost as the prototype for Switzerland's finishing schools for well-born, or anyway well-heeled, young ladies. The tax revenues provided them with an income, and as long as the money kept coming the nuns were probably not too bothered about the day-to-day running of the land.

Subsequent events in Uri are rather confusing and as such are typical of the general mêlée surrounding the birth of the Swiss Confederation. While the nuns of the Abbey of Our Lady collected the money, political overlordship was given first to the Zähringers and then, when that family petered out, to the Habsburgs when they acquired the governship of Zürichgau, an extensive district which included all three Forest Cantons.

The fact that most of the population were free peasants, and thus had the right to bear arms and to serve abroad gave them delusions of grandeur and importance. They believed they were free of all feudal obligations except, as has been seen in the context of ambiguous chains of command, to the emperor himself. The coronation of Rudolf as Emperor brought matters to a head: the emperor whom they were prepared to love, and the titular overlord whom they instinctively hated, were at a stroke one and the same person. Which would it be: love or hate?

The traditional version of events provides one answer. It says that Rudolf could have been loved if he had been willing to adjudicate personally over the theft of goats and other items of parochial business, but as emperor he was far too busy. He appointed agents to deal with such things, and they were not good enough for the proud free peasants. The conventional view is that the agents were "covetous and cruel tyrants who taxed, fined, imprisoned, and reviled the unfortunate inhabitants".

Right, William Tell shoots an apple off his own son's head, and bags a place in history.

The worst of these was a bailiff named Gessler, who thought it preposterous that a Schwyz peasant named Werner Stauffacher should presume to live in a fine stone-built house. Unforgivably, he said as much to Stauffacher's face.

Another of these tyrants, a certain Landenberg, was enraged when one of his servants was struck and had a finger broken while trying to unyoke some oxen he was expropriating from an Unterwalden farmer. The farmer's son, young Arnold, who struck the blow, ran away. Landenberg's response was to have the father's eyes put out. The offended home-owner, the fugitive son of the blinded farmer and an equally disgruntled resident of Uri, Walter Furst, met up at Rütli, a meadow above Uri lake, and there plotted their revenge. The number of dissidents grew until there were 33, "their hearts swelling with love for their country and hatred against tyranny".

Enter William Tell: In the meantime, Gessler was being as haughty and spiteful as ever. In the town of Altdorf in Uri he placed his hat on a pole in the marketplace and gave orders that all passing should show due reverence to it. William Tell now makes his debut by blatantly ignoring the hat and being arrested. The biting sarcasm in the exchange between a furious Gessler and the unrepentant Tell gets lost in translation, but the well-known outcome was Tell being ordered to shoot an apple off his son's head. The arrow was right on target, but that led to questions about a second arrow in Tell's quiver. "Had I injured my child," Tell told Gessler, "this second shaft should not have missed thy heart." Right, said the governor, lock him up!

Tell was taken in chains to Gessler's dungeon in Axenstein, which meant crossing the lake by boat. When a violent storm threatened to engulf the boat, Tell was unbound to take the helm. He was evidently as expert with boats as he was with bow and arrow. On reaching the shore he was able to jump out and push the boat adrift with his captors, including the appalling Gessler, still in it. Gessler and crew managed to save themselves, but by then Tell had vanished. He had not gone far, however. Tell knew the route Gessler would take back to his castle, and he was lying in ambush at a suitable spot near Küssnacht when the governor appeared. The arrow held in reserve found its mark through Gessler's heart. "This is Tell's shaft," gasped the dying Gessler.

The basic story and various embellishments, culminating in the dissidents in the meadow at Rütli taking their cue from Tell and launching a full-scale rebellion, paint a picture of freedom-loving Alpine republicans who were willing to submit themselves to a decent German king like Frederick II but were more than capable of delivering a devastating riposte to tyrants like the ghastly Habsburgs. "All this seems to have been invented," observed the Swiss historian François Guilliman in a private letter in 1607, "to nourish hatred against Austria."

Ironically, Guilliman was one of those responsible for nurturing the figure of William Tell, but the story owes its universal currency to a play by Schiller in 1804 and Rossini's well-known opera, which was first performed in 1829. Schiller, a German, never set foot in Switzerland and his knowledge of Swiss history was largely gleaned from Johannes von Müller's *History of Switzerland*, which appeared during the French Revolution. The William Tell story, which von Müller believed absolutely, was offered as Switzerland's contribution to the rampant spirit of Liberty, Equality and Fraternity.

"The first to challenge the fact that there ever was a man named William Tell, or a bailiff named Gessler," says the waspish Herold, "was saved from national disgrace and possible lynching only by the fact that his books were so dull and unreadable that few people were aware of their existence." His research was taken up by other historians, however, and the discovery of the original document of the Pact of 1291, detailed in the next chapter, swung responsible opinion behind Voltaire's observation that "this whole business about the apple is highly suspect". It transpired that very similar legends (the archer, the object on his son's head, the second arrow held in reserve) crop up in mythology over northern and central Europe and even in Asia Minor.

The truth of the matter would seem to be that the birth of Swiss liberty in 1291 was not a spontaneous explosion against Habsburg tyranny but a refinement of earlier alliances among communities who probably derived the idea of such leagues from Italy. In fact, some say, there was no Habsburg tyranny. Nevertheless, the inhabitants of the Forest Cantons would have had enough to alarm them in the remorseless expansion of the Habsburg estates which created a *de facto* cordon around them. The Swiss whom William Tell symbolised were undoubtedly exceptionally sensitive to the threat of outside interference: "Perched on their rocks, they developed the mentality of castle-owners rather than reasonable subjects."

Right, the most famous Swiss of all: William Tell, hero of Schiller's play and Rossini's opera.

The three Forest Cantons signed their "Perpetual League" pact on 15 July 1291, a little more than a fortnight after Rudolf's death. "Therefore, know all men," it proclaimed in Latin, "that the people of the valley of Uri, the democracy of the valley of Schwyz, and the community of the moutaineers of the Lower Valley, seeing the malice of the age, in order that they may better defend themselves and their own, and better preserve them in proper condition, have promised in good faith to assist each other with aid, with every counsel and every favour, with person and goods, within the valleys and without, with might and main, against one and all, who may inflict upon any one of them any violence, molestation or injury, or may plot any evil against their persons or goods..."

The declaration went on to lay down the basis of a legal code with the proviso that "we will accept or receive no judge in the aforesaid valleys, who shall have obtained his office for any price, or for money in any way whatever, or one who shall not be a native or a resident with us."

Rudolf died bitterly disappointed that he had not been able to secure the non-hereditary succession to the imperial throne for his son Albrecht, and the family reverted to being mere dukes when the crown went instead to Adolf of Nassau. The loss of imperial status made the Habsburgs a less imposing force in the eyes of the Swiss Confederation, which almost immediately entered into an alliance with Zurich and an anti-Habsburg coalition which sprang up in eastern Switzerland.

Zurich felt emboldened to attack Winter–thur, a Habsburg town, in 1292 and was severely defeated. The Habsburg Duke Albert added to the injury with a siege of Zurich, only to call it off when it appeared that the defenders had mustered a massive force. Tradition has it that the additional legions drawn up in battle array on the Lindenhof were actually the women of the city wearing armour and helmets.

Left, the Oath at Rütli, as perceived at the time of the French Revolution. Above, the Swiss "family tree" up to 1815.

Duke Albrecht regained the crown for the Habsburgs and, the Swiss feared, wished to settle a score with them. He was prevented from doing so by his nephew and a gang of Swiss nobles who waylaid him within sight of the ancestral Habsburg manor and stabbed him to death. All but one of the assassins, a certain Von Wart, escaped. He was put to death "amid frightful tortures" along with the exemplary execution of 1,000 presumably innocent locals on the orders of the king's widow Elizabeth, who then built the

famous monastery of Königsfelden on the spot where Albrecht was slain. On his death, the German crown slipped away from the family again, this time to Count Henry of Luxembourg.

Night of violence: The violence was not one-sided. In 1314 a band of Schwyz men, who had collectively been excommunicated a few years before, attacked the Habsburg-controlled Abbey of Einsiedeln at dead of night. They took the sleeping monks prisoner, broke into the cellar, drank themselves stupid and proceeded to smash the religious treasures, vessels and relics. At daybreak, still feeling the effects of the night before, they departed with their prisoners and the monastery's cattle. Habsburg exasperation was complete and the following year, in 1315, serious hostilities commenced.

Duke Leopold assembled at Zug an army which included contingents from Lucerne, Winterthur and, remarkably, Zurich. "The men of this army came together with one purpose," says Johannes Vitoduranus, a contemporary chronicler, "to utterly subdue and humiliate those peasants who were surrounded with mountains as with walls." Leopold seems to have been poorly advised in the choice of the route along which he advanced on Schwyz. On reaching the hamlet of Haselmatt, near Aegeri, his force

began the steep, frozen ascent of Morgarten. They took no special precautions beyond ensuring that they had enough rope to harness the cattle they expected to capture. Leopold's men, it was said, "resembled a hunting party rather than an army expecting serious warfare".

Above a particularly tricky part of the ascent – at what the Swiss have called their Thermopylae – the defenders were waiting for them. Weighed down by heavy armour, the Austrians and their Swiss allies barely had time to look up when an avalanche of rocks and tree trunks descended on them from the Figlerfluh, a spur on the ridge of Morgarten. The Confederates rushed into the confusion with their fearsome halberds, a kind of axe with a pick on the back. The Austrians could retreat only by the way they had come. The retreat turned into flight, the flight into slaughter. Many of those who escaped as far as a lake were drowned by the weight of their armour.

Peasants triumph: The battle of Morgarten, a victory celebrated in Switzerland to this day, was possibly the first triumph in medieval Europe of peasants on foot over mounted knights. "When the fight was over," the chronicle records, "the men of Schwyz pulled off the weapons of the killed and drowned, robbed them also of their other possessions, and enriched themselves with arms and money." The occasion was commemorated by the construction of a chapel to St Jacob, but perhaps the best epitaph is a quotation attributed to the Austrian duke's fool before the action: "You have taken counsel how best to get into the country, but have given no explanation of how you are going to get out again."

Morgarten revealed the martial instincts which came to dominate Swiss history well into the 19th century, hard to reconcile with the *volte-face* which has made Switzerland today a paragon of fastidious neutrality. Among the explanations offered for the fighting qualities of the Swiss are an unusually high protein diet and warlike sports. The Alpine peasant was certainly, by the nature of the terrain, physically very fit and the halberd a nasty weapon capable of splitting a suit of armour, but there is also the fundamental point that, like the great warrior nations of Africa, the Alpine Swiss economy was pastoral.

Small boys or women could, if necessary, do the work of shepherds perfectly well, as we have seen in the instance of the shepherdess who charmed good Queen Bertha. If the able-bodied male was not quite a parasite, he was at least economically dispensable and he offers an early example of migrant labour. Mercenary pay was high, in addition to a share of the loot, and as long as the money somehow got back to them, the family was able to manage very well without him.

The surprise victory over the Austrians did as much for the Forest Cantons' prestige among their peers as the defeat of the Persians did for Athens among the Greek city states in the 5th century BC. In 1332 Lucerne was the first town to be drawn into the Confederation, followed by Zurich (1351), Glarus and Zug (1352), and Berne (1353), making a total of eight members. After Berne, however, the rural cantons were wary of the balance tilting towards the cities, and no more cities were admitted until 1481. They even fought a civil war to prevent Zurich from acquiring the county of Toggenburg from the extinct family of that name. Zurich seceded from the Confederation but rejoined when not even the military assistance of Charles VII of France could stave off defeat.

A similar league was formed in Rhaetia, where the city of Chur joined surrounding villages and valleys in the "League of the House of God". The spread of such leagues was propelled by the bankruptcy of the smaller feudal lords in an economic climate devastated by the Black Death, bad harvests and starvation. Forced to pawn their feudal rights, they saw them being snapped up by prosperous cities. Berne bought the Hasli Valley from the impoverished lords of Weissenburg and with it the feudal rights over its inhabitants. Ironically, the new "lords" in such circumstances were in no hurry to extend to their acquired subjects the freedom which they valued so highly for themselves.

Successive Habsburg dukes never gave up the idea of reclaiming the Swiss lands lost to the Confederation and for a while succeeded in regaining Zug. Zurich was the main target, however, and it was only saved in 1351 by the intervention of the Forest Cantons. In time, the Swiss took the offensive. Lucerne launched attacks on surrounding Austrian strongholds, Zug on the castle of St Andreas near Cham, Zurich on Rapperswil, and Schwyz on Einsiedeln. In June 1386, Duke Leopold III, nephew of the loser at Morgarten, proposed to deal with the Swiss once and for all, at the Battle of Sempach.

Left, Swiss mercenaries. Above, Von Winkelried's heroic death in the Battle of Sempach.

A particular point of interest about the Battle of Sempach is that it involved Arnold von Winkelried, a national hero whose credibility very nearly went the same way as William Tell's when historians later sifted through the evidence. Again the Austrians took to the field in the full panoply of mediaeval armour; the Swiss infantry faced them in a wedge-shaped formation. Unusually, the Austrian knights dismounted and advanced on the wedge with their long lances levelled. The tactics seemed to work because, even with halberds 2½ metres (8 ft) long, the Swiss could not get close enough to strike. The Swiss were dropping like flies and defeat seemed certain when things took a miraculous turn. "A good and pious man," says the chronicler without mentioning names, stepped forward from the Swiss ranks. The Swiss are reluctant to believe that it was anyone other than Arnold von Winkelried. "I will cut a road for you; take care of my wife and children!" he cried.

The enterprising Von Winkelried spread his arms wide and threw himself forward, forcing a number of levelled lances to the ground. His comrades charged over his fallen body and through the gap to engage the enemy at close quarters, the style of

a family of that name living in Unterwalden at the time, although there is no hard evidence connecting any member of the family with the battle.

It also seems that at least five battles in Swiss history, albeit less famous ones than Sempach, were won against the odds by a hero employing exactly the same outspread-arms-and-diving tactics. One spoilsport, the 19th-century historian Karl Bürkli, went so far as to say that the whole story was lifted long after the event from an account of a battle at Bicocca, near Milan, in 1552. The hero of that action, another who threw himself on to a phalanx of spears, was actually named: a certain Arnold von Winkelried.

fighting at which they excelled. The weather played a part too. It was evidently a blisteringly hot July day, and in their iron suits the knights began to wilt. Duke Leopold, standing with the reserves, saw the Austrian standard wavering, plunged into the thick of the fight, and was hacked to death. When his body was laid out in the monastery of Königsfelden, the Swiss having won another resounding victory, it was noticed with some interest that his head, covered with long, reddish-gold hair, bore no visible wounds.

As for the courageous Arnold von Winkelried, a Dr Hermann von Liebenau established in 1854 that there was definitely

In 1389, after another Austrian defeat at Näfels, a seven-year peace treaty was signed at Vienna which gave the Confederation undisputed possession of conquered lands, which is not to say that the Habsburgs did not attempt to seduce Zurich back into the fold by various diplomatic subterfuges. A 20-year peace treaty signed in 1415 was an altogether more reliable indication of Austria's willingness to accept what had happened. Although the Confederation was still technically within the German Empire, the bond was growing meaningless. Germans began to refer to the inhabitants of the confederate states collectively as Die Schweiz, after Schwyz, the state which to them seemed most representative of their increasingly distant neighbours. The "Schweiz", for their part, began to refer to their confederation as an *Eidgenossenschaft*, the implication being that they were a separate nation.

The term *Eidgenossenschaft* first surfaces in the so-called Priest's Charter, which effectively told the clergy to mind their own business: "A priest who disobeys these injunctions shall be outlawed..." The Covenant of Sempach, drawn up after the battle, has been described as "the first attempt, made by any people, to restrain somewhat the fury of war, to regulate military disciples and leadership by intelligent, humane law." Five centuries before the Geneva Convention, it provided for the humane treatment of the wounded and included such clauses as: "Women should not be attacked unless they warned the enemy by an outcry or fought themselves, in which case they could be punished as they deserved."

Such codes hint at progress towards a constitution, yet the Confederation still fell some way short of a comprehensive government. It was a union of the loosest kind, in which the members were neither fully equal nor all bound to one another. Zurich kept a rather frigid distance from Lucerne, for example, and Lucerne from Glarus. The charters of the various states were individually very different. The rural cantons tended to be quite genuinely democratic, with magistrates appointed by popular assemblies, while in the cities the supreme power was lodged with the magistrate, who dispensed liberality downwards more or less as he pleased.

Nevertheless, during the 15th century Switzerland began to assume the proportions of a major European power. Its military prowess had already been amply demonstrated, now the economic foundations also looked solid. After the pan-European depression of the 14th century, the Confederation grew rich on cloth, wool and linen or, in the case of Zurich, silk. The attraction of money, as opposed to the barter goods which had generally been the currency previously, took precedence over political power.

This development was not quite as high-minded as it may appear, however, because much of the capital which created the new wealth was plainly and simply war booty, the fruits of victory over the richest ruler in Europe, Charles the Bold of Burgundy. Charles had fabulous wealth, but he was

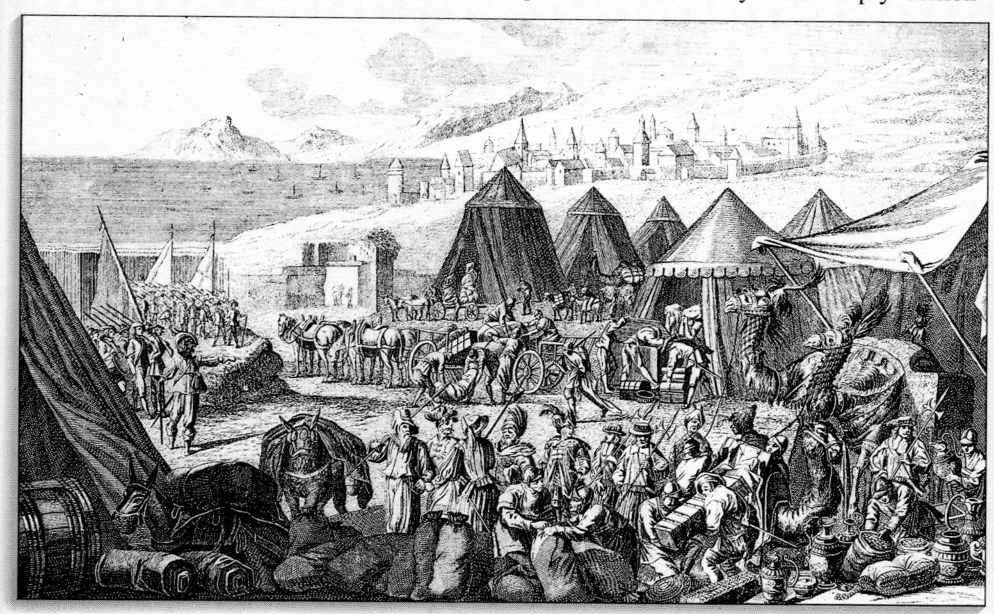

Left, Burgundian troops, Switzerland's next opponents. Above, Confederate troops grab the booty from the Battle of Morat.

obsessed in his rivalry with King Louis XI of France by the fact that he was only a duke. The Habsburgs had by then fallen on exceedingly hard times, but they had regained the throne of the Holy Roman Empire and Charles was more than ready to marry his daughter, Mary, off to Maximilian, the penniless son of the then Emperor Frederick, if the emperor was prepared to exercise his right to make him a king – any kind would do. With his eye fixed firmly on the Burgundy coffers, Frederick agreed to revive the extinct Kingdom of Burgundy for Charles, but on the very morning of the planned coronation, Frederick withdrew without one word of explanation.

Saddled with a redundant crown which had been produced at top speed and enormous expense by the royal jewellers, and with a betrothed but suddenly abandoned daughter, Charles the Bold went mad. He threw himself into a series of absurd adventures, and his fatal mistake was to be sucked into a wholly unnecessary war with the Swiss. For their part, the Swiss were so confident of their military superiority that they looked on foreign wars as unremarkable business opportunities. They did not realise that in this instance they were being manipulated by the notoriously wily Louis of France. The war was undertaken, says one historian categorically, "at the instigation of France, for the interest of France, and in the pay of France."

Hostilities commenced with Berne declaring war on Charles the Bold in the name of the whole Confederation. While Charles was away in Germany on another of his pointless expeditions, Bernese troops invaded Burgundy and took Héricourt. On his return, Charles marched on Berne by way of Lake Neuchâtel, pausing to take the town of Grandson and either hanging or drowning 412 prisoners. "It is a horrible, a fearful sight, that of so many dangling corpses," reported the Duke of Milan's ambassador with the Burgundian forces.

The first engagement proper at Neuchâtel took place on 2 March 1476 when, after an initial skirmish, the Burgundians were surprised by a sudden Swiss offensive, as described by the chronicler Petermann Etterlin. "Now, when the Duke of Burgundy saw the hosts descending the mountains, the sun just shone upon them, and they glittered like a mirror; at the same time the horn of Uri bellowed, and the war horns of Luzern (Lucerne), and there was such a roar that the Duke's men shuddered at it and retreated."

The retreat was so hasty and disorderly that the booty left behind was unbelievable. Among 420 pieces of artillery and a huge quantity of general stores, the Bernese chronicler mentions three great diamonds of inestimable value. He describes in great detail a golden casket containing holy relics including nothing less than pieces of the true cross and the crown of thorns. It was said that the booty included enough silk to enable the Confederate peasants to scorn clothing made from anything less for years. The loss of life was trivial.

Dire straits: Charles returned within a few weeks with a force of 25,000 men and laid siege to Morat, pounding the city with artillery fire which tore down part of the town wall and destroyed houses. Berne, which knew it would be next if Morat fell, sent an urgent appeal to the Confederates: "Dearest friends and brothers," it read, "were the need not so great, we should be loath to use such pressing and burdensome solicitations..." The Confederate forces marched to the relief

Left, Charles the Bold. Right, the founding of Basle University, 1460.

of Morat with a force as large as the Burgundian besiegers, who included a number of English archers. The result was one-sided: between 8,000 and 10,000 of Charles's men were killed, against a few hundred Swiss losses. The Swiss were disappointed that the booty was nothing like as good as that after Grandson.

The last chapter of the Burgundian war was fought not in Switzerland but at Nancy, although more than 8,000 Swiss fought for Charles's opponent, the Duke of Lorraine. Shortly before the battle, Charles agreed that his daughter Mary could after all marry Maximilian with no strings attached. He still owned a large chunk of Europe, but all his money had gone. Two days after the battle, a decisive victory for the Duke of Lorraine, a body was recovered from a frozen lake. It had been half-eaten by wolves but the exceptionally long fingernails – an affectation of Charles the Bold – left little doubt as to identity.

Dividing the booty: The spoils of the Burgundian war were colossal but their division, as far as the rural cantons were concerned, was so loaded in favour of the cities that the question of admitting yet more cities to the Confederation, in this instance Fribourg and Solothurn, brought the country to the brink of civil war. "Tempers were so hot," says Herold, "that only a saint could have calmed them down. Providentially, a saint appeared."

Niklaus von Flüe had forsaken his position as a magistrate, husband and father of several children to retire to a cave in a wilderness near Sachseln. For 20 years he had been sleeping on planks and using a log for a pillow. Some people believed that he lived on a diet of berries and roots; others that his sole form of sustenance was the bread of the holy sacrament. Even so, he seems to have kept himself remarkably well-informed about current affairs.

Notoriously given to platitudes like "Pure water does not flow through golden pipes", on this occasion he got straight down to business and within an hour had worked out a compromise which admitted the towns to the Confederation in return for abandoning their other alliances. He proposed a new covenant, the *Stanser-verkommnis* (Agreement of Stans), which would in future regulate the division of spoils. With that he returned to his cave. His canonisation followed some five centuries later.

The death of Charles the Bold and the disintegration of the Duchy of Burgundy in the 15th century was as momentous and unexpected as the collapse of the Soviet Union would be in the 20th. The Duchy was in reality an empire which included the Netherlands and Belgium and went all the way south to the Mediterranean. Now, the Low Countries were able to reassert their own identities and what had so recently been Louis XI's relatively insignificant kingdom assumed the dominant role in what became modern France. The role of the Swiss in bringing about Charles's demise was not as significant as his own bad judgement, but Swiss soldiers won great admiration and were perceived throughout Europe as the most useful to have on one's side.

The Swiss soldier, in turn, needed no second bidding. Swiss cloth was selling well abroad, but that represented the country's only export of any consequence. In moving into the first rank of European nations, Switzerland, like England, had to trade to survive. Christopher Herold's summary of the situation is crisp: "Beginning in the Middle Ages, [the Swiss] sold military service to foreign powers in the form of mercenaries. In order to exercise their military profession undisturbed and to enjoy its fruits in peace, they soon adopted a policy of neutrality – that is, the territory of Switzerland became neutral, while its citizens took part, on an impartial basis, in every European war for several centuries.

"Thus it happened that the Swiss, who now consider themselves the first free and peaceful nation of the Continent, gave their name to an occupation usually involving both servitude and belligerency. Just as now the word Swiss evokes in many minds the picture of a watchmaker or a cheese expert, there was a time when it meant, to most Europeans, a professional soldier, and a ferocious one at that."

ance was, with perfect impartiality, reaching for Maximilian's throat.

Maximilian's mistake was to offer the Swiss the hand of friendship. He suggested they forget about their Confederation and join instead the Swabian Bund, a new league headed by himself. War was soon raging along the whole line of the Rhine, from Basel to the borders of Vorarlberg and Graubünden, at the very idea. The so-called Swabian War lasted six months and was punctuated by the acts of valour now expected of Swiss troops. Thus Benedict Fontana, leading a charge on the supposedly impregnable fortress of An der Calven (Chialavaina) on the Tyroleàn border, gave

As we have seen, Charles the Bold's terminal difficulties began with a hitch in the proposed marriage between his daughter Mary and Maximilian, son of the Habsburg Emperor Frederick.

The marriage eventually took place and rescued Habsburg finances in what was undoubtedly their darkest hour. The Swiss soldier who had to a large extent paved Maximilian's way to a handsome inherit-

Left, Niklaus von Flüe known as Bruder (Brother) Klaus, was instrumental in the Agreement of Stans. Above, *Death and the Mercenary* from the Berne *danse macabre* by Niklaus Manuel.

his orders while lying on the ground, clutching at bullet wounds: "Onward, comrades! I count but for one man; today we are Rhaetians and allies, or nevermore."

The point of Fontana's exhortation was the liberation of Rhaetia from the German Empire and its incorporation in the Confederation. The effect of the peace treaty signed at Basel on 22 September 1499 was not only to secure that incorporation but to reduce the links between the Swiss Confederation and the Empire to a mere formality, a step tantamount to acknowledging its independence. Curiously, the Swiss continued to submit their charters for the sovereign's approval, accepted patents of nobility, and so on. Formal independence was not declared until the Peace of Westphalia 150 years later.

The Confederation's burgeoning prestige attracted applications for membership from Basel and Schaffhausen in 1501. Basel was so pleased to be accepted that the guards who had always been stationed at the city gates were replaced by a symbol of open arms in the person of a grandmother armed only with a distaff. The effect was rather spoiled by the old woman demanding a toll from anyone entering or leaving the city. When Appenzell joined the Confederation in 1513 the number of members stood at 13, and there it remained for the following three centuries.

The activities of Swiss mercenaries from the 15th to 19th centuries really belong to the history of other nations' problems rather than Switzerland's, but in the interest of symmetry it may be worth noting that having helped France and the Habsburgs in their difficulties with Burgundy, and having then turned on the Habsburgs, the Swiss again demonstrated perfect impartiality by taking up cudgels against France.

The Swiss actually began on France's side, the occasion being the invasion of Italy in 1494. The switch in their loyalties was the work of Matthäus Schiner, a man who began life as a street urchin but went on to become a cardinal and a confidant of Pope Julius II. The pope was of course alarmed by French ambitions in Italy. Schiner suggested to him that the Swiss might be open to an offer of money, indulgences and other incentives. They were: a five-year alliance between the Papal See and Switzerland was duly signed. The Swiss drove their recent allies out of Lombardy and reinstated the Sforzas in Milan, which became a Swiss protectorate. The French bounced back but the issue was settled, so it seemed, at the battle of Novara which decided the matter in 1513.

Two men with promising careers ahead of them were on the fringe of these events. One, acting as a kind of war correspondent, predicted that the Swiss would go on to conquer and rule the whole of Italy. That was Machiavelli. The other was a cynical observer at the peace negotations. "Here you might observe men's disposition – caution and cunning," he wrote. "They strive to puzzle one another with the view of drawing advantage from the confusion. They pretend to one thing, but hope to get another." That was the opinion of Ulrich Zwingli.

The presence of Zwingli, then an army chaplain, was of course a portent of the Reformation just around the corner, the last thing the Confederation needed at a time when divisions were piling up. The Confederation's brilliant military success was the ironic root cause. Success spelt confidence, and confidence removed the fear of foreign aggression. That fear had cemented the young Confederation, and without it the components were left with very little in common. Their only central institution was the Diet (*Tagsatzung*), and that had no authority to discipline neighbours who, under the

strain of a declining economy, were increasingly disposed to fall out.

The rural cantons were uncomfortably aware that the balance of power previously shared with the cities was slipping away. Zurich, Berne and Lucerne could between them field twice as many men as all the other cantons put together. Zurich, in particular, was behaving like a sovereign state under its "ambitious and readily bribed" Burgomaster, Hans Waldmann, "whose manifest opulence gave the lie to his affectation of republican simplicity".

Of humble origins himself and "Squire of Dubelstein" only by a fortuitous marriage,

Waldmann personified the contempt of the urban *nouveaux riches* for the agrarian peasants by ordering them to put down all their large dogs because they were spoiling the hunting.

Torture and execution: Five hundred peasants of Knonau marched on Zurich in protest and, taking Waldmann prisoner, gave him a taste of the rack in the Wellenberg state prison. Waldmann had spent some time in Wellenberg for youthful excesses, and there were not a few jilted mistresses who probably wished he had never been let out, but on this occasion the rack failed to extract a confession which would have invoked the death penalty. Undeterred, the city council

voted to let him die anyway. Thousands turned out to watch him being led to the block in a meadow outside the city walls. He is said to have looked back at the city longingly before lowering his head. "May God protect thee, my beloved Zurich, and keep thee from all evil," were his parting words. His death was followed by rioting and many more executions as the plutocrats tightened their grip on the city to the exclusion of the country districts. After centuries of debate

Left, Matthäus Schiner, bishop, cardinal and politician. Above, the Battle of Marignano, a crushing defeat for the Swiss.

Zurich finally elected a monument to Waldmann in 1937.

While enterprising merchants could amass fortunes in the towns, the economy as far as rural people were concerned was still all about mercenary soldiering. Unfortunately for them, mercenary work was no longer so readily available or profitable. Warfare was becoming too expensive for prospective employers. Developments like artillery, now essential, put the cost of even small wars beyond the means of minor, bad-tempered princes, traditionally the most regular source of employment. Moreover, the Germans had woken up to what they were missing and their mercenaries, keen students of Swiss techniques, were competing for what business there was.

Novara had been a great triumph for Swiss arms, but when Francis I acceded to the French throne soon afterwards and immediately marched on Italy to restore French honour, three cantons – Berne, Fribourg and Solothurn – refused to fight. Cardinal Schiner, his sacred mission yielding to the profane, took command of the depleted Swiss forces. The two armies met on the road to Marignano on 13 September 1515. Battle raged inconclusively until midnight, was broken off, and resumed at dawn. In the afternoon, the French destroyed the dykes holding back the Lambro and the plain on which the majority of the Swiss troops stood was suddenly flooded. The orderly retreat from this impossible predicament so impressed Francis that he ordered his men not to pursue. There was also some solace in the "Eternal Peace" concluded with France afterwards. The Swiss possession of Ticino was acknowledged, although the future "Italian" canton was not granted that status until 1805.

The trauma of defeat weighed heavily on the Swiss. The Diet tried immediately to raise another army, but the response was lukewarm. That afternoon on the road to Marignano saw France and Switzerland change places on the ladder of European power. A loose Confederation without a strong central authority was suddenly and dramatically exposed as an inadequate anachronism. Switzerland was reduced at a stroke from a great power to a small neutral state, and it was in no condition to face the schismatic wrench of the Reformation.

The impact of the Reformation was doubly hard on Switzerland because, while Martin Luther in Germany concentrated on theological matters and was content to leave politics to the princes, Ulrich Zwingli drew no such distinction between religion and politics. The kind of reformation he had in mind was a total overhaul of Swiss society, top to bottom. Zwingli, born in Wildhaus in 1484, was educated in Basel and Berne with a view to entering the church. He was a gifted student, the only note of criticism being that he was rather too fond of singing, a weakness reputedly common to the Toggenburger population. The more serious side of his character was reflected in correspondence with scholars like Erasmus in Holland.

Never a bookworm, Zwingli went campaigning in Italy, although he became increasing sceptical about the Swiss mercenary tradition and expressed his objections so forcefully that a public uproar made it prudent to retreat for two years to the abbey at Einsiedeln. The abuses within so appalled him that he re-directed his critical energies, and this brought him to the attention of the Zurich council, which had decided that the city's reputation for wickedness required a vigorous remedy.

Zwingli's first sermon as the newly appointed plebanus was a rousing address which had people talking about "a new Moses who had arisen to save his people from spiritual bondage". The scholar Platter, sitting in the congregation, "felt himself lifted off the ground by his hair". Unlike Luther, Zwingli did not challenge papal authority over the sale of indulgences and the like. He was at first more inclined to outline a new state modelled on the Greek ideal, but he came round to the view that in order to build a new society it was necessary first to destroy the old. His targets were the mass and the worship of images.

In 1524 Zwingli showed what he thought of clerical celibacy by marrying a rich widow, and in the same year he was supported by the government in ordering the removal of all pictures and images from churches. By cutting ties with the diocese of Constance, Zwingli created in Zurich what was virtually its own state religion. The reforms were adopted readily in the northern and eastern cantons, but the Forest Cantons were steadfastly conservative and Roman Catholic. The Reformation was to them a product of the cities and for that reason alone suspicious if not downright evil. The Forest Cantons issued a warrant for Zwingli's arrest in case he entered their territory.

The Swiss factions looked beyond their borders for support, the Reformers to the German states and the Catholics to Austria.

The split deepened and in 1529 Zurich declared war on the Forest Cantons. The confrontation of the two armies at Kappel was cooled at the last moment by urgent diplomacy. Tradition has it that Catholic troops placed a large bowl of milk on the boundary between Zug and Zurich, the Protestants reciprocated with bread, and between the two of them they had the ingredients for a party. Zwingli was disgusted at the peaceful resolution. He predicted that the Catholics would one day be the stronger party and then there would be no moderation or mercy.

In a way, Zwingli was right, because when the armies squared up again in the same place two years later the Forest Cantons had four times as many men as the Zurich force. On this occasion battle was not averted, and Zwingli was killed, along with many of his relatives and most of the Zurich city council. His body was quartered, burnt and "scattered to the wind". Leadership of the Zurich movement passed to Heinrich Bullinger, who found it expedient to concentrate on ecclesiastical matters and leave politics alone.

In one sense, John Calvin, the second giant of the Swiss Reformation, picked up where

Zwingli left off, but Zwingli's work was mainly about Zurich and the conversion of German-speaking Switzerland while Calvin's was about Geneva and French-speaking Switzerland. Calvin and Geneva were improbable bed-fellows. He was born in Picardy in 1509, "a northern Frenchman of superior intelligence and learning, but of a gloomy, austere disposition". The Genevese were the least austere people in Switzerland. They were gamblers, wine-lovers and kept a red-light district busy.

Left, John Calvin, reformed the French in Geneva. Above, Ulrich Zwingli, his precursor in Zurich.

Their moral plateau was a city statute which levied a modest charge on men who kept more than one mistress at a time.

Julius Caesar had recognised the strategic value of Geneva in its command of the gap between the Jura and the Alps, in other words covering both access to Italy via the St Bernard and Simplon passes and the gateway to Burgundy and France. After the collapse of the Roman Empire, the city was passed around various masters, but at an early date it became an episcopal see, the bishops reaching some kind of accommodation with the House of Savoy which controlled the territory all about. In 1421, however, Duke Amadeus VIII of Savoy usurped the see and it was entrusted to a motley collection of Savoyard hangers-on and royal offspring, not excluding bastard sons.

Geneva hotbloods: Rebellion against the Savoyards produced the three musketeers of Geneva's history: Bezanson Hugues, Philibert Berthelier and François Bonivard, the last immortalised – with poetic licence – in Byron's *Prisoner of Chillon*. They were a slightly anarchistic band of hotbloods known as the "Children of Geneva". The first was decapitated by the bishops in 1519, the second fled, and Bonivard, about whose life Byron knew very little, was imprisoned.

Bonivard was actually a turncoat Savoyard nobleman who at the age of 17 became, through his family's influence, the prior of the Benedictine abbey of St Victor just outside Geneva. The prior's job was to collect taxes. Not even affecting a clerical role, Bonivard contracted the first of four marriages, not to mention a considerably larger number of mistresses.

He was freed after the initial imprisonment over his association with Hugues and Berthelier but jailed again in 1530, this time in the dungeon of the castle of Chillon where he carved his name into the rock. Visiting the castle in the 19th century, Byron saw the carving and let his imagination run free with images of the poor fellow "to fetters confined" in the "damp vault's dayless gloom". Bonivard was in fact quite comfortable in the circumstances, being supplied with paper, ink and books to pursue his studies. We shall return to Bonivard and his dungeon shortly.

Wishing to rid themselves of the autocratic Savoyards, the Genevese turned to the Swiss Confederation, then at the pinnacle of its military prestige, and to Berne in particular. Berne was by then under Zwingli's influence and the price of its support was that the Genevese had to reform. Guillaume Farel, a fanatical preacher from Neuchâtel, was chosen as the man for the job.

Farel's arrival in 1532, two years after Bonivard had been locked up for the second time, precipitated a storm, the city dividing into supporters of the Confederation, known as the Eydguenots, and those who realised they preferred Savoy, the so-called Mamelukes. Egged on by Farel, the former invaded the cathedral in 1535, ripped apart everything except its walls, and led their dogs and mules inside the hallowed walls to add the proverbial insult to injury. Defrocked priests trampled on their robes while the beleaguered Catholics could only pray for a miracle. They claimed to have witnessed several, not least the Hosts of the Holy Eucharist levitating in the sky.

It was Geneva's misfortune at the height of this religious tension suddenly to become the coveted target of three avaricious neighbours: Francis I, the victor at Marignano, the Emperor Charles V and Geneva's supposed ally, Berne itself. Berne got there first with a force of 6,000 men but fear of French intervention inhibited them and saved the city from annexation. The Bernese forces captured the castle of Chillon, however, and Bonivard was led blinking into the sunlight.

Bonivard discovered that Geneva had changed in his enforced absence. His abbey had been seized and secularised, and the whole city looked gloomy. The difference was John Calvin, whom the fiery Farel had taken on to help him clean things up. For the moment, Calvin's proposed remedy was altogether too rigorous for the Genevese and in 1538 both he and Farel were banished. Farel returned to Neuchâtel and stayed there for the rest of his life, but within three years violent in-fighting on the Geneva council and the renewed threat of a Bernese occupation led to an invitation to Calvin to return. "Why should I plunge again into that yawning gulf," he wrote to Farel, "seeing that I dislike the temper of the Genevese, and that they cannot get used to me?" In the end he agreed – but on his terms.

Moral police: Calvin now set about his mission with a vengeance. The Genevese were less aware of the intricacies of his doctrine of pre-destination than of the impact of the Consistory, his tribunal of 12 civic worthies who passed judgement on all spiritual and moral matters, public and private. They had the power to enter houses on suspicion of depravity, and laid down the law on the clothes, including the colour, and on what people ate, which was to be no more than one dish each of meat and vegetables per day, no pastry and only local wine.

Girls were hauled before the Consistory for skating, a man for sniffing in church, and two others for talking business as they left church. A hairdresser was jailed for creating an ostentatious coiffure, and there was a total ban on dancing, games and all music except psalms. Drunkenness, blasphemy and agnosticism were put into the same criminal category as murder. The Spanish scholar Servetus unwisely passed through Geneva on his way to Italy. He was not only a Unitarian but unsound on infant baptism. Servetus was publicly burnt to death.

"The sword, the gallows and the stake were equally busy," writes a Swiss historian. "The jailer asserted that his prisons were filled to excess, and the executioner complained that his arms were tired. Within a period of three years there were passed fifty-eight sentences of death, seventy-six of banishment, and eight to nine thousand of imprisonment..." Calvin regarded any criticism of himself as blasphemy. One Pierre Amieaux, who muttered that Calvin was a bad man, was led through the city in his shirt, a torch in his hand, and was required to make a public confession of his wretchedness in three squares. "The dogs are barking at me on all sides," Calvin complained to a friend.

The recently-released "Prisoner of Chillon" had difficulty adjusting to the new moral climate. He was up before the Consistory for gambling, nodding off during

a sermon and wearing a nosegay behind his ear – "ill becoming to one of his age". Nevertheless, he was treated more leniently than his fourth wife who was charged with adultery: she was sewn into a bag and thrown into the Rhône. Curiously, Bonivard was commissioned to write the *History of the Reformation in Geneva*. Less surprisingly, it was not published until the 19th century.

In 1556 John Knox, the Scottish Calvanist, visited Geneva and described it as "the maist perfyt schoole of Chryst that ever was in the erth since the dayis of the Apostillis". By then, most of Calvin's opponents had bolted from the city, but his writings, which could be construed as a charter for capitalism in that they sanctioned the charging of interest on loans, went down well in Scotland and New England. No fewer than 24 printing presses ran day and night churning out his works in a number of languages. More than 2,000 of his sermons and 4,721 letters survive. "His religious enthusiasm was able to triumph over bodily ailments," says one of the more sympathetic biographers.

Last lecture: Calvin died in 1564, his parting words being a stern lecture to those who came to pay their respects. The institutions he left behind in Geneva were soon severely tested by the gentler form of persuasion employed by St Francis of Sales, the champion of the Counter Reformation. By eliminating the more scandalous abuses of the Catholic church, he managed to win back the entire countryside south of Lake Geneva. The city itself remained loyal to Calvinism and it was at the risk of his life that St Francis, while officially the Bishop of Geneva, paid one or two clandestine visits.

The Genevese took – and take – considerable pride in the way they saw off a perfidious attack on their religion in 1602 by Charles Emmanuel I of Savoy, who was re-

Left, Calvin and Farel in Geneva. Above, the death of Zwingli in the Battle of Cappel.

living the old Savoyard dream of making Geneva his own. The Savoyards crept up on the city on the night of 11 December and several were halfway up the walls when, the story goes, an old woman called La Mère Royaume saw what was going on and poured a cooking-pot of hot broth over their heads.

Another version of the story says it was a chamber-pot and the contents were not hot broth. Either way, the alarm was given, citizens in nightshirts rushed out and the invaders were beaten off at the cost of several lives. To guard against any repetition, Geneva signed a treaty with Henry IV of France, but the treaty did not come cheap. The city had to surrender to him its main agricultural hinterland, the Pays de Gex, and it was hard to imagine how the city would be able to feed itself.

Continual conflict: Unpleasant as the Reformation and Counter Reformation had been in Switzerland, the discomfort paled in comparison with the Thirty Years' War, which began at the start of the 17th century as a war about Bohemia and religion, developed into a trial of strength between France and the Habsburgs, and tore Central Europe to shreds. The Swiss cantons were neutral, but atavistic instincts were aroused by war swirling around them and the Swiss population were rooting for one side or the other.

When Gustavus Adolphus of Sweden brought his victorious Protestant army close to the border, the leader of the arch-Protestants in Zurich, Johann Jacob Breitinger railed against Swiss neutrality: "So do I condemn utterly our harmful and ridiculous temporising," he said, "and damn the ugly, shameful and loathsome Monster of neutrality. May God spit out the lukewarm, that is, the neutralists who are neither warm nor cold seeing that the Lord Christ holds such for his enemies in bright clear words when he says that he who is not for him is against him."

As the war continued, Breitinger would have found fewer of his fellow Swiss agreeing. Cattle and other exports fetched record prices in foreign markets too occupied with war to produce their own foodstuffs. Neutrality began to look like good business and, according to Jonathan Steinberg, "however much they may have hated each other, [the Swiss] were better off living together as neutrals that dying apart as enemies". The war also saw foreign troops taking short cuts across Swiss territory, and there was a flood of refugees, but ironically it was the not altogether welcome refugees, particularly the persecuted French Huguenots, who laid the foundations of the Swiss economy.

We have seen how Geneva had difficulty feeding itself with the loss of the Pays de Gex

to Henry IV of France. The Huguenots provided the solution. They were artisans, watchmakers and jewellers, merchants and, above all, financiers. In little more than a century, Geneva became one of the wealthiest cities in Europe. On the political front, the Peace of Westphalia, which concluded the Thirty Years' War, ratified Swiss independence. The Swiss states were no longer, even in the loose sense which had long been the case, part of the German Empire.

The Swiss, quiet and prosperous while the rest of Europe was at war, used the Peace of Westphalia as a cue to fight among themselves and let the economic advances slip away. It was almost as if the Confederation

needed an external threat to remain in one piece. Without it, the states went off on their own. Neuchâtel and St Gallen were paragons of unbending absolutism, Berne, Fribourg, Solothurn and Lucerne aped the oligarchies based on birth and inheritance. It was said that so many upstarts assumed "von" before their names that those who were truly well-born promptly dropped theirs. Only the Forest Cantons were remotely democratic. Society split along class lines too: a minor peasant protest against new taxation struck such a popular chord that a proletarian uprising exploded over much of central Switzerland. The peasants themselves were "hards" pitted against "softs", the former chopping off the beards, ears or both of those who were thought to be not pulling their weight. The poorly equipped peasants were no match for their common enemy, however, and both their principal leaders, Christian Schibi and Nicholas Leuenberger, were captured, tortured and executed.

Left, Calvin delivers his parting lecture on his death bed. Above, pimps and prostitutes were ostracised.

Second wave: The religious wars were fought all over again on slight pretexts. The First Villmergen War (1656) was sparked by the imperiously Catholic Schwyz sending three of the handful of Protestants living in the canton to be dealt with by the Inquisition in Milanits, and eventually had Berne and Zurich at war with all five Catholic states. War threatened in St Gallen in 1697 because Catholics wished to carry the cross upright in a procession through the streets. The Second Villmergen War, which again saw St Gallen in the thick of the action, was over who should provide the labour for the construction of a new road. The pope was drawn into the dispute and it was was only settled after a bloody victory by the combined Zurich and Berne armies.

The manipulative hand of Louis XIV of France was behind much of the religious ill-feeling of the 17th century. To begin with, he needed Swiss mercenaries – between 6,000 and 16,000 a year – for his wars and was prepared to offer commercial privileges in return. Switzerland ended up, though, as a dependency of the French Crown in all but name, and things might not have stopped there had France not been kept in rein by Britain and Holland. Swiss envoys were treated to lavish entertainment at the French court and it was said that they were beguiled into playing his poodles. The one celebrated exception to the sycophancy was the Swiss riposte to the king's remark that all the money he had paid for Swiss troops would have paved the road from Paris to Basle with gold pieces. "You forget, Sir, that with the Swiss blood spilt in the French service you might fill a canal from Basel to Paris."

In the 17th and 18th centuries the leading cities of the Confederation took on different characters. Zurich was the seat of liberal tendencies and intellectual progress, Berne of politics and finance, and Geneva of science. Zurich, like all fully-fledged members of the Confederation, had its subject lands, and the liberal tendencies stopped there to be replaced by the sort of patriarchal governor much admired by Goethe. Landolt von Greifensee, a case in point, "hated enlightened peasants and modern revolutionary ideas". He advocated compulsory church attendance and believed that the most rational form of social discipline was a good flogging. He toured his domain incognito, seizing drunkards and putting them into revolving cages until they sobered up.

French elite: Berne was resolutely French in language and manners. Its constitution was unashamedly élitist, with all power vested in 360 families, although natural wastage and scheming later reduced the number to less than 80. The middle class had no political rights but were given the run of trade, education and religion. The lower class, which included foreigners, were not permitted to own houses or have their children baptised in the city. They were not allowed to enter the market before 11 am, by which time their betters (or their betters' servants) were supposed to have done their shopping. Even then, they were forbidden to carry baskets in case they snagged the hooped skirts of better women, presumably those who were short of staff and had left their shopping a bit late. In 1744 a group of citizens led by a certain Henzi presented a petition asking for some of these regulations to be relaxed. Henzi paid for the presumption with his life.

Geneva, which we have previously seen under the heel of Calvin's Consistory, was rocked to its foundations in 1755 by the arrival of Voltaire. He was there, he said blandly, to see out his twilight years (he was then 61), but his curriculum vitae to date would not have been at all to the taste of the previously libertine but now thoroughly chastened burghers. His Jesuit education in Paris notwithstanding, he had been such a tearaway youth that his father was mightily relieved when he took a junior position in the French embassy in the Hague, but his diplomatic prospects were immediately dissipated by a lively affair with a French Protestant émigrée. In fact, he was sent home.

Voltaire's attempt at a law acreer was also short-lived; he found his métier in writing a wicked satire on the pompous Duke d'Orléans which earned him a six-month banishment from Paris. He continued to comment on the unfortunate man's character and was therefore brought back and, not for the last time, thrown into the Bastille. A spell in England opened his eyes to the intellectual tradition of Newton, Locke *et al.* He was writing impressively all the time, and on returning to France showed a hitherto unsuspected talent for making money, buying shares in the government lottery and selling corn to the army.

Voltaire's romantic attachments kept pace with his rising fame and fortune and earned him the patronage of Madame de Pompadour. Nevertheless, he was obliged to go on pricking personalities, including the Prussian Frederick the Great, for whom he happened to be working at the time, living in one of Frederick's palaces and drawing a pension of 20,000 francs. When Voltaire then showed up in Geneva, an unlikely place for someone with his kind of background, it was a matter of waiting to see what he would get up to next in spite of his protestations about being on the brink of death and wishing only to lead a quiet life.

In the event, Voltaire bought the estate Les Délices, pottered about his garden, was charming to everyone and on one pleasant evening invited a select group of Genevese society, including a number of city councillors, to meet his house-guest Lekain, the greatest French actor of the day. Lekain, Voltaire himself and his niece, Mme Denis, gave a reading from one of his works, *Zaïre*. "Never saw I so many tears shed," Voltaire wrote later, "never were the Calvinists so tender..." His mind was made up – Geneva must have a theatre! At his announcement of this, Geneva caught its breath. The Consistory fulfilled expectations with such an explosion of moral outrage that even Voltaire, to whom controversy was meat and drink, thought it prudent to decamp to Lausanne until things cooled down.

He returned quietly the following year and seemed to make amends by introducing the pious pastors of Geneva to another of his guests, M d'Alembert, co-editor with Diderot of the *Encyclopaedia*. The conversation on philosophical issues was courteous and the pastors left confident that they had made an excellent impression on Alembert. The seventh volume of the *Encyclopaedia* appeared the following year and the pastors were of course impatient to see what he had thought of them. What they read had them

Left, Voltaire, *bête-noire* of the Calvinists. Above, Jean-Jacques Rousseau.

spluttering and shaking the incriminating article and their fists at Voltaire, who promptly said he had not yet had the chance to read it, which was not to deny that he may have written some of it. "Do not retract," he advised Alembert gleefully in a private letter, "Your salvation, your conscience are at stake... The priests of Geneva will write to you [they had in fact appointed an ecclesiastical commission to do so]... I assure you that I and my friends will give them a good time; they will drink the cup to the dregs."

Strange to relate, the contentious article found space for a special plea. Geneva needed a theatre, it said – one which would "unite the wisdom of Sparta with the polish of Athens". The pastors were too anguished by observations like "the respect for Jesus Christ and for the Scriptures is, perhaps, the only thing that distinguishes the Christian doctrine of Geneva from pure deism" to care about Voltaire's theatre, but it raised the hackles of the other great man of letters in contemporary Switzerland and a fellow contributor to the *Encyclopaedia*, Jean-Jacques Rousseau. He did not object to theatres *per se*, he wrote in his Letter to Alembert on *Spectacles*, and in cities already stinking with corruption they probably did little harm. Geneva, however, was a unique virgin. Allow a theatre and the Genevese would surely start buying their wives expensive clothes and jewellery – the road to levity, ruin and perdition. Voltaire's theatre would turn Geneva into a whore. "Elections will be held in actresses' dressing-rooms and the leaders of a free people will be the creatures of a band of mountebanks."

Noble savage: Rousseau was Geneva-born, and although he had spent most of his life wandering about he claimed never to have lost his love for the city. Once, on leaving after a return visit, he was so overcome by emotion that he fainted. Rousseau combined sentimentality with a nasty streak of hypocrisy. He is best remembered for the resounding opening to his *Social Contract* – "Man is born free; and everywhere he is in chains" – one of the most influential books of the 18th century and an inspiration to the French Revolution. It had not yet been written at the time of his row with Voltaire over the theatre. He was then beating the drum of the nobility of savagery, the innocence of childhood, the wickedness of civilisation.

Voltaire was unimpressed. He said that on reading Rousseau he wanted to get down on all fours. Other critics have pointed out that Rousseau's damp-eyed adoration of childhood hardly squares with the fate of the five children he fathered by an illiterate servant, Thérèse le Vasseur. He despatched the lot to foundling hospitals.

Voltaire opened his theatre at Les Délices; the city closed it down. He tried again at several other locations, always with the same result. In the meantime, Rousseau's writings stirred popular dissatisfaction with Geneva's ruling elite into an open revolt. No lives were lost but, according to Voltaire, so many watchmakers left their workplaces

nobody in Geneva knew what the time was.

Geneva at last got a purpose-built wooden theatre in 1766 and the Puritans promptly put a torch to it. Voltaire swore that Rousseau was responsible. The flames attracted a crowd of citizens armed with buckets, but on realising that it was the theatre they are reputed to have emptied the buckets with a cry of "Let those who wanted a theatre put it out!" There was another famous fire in the city at roughly the same time – the public burning of *Emile*, a book laying down the principles of sound education, by Jean-Jacques Rousseau. Hounded out of town, the author was given no time to faint. Voltaire was among those who gratefully saw him off. The ironic outcome to this feud is that when Rousseau died, having gone completely off his head, he was buried in the Pantheon in Paris – alongside Voltaire.

Revolutionary shock: As France had long been Switzerland's most powerful ally, the Revolution sent shockwaves through the Confederation. It was opposed, naturally enough, by those with a vested interest in the divinely appointed social and political order: the cantonal governments, the privileged urban classes, the church and, of course, the French aristocratic refugees, most of whom congregated in Solothurn, Fribourg and Neuchâtel. It was supported, almost as naturally although in varying degrees, by the subject territories, the French-speaking parts (especially Vaud) and by Swiss émigrés in Paris. The opponents could have found an ally in imperial Austria, but there was always the fear of Austrian territorial ambition in Switzerland. France, whatever its government, was seen as the best available guarantee against Austrian aggrandisement. All in all, it suited Switzerland to be neutral.

Franco-Swiss relations, on tenterhooks because of the Revolution, were tested to the limit on 10 August 1792 when the Paris mob stormed the Palace of the Tuileries, where the job of protecting the French royals was in the hands of the Swiss Guard. It seems that once his personal safety had been secured, Louis XIV ordered a ceasefire, whereupon the mob turned on the guard and massacred nearly 800 of them. Ten days after the incident, the French Assembly dismissed the Swiss mercenaries serving elsewhere and sent them all home without pay. Many of them, particularly the officers, promptly switched sides, fighting for the anti-revolutionary coalition under Austrian command and British pay.

The Swiss revolutionaries in Paris, the so-called Helvetic Club led by the Vaudois Frédéric César de Laharpe (former tutor to the grandchildren of Catherine the Great in Russia) and Peter Ochs of Basle, shook off the general Swiss outrage at the massacre of the Guard to press for the French "liberation" of Switzerland. The French government was cautious. Almost the whole of Europe had imposed a blockade on France, and only the Swiss frontier was open to admit a long list of materials provided by undiscriminating suppliers in Austria, Italy and Hungary.

In 1798 French attitudes hardened under the growing influence of Napoleon Bonaparte. A pretext was found to occupy the southern shore of Lake Geneva, the first such foreign invasion in the Confederation's history. Laharpe, who had long borne a grudge against Berne, reminded Napoleon that the city possessed a treasure trove of gold. Berne was the military mainstay of the Confederation but, abandoned by the other members and paralysed by internal dissent, it could not withstand a French assault.

Sack of Berne: On 5 March the French army entered the city and went to work. The contents of the treasury were carted off in 11 wagons together with the city's three mascots, bears named Erlach, Steiger and Weiss.

The 10 city cantons acquiesced in the Helvetic Republic proclaimed by France, but the three Forest Cantons were defiant. They would be "burnt beneath their blazing roofs", they said, "rather than submit to the dictates of the foreigner". They were hopelessly outnumbered, however, and after the fall of Glarus and Schwyz the resistance focused on the town of Stans. The French commander called 9 September 1798 the hottest day of his life: "Like furies, the black legion of the French galley-slaves slew and raged the district through." The defiance ended in smoke and blood that night.

Left, *The Elephant Carousel* by Antoine Caron. The Elephant represents Geneva, the Turks sitting astride its back are Protestant infidels: both are under attack from Catholics. Above, Zurich at the time of the reformer Zwingli.

The Helvetic Republic was shaped territorially and constitutionally to suit the purposes of France. Bits of the south were chopped off and given to French-controlled Italy, Neuchâtel was completely cut off and Mulhausen was attached to France. The remainder were divided into 23 cantons under a rigidly centralised executive directory, as in France. The constitution duplicated the individual liberties introduced by the Revolution but these were less appreciated than the loss of local autonomy was mourned. The ultimate humiliation was the choice between signing a perpetual military alliance with France (effectively ending Swiss neutrality) and outright annexation.

The constitution was made unworkable by constant squabbling among the Swiss and six changes to it between 1798 and 1803 made no difference. "The sad but obvious truth was that the Swiss proved unable to govern themselves and unready to be a democratic nation," says the historian Christopher Herold. By 1803 Napoleon had had enough: they could have their quasi-sovereign cantons, their neutrality and even their judicial torture. The perpetual alliance was reduced to 50 years, and Napoleon reserved the right to recruit 16,000 men in Switzerland. Under his Act of Mediation Napoleon took the title Mediator of the Swiss Confederation and for a while the country was able to dress the wounds.

Educating the nation: One of the first paragraphs of the Helvetic constitution concerned education – "better than wealth and splendour" – and it rescued for posterity a pedagogue who was down on his luck. Rousseau's *Emile*, reviled in Geneva when it first came out, found at least one avid reader in Zurich, the youthful Heinrich Pestalozzi. Pestalozzi's name generally conjures up the image of "a benign and dishevelled father, surrounded by a happy flock of grateful children" (in Herold's words). The poor, he believed, should be educated in accordance with their poverty – no need to clutter the brain of a future farmhand or industrial worker with superfluous knowledge.

Rousseau's influence is all too obvious in Pestalozzi's thinking, although the experience of bringing up his own son made him wonder about Rousseau's maxim that a child should never be made to obey. Rousseau got rid of his five children, as we have seen, so this was pure theory on his part; Pestalozzi was rather more practical, though not sufficiently so to realise the glorious nobility of agriculture, as preached by Rousseau. He dutifully tried farming and was quickly bankrupt. It was sheer financial desperation that gave him the idea of turning the farm into an institute for waifs and strays. Their formal education took a distant second place to unpaid work in the fields, and even so he could not keep the place going.

Failure made Pestalozzi think again. He still believed that poverty was the preferred human condition, but he began to find circumstances in which wealth might be tolerable. His ideas poured out in *Evening Hours of a Hermit* and a four-part novel about a working couple, *Lienhard and Gertrud.*

Preceding pages: *The Famous of the Nation*, a painting of 1829. Left, cover of the confederate agreement of 1815. Above, Heinrich Pestalozzi, a teacher with a vision.

Pestalozzi's musings were interrupted by the French Revolution. He offered his services to the new French government but they were declined. Nevertheless, the revolution raised broad issues which Pestalozzi thought he ought to address, and the result was *My Researches of the Course of Nature in the Development of the Human Race*.

When French troops entered Switzerland in 1798 and established the Helvetic Republic, Pestalozzi again offered his services, and now they were accepted. The last stand of the Forest Cantons at Stans already mentioned, had resulted in many deaths and there were orphans to be taken care of. Unfortunately, Pestalozzi's orphan school at Stans lasted only eight months. He was appointed to another school at Burgdorf, but that position was equally short-lived. Unable to practise, Pestalozzi reinforced his theories through such works as *How Gertrud Taught Her Children* and *Instructions to Mothers on how to Make Their Children Observe and Speak*.

In 1805 the town of Yverdon in Vaud made a castle available for Pestalozzi to try again. His fame had spread through his writing and he was emboldened to say that with 200 disciples he could change the world. Impressed parents in France, England, Germany and Russia sent their children along as guinea-pigs, but the school was no more successful than its predecessors. A visiting Prussian inspector commented on an abysmal level of instruction and chaotic finances. When plans were drawn up to turn the school into a hospital, Pestalozzi cornered Czar Alexander I and offered to overhaul education in Russia.

Mrs Pestalozzi had on several occasions expressed the view that her husband was not all there, and he seemed to confirm suspicions at her funeral in 1815. Standing over her open grave, he launched into a sort of Socratic dialogue (providing both the questions and her answers) on whether he had made her as happy as he could have done. Eventually even his oldest supporters turned on him and in 1825 he had to close down the school. "His international fame as a teacher stands in strange contrast to his personal fate," says one study soberly. "His life was a series of disappointments."

The road to neutrality: The Congress of Vienna, convened to unstitch the Napoleonic Empire after its collapse in 1814, saw the Swiss patricians lobbying furiously to regain their former rights, and it was only through much banging of Swiss heads that the Big Four – Austria, England, Russia and Prussia – got them to agree to a loose federation. The cantons, now numbering 23, would be almost autonomous with just a few federal functions exercised by rota among Berne, Zurich and Lucerne. These deliberations were dramatically interrupted, however, by news of Napoleon's escape from Elba. Switzerland, whose neutrality was on the table awaiting ratification, was coerced into declaring war on France, the argument being that neutrality would be worthless if Napoleon were able to re-establish himself. The Swiss army invaded France on 3 July 1815, halted on the 22nd, and simply went home, an episode which the Swiss have fairly well succeeded in eradicating from national memory. With Napoleon finally disposed of, the Treaty of Paris recognised the perpetual neutrality of Switzerland on 20 November 1815.

Switzerland's borders were established as they are today. The Confederation lost Mulhouse but regained an enlarged Geneva, the Valais and Neuchâtel. The former territory of Basel was divided between Basel and Berne. While the international status and map of Switzerland were now secure, the domestic scene during the next 15 years of "Restoration" was chaotic. Cantons insisted on coining their own currency and customs barriers between them were so cumbersome that international traders used other routes.

In 1830, inspired by the example of the revolution in France, "Restoration" was transformed into "Regeneration", a curious misnomer unless it is understood to mean the regeneration of forces capable of turning confusion into utter chaos. Disgruntled peasants in the various cantons pursued their respective dreams which, apart from a general desire to cut the aristocracy down to size, reflected the spectrum of differences. The reactionary old order fought back with the kind of mindless logic which saw the French-speaking aristocrats in Fribourg demanding German as the official language because German it had been until 1798.

The Federal Diet was impotent, so much so that in 1832 seven cantons, including Lucerne and Zurich, formed a federation of sorts within the federation, and other groupings followed suit. These groupings then re-arrranged themselves so that the Confederation was effectively two bitterly antagonistic camps: "an ominous state of affairs, calculated to make every patriot tremble for the result..."

Left, planting the tree of liberty on Münsterplatz in Basel, 1798. Above, French troops near Hüningen.

Things nearly boiled over with the appointment of Dr D F Strauss to the chair of dogmatic theology at the newly formed university of Zurich in 1839. Dr Strauss was a liberal, the university having decided that it ought to keep up with the times. It was not a view shared by the watchdog "Committee of Faith". The appointment of Strauss was, it said, "so convulsing... that all minds saw themselves filled with horror as though smitten by an electric shock." Strauss was awarded a pension for his trouble, and resignation.

Aargau "set the whole country ablaze" by abolishing all monasteries and nunneries ,

thereby antagonising the pope and the Emperor of Austria whose ancestors had founded Muri, one of the monasteries in question. The compromise was to save the nunneries but to get rid of the monasteries. In 1844 Lucerne, one of the Catholic cantons, decided that its religious interests would best be served by handing over its education to the Jesuits. The comparatively undogmatic Jacob Burckhardt, then editor of the *Basler Zeitung* and later a distinguished historian, was moved to comment that "the Jesuits are a curse on all those lands and individuals who fall into their hands". More extreme Protestants launched guerrilla raids on the city, in one of which 100 para-military volunteers were killed and 1,900 captured. The seven predominantly Catholic cantons linked up as the *Sonderbund*, declared an Act of Succession and appointed a Council of War.

Prince Metternich, the Austrian Chancellor who had been one of the architects of the "new" Switzerland at the Congress of Vienna, watched these developments aghast. "Switzerland," he wrote, "presents the most perfect image of a state in the process of social disintegration... Switzerland stands alone today in Europe as a republic and serves troublemakers of every sort as a free haven. Instead of improving its situation by appropriate means, the Confederation staggers from evils into upheavals and represents for itself and for its neighbours an inexhaustible spring of unrest and disturbance."

The civil war pitted the 415,000 inhabitants of the seven Sonderbund cantons against nearly two million of the "Federal" cantons. The Sonderbund, moreover, was difficult to defend. The Forest Cantons held a strong central position, but Fribourg was completely isolated and Valais was connected to the others only by high Alpine passes. Understandably, the Federal forces picked off Fribourg first and then closed in on Lucerne from all sides. The city surrendered without a fight, and the others soon followed. The campaign was over within 20 days at the cost of 78 dead and 260 wounded.

The victors were lenient, the principal victims being the Jesuits, who were expelled. A new constitution was put to the vote, and although seven cantons opposed it they agreed to go along with the majority. The Federal Constitution of 1848 put foreign affairs and other institutions like the Post Office and Customs under central control, restricted mercenary activities abroad and ensured that for the first time all cantons had democratic institutions. The Swiss had a plausible national government at last and were in a position to catch up with the rest of Europe.

In the years that followed, Zurich played a prominent role in federal affairs, and under the dynamic leadership of its liberal mayor, Jonas Furrer, enjoyed an unprecedented cultural renaissance. The poet and novelist Gottfried Keller, a native of Zurich, returned in 1855 after a long absence abroad and could hardly believe his eyes. "It's frightful how the streets of Zurich pullulate with scholars and men of letters..." he wrote to a friend. "Two weeks ago in Zurich, we had a big spring festival in the Old Town, in which all the nations in the world, wild and tame, with Lola Montez, the Czar of Russia, Soulonque (the Emperor of Haiti), New Zealanders, Greenlanders, Bedouins, Bashibazouks, in short, whatever you can think of, paraded through the streets in the richest and most delicate decorated costumes, on horseback, in carriages, and on foot."

Some months later Keller was still so enjoying himself that he pretended to feel guilty. "I have already been present at various Zurich banquets," he wrote to another friend. "They cook well here, and there is no lack of subtleties, so that it was high time that I came home to preach morals and moderation to my countrymen, for which purpose, however, I had to taste things one after another in order to obtain a thorough knowledge of what it was I wanted to attack."

As Keller was writing these letters, the Swiss were feeling cocky enough to contemplate going to war with Prussia over the curious business of Neuchâtel, the first crisis of foreign policy the young state had to face. Neuchâtel had been something of an oddity since 1707 when, in order to spurn the advances of Louis XIV of France, it had put itself under the ducal sway of Frederick II of Prussia. It remained a Prussian possession even after admission as a canton in 1814; it was thus a monarchical enclave within a republican confederation. These royalists refused to join the federal forces against the *Sonderbund* in 1847 and were overthrown by republican sympathisers.

Two-day coup: The following year, however, the Great Powers reinstated the Prussian king as "Prince of Neuchâtel" as a bargaining chip in the nightmarish complications of the dispute between Prussia and Denmark over Schleswig-Holstein. The Swiss would have none of it and went on recognising the republican usurpers. On 2 September Count Frédéric Pourtalès usurped the usurpers in a royalist coup and Neuchâtel was Prussian again – but only for two days. A hundred or so royalists were taken prisoner in the counter-coup, which Frederick William IV of Prussia called a "slap in the face for all the monarchs of Europe". He mobilised, and the Swiss responded by raising a force of 30,000.

Napoleon III, who did not wish to see the Prussian army rolling up on his southeastern flank, offered to mediate, and from Britain poor Lord Palmerston, his brain still reeling with the complexities of Schleswig-Holstein, reminded Frederick William of the guarantees of Swiss neutrality. "Her Majesty's Government," he added, "would earnestly request His Prussian Majesty to consider how painful and distressing must be the spectacle presented by the military force of one of the great monarchies of Europe marching to attack a small but free State, in order to enforce rights which have been left in abeyance for eight years."

The agreement reached was that Switzerland would release the royalist prisoners, who would then go straight back to Prussia, Neuchâtel would be given full cantonal rights within the Swiss Confederation, and Frederick William would give up his sovereign rights for all time although he could, if he liked, go on calling himself Prince of Neuchâtel. It was the last of the old struggles between Swiss and foreign authorities.

Two other nagging problems remained: mercenaries and political refugees. The 1848 Federal Constitution had forbidden any more military capitulations (i.e. contracts to supply mercenaries) but it did not abolish those already in existence, two of which were with King Bomba of Naples and the pope. These meant that, whether they liked it or not, Swiss troops were mixed up in the wars of

Left, exchange of fire during the civil war between Basel District and Basel Town. Above, the Jesuits led the Conservative backlash.

the Italian Risorgimento, a situation which continued in defiance of the issuing of a new federal law in 1859 which tightened the ban on mercenary service.

In the same year a papal Swiss regiment was accused of atrocities after capturing Perugia; another unit was badly beaten the following year at Castelfidardo by an Italian army marching to join Garibaldi. About 4,000 Swiss "volunteers" fought in the American Civil War, mostly for the South, and 7,000 were killed fighting for France in World War I. Volunteering – even for the French Foreign Legion – was absolutely banned in 1927, the only exception being the Vatican Guard, founded in 1505 by Pope Julius II, whose contracts stipulate no combat duties.

The political convulsions of the mid-19th century created a flood of fugitives who chose to interpret Switzerland's internationally guaranteed neutrality as a safe haven for them. The country showed both profit and loss on its reputation as an asylum. It has already been seen how the French Huguenots virtually created Geneva's watch-making industry, and the intellectual climate obviously benefited from the presence of such luminaries as Richard Wagner. Very little could have been gained, however, from the arrival of Charles Bourbaki, the French commander of the Army of the Loire after his failure to break the Prussian line at Belfort in 1871. He was accompanied by 85,000 men who had to be quartered all over the country until the end of the war.

Swiss Napoleon: Louis-Philippe, the future "citizen-king" of the French, spent some years in Graubünden as M Chabaud, a mathematics teacher, but on assuming the throne he objected violently when Louis Napoleon, who later succeeded him as Napoleon III, claimed asylum in Switzerland. Napoleon was in fact a naturalised Swiss and had become a captain in the Swiss army. When the Diet refused to expel him, Louis-Philippe sent an army of 25,000 men to fetch him. Napoleon defused the danger by leaving Swiss territory and moving to London.

Louise-Philippe's actions reflected the not uncommon attitude that the price of Swiss neutrality was *not* harbouring fugitives. The Swiss of course did not agree and, at least to begin with, the majority of the population welcomed the refugees as martyrs, presenting them with gifts and trying to find them work. The welcome cooled when the volume swelled to thousands and, unable to find work, they became public nuisances. The character of the more prominent refugees changed too; instead of persecuted Protestants, they were men like Mazzini, Lenin and in time Mussolini. Geneva, a favourite haunt of refugees, had to put up with the Russian Bakunin and his flock of female nihilists.

The refugee question became a grave embarrassment to Switzerland, and its shadow today is the feeling, perhaps, that the vaunted secrecy of the country's banking system may shield rather too many unworthy causes.

In spite of difficulties with Neuchâtel, mercenaries and refugees, federal Swiss enjoyed internal peace, economic prosperity and a measure of respectability in foreign relations. Between 1848 and 1866 the only issue which seemed to require a constitutional amendment was the abolition of discrimination against Jews. Travellers began to take an interest in Switzerland, and in particular, the mountains. Albrecht von Haller, the Swiss poet, had sung the praises of the Alps as early as 1729 – until then they had simply existed and were to be avoided as far as possible. Although von Haller's theme

Above, Albrecht von Haller, poet of the Alps. **Right,** Henri Dunant, founder of the Red Cross.

The Red Cross

International Geneva, familiar to television viewers as the backdrop to so many peace conferences and summit meetings, is practically a state within a city. It is the address for scores of international organisations and even has it own postmark for their outgoing mail. Visitors should look out for the Red Cross Museum. It is no coincidence that the famous Red Cross which has fluttered above ambulances in countless wars is actually the Swiss flag with its colours reversed, nor that the Red Cross headquarters should be in Geneva. The two are closely linked, but the origin of that association is a largely forgotten story worth recounting.

Henri Dunant, the founder of the Red Cross (*pictured right*) , was born in Geneva in 1828 and went to Algeria at an early age to make his fortune as a grain speculator. He built several mills but, as the enterprise was under-capitalised, went back to Geneva to beguile investors, including his family, with tales of Algeria's fabulous potential under the French, who had just conquered it. He raised the capital but nothing went to plan. Dunant believed he was being victimised by French bureaucrats and decided to go to the top, to Napoleon III personally.

His efforts to secure an audience with Napoleon set something of a benchmark in sycophancy. He wrote a book which proved beyond a doubt that Napoleon was, among other things, heir to the Emperor Augustus, a fact only vaguely implicit in the title. It was *The Empire of Charlemagne Re-established*; or, *The Holy Roman Empire Reconstituted by His Majesty the Emperor Napoleon III*, by J. Henri Dunant, director and president of the Financial and Industrial Society of Mons-Djemila (Algeria), member of the Asiatic Society of Paris, of the Oriental Society of France, of the Geographic Societies of Paris and Geneva, of the Historical Society of Algiers, etc. Dunant had one copy printed, and then had to deliver it.

He managed to track down Napoleon in Italy on the eve of the Battle of Solferino. Understandably, the emperor had other things on his mind and, in the morning, so did Dunant. He found himself in the middle of one of the bloodiest battles in history – 33,000 casualties on the first day alone. Dunant was wearing a white suit appropriate to an imperial audience when he threw himself into washing wounds and generally helping as casualties poured in at the rate of 55 per minute. After two days and nights without sleep, the man in the now thoroughly bloodied white suit was a legend. By then it was almost irrelevant that Napoleon glanced at the book and said that for political reasons he could not accept it.

Dunant returned to Geneva and wrote a moving account of the horrors he had seen. A *Souvenir of Solferino* was a powerful plea for the creation of a neutral organisation which would care for the casualties of war. M Gustave Moynier, president of the Society for Public Usefulness of Geneva, read it and thought the idea good. Dunant toured Europe drumming up support; the result was the signing of the first Geneva Convention in 1864.

General Henri Dufour was in the chair, Moynier was vice-president, and Dunant was a spectator.

Three years after the foundation of the Red Cross, investors in the Algerian enterprise wanted to know what had happened to their money. Dunant was driven out of Geneva, bankrupt and a pariah. Wandering about penniless, he thought of other schemes like putting the Levant under Napoleon's protection and creating a Jewish state in Palestine. These came to nothing and pursuit by his creditors meant he could not stay in one place long.

In 1887 he returned to a semi-incognito existence in Switzerland, living like a hermit in the village of Heiden in Appenzell. A journalist discovered the fate of the founder of the Red Cross, and his scoop was quickly followed up by other newspapers. In 1901 the white-bearded hermit of Heiden jointly won the very first Nobel Peace Prize – seized on by his creditors as an opportunity to renew their claims. Embarrassed by the financial failure of one of its own, Geneva questioned his claim to have founded the Red Cross.

Dunant neither forgot nor forgave. When he died in 1910, he left all the Nobel prize money he had managed to preserve to charitable institutions in Norway and other parts of Switzerland. His remaining Geneva creditors got nothing.

was taken up locally by the likes of the Swiss historian Johannes von Müller (who inspired Schiller's tale of William Tell), the outside world remained largely indifferent.

John Ruskin, one of the most influential Victorian writers, therefore broke new ground with "mountains are great cathedrals of the earth, with their gates of rock, pavements of cloud, choirs of stream and stone, altars of snow, and vaults of purple travelled by the continual stars."

Tourist promotion: With that, an enterprising theatrical impresario named Albert Smith staged "Mont Blanc" at the Egyptian Hall in Piccadilly, London. Mont Blanc, of course, is in France, but the exhibits included genu-

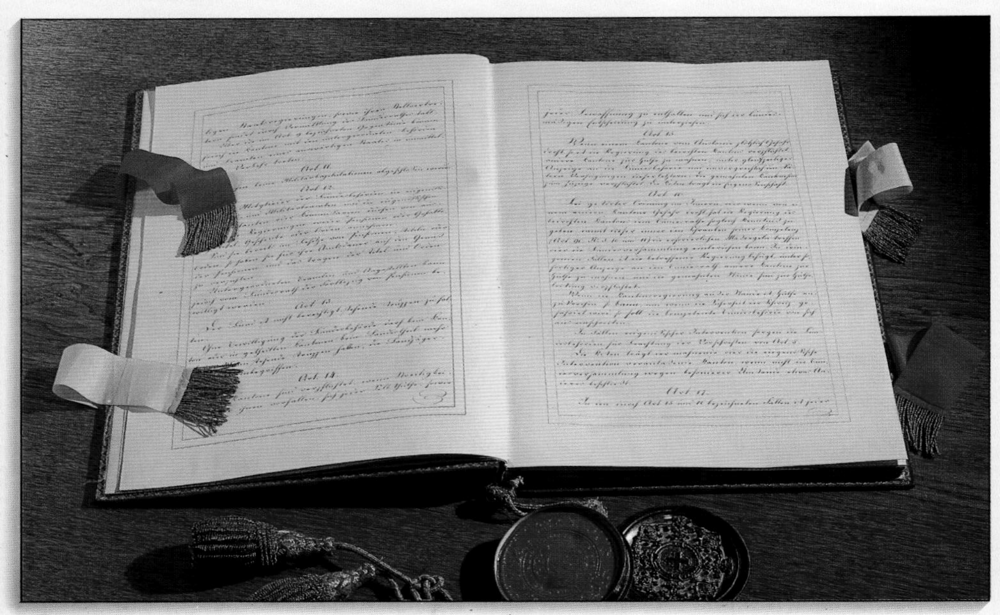

ine imported Swiss mountaineers in costume, and St Bernard dogs. Queen Victoria paid two visits, and the newspapers were suddenly full of advice on what the well-equipped traveller ought to take to Switzerland: *inter alia*, an umbrella, walking-stick, peppermints and a whistle. The Swiss Alpine Club was founded in 1863.

At the outset, no one considered going to Switzerland except in summer, but legend has it that in 1864 the manager of the newly acquired Kulm Hotel in St Moritz was describing the conditions in winter to four sceptical Englishmen spending an autumn evening around a log fire. In daylight in winter, he said, neither hat nor coat was necessary, and to prove the point he was willing to put them up at the hotel throughout the entire winter free of charge. If itwas not to their liking, he would pay their fares.

The hotel never looked back, but St Moritz itself was evidently not above criticism. "Built in an irregular untidy scrambly way with narrow dirty streets and terribly rough and jolty pavements," read one comment. "The great drawback," said another, "is the want of good food. The milk and the bread and the butter are good, but the meat is bad... For three months the only vegetables that we had were potatoes. In fact a person coming here for health gains greatly as regards climate, but loses greatly for want of good food and ordinary home comforts." The first form of entertainment was joy-riding downhill on *schlitten*, or toboggans, which were borrowed from villagers.

As long as the European balance of power remained stable, the independence and neutrality of Switzerland were safe and tourists could frolic in the Alps. When the balance was upset, cracks showed in the fabric. The Franco-Prussian war was a particular case in point because of the country's racial and religious composition. The political minority of Catholic Conservatives and the linguistic minority of the Radical-Democratic

French cantons were united by the dread of Protestant Germanisation, as exemplified by the growth of Prussia. The threat existed in the possible Germanisation of the federal government, so logically they dug in their heels in favour of cantonal autonomy. The division between Centralists and Federalists was therefore a racial and cultural one, championed respectively by the Vaudois Louis Ruchonnet and the Federal Councillor Emil Welti, the latter campaigning on the slogan "One law, one army".

The obvious outsider in the fundamental Swiss split was Ticino, the Italian-speaking canton, where Conservatives and Radicals were practically of equal strength. Complaints of dishonest electoral practices led to demonstrations, riots and bloodshed, and for a while civil war within the canton looked likely. Elections in 1889 to test some democratic innovations brought Ticinese living abroad streaming home to vote. The parties even chartered ships to bring hundreds of voters back from Europe and all the way from America. The result was a draw but, under the majority system, the Conservatives gained two thirds of the seats. The Radicals took the law into their own hands, seizing public buildings, imprisoning the Municipal Council and declaring a provisional government. Two battalions of federal troops and a promise of proportional representation calmed things down. In 1892, the Radicals were returned to power.

No sooner had Switzerland re-settled into internal calm than it felt the shadow of the formidable Otto von Bismarck. The problem, yet again, was Swiss political asylum, in this instance granted to German Socialists who continued to agitate against his government. A Prussian police inspector whom he had sent to spy on them was arrested and expelled. Bismarck demanded a withdrawal of the expulsion order and an apology, without which he would show the Swiss what he thought of their neutrality. The Swiss police were useless, he said, so among other measures he proposed to give the country a German police force. It seems that Bismarck was not jesting with his threat of war, but the Swiss repudiation was skilfully orchestrated by Numa Droz into an international issue and he quietly dropped it.

The size of Switzerland alone meant that the country could only ever be a pawn in the grand strategies swirling around it, but with the opening of the Gotthard Tunnel in 1882 it became an increasingly important pawn. The best route between the north and south

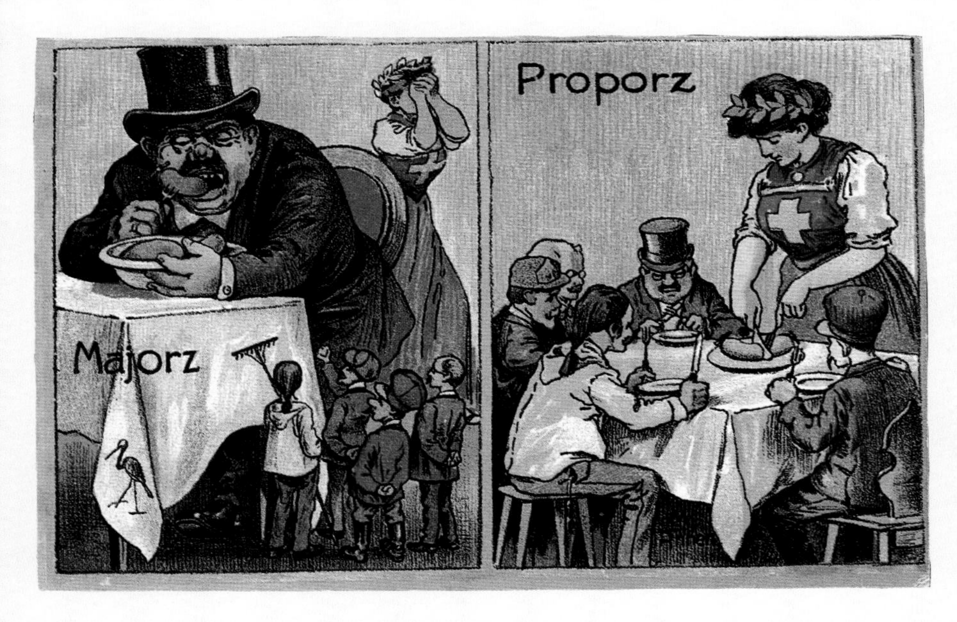

Left, the Federal Constitution of 1848. Above, campaign for proportional representation.

of Europe now ran through it, as did one of the most vital routes east-west. A neutral Switzerland provided one carefree flank for all its neighbours; the critical question was whether Switzerland had the will and the power to prevent its neutrality from being invaded by someone else. It was probably as much as Switzerland could do in this respect to announce large increases in the mobility and striking force of its army and, all the while, lend its neutral territory profitably as the seat for international organisations.

The new tunnels, roads and railways were bad news for farmers, or so it seemed. The military efficacy of embryonic Switzerland depended to a very large extent on a pastoral economy, that is to say non-labour-intensive stock-raising. Over the course of centuries, the Forest Cantons were joined and progressively dominated by others whose land was more conducive to mixed farming. Agriculture evolved so that by the middle of the 19th century the main activity overall was cereal production. In an isolated Switzerland, cereals were viable because farmers were cushioned by market forces. In a bad year, they produced less but prices went up accordingly so that the net result for them was more or less unaffected. The same could not be said for their urban customers, but they were a small minority of the population.

In the circumstances, cereal production increased so that the country generally had enough grain to cover domestic consumption for 300 days. Modern means of transport, however, exposed the Swiss farmer to competition from as far afield as Russia. Competition revealed that at the best of times Swiss production costs and prices were too high. In bad times, they were hopelessly out of touch with cereals which, thanks to better transport, could now be imported with ease. Swiss farmers turned to other things, and the cereal mountain at the end of the harvest shrank. By the end of the 19th century, the country produced only as much as would cover domestic consumption for six months.

Today, incidentally, if a farmer grows any grain at all it is likely to be for him and his family, no one else.

Swiss farmers realised that they had turned full circle. Conditions were still excellent for stock-raising and dairy farming, so they once again invested their energies in these. Some things had changed. The demand from abroad was not for horse-meat, as it had once been, but for beef.

Cheese sold so well that it eventually accounted for more than a third of agriculture exports. The dairy industry also produced two novelties which have since become synonymous with Switzerland – chocolate and condensed milk. The wine industry was not so lucky as, like cereals, it was up against foreign competition, especially from France. Some farmers obviously did extremely well, but there were enough exceptions to challenge the Free Trade axiom of the late 19th century. They broke ranks to press for, and ultimately achieve, protective tariffs.

Watch industry: The caricature of the Swiss national character as a laconic, self-sufficient man of the soil was rapidly being overtaken by events. At the end of the 19th century more than 90 per cent of the population was rural, but the typical Swiss was increasingly likely to have a job in textiles or chemicals, even if the factory in question was in a rural area. The watch and clockmaking industry, originally a home industry, was forced (especially after World War I) to adopt factory methods. The Geneva craftsmen bucked the trend by concentrating on precision instruments and luxury watches decorated by goldsmiths, but the industry as a whole went for volume, worked almost entirely for export and rose to control nearly 90 percent of total world production.

The causes of the subsequent decline in the Swiss market share are perhaps too obvious to warrant any great detail here. By the 1970s it had slipped to about 40 percent and was still falling as the Swiss franc gained against the currencies in the watch industry's main export markets. A falling dollar meant that competitive American watches were cheaper, and of course the entry of the super-efficient Japanese manufacturers re-wrote the rules from top to bottom.

What is less well-known about the Swiss watch industry is the way it fascinated Karl Marx and the Russian revolutionaries. It had him musing on the difference between "heterogeneous" and "organic" industry. Heterogeneous was the process by which some filthy capitalist merely assembled bits and pieces produced by honest workers in their various independent workshops. Organic manufacture meant the finished product of one worker being passed on as raw material for the next, eventually to emerge as a triumphant collective climax. The Swiss watch industry, by Marxist criteria, belonged to the former. Marx listed more than 100 specialists who independently – and of course "heterogeneously" – produced a watch. One was an engraver, another a mainspring maker, a third a polisher, and so on. Each was self-employed and independent.

Peter Kropotkin, a Russian prince turned nihilist, thought the watch industry was a microcosm of the cellular cantonal political system. "In a little valley in the Jura hills," he wrote in 1871, "there is a succession of small towns and villages of which the French-speaking population was at that time entirely employed in the various branches of watchmaking; whole families used to work in small workshops. In one of them I found another leader, Adhemar Schwitzguebel with whom, also, I afterward became very closely connected. He sat among a dozen young men who were engraving lids of gold and silver watches. I was asked to take a seat on a bench, or a table, and soon we were all engaged in a lively conversation upon socialism, government or no government, and the coming congresses."

Left, women making hay. Above, a poster supporting a woman's right to vote on cantonal affairs in Zurich.

In time, political conversation in Switzerland, as in the rest of Europe, hinged on the domino effect that began with the Habsburg Archduke Ferdinand's assassination in Sarajevo and resulted in World War I. The Franco-Prussian war in the 19th century had polarised Swiss society along French and German lines, and it was inevitable that the World War would re-open those wounds. The whole of the Swiss Army was mobilised as a show of strength to discourage invasion, but then the war effort ran into a snag which could probably have existed only in Switzerland. The law provided for the election of a Commander-in-Chief, with the rank of General, only in time of war or when the army was mobilised. The Federal Council elected Commander Ulrich Wille as Commander-in-Chief; Parliament voted for Colonel Theophil Sprecher. The choice was put to the nation, and Wille it was.

French-speaking Switzerland, as before, was suspicious of Germany, exceptionally so after its invasion of Belgium, and of the German outlook which had been gaining ground within the country. More than 220,000 "pure" Germans were living in Switzerland, half of them in Basel and Zurich alone. French-speaking Switzerland's sympathies were entirely with France and Britain. The Italian-speaking Ticinese were for Italy. For their part, German-speaking Swiss felt a kinship with Germany and admired its rise in technology, industry and commerce. Many deplored the invasion of Belgium but they still believed in Germany. "On general cultural grounds as well as political I believe that a German victory is desirable," wrote Karl Scheurer, head of the Military Department of Berne canton in August 1914. A month later, the German minister in Berne reported to his superiors: "From the very first day since the outbreak of war Switzerland has discreetly placed at our disposal her entire secret military intelligence service..."

The arrest and trial of two of General Wille's staff officers for passing secrets to the Germans and Austrians led to calls for his resignation, which did nothing for the morale of an army on uneventful, boring frontier duties. A few bombs were dropped but there were no serious breaches of neutrality. The real war, for Switzerland, was economic. Depleted agriculture was insufficient to feed the people and there was always the danger of being cut off not only from imported food supplies but also from the raw materials which kept industry running. An agreement with the central powers in 1915 provided for the import of German and Austrian goods but the Allies were not so cooperative. America guaranteed the supply of bread.

Some Swiss were ruined by the war, others did well. In the absence of foreign competition, it was like old times for farmers. The worst economic pressures fell on the working class. The bitterness of the workers was exacerbated by the large number of foreign-

ers who flooded in during the war – profiteers, deserters, conscientious objectors, and even more Russian revolutionaries like Lenin, Trotsky, Zinoviev, Axelrod and Martov. Their presence alone made Switzerland look like the revolutionary capital of the world, and Swiss socialists were impressionable. The idea of a general strike took shape.

The Federal Council moved quickly to stifle the strike. The army was sent into Zurich to prevent the Social Democrats from holding a demonstration to celebrate the anniversary of the Russian Revolution and the entire Soviet legation in Berne was frog-marched to the frontier. The strike was only partially effective, and the Social Democrats

succumbed to a federal order to call it off. Some of the strike leaders went to prison for short spells, but many of their demands, such as that for a 48-hour week, were quickly met.

League headquarters: Switzerland was enthusiastic about the proposed League of Nations after the war, and although it took no significant part in its creation, Geneva was selected as the seat of the League. Nevertheless, there was doubt whether Switzerland's neutrality would allow it to join; in 1920 the Declaration of London effectively bent the

Left, poster advertising the 1905 Wine-growers' Festival at Vevey. Above, General Henri Guisan.

rules to allow Switzerland in "by reason of an ancient tradition". The Confederation would not be called on to take part in military operations, but it would be bound to observe economic sanctions as imposed by the League. When the chance to join was put to the Swiss electorate, the Social Democrats described it as a choice between Woodrow Wilson and Stalin. Their preference did not need stating. The population voted in favour of joining, by 414,830 votes to 322,937.

The ambivalance of the Swiss position in the League led to all sorts of dilemmas, and with the League's manifest disintegration it was felt that the country ought to come out categorically for "integral" rather than "differential" neutrality. On 14 May 1938, just after the German "union" with Austria, the League passed a motion: "In consideration of the peculiar situation in Switzerland due to her perpetual neutrality, the League of Nations takes cognisance of the intention of Switzerland not to participate henceforth in any way in the application of sanctions provided for by the Covenant and declares that she shall no longer be called upon to do so."

With the prospect of war ever more likely, Switzerland took precautions against being caught out as before by filling its granaries. Neutrality in the event of hostilities was taken for granted, but sight of an official German training manual gave a shock: its maps put Switzerland firmly within the boundaries of the Third Reich. The German Swiss were no less alarmed than the rest and it made them realise that, after all, they were rather different from real Germans, certainly from Fascist Germans. Mussolini, having previously tried to persuade the Maltese that they spoke an Italian dialect and were therefore part of Italy (if anything, the language is more closely related to extinct Phoenician), told the Swiss Romansch-speakers that they were also really Italians. Romansch was hurriedly promoted to become Switzerland's fourth national language.

When war broke out, Switzerland's Commander-in-Chief was again elected, and the choice fell on the French-Swiss Henri Guisan of Vaud, a significant change from the previous German bias among the military. Mobilisation led to the call-up of 400,000 men, later increased to 850,000 with the inclusion of auxiliary services and the home guard, out of a total population of only four million. In the early stages of the war, Swiss troops took up their usual positions along the borders, but with the fall of France, which left the country completely surrounded by the Axis, Guisan adopted a strategy based on the Russian "defence in depth". The principle was that an enemy would be allowed to roll across the frontiers, where defence was difficult, in order to be met where conditions better suited the Swiss, in and along the Alps.

There is no doubt that the German High Command had plans for a Swiss invasion. They even had a codename, *Tannenbaum* (Fir Tree). Why they were not carried out remains a puzzle. One theory is that Hitler thought that the number of troops required could not be justified by what Switzerland represented in the way of raw materials. Moreover, he needed and already had the use of the Gotthard Tunnel to get coal to his Italian allies. The Swiss, he knew, had mined the tunnel and would blow it up at the first sign of an invasion, a potential loss which would make the invasion counter-productive. Hitler had a ready-made excuse to invade if he needed one: his troops had uncovered in French headquarters at La Charité-sur-Loire the terms of a secret agreement on the exchange of information between Swiss and French intelligence, an ironic postcript to World War I. In any case, after the Allied landings in North Africa and France, Hitler had other things on his mind.

On the economic front, Switzerland contrived to maintain neutrality with a balancing act of exquisite finesse. Goods of potential military value were supplied to both sides with perfect even-handedness; in return, the raw materials were made available to keep industry producing the goods in question. As before, Switzerland was a haven for fugitives, and countless Allied air crew shot down over central Europe were grateful for the Swiss route to the French Riviera, where a well-oiled escape organisation moved them west to neutral Spain and thence to Britain.

Post-war help: When peace was concluded, Switzerland devoted a generous proportion of its intact economy to post-war reconstruction. The full implications of Fascism in Germany and Italy ran deep. The various Swiss contingents seemed to decide that they were not bad bedfellows after all.

But the unified spirit of the war-time years was quickly upset by the effects of the Cold War. From 1948, the Communist party had a strong influence, and tensions between Communists and opposing factions caused a deep rupture in Swiss society. Nevertheless the economy purred from one boom to the next, propelled by huge reserves of capital and relatively cheap foreign labour. The question of giving the vote to women, a proposal discarded in 1959, but finally accepted in 1971, suggested the Swiss were not merely quaint, but antediluvian. Conservatives and the lower-middle classes broke a taboo by asking aloud whether the country really wanted so many foreign workers. Students no longer subscribed unquestioningly to the hallowed Swiss virtues, suggesting, for example, that they did without national service.

Even questions about the canton system, which most people assumed had been settled in 1848, arose in connection with the proposal to detach the Jura from Berne canton and make it a canton in its own right. To make matters worse, it emerged that Berne interests opposed to the change had bought votes to prevent it from taking place. And in Berne itself, the unthinkable. Elisabeth Kopp, first woman ever to be appointed to the federal government, left her post of Minister of Justice and Police in disgrace after phoning her husband and warning him to resign as director of a company being investigated for money-laundering. The scandal shook the country… and the proud image of the new Swiss woman. Students demonstrated at the drop of a hat, and on one memorable occasion, after dropping their trousers.

For the older generation especially, this was a lot to assimilate. The political and social stability of Switzerland is legendary. This is reflected in the results of the last parliamentary elections where one of the large political parties was regarded as winning a landslide victory when it won 5 percent more seats than it had done in the election four years before.

The Swiss, with their high standard of living and easy pace of life, have tended to regard themselves as being immune from the rest of the world. In 1997, the Swiss banking industry was found to have about $57 million in dormant accounts, many opened by German Jews before WWII, of which $8.6 million was in accounts under Swiss names.

Left, Swiss National Socialists in the Tonalle in Zurich. Above, Tamils protest against expulsion after being denied refugee status.

The Nazi Gold Scandal, as it became known, had a deep impact on the collective psyche but not a tangible one. The 1986 vote against becoming a member of the UN will, it is thought, not be reversed in the near future. As long as Switzerland remains one of the world's richest countries, it can be said that the average Swiss citizen will not be interested in big changes – especially if they will drag Switzerland into international or even European affairs – that might disturb the peaceful equilibrium of life.

HELVETIORU
DIE X AUGUSTI. II ET III
HAEC SUNT NOMINA EORUM QUI
FORTISSIME PUGNANTES CECIDERUNT.
DUCES XXVI.
MAILLARDOZ. BACHMANN. REDING. ERLACH. SALIS-ZIZERS.
H. DIESBACH. GOTTRAU. L. ZIMMERMANN. WILD. CASTELBERG.
GROS. P. GLUTZ. S. MAILLARDOZ. ERNEST. FORESTIER.
DIESBACH-STEINBRUGG. WALTNER. I. MAILLARDOZ. MULLER.
MONTMOLLIN. CASTELLA-ORGEMONT. CAPREZ. ALLEMANN.
CHOLLET. BOECKING. RICHTER.
MILITES CIRCITER DCCLX.
HUIUS REI GESTAE CIVES AERE COLLATO
STUDIO. C. PFYFFER
ARTE. A. THORV

DEI AC VIRTUTI
EMBRIS MDCCXCII
ENTI FIDEM FALLERENT
AMICORUM CURA CLADI SUPERFUERUNT
DUCES XVI.
S-ZIZERS. DURLER PFYFFER-ALTISHOFEN.
ERMANN. REPOND I. ZIMMERMANN.
A. ZIMMERMANN GLUTZ. GIBELIN.
ARDOZ: VILLE CONSTANT-REBECQUE.
BIERE. FORESTIER. LORETAN.
MILITES CIRCITER CCCL.
MONUMENTUM POSUERE.
OPERA.L.AHORN.
R1903 1943

FREISCHÜTZEN GEMPEN
SOCIETED DA TREGANTS
34

Chur
1874 Schützengesellschaft Flüh 1982

FABRIQUE DE CHOCOLAT
PH. SUCHARD
Fondée en 1826.
CHOCOLAT
U-S 4023
217
217.

The "Gnomes of Zurich" is an expression coined in the 1970s by a British Foreign Secretary who needed a quick explanation, and preferably also a scapegoat, for chaos in international money markets. The insinuation was of sinister manipulations behind a screen of state-sanctioned secrecy, and it reinforced the idea of the numbered Swiss bank account as the haven of drug dealers, terrorist organisations, Third World tyrants and shady tycoons generally.

This cynical view of Swiss banking, and the wealth derived from it, owes something to pure envy but the intriguing question remains: how can this small, landlocked country with hardly any natural resources be so rich? The country has consistently been one of the richest in the world, and often *the* richest, ever since the late Middle Ages.

How the money was acquired is a matter of history, but that still does not say how much has swilled through the vaults along the Bahnhofstrasse in Zurich. No one knows; certainly not the Swiss government. Gross national product and similar statistics compiled by the federal authorities go nowhere near the proverbial cash under the mattress, in this case what Swiss companies refer to in their balance-sheets – but do not quantify – as "still reserves".

Swiss law allows companies to be coy about their accumulated wealth, the reason being, according to the managing director of one such company, that if the truth were known there would be such a scandal that the government would be obliged to tax them. Hence the old joke that the only figure to be found in a Swiss company's annual report is the date. Companies are now more candid than they used to be, but there is still a portion of the iceberg whose vast size can only be guessed. It helps to know that the turnover of Nestlé alone, for example, has at times exceeded the entire federal budget. The two main banks are in another league again: their balance-sheets total roughly the GNP. At the last count, Switzerland had over 1,100 banks operating about 4,000 branches. A few years ago, a survey revealed that there were rather more banks than there were dentists. However, the economic crisis of the early 1990s also touched Switzerland. A lot of smaller banks had to be closed or have been overtaken by bigger ones.

As the history section of this book shows, the origin of Swiss wealth was plainly and simply booty, the haul of Burgundian jewels, silk and money after the battles of Grandson and Morat in 1476. The Swiss very nearly went to civil war in the scramble over who got the proceeds; it was averted, curiously, by the intervention of a wealthy native of Inner Switzerland Cobwalden, Niklaus von Flüe, who had previously given away his money to become a hermit.The Swiss who got rich in the 15th century could not hold a candle to the likes of the Fuggers in Germany, but their fortunes had the happy knack of surviving, whereas many German ones sank under religious wars. The Swiss remained neutral during the Thirty Years' War and even did very well out of it, mainly by supplying the belligerents with the goods

Preceding pages: the Lion monument in Lucerne; Wangen-on-the-Aare in canton Solothurn; rifleclubs' meeting. Left and right, a land known for luxury chocolate and numbered bank accounts.

which they were distracted from producing for themselves. Legendary Swiss neutrality is easily misconstrued: profitable, yes; pacifist, no.

Soldiering on: "The fashion of the Swiss for gunpowder on interesting occasions," Charles Dickens once mused, "is one of the drollest things." Presumably he had been leafing through history and seen that mercenary soldiering was for centuries the backbone of the Swiss economy. The country has always been dependent on imports to an unusually high degree, and to pay for these imports it has had to sell something abroad. Until the 19th century, Switzerland's most marketable asset was the fighting quality of its men. In view of Switzerland's modern image as the land of moderation and reconciliation – Geneva has turned peace conferences into a minor industry – the irony is doubly delicious. Swiss neutrality was originally and fundamentally the basis on which best to sell impartial mercenary services.

The Swiss mercenary was quality merchandise, and Swiss success is all about quality. It could not have been otherwise. With the need to bring in raw materials and then ship finished products out, Swiss industry has always been a hostage to transport costs. A 19th-century Swiss economist worked out that getting textiles to the nearest seaport cost Swiss exporters 10 times as much as their competitors. The solution was to concentrate on goods which were small, specialised luxuries and thus commanded a price high enough to include a generous profit margin. Watches were just the ticket, and Huguenot refugees from France knew how to make them.

One of Switzerland's sharper critics pays tribute to a combination of opportunism and dedication: "The very limitations under which the Swiss have been labouring for hundreds of years have developed in them several qualities which have become their second nature. For one thing, they are hard-working and tenacious; for another, they are frugal and thrifty. These qualities would not have been enough, however, if they had not also acquired an uncanny flair for seeing potential gains where unimaginative human eyes could detect nothing."

Watch workers: Decentralisation spread Swiss wealth around: Geneva and the Jura had watches, St Gallen embroidery, Zurich textiles, Basle dyestuffs, and so on. In the case of watches and embroidery, work was further decentralised by being farmed out to families to be done at home. "Watchmakers work as free men," declared one, but the arrangements did not always please children. "After supper," complained one12-

year-old worker, "I have to unravel until 10 pm; sometimes, if work is pressing, I have to ravel in the cellar until 11. Afterwards I say good night to my parents and go to bed. Every day is the same."

St Gallen, with a population of less than 8,000 but boasting no fewer than 60 embroidery operations, grew so rich in the 18th century that the abbot was able to spend half a million gulden adorning the pocket republic and still leave a quarter million, in cash, in his will. In 1813 a French priest wondered whether the abbey had not taken secularism a bit too far: "St Gallen is an entirely commercial city... From commerce is born avarice, not the sordid and bizarre avarice which forms skin-flints but rather the fatal habit of weighing sentiments on the scales of gold."

The Achilles' heel of an economy dependent on exporting pricey luxuries was the health of its foreign markets. War, depression or even changing fashion could strike a lethal blow. The embroidery industry, which at the beginning of the 20th century employed 100,000 people in the northeastern cantons, was wiped out by the economic malaise after World War I. St Gallen became a ghost town. More recently, in the financial turmoil of the 1970s , the collapse of many currencies while the Swiss franc stood firm had a devastating effect on the sale of Swiss watches. Resilient ingenuity, however, has since repaired much of the damage.

Left, in any language, money talks. Above, it also makes the world go round.

The chemical industry which now dominates Basel was largely the result of a professor at the local university experimenting with sulphuric and nitric acids and coming up with a synthetic material which formed the basis of plastics. The city's chemical giants, responsible for Valium among other products, are better off than the traditional industries because they import raw materials made cheaper by a rising Swiss franc.

The chemical giants – Novartis and Roche – have discarded the secrecy which once made their affairs as impenetrable as a numbered bank account. They are now probably no better or worse than large corporations anywhere.

Even the watchmakers have consolidated their operations to meet Japanese competition; so perhaps, as one economist has predicted, the days of the Swiss economy as an enigmatic freak are over. "The sturdy Alpine peasant has become a type of landscape gardener living off state subsidies... The country is full of foreign workers who will not go home... In short, the Swiss economy is like any other."

LANGUAGE

Surely the Swiss are effortless polyglots who switch between flawless German, French, and Italian and usually throw in serviceable English as well? No, not quite!

The Swiss-German majority, for a start, read and write a language they don't speak (German), and speak one which is neither official nor national (Swiss-German *Schwyzerdütsch*) and is incomprehensible across the border in Germany. Secondly, official French as disgorged in writing by bureaucrats makes purists cringe, while the vernacular French is not at all bad, although each area has its own idiosyncracies. Italian Swiss can speak standard Italian, the third official language, but generally use dialects which would draw blank stares in Italy. Romansch, national but not official, sounds something like a mixture of Italian and Schwyzerdütsch but is Latin and Etruscan.

Government documents are in the three official languages, while officials are addressed in the "national" language of the region. That is the theory; the practice is more complicated. The best way to make any sense of it is to follow the chronology.

Accidents of history: Romansch is a legacy of the Rhaeti, who resisted the Romans, and of the Romans themselves. It is used by only 50,000 Swiss in Graubünden and splits into five quite different dialects in the following areas: Upper Engadine, Lower Engadine, Vorderrheintal (Valley of Front Rhine), Rheintal and the region of Oberhalbstein. Romansch was declared a national language in 1938 to thwart Mussolini, who tried to argue that Romansch was Italian and Graubünden suitable for annexation.

German arrived in Switzerland with the Alemanni, who expelled the Romans, and Schwyzerdütsch is collectively three bands of the Alemannic dialect known as "Low", "High" and "Highest" Alemanni. The grammar is very different from standard German, a relatively recent convention created by Luther's translation of the Bible.

The Swiss read the Bible in Luther's German, just as they now read their newspapers and government documents in standard German, but they speak one form or another of Alemannic. Highest Alemannic is, appropriately, the dialect of people living in the very high Alps, and while they can understand the lower forms of Schwyzerdütsch, those lower down can't always understand them. The speakers of Highest Alemannic are favourite topics of cocktail-party chatter in the context of "you haven't heard an accent until you've heard theirs".

Accents speak volumes: Unlike accents in England, the varieties say nothing about class but they reveal where someone comes from and therefore their character. Thus a person is presumed to be aggressive if audibly from Zurich, witty if from Basel, and so on. The educated classes can speak and read standard German but are not inclined to do so. Radio and television use both German and Schwyzerdütsch: the former for international news and weather reports; the latter for sport. A Swiss-German must listen to sermons in Schwyzerdütsch but can pray only in German.

In literature and the arts, the situation gets more complicated. Swiss writers by their own admission generally come across as stilted when they write in German. Writing in dialect, though, may lead to different problems. A 20th-century playwright committed suicide because a work in his distinctive Aargauer dialect was boycotted, he believed, for no other reason. An attempt to restage the play in 1975 foundered on the difficulty of finding nine professional actors in Switzerland who could handle the dialect convincingly. Two Swiss-German postwar writers, Friedrich Dürrenmatt and Max Frisch, brushed aside such hazards to become better known to English readers and audiences than any contemporary German authors bar Günter Grass.

The history of French in Switzerland is a little less complex. In about AD 500, Helvetic territory split between the Alemanni and the Burgundians, who were also Germanic but gradually adopted the Latinian language, which became French. In so doing they earned the derision of those who remained loyal to Alemannic, and were called "Welsch", applied (as the Greeks did "barbarian") to anyone who did not speak their language. As for Romansch, that was

"Kauderwelsch" or, roughly, gibberish.

Those of Burgundian stock held their ground and today about one-fifth of the Swiss population speak French. They are concentrated in six cantons: Geneva, Waadt, Jura, Neuchâtel, and a large part of Fribourg and Valais.

The Swiss-French feel they are very much part of the cultural world of France and would only wish to take issue with Parisians over language on the matter of whether the "x" at the end of Chamonix, for example, ought to be pronounced. The Genevese think it should. There is one point which never fails to make French blood in Paris or Geneva boil, however, and that is what the Swiss-Germans do to their language.

Italian is the common language in Ticino and in parts of Graubünden, but even in these confined spaces it manages to get things into a twist. A census of the village of Bivio in Graubünden (total population, 260) revealed that the majority spoke Italian but there were enclaves of Romansch and Schwyzerdütsch. The village had both a Catholic and a Protestant church, and it was said that the pastors had to look at the congregation before deciding in which language to preach. Romansch or Schwyzerdütsch was an easy choice. The challenge lay with the Italians who all spoke Italian but divided between a form of Lombard (koine) and a Bergamasco dialect introduced over several centuries by shepherds in the Alps.

Local Italian dialects amount to private languages, so someone from northern Ticino would be completely baffled by what is said in the south. Let a Swiss-Italian academic have the last word: "If I have to go to the window of a post office and I speak Italian, I make the postal clerk understand that I want to ask for some information or buy a stamp and that I want our relationship to remain at this strictly official level. If I have to go back to the same window two or three times, and...if even a single allusion to the excessive heat or cold, to head-ache or sniffles, to the health of wife or children... should insinuate itself into our exchange, dialect is immediately used to underline the new sort of relationship between us."

Above, in Geneva dogs speak French: "I don't foul the pavements."

SPES

Swiss cuisine is like a chain of roadside restaurants run by an unequal partnership of Germans, French and Italians. The larger establishments along routes which since Roman times have been busy European thoroughfares tend to be under solid German management with a couple of French and Italian cooks brightening up the kitchen. Smaller inns in remote areas are more likely to be left almost entirely to the partner who happens to live locally. The larger places have correspondingly longer menus catering for all tastes; it is in the smaller establishments, where the specialities change from one valley to the next and according to season, that the discriminating traveller tucks in a napkin and gets down to some serious ethnic appreciation.

Not surprisingly, the flavour of regional cooking bends with the contours of Switzerland's linguistic topography. The basic geography is simple and logical: Frenchified in the west, Italianish in the south, Swiss-German elsewhere. Each of these regions is represented, however, in the collective pool of "typical" Swiss dishes. A consolidated menu might include two Zurich specialities, *Geschnetzeltes* and *Ratsherrentopf*. The former is strips of meat stewed in a thick sauce and served with Rösti; the latter is, literally, the "councillors' stew" of several kinds of meat and potato.

Other possible contenders are Lucerne *Chügelipastete* (pâté in a pastry case), *Papet Vaudois* (leeks with sausage), *Churer Fleischtorte* (meat pie), *Innerschweizer Älplermagronen* ("Alpine macaroons"), *Puschlav pizzoccheri*, Ticino *busecca* (entrail-and-vegetable soup), Goms *cholera* (bacon, leek, cheese and potatoes), Engadine *plain in pigna*.

The famous fondues and raclettes are considered in the accompanying article on cheese in general. The regional sweets which have become national are Zuger *Kirschtorte* (cake with Kirsch), Aargauer *Rueblitorte* (carrot cake), Glarner *Birnbrot* (pear bread), the Engadine *Nusstorte* (layer cake with a nut filling), Willisauer *Ringli*, Basler *Leckerli*, and Schaffhauser *Züngli*.

These national favourites have emerged from Switzerland's historical patchwork of rather isolated communities whose distinctive diets depended on what was available locally. By the 12th century the Bishop of Horburg, at least, seems to have overcome most barriers. Records have him sitting down to hams, the head of a pig and its trotters in brawn, savoury mince (*Gehacktes*), and several kinds of sausage. That was the first course; he then moved on to smoked beef with cabbage, roast neck (*Schluchbraten*), pot-roast, venison, millet cooked in blood, larded shoulder of pork and various milk and egg dishes.

Regional patterns formed more distinctly in the 16th century. In Ticino, the Italian south, people ate rice imported from the Po plain with home-produced pork, goat's milk, chestnuts and wine. In the Valais, the emphasis was on bread, cheese, drief beef and wine, the monotony relieved by the introduction of some marvellous beans left behind by the Turks after their unsuccessful siege of Vienna. When the Austrians worked out what to do with them, the result was coffee. The other legacy of the Turks, known as *granturco*, was corn, which quickly established itself in Grisons and Ticino.

In the Lowlands, a large part of the diet was a purée made from millet. As puzzled as the Austrians had been by the mysterious Turkish beans, the Swiss at first used a novelty from America merely as a decorative plant. It was only in a lean period in the 18th century that they recognised that the potato made a reasonable meal. It never looked back. Cooked in its skin or as a purée, the potato is a feature of many dishes today in the northeast and northwest. In Aargau and Berne the tradition was born of par-boiling, slicing into strips and frying the potato, the result known as *Rösti*. The preference in western parts is *au gratin*. Ticino shunned the potato but was enthusiastic about corn which, as polenta, became one of the staples.

Preceding pages: family at table (1643). Left, farmers demonstrating the five senses (around 1796). Above, on the way to the dairy.

A calendar is almost as useful as a good map to make the most of the rich variety of Swiss regional dishes because many specialities are tied to a particular holiday or festival. The following pointers are necessarily highly selective.

New Year: In Ticino, *zampone*, a stuffed pig's trotter with lentils; in Graubünden, especially the Engadine, varieties of smoked pork with vegetables in a barley soup. *Beinwurst* is not, in spite of the name, a conventional sausage but a skin filled with smoked pork, herbs and wine according to the "secret" recipe of the butcher concerned.

Shrove Tuesday: Everywhere, delicacies fried in oil – *Fasnachtschüechli*, *Schenkeli*, *Zigerkrapfen*, *Schlüferli*, *Rischeulen*i and so on. In Ticino, cooks celebrate Shrove Tuesday by preparing huge pots of saffron risotto in the village piazza. By midday the whole village will have turned out for a free helping together with *luganighe* (garlic pork sausages). The piazza is laid out with tables; the festivities go on all day and into the night. In Protestant Basel, the celebrations start in the early hours of the day before. All lights in the city are turned off for 4am when hundreds of piccolos and drums strike up simultaneously to herald the Morgenstreich. A pre-dawn procession by lantern-light is the start of a three-day carnival in which revellers, many wearing masks, pack restaurants for the traditional gruel, brown-windsor soup and onion and cheese tart.

Easter: An alternative to the ubiquitous lamb is *Gitzi* (kid). Many families troop off into the countryside in search of young dandelion plants, whose succulent leaves make a delicious salad.

Autumn: Having just returned from their summer holidays, half the country's cooks seem to vanish again on the bugle-call signalling the start of the shooting season. Some may conscientiously drop off their trophies at the office, but most of the "chamois" (the goat-like Alpine antelope) on menus at this time of year is likely to have arrived frozen from somewhere like Australia. The origin of the ingredients may be suspect, but the preparation of venison is expert and delicious.

Metzgete: Once merely the day on which farmers slaughtered their animals, Metzgete has become a gastronomic event, an occasion for restaurants to stack the proverbial groaning table with ham, bacon, an immense selection of sausages and various parts of the noble pig tagged as *Wädli*, *Öhrli*, *Schnörrli* and *Schwänzli*. The Berner Platte, which has made this day its own, consists of bacon, sausages and ham served with sauerkraut and potatoes.

Wine was introduced by the Romans, but it was not until the 9th century that the beer-drinking laity obtained it from the clergy who used it, of course, for liturgical purposes. By the 19th century production had grown so indiscriminately, and the results become so indifferent, that consumers went back to drinking beer. A wine statute in 1953 imposed rigorous quality controls and since then Swiss wine has improved immensely.

Most wine is produced in the west and the Valais, about three-quarters of it white. The wine produced around Lake Zurich and in the Thurgau and Schaffhausen areas is predominantly "Blauburgunder" with smaller quantities of a Riesling-Sylvaner hybrid. Ticino specialises in reds made from the Merlot grape, and most restaurants offer a house-wine as *nostrano* – "one of ours". These are usually home-pressed blends, comparatively cheap, and delicious.

Spirits took some time to recover from being blamed for the epidemic of alcoholism in central Switzerland in the 19th century, and even in the early part of the 20th century some of the stronger concoctions – including absinthe – were banned. The reputation of spirits such as Kirsch, Pflümi, Mirabelle, Marc, Grappa, Enzian and Chrüter has long since been rehabilitated.

Left, absinthe was once a major export. Right, raclette in Saas Fee.

CHEESE

"Swiss cheese" – that of holes and tired jokes – is Emmentaler and just one of hundreds of different varieties. To put the jokes to rest, the holes are bubbles made by carbonic acid during the four-month fermentation process. The more symmetrical the holes are, the more expert the fermentation.

The Swiss were making cheese before their recorded history began, and as Roman records indicate that the cheese they imported over the Alpine passes had holes in it, it was almost certainly a kind of Emmentaler. Perhaps the Romans started the jokes too.

In any case, Emmentaler is now produced in Germany, France, Austria, Finland, Argentina, Australia, the USA and no doubt in many other places as well. The appearance is similar, but even identical processing cannot achieve the flavour imparted by the Alpine herbs which the cows eat on the high pastures during the summer months.

With the end of the Pax Romana, the Swiss must have used goat's milk for their cheese because only goats would have survived all year round at the kind of altitude to which herdsmen were restricted by hostilities below. It was only the security brought about by the military victories at Morgarten and Sempach in the 14th century that created safe grazing for cattle in the Forest Cantons, Entlebuch, the Oberemmental, the Bernese Oberland and the Gruyère region, the heart of the future dairy industry. At a later stage in their history, the herdsmen had to decide between growing cereals for their own consumption or devoting the acreage to grazing. The cows won.

"The products that can be obtained from milk and from cattle are the precious and divine materials of our mountains and bring gold, silver, and much wealth into our country," wrote a 17th-century chronicler of Lucerne.

After Emmentaler and Gruyère, the best known cheese is Sbrinz, a hard variety which becomes easily digestible after being left to ripen for about three years. On a smaller scale, Schabziger from Glarus, Vacherin Fribourgeois, Tomme Vaudoise, Tête de Moine, Appenzell Rässe and the Ticino Formaggini are notable delicacies.

The popularity of cheese fondues in general and raclettes of Valaisan cheese in particular has spread well beyond Switzerland in recent years. Some of the contraptions now used to melt the cheese are designed along the lines of an electric chair, but in fact both fondue and raclette are ancient dishes. Dairymen stuck in the Alps used to melt their cheese and mix it with milk; it was the Valaisans who first introduced the refinement of pouring it over potatoes.

Purists insist that the raclette should use halves of Goms cheese only which are scraped after being melted by an open fire or a large charcoal oven. Potatoes (often in their jackets), pickled onions and gherkins are among the approved accompaniments. Fancy equipment erected on individual tables, exotic sauces and so on are frowned upon and polite visitors are likely to find that they are left with no choice in this respect.

The Cresta Run

Before the motor-car and aeroplane, the fastest men on earth were an amiable group of eccentrics including the author and literary critic John Addington Symonds (Harrow and Oxford) who was in a "miserable state of health mentally and physically" and, strictly speaking, should have been tucked up in bed in the Swiss hospital in which he was staying.

Instead, Symonds and company, some of whom were also in Switzerland on doctors' orders, begged and borrowed *schlitten* which the Swiss used as their ordinary means of winter transport and, hurling themselves down a hill near the Belvedere Hotel in Davos and down the Clavadel Road leading to Klosters, invented the sport of tobogganing and hence its offspring, bob-sleighing.

By 1903, the year in which the Wright brothers nursed *Kitty Hawk* into the air, they were attaining speeds of some 80 miles an hour. This was at a time when motor-cars were still being preceded by pedestrians waving red flags.

An entry in Symonds's diary is one of the earliest references to how the sport started. After a dinner which lasted until two in the morning, complete with a zither and guitar player, he and two friends "descended on one toboggan in a dense snow-storm. It was quite dark and drifty beyond description." They got down all right, the diary notes, but not so "Miss I" who was on another toboggan. She completely lost control, flew over a photographer's hut and landed "on the back of her head on the frozen post-road. I fully expected to find her dead. She was only stunned, however."

The original *schlitten* was simply a pair of flat iron runners screwed to a wooden frame on which riders sat upright. Canadian settlers discovered that the Indians used something similar, and in 1870 they were tearing down Mount Royal in Montreal.

The English invalids founded the Davos Tobogganing Club in 1883 and in that year issued a challenge to all other nationalities to a race down the twisting road from Davos to Klosters. Two Australians, one Canadian, two Germans, one Dutchman and 12 Swiss accepted. The race was a dead heat between the Australian, one George Robertson, and the conductor on the Klosters post-coach, Peter Minsch.

In the meantime, the St Moritz invalids had also made a rough and ready run alongside the Kulm Hotel. The general standard of behaviour among these invalids was very open to reproach: "A good deal of gambling and drinking took place at times and flirtation led to many scandals, all of which used to stop when the spring came and the invalids scattered with the melting of the snow."

Realising the commercial potential of the new craze, the owner of the Kulm Hotel contributed towards the cost of building a better run to woo custom away from Davos. The result was the most famous toboggan run of all, the Cresta, and competitions between the two fledgling resorts were soon being organised on a regular basis.

The 1886 competition provided a sensation. Up until that year riders had invariably sat upright on the toboggan but, as the local *Alpine Post* newspaper dramatically reported: "Mr Cornish... lay his body on the toboggan, grasping its sides well to the front, his legs alternating between a flourish in mid air and an occasional contact with mother earth... To see him coming head first down the leap is what the Scotch call uncanny... Unfortunately, however, he came to grief more than once during the race, though the extraordinary quickness of his recovery astonished the onlookers."

The following year provided an even greater thrill. A New Yorker, a Mr L.P. Child, "who had considerable experience of tobogganing in the United States", asked a local carpenter to run up a toboggan to his own specifications. He named it *America*. It was long, low, built of solid wood and had spring steel runners attached fore and aft.

Mr Childs thrashed the opposition down the Clavadel road. The shocked regulars wanted the device banned, but others could see the writing on the wall and rushed off to see their carpenters. The genesis of the bob-sleigh was a Mr Wilson Smith asking the blacksmith if he could link up two Americas.

Tobogganing was for some years confined to a closed circle of *aficionados*. But a series of articles carried in *The Bystander* in 1905 brought the sport to the attention of a much broader audience. "To attempt to explain tobogganing from any logical basis is absurd," it was stated.

"Tobogganing itself is absurd. It glories in being absurd... The Cresta, after all, is not so extravagant as tiger-shooting, but it provides hardly less excitement and certainly no fewer perils. If the measure of a sport's excellence lies in the proportion of danger which it holds for its pursuers, then the Cresta ought to be well up in the list."

Tobogganers seemed routinely to die, but it was from tuberculosis or whatever complaint had brought them to Switzerland, and the sport, in the first instance. The first death to occur on the run was that of a 27-year-old British Army captain, Henry Pennell, who had ironically won the Victoria Cross on the Indian North West Frontier. The second death followed less than a month later and involved another heroic character, Count Jules de Bylandt, a Dutch big-game hunter. De Bylandt crashed into the level crossing which controlled traffic where, before a tunnel was built, the run crossed a road.

The scene of Captain Pennell's accident was a particular curve, known as Shuttlecock, which caused so many horrific high-speed tumbles that in 1934 a club was formed, and an annual dinner given, by those who survived. As is the custom of such clubs in other spheres, members instituted their own peculiar rites. Members wore elbow pads over their dinner-jackets and adopted a somewhat obscure and not-very-catchy motto: "Here's to it, and do it, and do it again. If you don't do it when you come to it, you may not be able to do it when you want to do it again."

The 1928 Winter Olympic Games were held in St Moritz and six nations took part in the toboggan event. The British regarded the Cresta as their pet invention and entered two lords, Brabazon and Northesk, but the former was eliminated by a crash at Shuttlecock during practice which left him with broken ribs and a badly bruised face. In the end the event was won by two American brothers, Jennison and Jack Heaton.

Over the years since the 1928 Olympics, the Cresta Run has been tackled by any number of celebrities, some of them lulled into trying by an oleaginous veteran who would sidle up to visitors to St Moritz and say: "Let me introduce you to a sport that requires no work at all. All you have to do is lie on a toboggan..."

There is a story that Errol Flynn stopped at Shuttlecock, knocked back a glass of champagne proffered by an astonishingly beautiful blonde, and continued to a chauffeur-driven Rolls-Royce at the bottom. Brigitte Bardot used to be a familiar sight at the Cresta while she was married to Gunther Sachs, the industrialist and pillar of the club in more recent years.

The Cresta is not all about fabulous wealth and glamour, however. The most successful rider of the Run's history, and therefore by definition the most absurd, was Nino Bibbia, the who hailed from St Moritz and was a greengrocer.

Left, poised for adventure. Above, one lady and many gents in the end-of-season photograph.

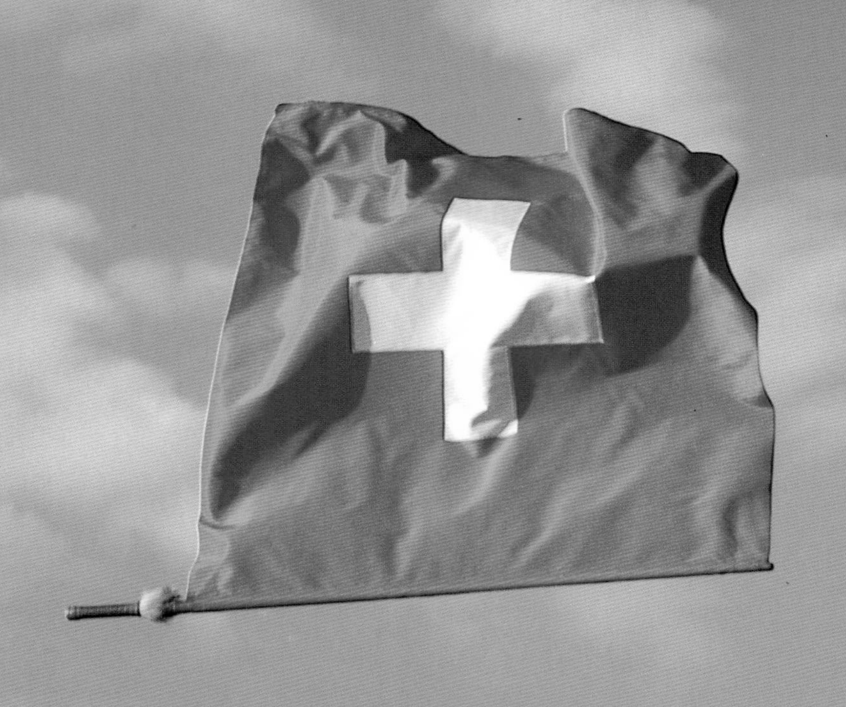

PLACES

The sharp divisions in the landscape and the major differences in elevation make a trip to Switzerland a rewarding experience almost any time of year. While Eastern Switzerland and the Lowlands, with their blossoming orchards and lush meadows, show themselves to best advantage in spring, in the summer visitors would tend more towards seeking out the banks of the country's numerous lakes.

Surfers and yachtsmen in particular prefer Western Switzerland, or the ice-cold, yet always breezy Alpine lakes of Inner Switzerland or the Grisons. Autumn can be enjoyed in many different ways: in the vineyards of the Valais or the Vaud, in the bright yellow larch forests of the Engadine, in the southern valleys of the Grisons or in the Ticino where, even in October, the days tend to be a lot longer and the fog a lot thinner than in the rest of Switzerland. Finally, the winter season provides innumerable possibilities, throughout the entire Alpine region, for participating in sports or for trudging off through the snow.

Switzerland may be small, but it still has many different regions, and there is the great danger of simply following the main through-routes and of crossing the country in a very short space of time without actually having got to know it any more closely. That is why this Insight Guide has been organised in such a way that the most widely differing areas can be reached from a large city or a regional centre respectively via comfortable day trips in all directions. If you find somewhere you particularly like, you can simply stay a little longer – and will, in so doing, doubtless discover supplementary curiosities that this book, however comprehensive it may try to be, neglects to mention.

In contrast to tourists of the past, who were compelled to explore the still undiscovered Alpine country of Switzerland on foot, on the backs of mules, or in coaches with little if any suspension, today's travellers have an astonishingly thorough and comprehensive traffic system at their disposal. Thanks to the many and varied means of travel available – whether rail, bus, cable railway, or boat – it is very tempting simply to leave the car at home, and to get to know really large areas of the country in a relatively short time. Every railway station in Switzerland can provide detailed information about these types of round-trip, and combination tickets for various different types of transport are available everywhere.

Preceding pages: Lucerne by night; on the Obergabelhorn; Foroglio in the Val Bavona; landscape in Appenzell. Left, Alpine flag-waving.

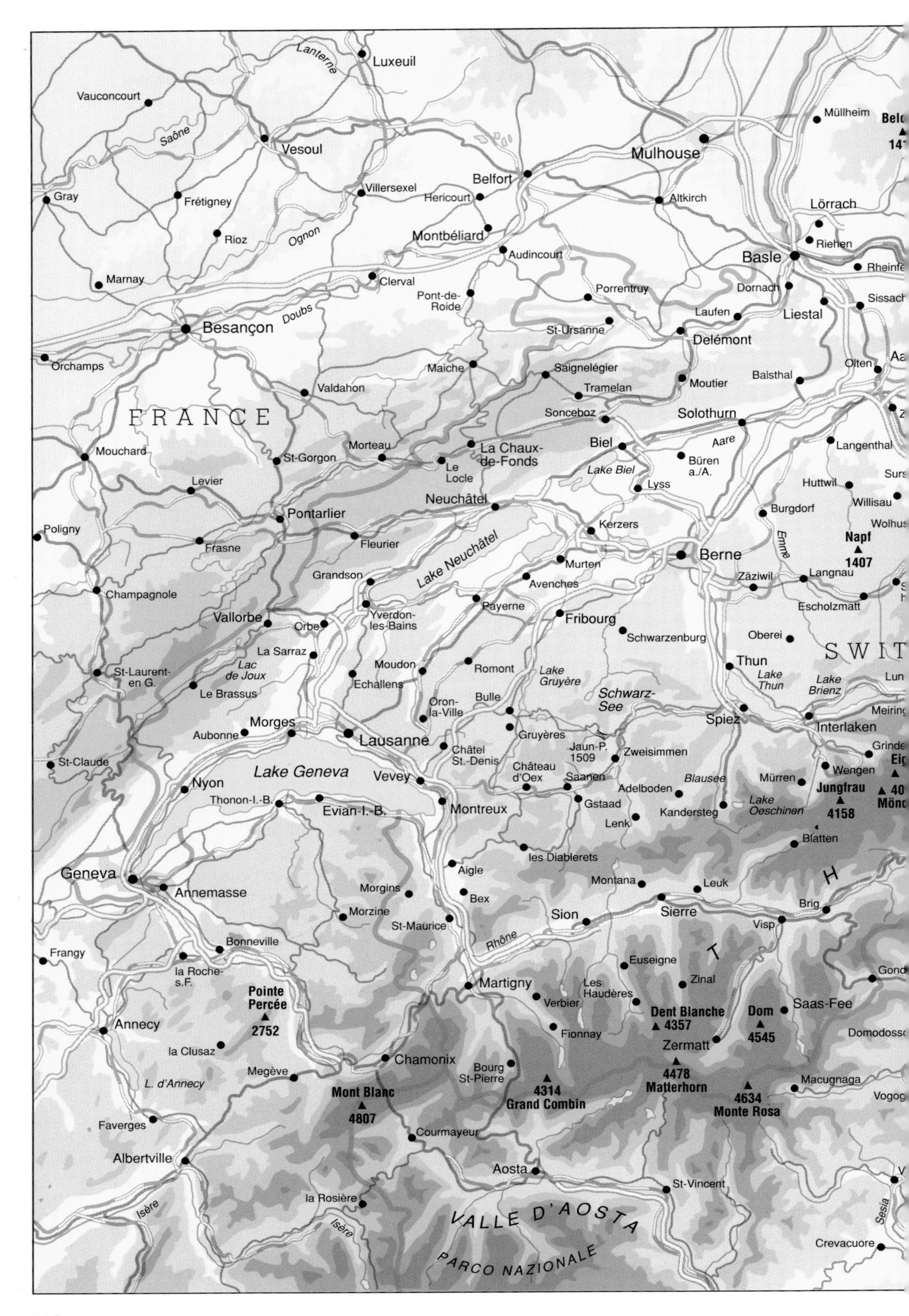
Luxeuil
Lanterne
Vauconcourt
Saône
Vesoul
Mulhouse
Müllheim
Belfort
Gray
Frétigney
Villersexel
Hericourt
Altkirch
Lörrach
Riehen
Rioz
Ognon
Montbéliard
Audincourt
Basle
Marnay
Clerval
Pont-de-Roide
Porrentruy
Dornach
Sissach
Besançon
Doubs
St-Ursanne
Laufen
Liestal
Delémont
Orchamps
Maiche
Saignelégier
Moutier
Balsthal
Olten
Valdahon
Tramelan
FRANCE
Sonceboz
Solothurn
Aare
Mouchard
Morteau
La Chaux-de-Fonds
Biel
Langenthal
St-Gorgon
Le Locle
Lake Biel
Büren a./A.
Levier
Lyss
Huttwil
Willisau
Neuchâtel
Burgdorf
Pontarlier
Poligny
Kerzers
Napf 1407
Frasne
Fleurier
Lake Neuchâtel
Murten
Berne
Emme
Grandson
Avenches
Zäziwil
Langnau
Champagnole
Payerne
Escholzmatt
Yverdon-les-Bains
Fribourg
Vallorbe
Orbe
Schwarzenburg
Oberei
SWIT
La Sarraz
Lac de Joux
Thun
St-Laurent-en G.
Moudon
Romont
Lake Gruyère
Lake Thun
Lake Brienz
Le Brassus
Echallens
Schwarz-See
Bulle
Oron-la-Ville
Spiez
Interlaken
Morges
Aubonne
Gruyères
Lausanne
St-Claude
Châtel St.-Denis
Jaun-P. 1509
Zweisimmen
Wengen
Lake Geneva
Château d'Oex
Vevey
Saanen
Blausee
Mürren
Jungfrau 4158
Nyon
Adelboden
Thonon-l.-B.
Evian-l.-B.
Montreux
Gstaad
Kandersteg
Lake Oeschinen
Lenk
Blatten
les Diablerets
Geneva
Aigle
Montana
Annemasse
Morgins
Leuk
Bex
Brig
Morzine
Sion
Sierre
St-Maurice
Visp
Rhône
Bonneville
Frangy
Euseigne
la Roche-s.F.
Zinal
Martigny
Pointe Percée 2752
Les Haudères
Verbier
Dent Blanche 4357
Dom 4545
Saas-Fee
Annecy
Fionnay
Zermatt
Domodosso
la Clusaz
Chamonix
Bourg St-Pierre
4478 Matterhorn
Megève
4314 Grand Combin
Macugnaga
L. d'Annecy
Mont Blanc 4807
4634 Monte Rosa
Faverges
Courmayeur
Albertville
Aosta
St-Vincent
Isère
la Rosière
VALLE D'AOSTA
Sesia
PARCO NAZIONALE
Crevacuore

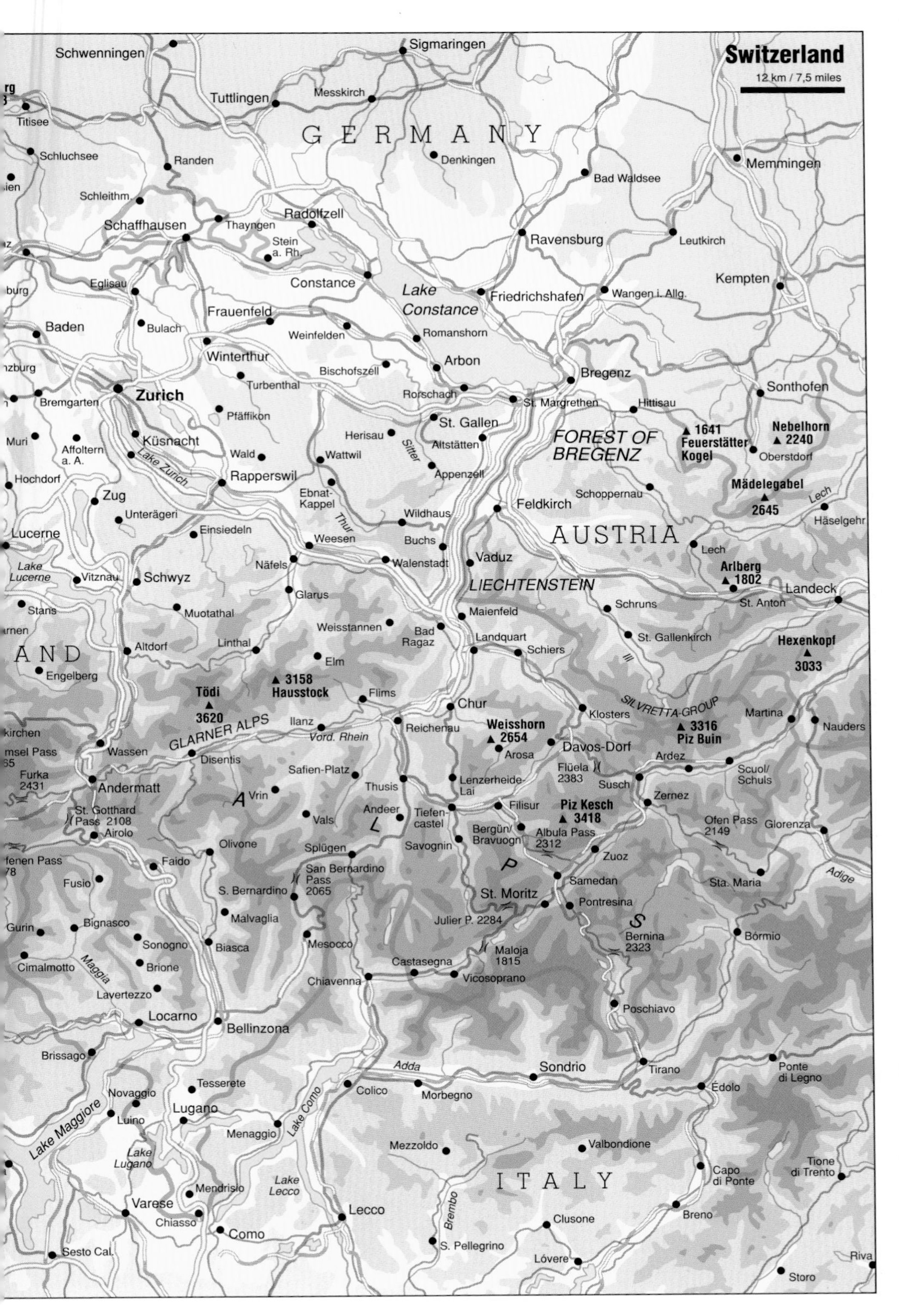
Switzerland
12 km / 7,5 miles
GERMANY
AUSTRIA
LIECHTENSTEIN
ITALY
Schwenningen
Sigmaringen
Tuttlingen
Messkirch
Titisee
Schluchsee
Randen
Denkingen
Memmingen
Bad Waldsee
Schleithm.
Radolfzell
Schaffhausen
Thayngen
Stein a. Rh.
Ravensburg
Leutkirch
Eglisau
Constance
Lake Constance
Friedrichshafen
Wangen i. Allg.
Kempten
Frauenfeld
Bulach
Baden
Weinfelden
Romanshorn
Winterthur
Bischofszell
Arbon
Bregenz
Turbenthal
Zurich
Bremgarten
Pfäffikon
Rorschach
St. Margrethen
Hittisau
Sonthofen
St. Gallen
Muri
Affoltern a. A.
Küsnacht
Lake Zurich
Wald
Herisau
Wattwil
Sitter
Altstätten
FOREST OF BREGENZ
▲ 1641 Feuerstätter Kogel
Nebelhorn ▲ 2240
Oberstdorf
Hochdorf
Rapperswil
Appenzell
Zug
Ebnat-Kappel
Schoppernau
Mädelegabel
▲ 2645
Lech
Unterägeri
Thur
Wildhaus
Feldkirch
Häselgehr
Lucerne
Einsiedeln
Weesen
Buchs
Lech
Lake Lucerne
Näfels
Walenstadt
Vaduz
Arlberg
▲ 1802
Landeck
Vitznau
Schwyz
Glarus
St. Anton
Stans
Muotathal
Schruns
Maienfeld
Weisstannen
Bad Ragaz
Landquart
St. Gallenkirch
Hexenkopf
▲ 3033
Altdorf
Linthal
Schiers
Engelberg
Elm
Tödi
▲ 3620
▲ 3158 Hausstock
Flims
Chur
SILVRETTA-GROUP
Klosters
Martina
Ilanz
GLARNER ALPS
Vord. Rhein
Reichenau
Weisshorn
▲ 2654
Arosa
Davos-Dorf
▲ 3316 Piz Buin
Nauders
Wassen
Disentis
Ardez
Andermatt
Safien-Platz
Thusis
Lenzerheide-Lai
Flüela 2383
Susch
Scuol/ Schuls
Furka 2431
Vrin
A
Zernez
St. Gotthard Pass 2108
Airolo
Andeer
Tiefen-castel
Filisur
Piz Kesch
▲ 3418
Vals
L
Bergün/ Bravuogn
Albula Pass 2312
Ofen Pass 2149
Glorenza
Olivone
Splügen
Savognin
Zuoz
Faido
San Bernardino Pass 2065
P
Samedan
Sta. Maria
Adige
Fusio
S. Bernardino
St. Moritz
Pontresina
Malvaglia
Julier P. 2284
Gurin
Bignasco
S
Bernina 2323
Bórmio
Sonogno
Biasca
Mesocco
Maloja 1815
Cimalmotto
Maggia
Brione
Castasegna
Vicosoprano
Chiavenna
Lavertezzo
Poschiavo
Locarno
Bellinzona
Brissago
Adda
Sondrio
Tirano
Ponte di Legno
Tesserete
Colico
Morbegno
Édolo
Novaggio
Lugano
Lake Maggiore
Luino
Menaggio
Lake Como
Mezzoldo
Valbondione
Lake Lugano
Tione di Trento
Capo di Ponte
Mendrisio
Lake Lecco
Varese
Lecco
Brembo
Breno
Chiasso
Clusone
Como
S. Pellegrino
Sesto Cal.
Lóvere
Riva
Storo

BASEL

The best place for an extensive view of Switzerland's second-largest city is the Pfalz, an ancient stone terrace right behind Basel (Basle) Cathedral. There are two ways to get to it.

Tram number 1 or 8 will take you from the railway station to Schifflände, by the main bridge over the Rhine, the Mittlere Rheinbrücke. From there, you walk up Rheinsprung, a narrow street lined with local-authority offices and quaint 15th- and 16th-century houses, to the **Münster** (Cathedral). If you need a rest after the five-minute climb, there's plenty of shade in the square (Münsterplatz) from the 34 chestnut trees planted at regular intervals. Or you can break your journey at the **Museum of Culture** (Museum der kulturen), in Augustiner-gasse ("Museum" above the entrance).

The fun way is to cross the bridge (note the tiny chapel in the middle) and turn off to the right, down Oberer Rheinweg, a pleasant tree-lined stretch of embankment. In a few minutes you come to the "Leu", one of four quaint wooden ferry boats that cross the Rhine, moored opposite the cathedral. For a modest sum, you are transported shakily but safely to the other side of the river, the current struggling against the steel overhead wire.

The next bit is more strenuous – just over 100 steps up to the tree-shaded bastion of the **Pfalz**. From up here, Basel is almost indecently exposed to view, though what we see is mainly the area of **Klein-Basel** (Little Basle), the industrial area. Apparently there are inhabitants of **Gross-Basel** (Great Basle) who have never been to this section of the city in their entire lives. However, Basel is full of such stories, and it tends to thrive on them.

A closer look: Klein-Basel first came into being after the river was bridged in the 13th century. The advent of industry brought workers' tenements along with it. People's faces are far more colourful here in every sense, as are the *beizen*, the restaurants typical of the area, even though, like almost anywhere in Europe, the area has its share of nasty-looking pizzerias, pubs and fast-food restaurants. The night life here in Klein-Basel, and all it entails, is upbeat by Swiss standards. The girl dancers are as friendly as they are anywhere else in the world, while the drink prices are somewhat steadier. The ladies at the bar are astonishingly cosmopolitan, and can speak several languages.

The main reason is that Klein-Basel is a meeting-place for the whole world – which may sound like a wild exaggeration, but it isn't. Klein-Basel contains the **Messe Basel**, a trade fair known for its free samples, the largest exhibition centre for hundreds of miles and one of the three most important centres of this kind in Europe. All types of industry the world over scramble to book a place here. Most important is the **Art** – the biggest art fair in the world – and the **World Jewellery and Watch Fair**. While the exhibition is taking place it is practically impossible to find any hotel vacancies in the area.

receding ages: asnacht in asel. Left, asel's olourful own Hall. ight, untain itside the eatre, by ulptor Jean nguely.

From the Pfalz, you can see the Rhine below, forming a long, drawn-out loop, with both ends fading away into the distant horizon. It is here that the river forms its great right-angled bend, or "knee", before it wanders off northwards for good.

Often, just as you're feeling like getting your camera ready for a picture up here, you hear the dull thud of a ship's diesel, and a freighter, loaded to the gunwales, pushes its way upriver against the current and squeezes itself underneath one of the low arches of the Mittlere Brücke.

Where three countries meet: Far beyond Klein-Basel, over to the left and shimmering misty-blue in the distance, the outlines of the Vosges can be seen, those mountains steeped in history, that divide Alsace from Lorraine; and over to the right you can make out the first friendly ridges of Germany's Black Forest. If Gross-Basel were not inconveniently blocking the view to the south, the heights of the Jura mountains would also be visible.

Long ago, the Celts determined certain points in the Jura, the Vosges and the Black Forest and defined an astronomical triangle. Standing on the Pfalz, one is exactly at the centre of it. This is the place that made Basel what it is today. Up here, the original Basel is at your feet; here, protected by the still unconquered Rhine, the Celts, the Romans and the Alemannians made enemies, made friends, fell in love and interbred. And what remains is the quintessence – or is it perhaps the sediment? – of several cultural epochs. Those peoples all met here on the rocky bastion of the Pfalz, and the people of Basel are the result.

The *Basler* is an unusual and unique mixture, a relic of history. Situated as he is on the "knee" of the river, he looks across at the plateau of the Upper Rhine, his cultural breeding-ground, to which he has not belonged politically since 1501. Swiss national territory and the above-mentioned cultural region have only a small amount of land in common – the city state of Basel. It is like an island, whose inhabitants, despite being

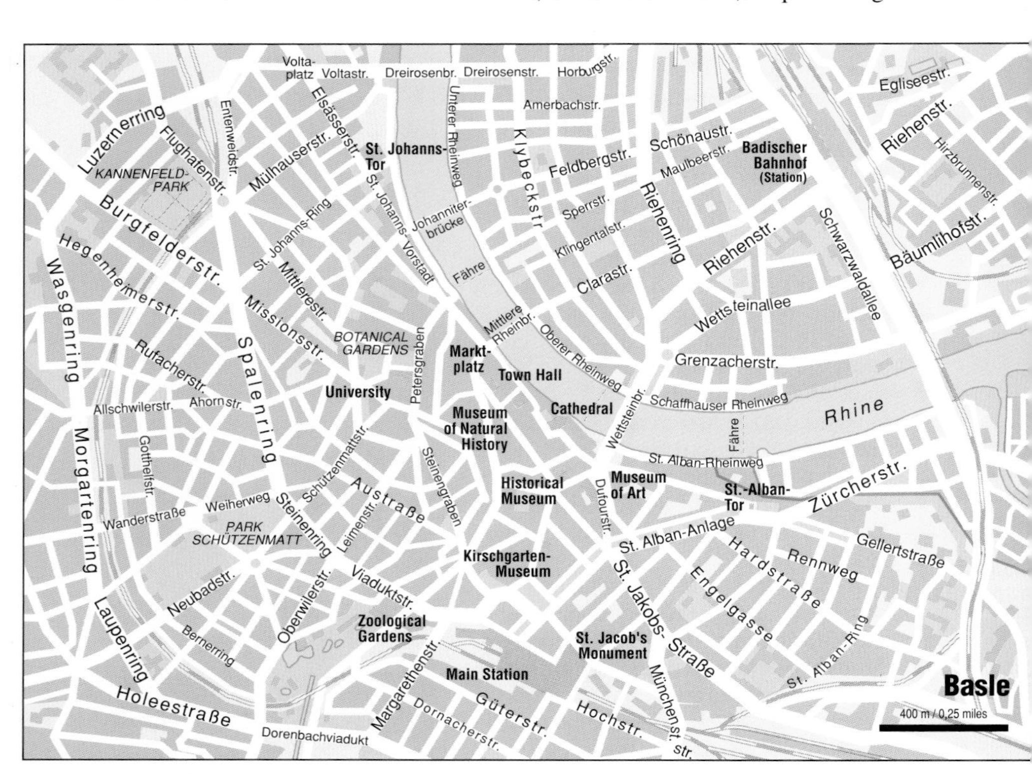

exposed to three different countries, are not noted for their openness: they are much happier keeping themselves to themselves, and they are good at hiding their introspective natures behind that special bitter-sweet sense of humour for which they are known among their fellow Swiss.

Adding to Basel's unique atmosphere are the many available ways of leaving it – it has a bi-national airport, a German, a French and a Swiss railway station. Despite, or perhaps simply because of, the frontiers, the opportunity to escape and leave everything behind has always been an option that was readily available.

Because of this, individuals undergoing some kind of spiritual exile have always felt very much at home in Basel, from Erasmus of Rotterdam to Karl Jaspers, from Hans Holbein to Rolf Hochhuth. The city's wealth of culture, its well-stocked museums, its archives and its antiquarian bookshops make it a more than desirable place for a stranger to put down roots. From 1521 on it was the principal centre of humanism and attracted distinguished scholars and teachers from diverse backgrounds.

Fasnacht: The city's three-day Lenten festival is the one chance, albeit a rather strenuous one, to get a whiff of the real Basel and its inhabitants. *Fasnacht* in Basel has nothing to do with *Fasching*, or carnival time.

Rather, it is a contrast to it, an event with a kind of defiance about it, held at the time when the Catholic areas have already begun a very serious period of fasting. Tens of thousands of men and women from Basel take part in the *Fasnacht*. It is not a public festival, though. Nobody dances in the streets to celebrate. The spirit of the *Fasnacht* – and in Basel it is a very powerful spirit indeed – is sombre.

This might suggest that Basel's *Fasnacht* is an ancient custom: well, yes and no. Of course, like all Lenten celebrations in Christian cultures, its roots are pagan. But after the Reformation *all* such festivals in Basel were banned. *Fasnacht* in its current form has been

erry across he Rhine, vith Basel athedral n the ackground.

going for only about 60 years, though many people claim the custom is well over a century old.

Fasnacht begins on the Monday following Ash Wednesday. At exactly four o'clock in the morning, all lights in the city are extinguished, and the participants, the *Fasnächtler,* organised into small groups, begin beating drums and playing pipes, in the glow of their lanterns. People pour on to the streets to witness their procession. The high, piercing sound of the piccolos, blending with the threatening rumble of the heavy Basel drums, evokes the days when Switzerland was one of Europe's great military powers.

The sight of the procession sends a shiver down the spine of the most cynical beholder. Darkness and the cold add to the eerie effect. However, the masks they wear (make-up is not used in Basel) and their lavish-looking lanterns and costumes inject a more robust dimension to the event. This is the so-called *Morgenstreich*, "morning prank", heralding a three-day event that everyone has been feverishly awaiting for months. In the *Morgenstreich* there can be sensed a deep and heartfelt anger at life's injustices, and a disgust with everyday realities. The city is shaken. In former times Basel's *Fasnacht* was a protest, a rebellion against those who did not need to go out into the streets to demonstrate power and influence.

Everyday life in Basel: But perhaps you have neither the time nor the inclination to get to know the ordinary people of Basel. After a tour of this port-city upon the Rhine, with its two giant chemical concerns of Novartis (a merger between Sandoz and Ciba) and Roche, which have turned Basel into the pharmacy of the world, you might feel that you have seen enough; that you have heard enough about this city of humanists and Nobel prize-winning scientists, about Nietzsche's lectureship at the university, about the cultural philosopher Burckhardt, about the painters Holbein and Böcklin, about the mathematicians Bernoulli and Euler, about Hermann Hesse, who wrote *Steppenwolf* here;

The Wildtsche Haus.

and enough about the successful matings at Basel's **Zolli** (zoological garden), which is built on the spot where Basel's very last public decapitations were held.

You may also have had enough of admiring the cityscape and the spacious 18th-century, such as the Wildtsche Haus on Petersplatz, perhaps, or the **Haus zum Kirschgarten** which forms part of the Historical Museum. After these dry sites it may be time to adjourn for a beer or a glass of wine.

Basel is located in the middle of some of Europe's greatest vineyards. The grape-rich areas of Alsace and Baden, and the wine regions of Lake Geneva, the Valais, the Ticino and Eastern Switzerland, form a garland around the "knee" of the Rhine. But the *Basler* drinks beer – exceptions only serve to prove the rule – and he does so for two main reasons. Firstly, because enjoying a good glass of wine is quite out of keeping with his puritan heritage. And secondly, because wine quite simply costs more, and *Baslers* don't like spending too much money on their pleasures.

Shopping: Fully refreshed, you might want to take advantage of Basel's excellent shops. First, head for **Marktplatz** (marketplace), where stallholders rub their hands behind heavily laden stands, extolling the merits of their flowers, fruit, vegetables, bread and cheese, where the red of the apples merges into the colour of the splendid **Rathaus** (Town Hall), and swarms of pigeons flutter everywhere.

The main wing of the Rathaus is in late Burgundian Gothic style, and the notable clock (1511–12) is the work of a local craftsman known as Wilhelm. The wing on the left-hand side and the tower on the right are both 19th-century additions.

On the corner of Marktplatz and Freie Strasse is the guild house of the wine merchants, the Renaissance-style Geltenzunfthaus (1578), and close by (at No. 25) is the guild house of the locksmiths, dating originally from 1488 but decorated in baroque style in 1733.

The area between Marktplatz and **Barfüsserplatz** contains the city's best

View of Basel's river port on the Rhine.

shops, chic designer boutiques and exclusive department stores. Since most of the narrow streets are closed to cars, this is a pleasant place to walk and even large amounts of shopping can be lugged around safely.

In Barfüsserplatz itself, you will find the 14th-century Barfüsserkirche (church of the barefoot friars), now successfully converted into the **Historical Museum**.The old church contains an interesting collection of exhibits relating to the history of culture in Central Europe. Among the more notable exhibits are the late Gothic tapestries and the so-called "Lällenkönig" (Babbling King), a crowned head with movable tongue and eyes.

Just a stone's throw from Barfüsserplatz is one of the city's cultural highlights, the Museum of Art. On the way there, we pass the restless **Theaterbrunnen**, (Carnival fountain), by the late Jean Tinguely, one of Switzerland's best-known sculptors, whose career began here in Basel. Behind the fountain, the **Stadttheater** (municipal theatre), every side of which looks like the back, pushes its way aggressively into view. The **Museum of Art** lies a five-minute walk away.

Auguste Rodin's *Les Bourgeois de Calais* welcomes visitors to the oldest art collection in the world. This museum was opened not by royalty but by burghers. Originally based on the private exhibition rooms belonging to Basilius Amerbach, it includes the most extensive collection of works by Konrad Witz and Hans Holbein the Younger (1497-1543).

An outstanding collection of 19th- and 20th-century art includes work by Gauguin, Van Gogh, Chagall, Paul Klee, Max Ernst and Kandinsky, to name just some of them. Two Russians, Dostoyevsky and Lenin, are both reputed to have spent hours in front of Holbein's painting *The Body of Christ* on their visits to Basel. Naturally Arnold Böcklin, a native of the city, is also well represented. The museum includes several paintings by Picasso. They were purchased with city funds after the

Inn sign in the country town of Liestal.

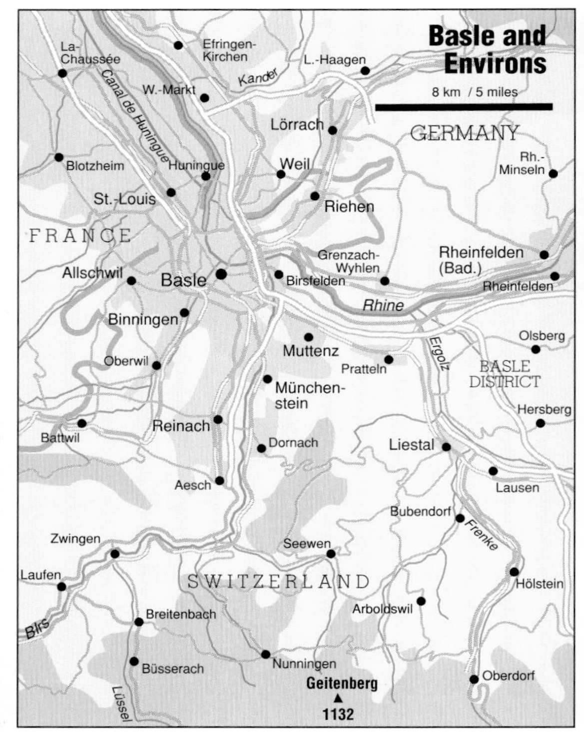

people of Basel took a democratic vote on what to buy for the museum. Picasso was so touched by their admiration that he donated several more of his works to the museum.

Basel's wealth of museums caters for every possible taste. The city offers a choice of no fewer than 36 museums, of varying degrees of importance. This is partly due to the fact that the Basel area established its own special form of patronage, and the people from the wealthy aristocracy, the so-called *Daig* (from the word *Teig*, meaning dough), discreetly supplied the exhibition rooms at regular intervals. Sometimes a particularly wealthy benefactor would commission an entirely new museum.

The **Museum of Contemporary Art** (60 St. Alban-Rheinweg) is well worth a visit. It was built for the country's richest woman, Maya Sacher. The Sacher family are the principal patrons of art in Basel.

Outside the city: Anyone who decides that they'd like to get away from the city for a while has a whole range of worthwhile destinations to choose from. The ruins of the Roman town of **Augusta Raurica** are particularly impressive. They include two theatres, some temples and a genuine Roman brothel dating from the time of the occupation.

Rheinfelden, founded by the Zähringen family, can be reached by steamer. A relaxed, small-town atmosphere, set against a delightful backdrop, awaits the visitor. The **Goetheanum**, headquarters of the anthroposophian movement, is in **Dornach**, and is world-famous for its Waldorf and Steiner schools.

Also worth mentioning are **Riehen**, **Sissach**, **Münchenstein**, **Bottmingen**, and **Binningen** with their country seats and mansions; not forgetting castles such as those at **Pfeffingen**, **Waldenburg** and **Dorneck**; and finally, delightful little towns and villages such as **Liestal**, **Gelterkinden** or **Pratteln**.

All these places are relatively close and a day trip from Basel could take in several, as well as the delightful countryside – at its most glorious when the cherry-blossom is out in April.

Horse and plough in the canton of Basel.

22. September

THE JURA

According to geologists, the Jura mountains are among the youngest on the planet. Some150 million years ago the Jura, an unusually complex mountain range, rose like a reef from the endless sea, much like the neighbouring Alps. Ferns, conifers and ginkgo trees carpeted the slopes of the new land, and the first of the flying dinosaurs circled above its peaks; then came the first birds, small carnivores and mammals; the seas teemed with giant dinosaurs, fish, snails, ammonites and innumerable tiny life-forms. Fossils, the petrified proof of these creatures' existence, can be seen today in their tens of thousands in the numerous village museum collections of local history.

In the eyes of the average Swiss citizen, the Jura represents nothing more than the Confederation's 26th and most recent member (born on 24 September 1978). Much has been written about the labour pains involved.This region in the northwest of Switzerland, which possesses three Jura lakes, has always been, and will continue to be, politically divided. The variations of the landscape are reflected in the diversity of the region's inhabitants.

Switzerland and France both have a share of the Jura mountain range. For the French, as for the Swiss, it is known simply as *Le Jura*; neither has made any effort to distinguish between the two parts by name. But anyone after a more accurate idea should not overlook the fact that these limestone mountains actually extend right across the canton of Schaffhausen and as far as the Franconian Jura in Germany. The mountain range reaches its widest point in the Bernese and Solothurn Jura, where as many as 10 ranges succeed one another, and where the longitudinal valleys are by no means of equal width.

John Ruskin, writing about the Swiss landscape, in particular the Jura, in 1885, had this to say: "With all my Tory prejudice (I mean, principle), I have to confess that one great joy of Swiss – above all, Jurassic Swiss – ground to me, is in its effectual, not merely theoretic, liberty. Among the greater hills, one can't always go just where one chooses – all around is too far, or too steep – one wants to get to this, and climb that, and can't do either – but in Jura one can go every way, and be happy everywhere... All Switzerland is there in hope and sensation, and what was less than Switzerland was in some sort better, in its meek sincerity and healthy purity."

Anyone looking across from central Switzerland at this bluish mountain range to the northwest can understand why people call the Jura the "blue mountains". So what more fitting place to begin a journey through the Jura than the Blauenberg, which separates the rift-valley of the Rhine from the Tertiary basin of Laufen? It extends westwards from the gorge at **Angenstein** in the **Birs Valley** to the **Lüssel Valley**, 18 km (11 miles) away, where it leaves Switzerland for France.

Raurici and knights: Walking out here, and looking at the steep walls of rock

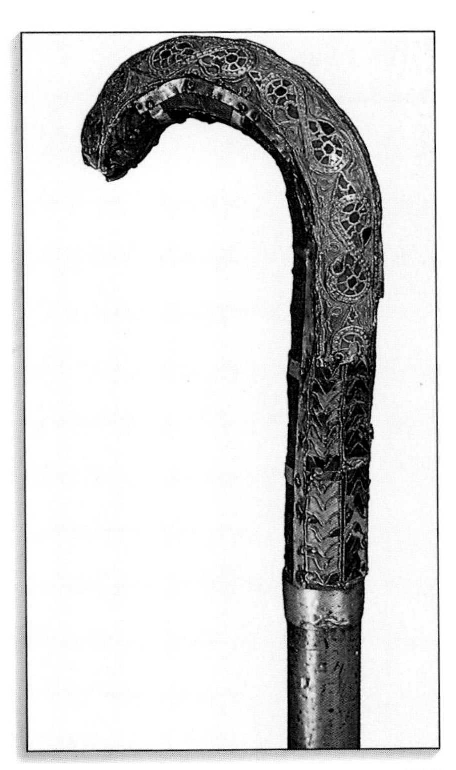

Preceding pages: the "Jurassian folk festival" in Delémont. Left, cherry blossom in the Passwang region. Right, St Germanus's crosier, an early Christian treasure.

where dark pine forests and mountain slopes alternate so dramatically, one tends to think of ancient legends about the old Raurici, their druids and their menhirs. The people of the Jura are happy to describe themselves as being descended from the Raurici. This Celtic tribe had moved southwards through Europe with the Helvetii, their aim being to find a more accommodating home than the northwestern Jura, but had been intercepted in 58 BC by Roman legions at Bibracte. The defeated hordes were sent back north and forced to resettle the regions which they had previously put to the torch.

Today, the very active Society of Friends of Raurician History from the German-speaking region continues to keep the Celtic heritage alive.

Vital passes: The Romans also influenced the area, seeing it as vitally important strategically. It was they who fortified the crossings from the Belfort Gap into the Alps, vital mountain passes which, centuries later, the Habsburgs of Austria and the bishops of Basel were equally keen to protect. Castles were built along the length of the passes at great expense: **Alt Biederthal**, today simply known as "Burg", **Blauenstein**, **Pfeffingen**, **Frohberg**, and **Angenstein**, most of them now in ruins. To the untrained eye, **Rotberg**, situated in the rear part of the Leimen Valley, appears to have remained intact. Appearances deceive. This castle, now a youth hostel, was restored after the outbreak of World War II in accordance with contemporary conceptions of "romantic chivalry" – unsuccessfully so, in most people's opinion today.

We can already see the broad plateau of **Mariastein**, the second most important pilgrimage shrine in Switzerland (the most important being Einsiedeln). The Jura rises up, right next to the French frontier, and forms the **Landskronkette**. The mighty ruin of **Landskron**, one of the landmarks of the **Birsig** or **Leimen Valley**, was a victim of the Napoleonic wars in 1813.

One of the most curious sites hereabouts is the **Benedictine Monastery**

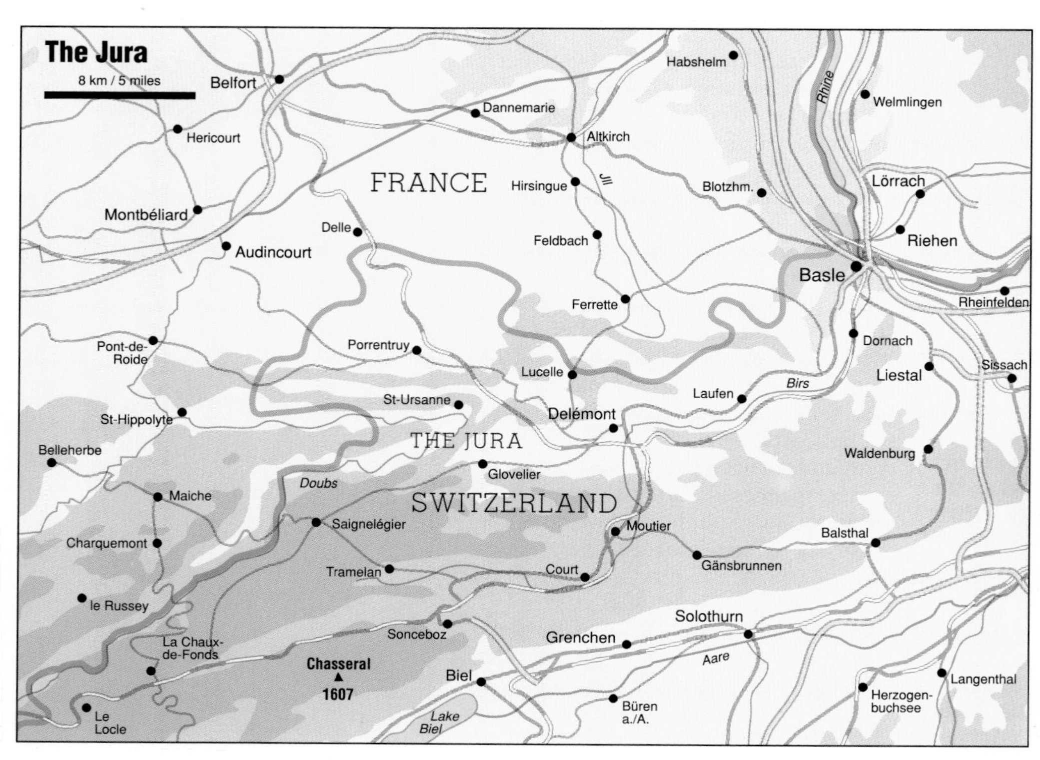

of Mariastein, built in late Gothic style in 1648, a time when that style of architecture had long since been supplanted by the Renaissance. The facade, however, is neoclassical, and the interior neo-baroque. All in all, the monastery is an instructive place for anyone wanting to take a crash course in the history of European church building. The main attraction, however, is the Gnadenkapelle, a chapel built into a cave below the church.

Along the River Birs: People who know the Jura well are apt to contradict John Ruskin's verdict on the area, saying that with all its dark valleys, inaccessible heights and sometimes rather damp depths it is an unfathomable kind of place. It is certainly not as easy to get to grips with as, say, the Upper Rhine Valley, nor can it be called homogeneous – after all, more than half a dozen Swiss cantons have a stake in its territory. The population is just as diverse: mountain dwellers, with and without bushy beards, who alternate between speaking German and French; artists, many of whom have taken over farms in the region; city dwellers escaping from the stress of everyday life; dropouts, alternative farmers, and many others, all of them in search of a better quality of life.

Nevertheless, gaining access to this well-known, and yet seldom visited sanctuary is relatively easy for travellers. All they need do is follow the course of the **Birs**. A good place to begin an adventure in the Jura is where the Birs narrows at Aesch, a real Swiss "cluse", with **Schloss Angenstein** towering above it.

In the old days, anyone wanting to go through the mountains followed the course of rivers – the Birs; the Sorne, the Suze, the Alleine and the Doubs have been lifelines from time immemorial. These days, the express train from Basel to **Laufen**, the main town in the German-speaking Laufen Valley, takes 18 minutes. On the way, it passes the odd-looking **castle** near **Zwingen**. Laufen – its name comes from the word *Lauffen*, meaning waterfall – has a very neat and

Market day in Laufen.

tidy appearance, and is an efficiently-run industrialised town.

A counterpart to the Blauenberg is the **Gempen Plateau** to the east; the Birs runs through much of this, too. Several delightful villages can be found on its ridges, including **Seewen**, with its well-known **Museum of Musical Automata**, the largest collection of its kind anywhere in Europe. The Gempen Plateau forms part of the area beyond the mountains known as **Schwarzbubenland**, in the canton of Solothurn; the people here still like to say that they live "in the mountains".

The largest town in the area is **Breitenbach**, down in the Lucelle Valley on the **Passwangstrasse**, a magnificent panoramic route running between Laufen and Balsthal, with a view of the **Hohe Winde** (1,204 metres/3,950 ft), the highest point in the Schwarzbubenland. The ancient capital of the region, however, is **Nunningen**, where the local lords from Solothurn used to rule from **Gilgenberg Castle**, taking advantage of its commanding location in the landscape. Another impressive-looking ruin, **Neu-Thierstein**, lies down in the Lucelle Valley, on a rocky outcrop above the Passwangstrasse: it was once the seat of the rulers of the lower and middle Birs Valley.

The Lucelle river hurries down from the Passwang to join the Birs. Another interesting stream, coming from the Pleigne plateau, flows towards Laufen and into the broad Laufen basin where it joins the Lucelle. **Lucelle Abbey**, a Cistercian monastery once famous the world over, used to stand on its banks, in the narrow, but highly picturesque Lucelle Valley. Now only a few remains of the monastery walls prove that it stood there at all. Another clue to its existence is the nearby small lake, the **Etang de Lucelle**, which used to serve as the monastery's carp pond.

Gateway to the "French-Swiss" Jura: One remarkable feature of this region is the "international route", which passes through mountain country belonging to Berne, Solothurn and France and then leads over to Porrentruy, in the Ajoie.

The Marché Concours horse show in Saignelégier.

For most Swiss people, the Jura begins "politically" at **Charmoilles**, but geographically it begins at **Soyhières** – which lies exactly on the German to French linguistic boundary.

Of course, it is not only the language that makes the difference so noticeable: the whole atmosphere has a definite "French-Swiss" flavour to it, which is shaped at least in part by the town of **Delémont**, the capital of the republic and canton of Jura.

Anyone approaching Delémont from Basel is greeted on his exit from one of the numerous gorges of the River Birs by the **Vorbourg**, a ruined castle situated on a rocky spur, which also has an important pilgrimage chapel.

The Birs actually curves around the capital, and Delémont itself lies at the mouth of two rivers: the **Scheulte**, that flows down from the **Scheulte Pass** connecting the **Gulden Valley** in the canton of Solothurn with the Delémont basin, and the **Sorne**, that flows down from Bellelay. It was not that long ago that countless watermills, ironworks and sawmills were still in operation on their banks. The hill on which the Vorbourg stands affords a magnificent view. The capital – a blend of the old and the new – lies at one's feet. Beyond it, in the distance, it is possible to make out the wild and jagged-looking series of ravines at Moutier, the **Gorge of the Birs**, and the quiet villages dotted across the Delémont Valley.

The Grand-Rue, without a doubt the finest street in Delémont, makes it obvious why the bishops of Basel elected to build a château here, around the year 1716, as their summer residence.

The people of the Jura have always held their public gatherings in front of the **Maison Bennot**, which today houses the excellent **Musée Jurassien** (Jura Museum).

Industry in the southern Jura: A few kilometres past Delémont the Birs becomes fully Bernese – as it was in the Laufen Valley – and remains so right up to its source, for here the river flows on through the **Moutier** region, one of the three regions that stayed under the

Farmhouse in the Franches-Montagnes.

jurisdiction of the "old canton", namely Berne, following the country-wide plebiscite that gave the Jura autonomy as the 26th federal state of Switzerland – the first change of cantonal boundaries in 163 years.

Access can be gained to the Upper Birs Valley, or **Grandval** as it is sometimes called, via the gorge of Moutier, the Gorge of the Birs – here, one is confronted with magnificent natural scenery. The regional capital of **Moutier,** however, could not be more of a contrast. Since the turn of the century, this neat and tidy little town has developed into the industrial centre of the Jura (machines, appliances, watches) – a consequence of the tunnel that was built through the Grenchenberg.

The valley basin of Moutier was already an important cultural centre in medieval times. The **Moutier-Grandval Monastery** stood here, and had its heyday in the second half of the 9th century, when great scholars used to teach there. The *Great Bible of Moutier-Grandval,* now in the British Museum, still testifies to the enormous influence this monastery must have had as a centre of learning.

The gorge at Moutier is certainly complemented by the one at **Court**. Both are natural traffic hindrances, and their military significance was known in Roman times. The gorge at Court separates the Delémont basin from the **Vallée de Tavannes**, which is situated between the mountain ranges of **Moron** (1,124 metres/3,687 ft) and **Montoz** (1,328 metres/4,357 ft). The mountains are ideal for walkers and mushroom-pickers, but the valley itself, heavily industrialised, has a sober, almost strict atmosphere about it; it seems the Muses make only the odd flying visit to this uppermost section of the Birs Valley.

Barren and bare: The people of the Jura love horses. And since it is particularly easy for horses to find footing on ground that is not too hard, the plateau of **Franches-Montagnes**, 1,000 metres/3,000 ft above sea level, is considered horse country.

As if this still needed to be proved, the

The high moor of Etang de la Gruère.

Marché-Concours, Switzerland's largest horse show, has been held in **Saignelégier** on the second weekend in August every year since 1897. With its races and equestrian games, it has become a national attraction. The Franches-Montagnes region extends from the Delémont basin all the way to La-Chaux-de-Fonds in the canton of Neuchâtel.

The air up here is more noticeably bracing, the landscape starker and more barren. Delightful meadows alternate with dark forests of fir-trees and with small villages, some of them still very secluded, whose characteristic farmhouses have broad, only very slightly sloping roofs. Particularly fine examples of these can be found in **La Bosse**, **Lajoux**, **Muriaux** (which has a motor museum), **Le Noirmont**, **Les Prailats** and **Les Bois**.

The Franches-Montagnes region is also considered excellent for hiking, and a well-developed network of footpaths guides the visitor to places of natural beauty that are still largely intact, despite human intrusion. The botanical wealth of mushrooms (including many edible varieties) to be found here is much appreciated by connoisseurs. Efforts have been made recently to increase the popularity of the Franches-Montagnes in winter, too, as a local recreation area for cross-country skiers, dog sleds and so on. Saignelégier, the main town in the region, has a leisure centre, complete with swimming pool, sauna and skating rink.

One peculiarity of the Franches-Montagnes region is its lack of any famous river: the rain instantly seeps away into the soil. It is on its eastern border, where the former **Abbey of Bellelay** stands (once just as much a centre of learning in the Jura as Moutier), that the River **Sorne**, which leads down into the Birs, has its source; it flows through the wild and romantic **Pichoux Gorges**, whose waterfalls were a great favourite with landscape painters of the 18th and 19th centuries. **Bellelay**, founded in 1136, was rebuilt in the baroque style in the 17th and 18th cen-

Porrentruy.

turies. Its monks are supposed to have invented the famous *Tête de Moine*, an aromatic cheese highly esteemed in Switzerland.

Very characteristic of the Franches-Montagnes region are, however, its many high moors. The most famous of these is probably the **Etang de la Gruère** below Saignelégier. Formerly a mill-pond, today it is a moor lake of incomparable beauty, with an unparalleled variety of different species. Also worth a visit is the delightful **Jura Farming Museum** at Les Genevez.

Dark beauty: Far away to the west, in France, the **River Doubs** has its source. It enters Switzerland at Les Brenets in the canton of Neuchâtel, and then forms a natural border with France that extends for 45 km (30 miles). It has cut a deep bed, almost a canyon in fact. Many of the municipalities of the Franches-Montagnes region have land that extends down to its lonely banks. The river is of opalesque beauty, flowing darkly onwards and seldom interrupted by weirs. The only important village actually lying on the Doubs itself in this dark valley is **Goumois**, a border crossing.

But at Soubey, where anglers can be found in their hundreds at weekends, the landscape starts to open up again, and soon the river changes course, no longer heading for the Rhine but for the Saône. Inside the curve it describes here nestles the historic town of **St Ursanne**. An ancient bridge connects it with the Clos-du-Doubs. St Ursanne is one of the few medieval towns with three intact town gates, and it also has a rather well-preserved Romanesque-Gothic **Collegiate Church** which is one of the most beautiful buildings in this part of Switzerland. It has a Romanesque crypt and Merovingian sarcophagi.

At **Ocourt**, where an unusual-looking church can be seen standing in the middle of some fields, the Doubs leaves Switzerland.

The Ajoie: It takes the local train 44 minutes to get from Delémont to Porrentruy, via Courtetelle, Courfaivre, Bassecourt, Glovelier, St Ursanne and Courgenay. The train even heads

Boncourt, the fag end of Switzerland.

underground for a short time, through the tunnel beneath the pass of **Les Rangiers**, the Rhine-Rhône watershed, 856 metres (2,808 ft) above sea level. Les Rangiers itself is an important traffic artery, with routes leading off towards the Delémont Valley, the Franches-Montagnes region, St Ursanne and the Ajoie.

After passing hilly grazing land, coniferous forest, stretches of almost alpine-looking grass, and St Ursanne down in the valley basin, the train reaches **Courgenay**, in whose Hôtel de la Gare the young woman known as Petite Gilberte, immortalised in film and song, used to console the Swiss soldiers who had to guard the country's borders during World War I.

Then the broad meadows of the **Ajoie** come into view. Geographically, this "promontory" jutting far into France is not a part of the Jura, because it lies at the foot of the mountains; but politically, it belongs to the Swiss canton of Jura. The landscape here is gentle and spacious; not only can you sense the proximity of Burgundy, you can smell it in the air, too.

Simon Nicolas de Montjoie, prince-bishop of Basel.

There's also a touch of Burgundian blue in the sky above the town of **Porrentruy**, the residence of the bishops of Basel since the Reformation in 1528. It must not be forgotten after all that the region referred to somewhat all-embracingly these days as "the Jura" is largely identical with the former bishopric of Basel.

Seen from the castle tower above it, the centre of Porrentruy is very similar to the old part of Berne. The town, which today has a population of roughly 8,000, received its first real impetus from the freedom charter granted to it in 1283 by Rudolf von Habsburg, and still retains some of the flavour of its past. One can sense it most strongly when one stands next to the **Porte de France** and looks up in the direction of the spacious **château**. This has been rebuilt several times, largely in Renaissance style. The buildings that once housed the castle guard, the mint and the chapel are sadly no longer preserved – unlike parts of the **Episcopal Gardens**, and the pavilion of Princess Christine of Saxony (1697). There is also a 13th-century **refuge**.

Other famous sights include the former **Jesuit College**, the partly Romanesque **Church of St Pierre** in the upper part of the town, the **Town Hall** and also several feudal houses.

The main river in the Ajoie region is the **Allaine**, which splashes its way towards the Rhône and leaves Switzerland at **Boncourt**.

Very close by are the mysterious **Grottoes** at **Milandre**; legend has it that a beautiful maiden emerges from them from time to time. You probably won't see her, as the grottoes are closed to the public. But you can get to the ones at Réclère, on the border formed by the Doubs, and also visit the prehistoric park there. Finally, situated diametrically opposite, are the ponds belonging to the old pottery town of **Bonfol**. This is where to find the best *Dammassine*; the traveller can relax after his many explorations with a glass of this delicious schnapps.

Zuber

EASTERN SWITZERLAND

"Switzerland," the saying goes in Berne, Zurich, Basel and Lucerne, "ends at Winterthur." It's a monumentally arrogant statement that really amounts to nothing less than this: the eastern part of the country is basically of very little relevance to the way the Confederation sees itself, and if the country were ever forced to relinquish any of its territory, the east would be the first part to come under consideration, since it is almost a part of Germany anyway.

In the opinion of the average Swiss citizen, Eastern Switzerland is only of secondary importance industrially, culturally and touristically – and on top of that, the eastern Swiss have a dialect that is considered by much of the rest of the country to be shrill, sharp and quite simply unpleasant. In short: Eastern Switzerland is seen as a border region.

As with most sayings, the *vox populi* expressed here is, of course, first and foremost, merely an expression of ignorance; Eastern Switzerland need not fear either industrial or cultural comparison with other parts of the country. Measured in terms of industrial output alone, the cantons of Eastern Switzerland – not including the two Appenzell half-cantons – occupy a solid mid-field position.

But the special characteristic of this often neglected part of the country is its landscape and cultural heritage.

Thurgau, with its meadows, forests, fruit plantations and monasteries has been spared the excesses of industrial expansion. If one disregards the clusters of detached family houses that seem to have sprung up almost overnight along the motorway to Zurich, many of the small towns and villages in Thurgau still seem draped in history. The sheer weight of the past is instantly felt in **Schaffhausen** and **Stein am Rhein**, with their medieval half-timbered houses and their fortresses. The monastery town of **St Gallen**, both baroque and sober-looking, reflects this double aspect of the people of Eastern Switzerland. The landscape in the two **Appenzell** half-cantons, with its lush green hills and neat farmhouses set against the imposing backdrop of the Alpine massif, delights the eye with a charm that is rare nowadays. And the area around the broad expanse of **Lake Constance**, with its colourful, flowery parks and vine-covered slopes alternating with reeds and marshes, with its fields and orchards, its forests, meadows and historic towns, fishing villages and wine villages, is a scenic oasis on a scale scarcely equalled anywhere else in Switzerland.

Thus, in terms of landscape and history, Eastern Switzerland seems able to exist quite happily without the approval of the rest of the country.

There is, however, a grain of truth in the quotation at the beginning of this chapter: a part of the country with a character all its own actually does begin beyond Winterthur. Eastern Switzerland is a Swiss creation that is not so much oriented towards Zurich or Berne – the industrial and political centres of Switzerland respectively – as towards the cultural region of Lake Constance,

Preceding pages: the abbey library in St Gallen. Left, the Moors' Fountain in Schaffhausen. Right, Wine Festival in Döttingen.

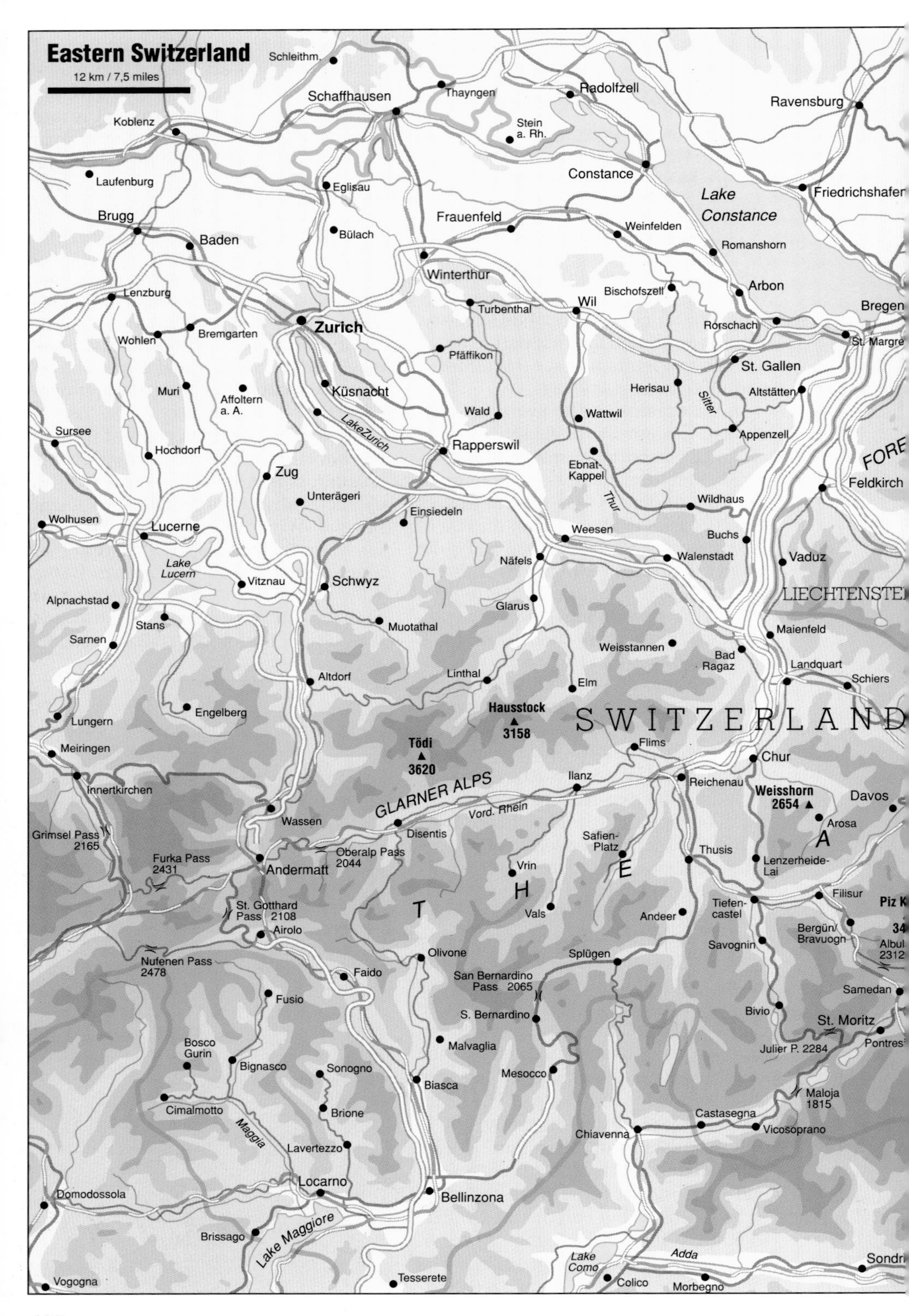

Eastern Switzerland
12 km / 7,5 miles
Schleithm.
Schaffhausen
Thayngen
Radolfzell
Ravensburg
Koblenz
Stein a. Rh.
Laufenburg
Eglisau
Constance
Lake Constance
Friedrichshafen
Brugg
Baden
Bülach
Frauenfeld
Weinfelden
Romanshorn
Winterthur
Arbon
Lenzburg
Bischofszell
Wil
Turbenthal
Bregen
Zurich
Wohlen
Bremgarten
Rorschach
St. Margre
Pfäffikon
St. Gallen
Muri
Affoltern a. A.
Küsnacht
Herisau
Altstätten
Sitter
Wald
Wattwil
Sursee
Lake Zurich
Appenzell
Hochdorf
Rapperswil
Zug
Ebnat-Kappel
FORE
Feldkirch
Unterägeri
Thur
Wildhaus
Wolhusen
Einsiedeln
Lucerne
Weesen
Buchs
Näfels
Walenstadt
Vaduz
Lake Lucern
Vitznau
Schwyz
LIECHTENSTE
Alpnachstad
Glarus
Stans
Muotathal
Maienfeld
Sarnen
Weisstannen
Bad Ragaz
Landquart
Altdorf
Linthal
Schiers
Elm
Engelberg
Hausstock 3158
SWITZERLAND
Lungern
Tödi 3620
Flims
Meiringen
Chur
Innertkirchen
GLARNER ALPS
Ilanz
Reichenau
Weisshorn 2654
Davos
Vord. Rhein
Wassen
Arosa
Grimsel Pass 2165
Disentis
Safien-Platz
A
Furka Pass 2431
Oberalp Pass 2044
Thusis
Andermatt
Vrin
E
Lenzerheide-Lai
H
Filisur
Piz K
St. Gotthard Pass 2108
T
Tiefen-castel
Vals
Andeer
Bergün/Bravuogn
Airolo
Albul 2312
Olivone
Splügen
Savognin
Nufenen Pass 2478
Faido
San Bernardino Pass 2065
Samedan
Fusio
Bivio
S. Bernardino
St. Moritz
Malvaglia
Pontresi
Bosco Gurin
Julier P. 2284
Bignasco
Mesocco
Sonogno
Biasca
Maloja 1815
Cimalmotto
Brione
Maggia
Castasegna
Chiavenna
Vicosoprano
Lavertezzo
Locarno
Domodossola
Bellinzona
Brissago
Lake Maggiore
Lake Como
Adda
Sondri
Vogogna
Tesserete
Colico
Morbegno

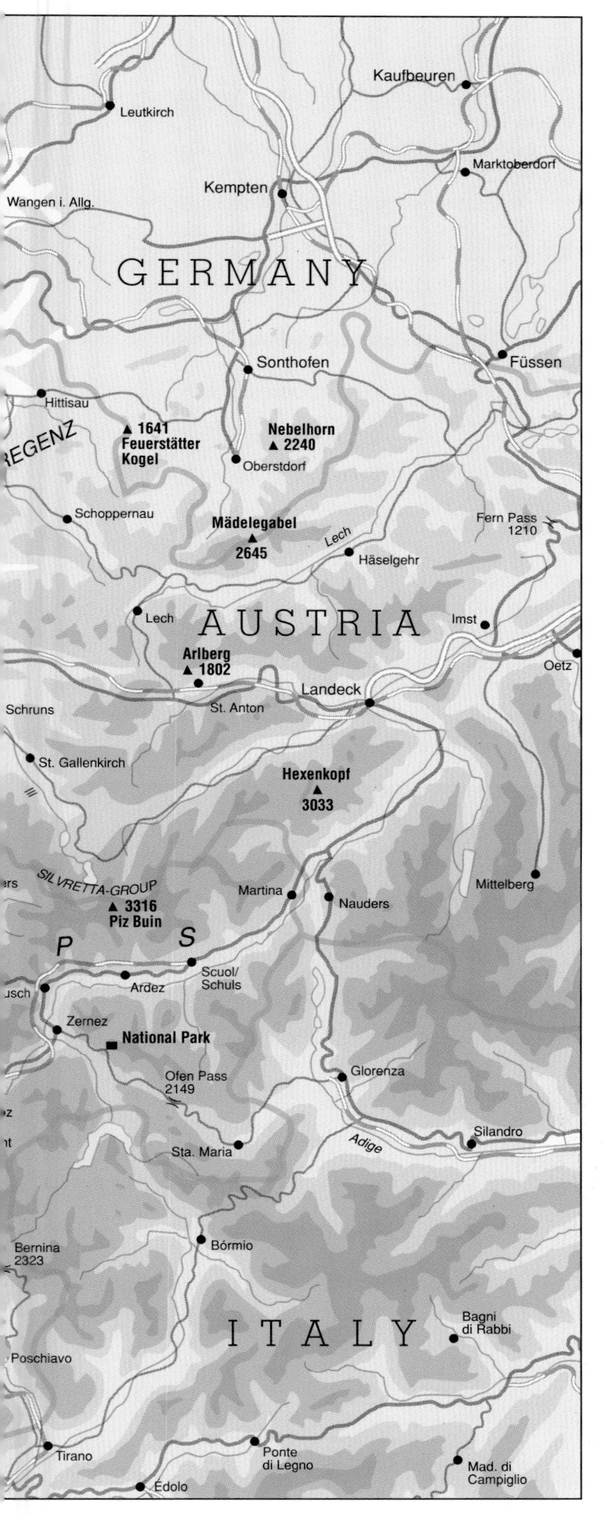

with the three countries (Switzerland, Austria and Germany) surrounding it; that is where its cultural identity lies.

The Lake Constance area has very little to do with with national borders. Here, in the basin formed by the "Swabian Ocean" (as Lake Constance is popularly referred to), the common Alemannian culture, the unique geographical location and strong trading history have contributed to the formation of a region that every now and then gets described, perhaps somewhat exaggeratedly, as "the cultural heart of Western Europe".

Ancient unity: At one time the Alemannian region was unified, and vestiges of this unity survived in Central Europe until quite late in history. Eastern Switzerland's city of St Gallen, for instance, had its very own policy of alliances, mostly directed towards southern Germany, right into the 14th century. Throughout the 1st millennium AD, the abbey in St Gallen played a leading role in the region, indeed it was among the most important abbeys of the Carolingian and Ottonian Empires.

Just how closely related the regions around the main national borders really are can be seen from the following example taken from more recent history: 50 years ago, in a referendum, the majority of the citizens of Austria's Vorarlberg region declared themselves in favour of annexation with Switzerland. However, the central governments in Vienna and Berne were not eager to comply with their wishes, and so the dream of unification in the Rhine Valley was never fulfilled.

The people of Eastern Switzerland don't mind being seen as a peripheral appendage by their fellow Swiss. What really hurts them, however, is the arrogance that has left them neglected as far as politics, industry and tourism are concerned. But there are advantages, especially for the independent tourist: whoever travels into Eastern Switzerland can discover a region off the beaten track that is full of beauty, some of it obvious, some of it subtly hidden away.

Around the Rhine: The city of **St Gallen**, the largest in Eastern Switzerland, can be reached quickly and easily from Zurich by motorway or inter-city train, but anyone with time to spare would do well to make a detour.

The traveller can, for instance, make his way into Eastern Swiss territory via either **Rapperswil** on **Lake Zurich**, or the **Toggenburg**. He can also go via the **Linth Plain**, **Lake Walenstadt** and the **Rhine Valley**; but probably the most delightful route is the one that starts off by going north and then, following the course of the Rhine, describes a huge curve before entering the depths of eastern Switzerland. Travellers choosing this route will have a chance to become acquainted with magnificent landscape, and can travel through many historic little towns before the broad basin of Lake Constance finally opens up before them. This is perhaps the ideal way to enter the cultural region of Eastern Switzerland.

The first stop on this route is **Neuhausen**, an industrial suburb of Schaffhausen as well as the starting-point for a descent to the **Rhine Falls**, one of the most spectacular natural sights in the country.

The falls inspired William Wordsworth in 1821:

The Virgin-Mountain, wearing like a Queen,
A brilliant crown of everlasting snow,
Sheds ruin from her sides; and men below
Wonder that aught of aspect so serene
Can link with desolation. Smooth and green,
And seeming at a little distance, slow,
The waters of the Rhine; but on they go
Fretting and whitening, keener and more keen;
Till madness seizes on the whole wide Flood,
Turned to a fearful Thing whose nostrils breathe
Blasts of tempestuous smoke...

This grand spectacle of crashing water and flying spray can be enjoyed from many different observation points at the foot of the falls. However, anyone who

The Rhine Falls near Schaffhausen.

wants a real close-up of the thundering mass of water – at peak times it can reach 1,250 cubic metres/sec (37,500 cubic ft/sec) as it crashes over the 150 metre/500 ft-wide cliffs – can travel by ferry either to the rock in the middle or to **Wörth Castle**, which used to be the customs house for Rhine shipping. **Schaffhausen**, with its 34,000 inhabitants, is also sometimes called the *Rheinfallstadt*, because of the falls, and sometimes *Munotstadt*, too, because of the Munot Fortress that towers above the town.

A stroll through the town reveals that, despite industrialisation (watches, textiles and machinery), Schaffhausen has managed to retain many of its historic buildings. The "old town", however, is actually quite new: a fire almost completely destroyed the medieval section of the town in 1372, but it is one of the best-preserved townscapes in the whole of Switzerland.

The oldest civic buildings in the town thus go back to the late Gothic period, but the main emphasis is on the baroque and rococo styles. The 170-plus oriels – richly ornamented projecting windows on upper floors – date from this period too and are styled in many different ways, reflecting the various epochs.

One place certainly worth a visit is the **Haus zum Ritter**, containing copies of frescoes by the Schaffhausen artist Tobias Stimmer. The old part of the town is full of Gothic buildings, rows of magnificent residential buildings and guild halls. Oriels, ancient fountains, small squares and sleepy corners can all be discovered during a stroll here. One of many rewarding sights is the **Reformed Minster**, part of the former Benedictine monastery of **Allerheiligen**, a masterpiece of Romanesque architecture in the town centre. The monks left the monastery centuries ago during the Reformation, and the buildings now house a museum. Nearby, a former textile factory has been transformed into the **Hallen für neue Kunst** (New Art Halls). This outstanding museum of contemporary art exhibits key works by 12 leading international artists from the

The wine village of Wilchingen.

1960s and 70s. Among the artists represented in the 5,500 sq metres (59,000 sq ft) of space is Bruce Nauman and Joseph Beuys, who is represented by his most famous installation *Kapital.*

A paved path leads up to the **Munot Fortress**. This circular fortress was built between 1564 and 1589 as a bastion against Germany, to defend Schaffhausen, the only estate on the right bank of the Rhine held by the Confederation. It was built according to the principles outlined in Albrecht Dürer's theory of fortification of 1527. The fortress is 49 metres (161 ft) in diameter. From the battlements one can enjoy a unique all-round view of the town; at their foot lies a fragrant rose garden.

Swiss vineyards: Anyone with time to spare in Schaffhausen can embark on various excursions: to wine villages such as **Wilchingen** to the south, or to the mountains of the **Randen**, the easternmost part of the Jura mountain range, or across the vineyard slopes of the **Klettgau**. This quiet border region of Switzerland is an excellent place for walking tours, and the Klettgau is famed for its wines. Here, around the smart little village of **Hallau**, we find the largest continuous wine-growing area in Eastern Switzerland, covering nearly 300 hectares (750 acres), and a museum of wine-growing. From time immemorial there has been far more red wine produced here (Blauburgunder) than white (mostly Rieslings and Sylvaners). Just as delightful as Hallau is Wilchingen, the second-largest wine-growing area in the canton.

The section of river between Schaffhausen and Stein am Rhein is considered one of the finest in Europe: largely unspoilt natural scenery, and historic sites such as the former monastery estate of **Paradies**, or the former monastery of **St Katharinental** never fail to enchant the eye of the beholder. **Stein am Rhein**, at the gateway to the Untersee (one of the western arms of Lake Constance), is yet another gem of medieval architecture. It would be pointless to try to sum up this famous region in just a few short lines. Here, simply, are

Oriel windows and painted facades in Stein am Rhein.

a few notes at random: the former **Benedictine Abbey of St Georgen** is considered to be one of the best-preserved medieval abbeys in the entire German-speaking region. The reformed **Parish Church of Burg** (first mentioned in a document dated 799) is the oldest church in the Schaffhausen area. **Rathausplatz** with its large, 10-cornered fountain, the **Marktbrunnen**, strikes the observer immediately because of its magnificent facades and the sheer quantity of frescoes and oriels. Particularly worthy of note among this wealth of paintings are the frescoes on the **Gasthaus Roter Ochsen**, on the **Haus zur Vorderen Krone** and on the **Haus zum Weissen Adler**, to the left of the Town Hall.

At Rathausplatz, the main street connects with the lower part of the town. Half-timbered houses, such a feature of the whole Lake Constance region, here determine the character of the townscape. The heavy oak beams bend beneath the weight of the centuries; sometimes entire house facades seem to be on the point of collapse. We now reach the **Untertor**, which once formed part of the medieval fortifications, as did the **Thieves'** or **Witches' Tower** at the lower end of **Choligasse**.

Stein am Rhein is the kind of place that invites one to stay on longer. After a stroll past the playful facades, visit the **Klostermuseum St Georgen**, the **Doll Museum**, or the **Lindwurm Museum** with its 19th-century agricultural exhibits. And then why not take a break in one of the town's numerous wine taverns, which radiate *Gemütlichkeit* with their oriels and Gothic wooden ceilings.

Lake Constance: Try observing the landscape from the heights of the Seerücken on an autumn day when the light is fading and the Untersee has turned a dull and tired-looking grey: water and sky blend into one another perfectly. The **Höri Peninsula** takes on the appearance of a smudged pencil drawing, and the island of **Reichenau**, with its Benedictine monastery founded by St Pirmin in the year 723, can only just be made out in the distance. The sights of the Untersee are not only con-

Regatta on Lake Constance.

fined to culture and history, though; the landscape has an aura so powerful that it seems to be quite out of this world. The idyllic villages on the Untersee also exude great tranquillity: **Mammern, Steckborn, Berlingen, Mannenbach** and **Ermatingen.**

On the gentle slopes surrounding the lake the traveller is greeted by imposing-looking country houses steeped in history. Surrounding the quiet bay in Mammern is the huge park (90,000 sq metres/295,000 sq ft) belonging to **Schloss Mammern**, where knights, and later the abbots of Rheinau, once resided. Also forming part of the castle, which today houses a clinic, is a **baroque chapel** dating from 1749 that contains noteworthy frescoes.

Salenstein, with its medieval core, rises high above Mannenbach. And further on, on the way to Ermatingen and at one of the finest points of the Untersee, **Schloss Arenenberg**, partially hidden by the trees of a park, can be seen at the top of a steep drop. Its modest exterior belies the fact that it is steeped in history, in particular world history of the last century: the castle bears witness to the life and works of two French emperors. After Bonaparte's downfall Hortense de Beauharnais lived here with her son, who was later to become the Emperor Napoleon III. After the latter's abdication, the fêted Empress Eugenie used to enjoy spending time at this country seat.

The furnishings at Arenenberg bear witness to that period: a marble statue of Napoleon, Empire furniture, obviously influenced by the Egyptian campaign, and court portraits featuring all the finery of the Deuxième Empire are just a few of the numerous royal relics in this otherwise very "un-royal" region.

In contrast, there are the simple farming hamlets on the Seerücken, and the villages down by the lake, where fishing is still a favourite pursuit of the local populace. *Kretzer* or *Egli*, fried in butter or baked in oil, and accompanied by a fruity Riesling or Sylvaner from the region, is a typical speciality. Many a restaurant here can pride itself on a

Half-timbered house in Thurgau.

distinguished past. The **Hotel Adler** in Ermatingen – an imposing-looking half-timbered building – is the oldest hotel in the canton of Thurgau; Alexandre Dumas, Ernst Jünger, Thomas Mann, Graf Zeppelin, Hermann Hesse and Henri Guisan, the general in command of the Swiss army during World War II, all dined here at one time.

The "Swabian Ocean" continues along its shore, and a small detour can be made to the German island of **Reichenau**. At **Kreuzlingen** the lake widens, the banks slope more gently, the landscape loses something of its charm and industrialisation increases. Nevertheless, it is worth visiting the small town of **Arbon**, or *Arbor Felix* as it was known in the ancient world, with its **Fort**, its **History Museum** – which contains finds from Neolithic and Bronze Age lake dwellings as well as from Roman times – and its promenade, a fine place for a stroll. To the southeast is **Rebstein** which has a small castle

Carthusian monastery: By branching off to the south of the Untersee and crossing the ridge above the lake, visitors can reach the **River Thur** and **Frauenfeld** by means of footpaths. The old town of the capital of the canton of Thurgau is dominated by buildings from the period after the fires of 1771 and 1778, which reduced the number of medieval houses in the town to those between the **Town Hall** and the Reformed church. Another relic of medieval times is the **castle**, which stands on a sandstone rock above the banks of the **Murg**. Here, in the centre of the canton, it is not far to one of the finest and best-preserved monastic complexes of Eastern Switzerland. In **Uesslingen**, set into the hilly landscape, lies the former **Carthusian Monastery of Ittingen**. Founded in 1152 as an Augustinian priory and rebuilt in several stages from the mid-16th century, the monastery is a unique mixture of styles. Since 1982 it has been used as a conference and cultural centre, and the restored buildings house a **Carthusian Museum** and the Thurgau canton **Museum of Art** (which also features a collection of naive art).

The small castle of Rebstein.

As already mentioned, Thurgau is not a canton with two or three breathtaking "highlights". The sights here are evenly distributed – almost democratically so.

Most Swiss are only vaguely familiar with the towns in the cantons of Thurgau, and St Gallen, often seeing them simply as landmarks on the way to somewhere else. **Wil**, which lies halfway between St Gallen and Winterthur, to give but one example, is a very ordinary little town, with next to no tourism. Wil possesses a faceless agglomeration of houses, and streets that are totally devoid of people the moment the shops have shut. The old town, in contrast, lies on a hill at the bottom of the valley, and is remarkably unspoilt. The Catholic **Parish Church of St Nicholas** can be admired here, as can the **Dominican convent** and also the **Baronenhaus**, the most important neoclassical residence in the canton of St Gallen. Stopping here for a while, off the beaten track, means experiencing something of genuine Swiss everyday life, which always has something of a provincial flavour to it.

Finger of God: According to local history books, the "decisive factor in the founding of St Gallen was not based on any strategic or industrial considerations – it was the finger of God." This refers to the saga in which the Irish monk Gall, in the year 612, was wandering through the "wild valley of the Steinach" and fell into a thorn-bush; he interpreted this as an unmistakable request to spend some time here. A bear helped Gall to build the monastery he founded, and the bear thus became the heraldic animal of the city of **St Gallen**.

Such is the story anyway, and it is probably futile to dispute its authenticity. There are actually no external conditions whatsoever to justify the founding of the city. St Gallen does not lie on a river, (if one disregards the Steinach, which is little more than a stream); in fact St Gallen, the economic centre of Eastern Switzerland, lies somewhere in the middle of a no-man's-land, jammed between the Rosenberg hills and the beginnings of the Alps sloping up towards the Appenzell district. Indeed,

Muttergasse in St Gallen.

had that Irish monk not stumbled into the thorn-bush all those years ago, it is hard to imagine how else St Gallen could justify its presence today.

Be that as it may, St Gallen's main cultural significance lies in sacred art of the type to be found in, say, the **Collegiate Church** and the **Abbey Library** (*see page 155*). The city traces its beginnings back to the 15th century, when a ring of houses was erected around the newly-built monastery precinct after a fire. The town, now famous for its textiles, then developed from this centre, dominated by the baroque church, in a northwesterly direction. St Gallen also contains a series of exceptionally successful baroque facades. The **Zum Greif** house (22 Gallusstrasse) has a carved baroque oriel with scenes from the Old Testament. Further examples are the house at **7 Bankgasse**, the **Haus zum Pelikan** (15 Schmiedgasse) and the **Schlössli** (42 Spisergasse).

From the 15th century onwards, St Gallen developed into a prosperous centre of the linen trade, and then of cotton and embroidery, before facing almost total industrial collapse during world economic crisis, the effects of which are still continuing. Today's St Gallen does boast a college, but the canton has so far not decided whether it wants a fully-fledged university or not.

St Gallen does, however, have its charms – even if many of them are hidden ones. Its industrial prosperity is far more apparent. The textile industry may be past its prime now, but many medium-sized firms serve to maintain the region's wealth. The town centre has been largely turned into a shopping precinct with innumerable shops and boutiques concealed behind historic facades. As well as possessing many aesthetically pleasing sights, St Gallen also has quite a few buildings of no architectural merit. One example is the town hall next to the railway station.

A more successful symbol of the town is the *Hochschule für Wirtschafts- und Sozialwissenschaften* on the Rosenberg, one of Europe's best-known institutions for the training of upper management.

Appenzell: driving cattle down from Alpine pastures.

The easiest place to get a real sense of St Gallen is in the numerous wine taverns situated on the first floor of the buildings in the old town: in the **Bäumli**, the **Neubädli** or the **Goldenes Schäfli**, the only guild building to have survived. With its sloping floor and its late Gothic beamed ceiling, the "Schäfli" is one of the most original taverns in Switzerland. And a definite "must" on any visit here is a real St Galler *Bratwurst*, sausage with onions and *Rösti*, because the *Bratwurst* they make here is nearly as famous beyond the canton's borders as the lace for which the city is internationally renowned.

The two Appenzells: The journey from St Gallen into the canton of **Appenzell** is almost like a purification. One leaves the lowlands behind, and climbs up into a landscape of almost painful serenity. The mountain scenery is quite idyllic: the hilly landscape spreads out like a green carpet, all the way up to the mighty **Säntis** mountain peak. The small farms are characteristic of the area. The villages here grew up around the churches, a large number of which were built by members of the Grubenmann family of master builders, but there are no communities of any size to be seen anywhere.

This region is famous for its traditional arts and crafts: men and women, using brushes and paints, scissors, looms and embroidery frames, have been creating small masterpieces for years on their remote farms, which today are much sought after by museums and collectors alike. It was here, in this Swiss pastoral landscape *par excellence*, that the original and unmistakable art form known as *Senntumsmalerei*, or "herd-painting", a variation of farm painting, was able to flourish around the middle of the 18th century (*see page 151*).

Appenzell country is a region without a real centre. **Appenzell**, the capital of the Catholic half-canton of Innerrhoden, is really little more than a village. The main town in Ausserrhoden, **Herisau**, is also a village, albeit a slightly larger one. But no Appenzeller likes to see himself that way; he's either a *Vorderländer* from **Heiden**, a *Mittelländer* from

The hilly landscape of Appenzell.

Teufen or just a *Hinterländer* from **Herisau**. The most likely place for Appenzellers to meet is St Gallen – though they don't actually care for St Gallen all that much, for Appenzellers are rather stubborn by nature, and tend to be quite scornful of the rest of the world. Yet strangers are welcome here – as long as they bring in the money, that is. Appenzellers are not the kind of easy-to-get-along-with mountain folk you'd imagine them to be; on the contrary, their obstinate nature is as hard to understand as their nasal dialect.

On the other hand, it was these very characteristics which gave rise to their unique customs in the first place; they have promoted a rich peasant culture, ranging from music for strings to herd-painting and immune to all contemporary fads.

Anyone visiting Appenzell country would do well to drive along the minor roads here, which are full of bends, or better still, hike along the simple footpaths of the region. Trogen, Heiden, Gais, Urnäsch and Appenzell are all equally representative of Appenzeller culture in their different ways. **Urnäsch**, for example, is famous throughout the region for its New Year processions which still take place according to the Gregorian calendar.

On 13 January, the "ugly" and the "handsome" *Silvesterkläuse* (hobgoblins) march through the streets. Scenes from everyday rural life are depicted in artistically carved miniatures on their head-dresses, which can sometimes be as large as a wagon-wheel. The sheer number of taverns in Urnäsch is astounding: one per hundred inhabitants. It is here that the Appenzellers like to sit around and drink cider, or coffee with schnapps.

The fact that the village square is lined with particularly fine-looking timbered buildings comes as no surprise in Appenzell. As well as this, Urnäsch also has a **Local History Museum**; another similar museum, only more modern and also more extensive, can be admired two villages away in **Stein**. Incorporated into it is a *Schaukäserei*,

The "Silvesterkläuse" in Urnäsch.

or cheese exhibition, providing first-hand experience of how Appenzell cheese is produced.

Trogen, which like Gais has won many "best-kept village" awards, prides itself like many other villages in Appenzell on its square. This is where, alternating every two years with the village of Hundwil, all the inhabitants of the canton can come and vote for their government and help decide on cantonal affairs. For hundreds of years, it had been the rule for men to wear a traditional sabre to the event (an army bayonet was also accepted). But in 1990, the women of Ausserrhoden were finally allowed to take part – and from then on, a voting card replaced the sabre as means of entry.

Then it was the turn of the women of Innerrhoden, who took their case to the Federal Court, where they won.

Not to be missed in the village square at Trogen is the **Reformed Church**, a particularly successful piece of work by Hans Ulrich Grubenmann, and it forms a fine backdrop on the last Sunday in April for the administrative council meetings. Other sights include the **Zellweger-Haus** at the entrance to the village square, the neoclassical **Town Hall** and house number 43, the oldest in the square. South of Trogen is the **Pestalozzi Village**, where war orphans of all nationalities have found refuge over the last 50 years.

On any trip through Appenzell country, a visit to the main town of **Innerrhoden**, Appenzell, should on no account be missed. This town, restored at great expense, contains delightful, brightly-painted patrician houses, as well as a finely preserved village square. The **Alpstein** massif, a popular hiking area with its soft Alpine pastures, emerald-green lakes and numerous peaks, is very close. Beyond Herisau, the landscape climbs over wooded hills all the way up to this limestone mountain range.

Primaeval hunters used to seek refuge from bad weather in the prehistoric settlement in the **Wildkirchli Cavern** along its flanks; a **meteorological observatory** has been in operation on top of

Local herd-painter Josef Manser.

Sacred Cows

Senntumsmalerei, or herd-painting, occupies a very special place in Swiss folk art. The folk art of Europe has nothing comparable to it. The special quality of this culture of alpine farmers has its roots in Switzerland's historical structure: its topography, its natural features and its climate made the Lowlands ideal for farming. The cow did not rank very highly here, and providing for it was left to the women and children exclusively. The *Bergbauer*, or mountain farmer, on the other hand, from the high valleys, was engaged in a constant struggle for survival and had to produce everything himself. But although for him the cow was more important than it was for the Lowlanders, "das Hirten" was also considered women's work.

In between these two extremes lie the grass-covered, pasture-farming and Alpine farming areas: the eastern and western foothills of the Alps as well as the Bernese Oberland, Urschweiz (Uri, Schwyz, Obwalden and Nidwalden), Glarus, and the St Gallen Oberland. The people here have lived from cattle-breeding and cheese production from time immemorial; economic thinking in general, as well as manners and customs, have all revolved around the cow. Other regions had more firmly rooted co-operative agricultural traditions, but every farmer from the Appenzell or Toggenburg areas, which have extremely high numbers of individual farmsteads, was seen as his own lord and master looking after cattle-breeding and cheese-making all alone. Alpine dairy farming here is definitely a man's business; the women tend to earn cash from domestic crafts.

Farming tools were being decorated as early as the 18th century, mostly through carving. At the beginning of the 19th century, *Fahreimer* (wooden pails carried on the way up the Alp by the two foremost herdsmen) began to have their bases decorated by means of a colourfully painted circular piece of wood which fitted into the bottom of the pail. These *Fahreimerbödeli* were only ever used on trips up the Alp, and were otherwise very carefully preserved. They usually bore the names of at least one herdsman and one cow, as well as the owner's name and the year in which they were made. There is also the *Sennenstreifen*: a long board, or a long strip of paper, depicting a cattle drive to Alpine pastures, which used to hang either above the door to the cowshed or in the living-room. A third early form was the so-called *Wächterbild*, an enormous portrait of a herdsman painted on the outside of window shutters.

Senntum-Tafelbilder, small paintings usually done on either card or paper, play a major part in Eastern Swiss herd-painting. Themes include cows, herdsmen, farm-hands, buildings and landscapes. The cattle drive up the Alp is again a favourite here. But there are also many pictures of farmsteads, and often of country inns too, and scenes of cattle markets and herdsmen playing card games keep turning up. Dozens of men and women made a name for themselves doing this from the mid-19th century up to World War II, and their many works can today be admired in museums.

the Säntis since 1887. For less enthusiastic climbers, there is a cable car here, and on the **Hohen Kasten**, the **Ebenalp** and the **Kronberg** as well.

The Toggenburg, the Rhine Valley and Lake Walen: The canton of St Gallen, including the Appenzell region, stretches across the Rhine Valley and the Toggenburg up to Lake Walen.

To the west, the canton extends as far as Lake Zurich. The canton of St Gallen is the sixth-largest in Switzerland, with a surface area of over 2,000 sq km (772 sq miles).

The canton, between the lake and the edge of the Alps, is made up of various different regions. The **Toggenburg**, like the Appenzell region, is a popular area for hiking (**Wildhaus**, **Unterwasser**, **Alt St Johann**); in wintertime it is a popular destination for skiers. Wildhaus also features the **Zwinglihaus**, birthplace of the famous reformer Zwingli, and one of the oldest wooden houses in Switzerland.

In the **Rhine Valley**, wine villages such as **Berneck** and **Balgach** can be found off the main road, then the journey continues southwards along the Rhine to **Werdenberg** with its castle, as well as the oldest wooden housing settlement in Switzerland, if not Europe.

On the way to **Sargans**, one sees its defiant-looking **Castle** marking the end of the St Gallen part of the Rhine Valley – today it houses a youth hostel as well as the **Sargans Museum**. Over to the left one can catch a glimpse a different country entirely: the **Principality of Liechtenstein**.

This small state, which joined the UN only in 1990, has made a name for itself over the past few decades in particular as a domicile with low tax liability for numerous firms, many of which exist only on paper. But a detour here is very rewarding, not least for the visitor in search of culture.

The capital, **Vaduz**, where the reigning prince's family has lived since 1939 in the castle of the same name, contains the **Liechtenstein Museum of Art**, which was presented to the state by the present prince's grandfather. It contains several remarkable works of art from the Dutch, Flemish and English schools. For those interested in philately there is also the **Liechtenstein Postage Stamp Museum**, situated in the so-called *Engländerbau* at 37 Stadtle.

From Sargans one can also reach the "international spa town" of **Bad Ragaz**, and **Pfäfers**, where Paracelsus was the first ever spa doctor, and where the reformer Zwingli used to go to cure the rheumatism and gout he contracted on military campaigns. Travellers may feel nostalgic here, especially if they dare venture into the wild depths of the **Tamina Gorge**; visitors to this famous health resort once used to be lowered hundreds of metres in baskets into its healing waters.

The journey then continues on to Lake Walen, via **Walenstadt** to **Weesen**, for instance, or to **Quinten**. In Quinten one can find kiwi fruit growing, as well as persimmons and figs, and even almond, acacia and sweet chestnut trees flourish in the more sheltered areas. Here, travellers find themselves at the gateway to the south.

Below, a holiday chalet in Braunwald. Right, Alt St Johann, under the Silberplatten.

THE POWER OF ST GALLEN

The baroque monastery area of St Gallen bears magnificent witness to the final flourishing of one of Europe's most important abbeys, its history stretching back over more than 12 centuries. In AD 612, an Irish itinerant monk named Gall built a wooden chapel and a cell, in which to live and sleep, here in the Steinach Valley, which at that time was still thickly overgrown with forest. In 747 a Benedictine monastery was erected on the site, which was to form a focus of Western culture for the next three centuries.

The original 8th-century stone sanctuary was replaced at great expense between AD 830 and 867 by three churches built together along the same axis, with the Gozbert-Minster to the east and the Gallus crypt situated under the choir.

The abbey subsequently became a great centre of ecclesiastical power. But in the 15th century it suffered some reverses, losing some of its power and property, including Appenzell.

As a result, it developed into a self-contained state ruled by prince-abbots. Their reign continued until 1798 when the French marched into the city. The monastery was disbanded, but in 1847 its minster was elevated as the cathedral of the newly-formed diocese of St Gallen.

The abbey that can be seen today was freely modelled on the famous plan that can be found in the abbey library. Instead of the western choir, a helm roof with a chapel consecrated to St Michael was attached to the upper floor. It also acted as a porch for the Otmarskirche, the western crypt of which was restored in 1967 and is the only part to date from the early Middle Ages.

In 1721, Caspar Mosbrugger submitted his plans for the new collegiate church, dedicated to St Gall and Otmar. Other noteworthy architects of the Vorarlberg region, such as Gaspare Bagnato and Johann Michael Beer von Bleichten, later took part in the planning. The nave and rotunda were built in 1755 by Peter Thumb, and the new choir with the twin-towered facade was added in 1761 under the supervision of Johann Michael Beer von Bildstein. This facade, in the lively three-dimensional attitude of its cut stone jutting powerfully into space, still reveals a certain baroque tension, but the interior, a central rotunda with a symmetrical series of cupolas in the nave and the choir, shows distinct signs of the incoming neoclassical style.

The most magnificent room in the 18th-century abbey buildings is undoubtedly the elegant abbey library, again by Peter Thumb (1758–67), one of the main exponents of rococo architecture in Switzerland. The long, rectangular hall is crowned with an axial vault. Its pilasters, surrounded by bookshelves and the winding gallery, create a kind of rhythmical movement which is reflected in the plaster mouldings, the paintings and the inlaid floor.

The abbey library contains one of the most important collections of manuscripts in the world, and includes documents dating from the time of the Carolingians.

A particular rarity is a collection of 15 Irish manuscripts from the 7th to the 12th centuries. Especially famous are the *Folchart Psalter* and the *Golden Psalter*, from AD 864–872, and the *Evangelium Longum* with ivory plates by Tuotilo, from around AD 900. There are also 19 illuminated Renaissance codices.

It is above all in the monastery precinct that architectural creativity reached its zenith, uniting the skills of builders of both church and castle in the prevailing baroque style. It was the apogee of the energetic forces that took hold at the end of the 17th century and the beginning of the 18th, when an unpresaged explosion of new building activity occurred across the whole area of Catholic Switzerland.

In mighty abbeys as well as in modest convents, the old churches were demolished or radically altered, and replaced by huge, flamboyant rooms festive and cheerful, they contained the creations of sculptors, painters and artisans, and provided a rich backdrop for all the other arts that filled the space: music from the daily liturgy or ceremonial masses, oratorios and passions, poetry and the theatrical aspect of the church, the choreography of the festive marches and processions. But even in their frivolity they managed to continue to evoke something of the sublime.

wetrok

4
CSUKA

ZURICH

The bustling metropolis of swiftly gliding trams and greystone banking houses, of cosmopolitan restaurants on the great stone banks of the swiftly-gliding snot-green (mucus mutandis) Limmat River, of jewelled escarpments and refugees of all kinds.

—Tom Stoppard, *Travesties,* 1975

One sometimes gets the feeling that Zurich is Switzerland itself, and that everything else – Lake Constance, the snow, the mountains and glaciers all the way to Lake Geneva – is no more than a picturesque wrapping, a recreation area for the hard-working inhabitants of the city's rich. Zurich is seen, especially by the people who live there, as Switzerland's heart that gives pulsating life to the entire country.

Zurich's own form of Schwyzerdütsch – Züridütsch – has a wider audience than the other main regional dialects (Bärndütsch, Baslerdütsch, Bündnerdütsch and Walliserdütsch). It is spoken by the announcers on Switzerland's public radio programmes, most of which are produced in Zurich, not to mention the private "easy listening" stations Radio 24, Radio Z and Radio Zürisee. But not only the country's language and radio comes from Zurich. Its television, too, is based here; and it is no coincidence that films made for television are shot either in or around the city. What happens in Zurich is soon imitated in other parts of the country.

So all this justifies the special treatment given to Zurich itself in this chapter, which really should have been about "the city and canton of Zurich". The *Zürcher* is not a clearly definable Swiss type, but there are some things one discovers on very close examination of Switzerland's "second capital" that also apply, in somewhat modified form, to the country as a whole.

This of course does not mean that the outskirts of the city, only briefly touched on here, or the canton, should be neglected. But the first thing a visitor wants to do in Zurich is to take a look at the city; what he finds in the countryside outside it – often in the most picturesque places – tends to be a reflection of the entire rural landscape of the Lowlands: villages and small towns which have delightful old centres but are surrounded by scars left by the building boom and the city dwellers' rush to live in the countryside. A whole variety of housing estates and blocks of flats, marked by very forced attempts at originality, often make the outskirts of villages resemble nothing more than three-dimensional architectural showcases.

Arrival in Zurich: Travellers who approach Zurich by air will land at **Kloten Airport**, which is the largest in Switzerland (of course, everything Swiss, apart from the mountains, is bigger in Zurich). They then move into a hotel room and wonder how best to get to know the city.

One possible starting-point is where this large Swiss city is known as "Dörfli", in **Niederdorf**, and the best time is towards evening. Here is a narrow street

Preceding pages: strong-room at the Julius Bär bank in Geneva. Left, the Limmat quay in Zurich. Right, early-morning travellers on Lake Zurich.

in the old town, traffic-free, with over 30 streets intersecting it; narrow Gothic houses, some looking as dingy as they have always done, bakeries, delicatessens, tobacconists, second-hand bookshops and antique shops. It is an area still populated by almost 5,000 people: young, fashionable people who have set up house here to inject new life into the heart of the city, and older people who were born here and who have chosen to stay, keeping their original "village spirit" alive for as long as they can. But it is also an area where one meets a lot of people out just for amusement. Niederdorf is Zurich's oldest entertainment district.

The place doesn't really pick up momentum until about eight in the evening. Until then there are still places vacant in the restaurants and at the pavement cafés; the street musicians are still busy tuning up and adjusting their costumes, the prostitutes and go-go dancers are drinking coffee at the bar. But by eight at the latest, everything is in full swing; crowds of people fill the streets, the beer is flowing Munich-style, the wine Paris-style, the bars are full of jazz, yodelling or rock music. Most of the activity stops at around midnight, but it continues on a more diminished scale until at least two o'clock in the morning in a few select nightclubs.

Zurich wakes up every morning at the **Main Station**. A sea of people, in dark-blue suits or brightly-coloured dresses and carrying attaché-cases, flows into the city from the suburbs, which are continuing to eat their way further and further into the green outlying areas to the west, north and east. Every morning, in they stream: businessmen, secretaries, managers, bank clerks, lawyers and sales staff, in a silent, hurried procession that would do honour to the Zwinglian work ethic.

The **Bahnhofstrasse** lies at the economic centre of the city. Some call it the finest street in Europe, and even though other fine cities possess their own special streets, the people of Zurich are particularly proud of this one. It extends from the main station to the lake, bend-

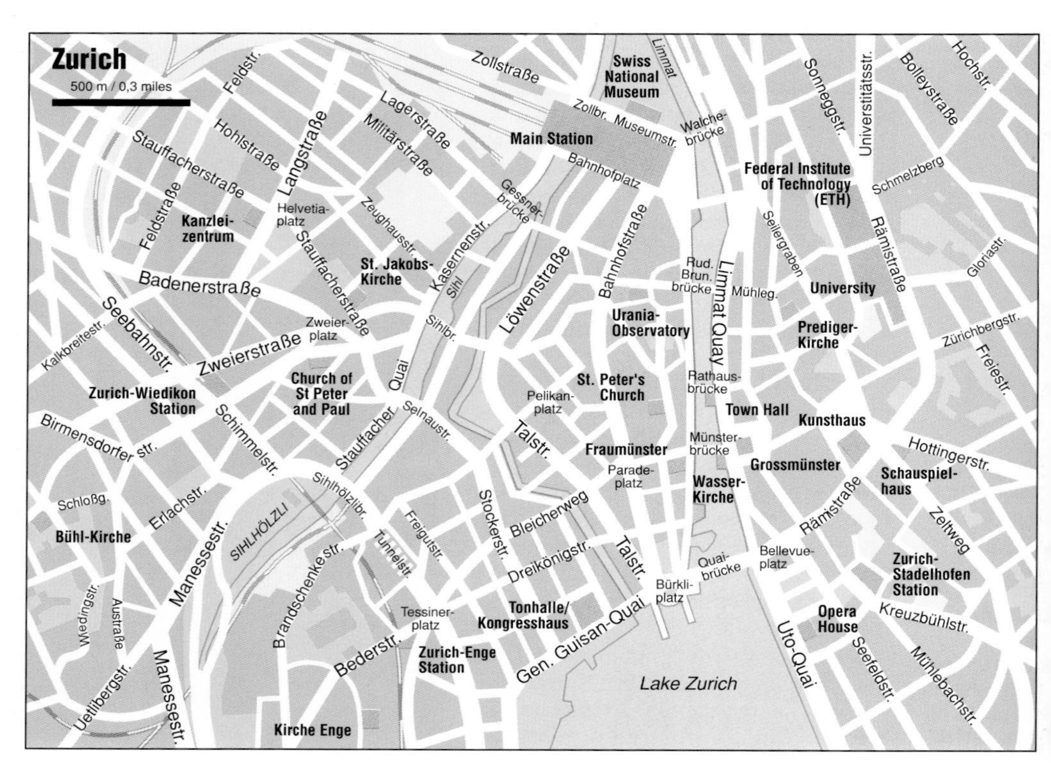

ing slightly on the way, and though only a kilometre (half a mile) or so in length, it offers the dazzling consumer temples of Globus and Jelmoli as well as the head offices of the "Gnomes of Zurich", in other words the five largest banks in Switzerland.

Money markets: Zurich has the third-largest stock exchange in the world after Tokyo and New York; gold and silver are traded and stockpiled here and have their international prices fixed, but just which potentates from the east and the west are either laundering or accumulating their money here is shrouded in secrecy – Swiss banking secrecy, something that the Swiss themselves are actually rather proud of, since it gives their otherwise decent little land a whiff of wickedness.

An embodiment of everything Swiss, the Bahnhofstrasse has all the Swiss virtues of order, cleanliness and punctuality. In fact everything is so squeaky clean that, as James Joyce once put it, you can eat minestrone off the street here without needing a plate. An everyday pair of trousers, or a simple shirt gets displayed in the shop windows like a masterpiece at the Louvre. Everything one can never afford to buy can be found here. The necessary loose change for such purchases can be obtained within the portals of the MBS – the biggest of the famous Swiss banks. These are also worth a visit; all you have to do is act as if you're about to raid your secret bank account. On the subject of shop windows: there is scarcely any city in the world, be it Tokyo, London or New York, with such a luxurious and carefully-packaged range of consumer goods as that to be found here in the magic shopping enclave bordered by Bahnhofstrasse, **Storchengasse** and the **Limmat River**.

One should not, however, burden oneself with too many shopping bags before crossing one of the bridges to the other bank of the Limmat. Here, under the roller-blinds of the south-facing facades of the old houses, beside the quiet river and the consequently even louder roar of the traffic, Zurich has an

At the opening of the Cartier Boutique.

almost Mediterranean feel to it. Between **Bellevue** and **Central** there is more than enough room to eat outside on summer evenings and, moreover, to see and be seen while consuming *coupes* (ice cream) and *cüplis* (glasses of champagne).

While strolling here, it is worth taking a look at the guild buildings, **Zunfthaus zur Saffran** and **Zunfthaus zur Zimmerleuten**, and the **Zunfthaus zum Rüden**. Via the Quaibrücke, one finally reaches the bottom end of Bahnhofstrasse again and the main station, into which most of the population of the centre of the city rapidly vanishes from 4.30pm onwards.

Evening life: Yes, evening rather than night life, because things tend to end far too early in Zurich. This is why the evening has to be prepared for all the earlier, especially as far as food and drink are concerned. However, if an unforgettable meal is what you're after, it's best not to be too optimistic. To have your palate tantalised by those famous *cordon bleu* cooks not only costs a lot but also requires enormous patience. If you are offered a table on a Friday or Saturday without having first telephoned or at least had a longish drink at the bar, you can be almost certain you are in The Wrong Place.

But there are scarcely any such wrong places to be found in neighbouring Niederdorf and around the **Langstrasse**. They're all stylish and consequently jam-packed. If you want good food and space to breathe it's often best to head further afield. The occasional insider's tip-off is likely to send you in the direction of the outer districts, where lower rents mean that daring proprietors and chefs can afford to be a little more experimental.

After the evening meal it's worth taking a constitutional (or should that be too much to ask, a three-minute trip on the Poly-Bahn funicular from Central) to the so-called **Polyterrasse**. Here we see Zurich nestling below us, its brightly-lit landmarks towering out of the sea of lights: the **Predigerkirche**, a Gothic church, in the foreground, behind it the

The Town Hall in Zurich.

Romanesque-Gothic **Grossmünster**, with its twin towers, cut down to size somewhat after an 18th-century fire, and on the other bank of the Limmat, the rococo **Zunfthaus zur Meise**, a jewel-box of a building, alongside the slim Gothic grandeur of the **Fraumünster**, (once part of a nunnery), and also the tower of **St Peter's Church** with its eye-catching clockface (8.7 metres/28 ft in diameter), Europe's largest.

A little architectural history: This begins on the **Lindenhof**, a small hill on the left bank of the Limmat with a fine view of the Limmat Quay, the **University**, in the distance, and the Federal Institute of Technology (ETH). It was here on the Lindenhof that remains of the Roman "Turicum" were found: a customs post and a late Roman settlement based on a fort.

Nestling around the Lindenhof, on various levels, is the most ancient part of the medieval town. The small streets are lined with high, very narrow houses. The city walls were moved several times to accommodate the growing settlement, and it was in 1642, within the span of a single generation, that vast entrenchments were constructed.

As early as the baroque and rococo periods – several buildings in the **Stadelhoferstrasse**, and the **Haus zum Kiel** and the **Haus zum Rechberg** in Hirschengraben date from this time – a new wealthy class of textile merchants and industrialists had shaken off their restrictive fetters and built themselves rural seats either in the nearby countryside, among the former entrenchments, or even further afield, out on the banks of the lake, away from the eyes of city society. Fine examples include the **Muralten Estate** (*Muraltengut*), the **Palace** (*Schlossgut*) on the **Au Peninsula**, and the country seat of **Schipf** in **Herrliberg**. It was when the trenches eventually disappeared in 1833 that Zurich began to develop into the Swiss-German metropolis it is today.

Outside the old town, on the former Schützenplatz, Zurich began to improve its links with the rest of Europe. The large, bright railway station hall – which

The PTT telecommunications centre in Zurich-Altstetten.

has been the subject of extensive renovation – was considered an architectural achievement of European significance in its time.

One should spare a glance for the architecture on Bahnhofstrasse, too: the (later purified) Art Nouveau facades of the department stores of **Manor** and **St Annahof**, the early iron construction of **Jelmoli** (Zurich's first-ever glass palace), the **Bank Julius Bär**, modelled on an Italian *palazzo*, or the head office of the **Credit Suisse bank** which takes up one whole side of the **Paradeplatz**.

The modern architect Arnold Bürkli used the excavated material from the city's many new building sites to fill in the large quay area at **Bürkliplatz** by the lake. Here we find what is unquestionably the finest post office building in all Switzerland, and beside it the Renaissance *palazzo* of the **Fraumünsterpost** and the Renaissance-style Stadthaus, as well as the city's most luxurious hotels, such as the Baur au Lac and the Savoy, and also, not too surprisingly, the head offices of the country's largest insurance companies.

Fine museums: Zurich, along with Winterthur, is among the leading museum cities of Europe. The morning goes by like a flash in the **Kunsthaus** on **Heimplatz**, where one can race through two millennia of European art history. The basic collection belonging to the *Künstlergesellschaft*, (Society of Friends of Art) founded in 1787, has been further extended by purchases as well as generous endowments by private collectors, and now offers a remarkably comprehensive documentation of European art history. Also worth visiting: the nearby **Prints and Drawings Collection** at the **ETH**, and also the various exhibitions at the **Museum für Gestaltung**.

It is hard to overlook the large and cumbersome **Swiss National Museum**, a castellated building erected in 1893. Inside it one immediately notices the enormous fresco by the young artist Ferdinand Hodler, which caused a nationwide uproar and gained him international acclaim. The collection, on dis-

Inside the "Container" design centre.

play in over 100 different rooms inside this labyrinthine building, includes archaeological finds, Roman relics, sacred and profane cultural artefacts dating from the Middle Ages, heraldic shields, and a whole series of rooms and halls furnished in the styles of the 15th to 18th centuries.

Around the lake: The lakeside can be reached from Bürkliplatz via a few shady walks – first following **General-Guisan-Quai** and Mythenquai, then crossing **Belvoir Park** – until one reaches **Villa Wesendonck**, situated on a small rise in **Rieterpark**.

The name is familiar: it was here that Richard Wagner set his famous *Wesendonck Lieder* to the words written by his beloved Mathilde. Not only Wagner, but also Franz Liszt, Gottfried Semper, Johannes Brahms and the Swiss poet Conrad Ferdinand Meyer were guests at this villa, which today houses the **Rietberg Museum**. It contains more than 2,000 cultural artefacts from faraway countries, which make one forget Zurich completely.

Equally exotic is the **Succulents Collection**, situated on the nearby **Mythenquai**, with over 5,000 magnificent plant specimens from Africa, South and Central America. If that was not enough, try the **Botanical Garden** on the other side of the lake. Its greenhouses and the University's herbarium housing one and a half million plants offer a real oasis of tranquillity after an eventful day.

Music and opera: Two buildings are worth visiting even if there isn't anything on that you want to see: the **Opera House** at **Bellevue**, restored at a cost of over 60 million francs, on the other side of Sechseläutenplatz, and the **Tonhalle,** in Gotthardstrasse, with its magnificent organ and unusually clear acoustics. Both buildings contain so much stucco and painting that the eye can happily take over from the ear during any boring stretches. But no criticism is intended here of Zurich's two orchestras; both of them are so generously supported by public funding that quality is assured, especially since the programme tends to

Zurich by night.

get repeated a little more often than the critics would prefer – another reason why the two institutions continue to be one of the favourite subjects of public discussion.

The political and cultural scene has calmed down a lot since the so-called Zurich troubles of the mid 1980s when protestors threw paint-bombs at the Opera House in an attack on "bourgeois" values. Some of the erstwhile rebels have fallen through the social net completely, while others, more successful, are now sitting on the city parliament, or own chic boutiques and art galleries; some of them even receive considerable amounts of public money as artists in order to enliven the city's established cultural life.

The centres of their activities are the **Rote Fabrik** (a former factory), the **Reithalle Gessnerallee** (once an army barracks), and the **Kanzleischulhaus**, previously a school and deprived of further funding from the public purse as an arts venue after a vote was taken in the autumn of 1990.

The highlight of musical and theatrical life for many people is the 10-day **Theaterspektakel** which takes place in August and September, when the very best in experimental productions from all over the world can be seen at the alternative culture venues. Others consider the peak of the season to be the **Internationale Junifest wochen**: every June, under the patronage of the city's president, a cultural theme is given wide-ranging treatment, and its various aspects, from painting to theatre, can be experienced in the city's various official cultural centres. Highlight number three in the year is the **Jazz Festival**, held at the end of October.

Pop and jazz concerts usually take place in the rather gloomy **Volkshaus**, the somewhat run-down Rote Fabrik or the relatively sterile Kongresshaus, annexed to the Tonhalle. Most enjoyable, though rare, is the loud music that can be heard in the restored and very jingoistic-looking **Schützenhaus Albisgüetli**, an extravagantly laid out, wooden Valhalla with its own tower and other

Every district has a brass band.

wartime paraphernalia. The huge rock concerts that are held in the **Hallenstadion** attract coachloads of fans, many travelling to the venue from Germany and Austria.

And the discos? Rather feeble, say those who have experienced the clubs of other major European cities: the international village of Zurich is still paying homage to the 1960s and early 1970s, but that has a charm of its own, and it can certainly be bearable for one night. Dancing is preferable to hiding in a hotel, anyway, and it can go on until 2am weekdays, and until 4am on Fridays and Saturdays.

The most popular cinemas are, as usual, the ones that show films in the original language, from the latest Hollywood box-office hits, and established classics, all the way to the outermost fringes of the avant-garde.

Despite the distinct lack of cinemas, and the fact that nearly every television set in Zurich has access to cable television, the city is still very much a cinema city, where seeing the latest film is a must if you want to keep up with the cultural and social scene.

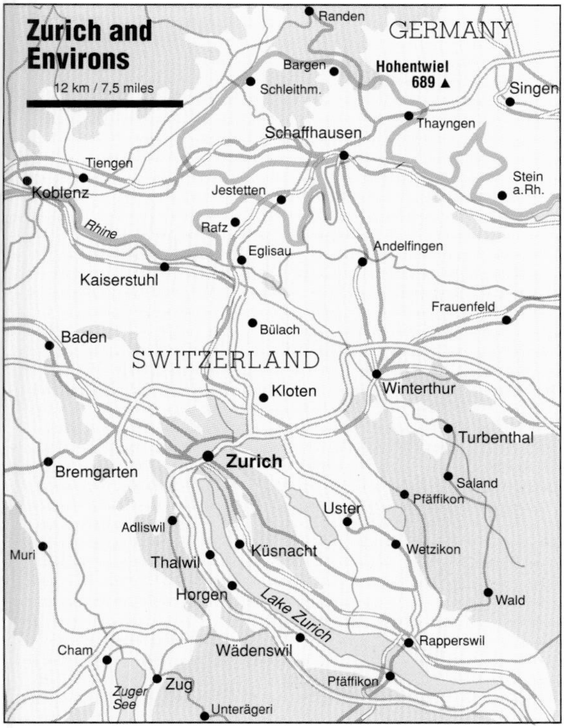

The Swiss stage: The **Schauspielhaus** is part of established cultural life in Zurich, but is less subject to public criticism than other such venues. Its productions are less expensive and its tradition so venerable that it is unquestioningly accepted by all and sundry. It still represents the cosmopolitan side of a city that welcomed, more or less heartily, the great artists and thinkers banned from the German Reich.

The Schauspielhaus, in its time a bastion of anti-fascist resistance, used to put on premières of Brecht plays with star casts, and right up to the 1960s was famous for its modern classics by Swiss authors Max Frisch and Friedrich Dürrenmatt.

The programme today ranges from Shakespeare, Schiller and Goethe to contemporary young Swiss playwrights. Underneath the building, in the Schauspielhauskeller, there is a venue for fringe theatre. This offers a politically and artistically far more daring programme. Though the "Keller" is a big success among younger theatre audiences, its economic future is by no means assured.

Around this large building, a series of small, yet no less significant, theatres are found. The largest of them, the **Theater am Neumarkt**, can even afford its own ensemble for performances of works by modern authors. The **Theater an der Winkelwiese** and the **Theater Heddy Maria Wettstein**, both situated in a marvellous Art Nouveau villa, stage plays and one-man shows. The atmospheric **Theater Stok** usually features literary collages.

The **Bernhard-Theater**, next to the Opera House, offers a very varied programme of entertainment that ranges from musicals to talk shows and esoteric lectures. The **Theater am Hechtplatz** features cabaret and *chanson*, and there is also the **Zurich Puppet Theatre** as well as the **Theatersaal Rigiblick**, which offers mainly modern dance and contemporary theatre.

Folk festivals: The high point in Zurich's festival calendar is the **Sechse-**

läuten in April. It is one of those strange folk festivals that divides popular opinion in two: one half takes part in it enthusiastically while the other half avoids the city like the plague on the days it takes place. Each year, the Sechseläuten opens up the old tensions between Zurich's traditional, Protestant, landed classes (usually better off) and the generally younger, left-wing section of the population.

During the Sechseläuten the medieval order of the guilds is celebrated in just as exaggeratedly idealistic a manner as it was in the 19th century, when the festival was "invented". All the city's notables, dressed in a range of historical costumes representing the various artesans, take part in a procession. On horseback or in carriages, they parade through the crowded streets. The idea is to represent "permanency in change", as the official definition has it. The guilds then ride around a snowman, made of cotton-wool, known as "Böögg" – an allegorical symbol of winter. In similar fashion to England's Guy Fawkes, he is perched on a funeral pyre, which is subsequently ignited. Scarcely any other festival anywhere could be more revealing of its social background and more over-obvious in its intentions, almost to the point of self-caricature; certainly no other festival has survived change so effectively over the years.

Much the same is true of the **Knabenschiessen** held in September, when schoolboys – and, in a break from tradition, girls – take part in a shooting competition, using live ammunition at a range of 300 metres (1,000 ft). The winner of the contest is proclaimed "Champion Marksman". However, the main attraction on the Albisgüetli shooting range is a miniature town of booths and sideshows, the largest *chilbli* (fair) in all Switzerland. The Zurich **Fasnacht** (carnival) is altogether a more subdued affair and not a patch on the one in Basel. Despite several attempts, it still has not managed to gain a real foothold in puritanical Zurich.

Living in Zurich: Not all that much remains of the magnificent villas in the

Lake Zurich and the island of Ufenau.

Enge, the Weinbergstrasse and the Riesbach quarter of town. Despite this, there is a walk that leads up from the lakeside to the **Dolder Grand Hotel** (Art Nouveau) and the residential area of middle-class Zurich. Those who live here usually either inherit their houses, possess a personal fortune, or the have letters AG after the name of the company they own. In the silence that hangs over these town houses and villas you can almost hear the interest and dividends piling up, assuring both children and grandchildren of a decent standard of living. Up here on the so-called **Zürichberg** (Zurich's "mountain")the view stretches for miles into the distance, right across the city. The suburban sprawl will soon extend the entire length of the lake all the way to Rapperswil.

The shadier sides of the city face away from the lake. They begin in the former Limmat swamps, on either side of the railway line leading westward from the main station: shabby, gloomy blocks of flats which once provided shelter for the rural immigrants from the Catholic cantons, and later for those from Italy.

No other street in the city is livelier, day or night, than the **Langstrasse**. It runs through an ethnically mixed area with a dazzling variety of lifestyles. In the daytime there are the Turkish and Italian delicatessens, and the Hong Kong second-hand clothes and shoe shops; in the evening there are the restaurants with their exotic specialities, and the *Beizen* and bars.

Far into the small hours, the pimps patrol the narrow streets in their limousines, keeping an eye on a host of glittering girls from all over the world and giving the city's right-thinking moralists something to complain about.

Because the seething life here is so attractive, and districts four and five are so close to the city centre, rents are rocketing, and many foreigners are having to move out while newcomers move in. If Zurich has any New York-style artists' lofts, then this is the place to find them. The latest sign of gentrification in

Market girl in Winterthur.

Winterthur: City Of Art

The city of Winterthur was founded in 1170 by the Kyburgs, but it had its origins in the Gallo-Roman camp of *Vitudurum*. It has been unlucky more than once in its history: in 1467 the Habsburgs pledged this market town (*pictured below*) to Zurich, and ever since that time it has been in a state of permanent rivalry with its more powerful neighbour, the canton's capital, which lies only 25 km (15 miles) away, and which has jealously guarded its civic privileges.

It was, however, this competition that acted as a catalyst for Winterthur's industrialisation during the 19th century, after protectionist trade barriers had been removed.

It all began with the textile industry – Europe's first ever textile factory was in Winterthur – which soon extended its sphere of activities to towns in the Zurich Oberland situated beside rivers, and the hydraulic power they provided. Textile manufacturing then led to the textile machine industry, and diversification followed: Winterthur produced turbines for power stations, ships' propellers and engines, and then locomotives and railway carriages. Paradoxically enough, it was the planned expansion of the Swiss rail network that ended up isolating Winterthur from the major transport routes so that it was finally beaten by its successful competitor, industrialised Zurich. Meanwhile, another facet of the early stage of rapid industrial expansion was the need for a lifestyle and a culture appropriate to individuals' personal standing. This manifested itself in various buildings as well as in private patronage in music and the fine arts, something which has formed the basis of Winterthur's reputation as a centre of culture to this day. There are several museums. Dr Oskar Reinhart's collection takes up two whole buildings: the "Römerholz" collection and the "Oskar Reinhart Foundation". The striking thing about both is not only the sheer number of works of art on view, but also their quality, ranging from the old masters right through to modern classics. Artists whose work features in the museum include Brueghel the Elder, Rubens, Rembrandt, El Greco and Goya and several 19th-century French artists.

There are three relatively new museums: the **Fotomuseum** – the only one in German-speaking Switzerland,the **Watch Collection Kellenberger** which includes the world-famous console watches of the Liechti watch dynasty and the Villa Flora which has master works by turn-of-the-century artists such as Cézanne, Van Gogh, Matisse, Renoir, Rodin, Vallotton and Toulouse–Lautrec.

One relic of prosperous 19th-century Winterthur, apart from its industry (which is still active), is the delightful – and still intact – old town, which more than stands up to comparison with that of Zurich. The Marktgasse, with its late Gothic and baroque town houses, has been turned into a pedestrian precinct, and is so lively in its own provincial way that a shopping trip here can be a lot more enjoyable than one undertaken in Winterthur's larger, and thus more hectic, neighbouring city of Zurich.

this former workers' district is the nearby **Kunsthalle** has made a name for itself with varying exhibitions of international contemporary art. The **Seefeld**, too, that stretches from the opera house to Mühle Tiefenbrunnen, has become similarly trendy: here are *Beizen* one has to be seen eating in, shops one has to be seen buying clothes in, and the time-honoured, wooden **Utoquai Swimming Baths** – the only place to be seen swimming in if one's scantily clad body is worthy of being seen at all.

The drug scene: Conflicts tend to surface more frequently and violently in Zurich than elsewhere in Switzerland. The housing shortage, noise levels, car exhaust emissions – whatever is currently bothering the population – is expressed here in its own special way. The "Globus riot" of 1968, when Zurich's students attempted their own version of the May riots in Paris, the "movement" of 1980, when young people hurt by the recession in the 1970s showed a new creativity – these have not been the only major disturbances in this city. Still unsolved, and more urgently in need of solution than ever before, is the drug problem, which has now been around since the 1960s. Gone are the days when the police had only to hunt down ordinary pot-smokers; today the problem is a tough heroin and crack scene. Many feel that the police are not up to dealing with the problems, and level the same criticism at the government, whose response until recently has been to turn a blind eye.

The city's main drug area used to be Platzspitz, which – following official intervention – became a public park, clear of undesirable elements. The dealers and addicts are now to be found in other parts of town. Middle-class society seems to be better at managing money than dealing with the drugs problem.

Anyone who hasn't seen more than enough by now, or who hasn't already shopped till they've dropped, will find what they are looking for in the amazingly varied shopping centres in **Spreitenbach**.

It is a residential area and a working

Painting by Albert Anker, from Winterthur's Reinhart collection.

area: a typical agglomeration stretching to the west to Baden, Brugg and Aarau and – in the opposite direction – as far as Winterthur and beyond. This is where the lower middle classes live out their T-shirted *Gemütlichkeit* with their families. They are the kind of people that one often meets on holiday, or finds oneself sitting next to on the S-Bahn, and thinks of as the typical Swiss. These concrete housing estates, which were built in the 1960s and 1970s, contain more yodellers, accordion players and wearers of traditional local costume than all of the mountain cantons put together.

The surrounding countryside: Typical Swiss countryside – that of the popular image – lies close to Zurich. The American writer F. Scott Fitzgerald commented on this quality in *Tender is the Night:* "In Zurich there was a lot besides Zurich – the roofs upled the eyes to tinkling cow-pastures, which in turn modified hilltops farther up – so life was a perpendicular starting off to a postcard heaven."

The citizens of Zurich tend only to dream of the country. They seldom actually go there, and when they do they soon find themselves heading back the way they came.

The fact that **Reppischtal**, the **Türlersee**, the **Greifensee**, the **Forch**, the hills of the **Albis**, the **Etzel** and the **Pfannenstil** tend to be considered suitable only for Sunday outings by the citizens of Zurich shouldn't put visitors off. They offer excellent hiking opportunities: and enthusiasts can try taking a trip up Zurich's local mountain, the **Uetliberg**, for a magnificent panorama of city, lake and Alps, then following the footpaths across the wooded cliffs, across the *Seedamm* to **Rapperswil** (around 50 km/30 miles).

This small country town, once so important that on one occasion it actually went to war against Zurich, is quite delightful with its striking-looking castle and its quay, where hotels and fish restaurants, boasting all the charm of establishments on a genuine Italian *piazza*, tempt visitors to spend the night. The *Stäfner Clevner* and other wines

The former Cistercian abbey at Kappel am Albis.

from Lake Zurich are sure to put one in the right frame of mind.

The way back into the city leads along the "Gold Coast", so called because of its high incomes and correspondingly low tax brackets.

Whether hardened five-star travellers will be much impressed by the country towns of **Regensberg**, **Grüningen** or **Eglisau** is hard to ascertain; as is the appeal of the **Roman citadel of Irgenhausen**, the **Fahr** and **Kappel** monasteries or the wine villages of **Marthalen**, **Oberstammheim** and **Unterstammheim**. But a real "must" of any journey through Switzerland is a country walk through the Lowlands.

Painters' lake: Lake Zurich, which reaches almost into the heart of the city itself, is also – strangely enough – considered part of "Zurich Land". With its gentle shores, and the Alps in the distance which tend to look even bigger and closer because of the *Föhn* (a warm southerly wind), it inspired J.M.W. Turner to paint some of his best "skyscapes". Just sit back and travel on one of Lake Zurich's nostalgic paddle-steamers, complete with its own restaurant, across to the taverns on the **Au Peninsula** or to the romantic island of **Ufenau** – though it's rather more distinguished to drop anchor in front of one of the numerous and very well-maintained fish restaurants in one's own personal motor yacht.

You may wonder how it is possible to complete this entire programme during only a short stay here. The answer is simple: take the excellent Zürcher Verkehrsverbund. It is important, though, to remember to take plenty of small change along with you: manned ticket-offices – apart from those in railway stations – are relatively thin on the ground, especially in the remote spots, and often you will need to buy tickets from an automatic ticket machine. It is also a good idea to keep a plan of the various transport networks handy, because the machines are not exactly helpful. There again, the people of Zurich generally are – and usually speak several languages into the bargain.

Rapperswil: a view of the castle and the town.

UNDISCOVERED GLARUS

In 1755, Konrad Schindler, a doctor from Basel, wrote a dissertation about green cheese. The author must have been familiar with the valley that his fellow Swiss refer to with fond condescension as the "Zigerschlitz" – because of its green *Schabziger* cheese, which is supposed to be one of the oldest known types of hard cheese in the world.

The area in question is the canton of Glarus, measuring all of 684 sq km (264 sq miles), whose uncontrolled hordes managed to defeat a Habsburg army in 1388 and thus secure their independence as part of the Confederation. The valley, almost 40 km (25 miles) long, has from time immemorial only ever provided meagre nourishment for those who settled there – Rhaeto-Romans, then Alemannians. The people of Glarus, known as *Glarner*, have made a habit of emigrating from Switzerland, and have helped to found several settlements in Eastern Europe as well as overseas (the most famous probably being New Glarus in Wisconsin, USA). Wherever you travel, even in the most remote corners of the world, it is surprising how often you will meet Glarner.

However, the popular *Schabziger* cheese, which is absolutely delicious when used in special *gratins*, is not considered the oldest denizen of Glarus. The very oldest, if folk legend is to be trusted, is actually a wind: the *Föhn*, to be precise. True, it occurs in Inner Switzerland, in Graubünden and elsewhere too; but it has set fire to a particularly large number of houses in the canton's 30 villages or so. The city of Glarus – which has an art museum with works from 19th- and 20th century Swiss artists – was almost completely burned down in 1861. (The picture opposite shows the ruins that remained.) That was not the first time the museum had burned down. It was rebuilt to a regular grid-pattern with many fine neo-classical buildings like the one pictured below.

As well as the *Föhn* and *Schabziger*, another aged institution is the Glarus *Landsgemeinde*. This deeply democratic community meeting is still popular in this canton situated between the Linth Plain, Lake Walen and the Tödi, despite all attempts to abolish it, just as in the half-cantons Appenzell Innerrhoden and Appenzell Ausserrhoden, each citizen – male or female – can sit in the "Ring" and openly criticise the canton's government, or even table their own motions.

Before the Walenseestrasse had been dug along the bank of the lake, when the mouth of the River Linth was an unspoilt natural paradise, the road leading from Mollis over the Kerenzer Berg still provided the best opportunity for lowlanders to reach the winter sports resorts in Graubünden.

These days, however, Filzbach and Obstalden, the two villages up here, are largely free of traffic, and because of its remoteness the region is ideal for hikers.

The first ever ski-jumping in Alpine winter sport took place in Glarus, whose ski club, founded in 1892, is the oldest in Switzerland. The *Pragellauf*, a cross-country skiing event that led from the Muota Valley in the canton of Schwyz across to the

Klöntalersee, a real Alpine gem, and then to the main town of Glarus, was for many years the most popular in Switzerland. In fact, its winter sports and mountain climbing have made Glarus very much for those in the know. Elm, in the Sernftal, which is generally referred to as the Kleintal because it forks away from the Linth Valley at Schwanden, is where the American and Swiss women's downhill skiing teams train from time to time. It was here, in 1799, that the Russian general Suvorov and his troops, in a hopeless situation, made their daring attempt to cross the Panixer Pass into Graubünden with horses and cannon. Elm has managed to retain its former appearance and has been given a medal for it.

The risk of avalanches was high in the villages of the so-called "Y-valley" in former days. The kilometres of continuous hiking and cycling trails. It's hard to believe that as recently as the 18th and 19th centuries this canton was the most highly industrialised in all of Switzerland (producing textiles), as well as one of the most prosperous, along with Zurich and Basel. But the people of Glarus remained conservative; even Ulrich Zwingli, the reformer, who was a pastor in Glarus for a time, had difficulty changing the minds of these people famous for their "bull-headed" stubbornness.

The history of the textile industry and of the early phase of industrialisation is well documented in the newly-refurbished cantonal museum, situated inside the remarkable Freuler-Palast in the town of Näfels. It was in the service of the French kings that the Freuler family and their relations made their fortune, which in turn enabled Kaspar Freuler

mountains here – if one bears in mind the natural difference between the valley floor (660 metres/ 2,000 ft above sea level) and the highest mountain, the majestic Tödi (3,614 metres/12,000 ft above sea level) – are extremely high indeed.

The Tödi seals off the relatively narrow valley. The furthest village inside the valley is Linthal, and high above on the mountain the River Linth has its source; further down, after it has flowed out of Lake Zurich, it is known as the Limmat. Linthal is a village on a pass, too. The Klausen Pass, Switzerland's longest, leads from here over into the Schächen Valley in the canton of Uri. It was here that the European Mountain Car Rally Championships were held in 1922 and 1934.

The canton of Glarus is a paradise for hikers, with its gorges, forests, alps, lakes and over 100

(1590–1651) to construct what has come to be known here modestly as "the big house" in his home town of Näfels. Many questions remain. Who designed the building? Where did the craftsmen who created the stucco ceilings and the stone staircases come from? Who furnished the rooms so majestically, and what made Kaspar Freuler build a palace on such a scale in Glarus when he was actually hardly ever there? All these questions remain unanswered; nothing has been passed on.

There are several other aspects of the canton of Glarus too – such as Braunwald, a spa town closed to cars, built on various rocky terraces with fine hotels and guest houses. The resort affords unparalleled views, and the hiking opportunities here are excellent. Braunwald is the very model of an Alpine resort, with all that this entails.

GRAUBÜNDEN

Preconceived ideas about the Bündner (the people of the Graubünden) tend to be flattering. This may be because the Bündner are few and far between – there are only 176,000 of them – making it harder to get at the truth. Another reason for their favourable image might be because they happen to inhabit the most beautiful portion of Switzerland, known to the tourist trade as "Switzerland's holiday corner", an area laced with palm trees and boasting 150 valleys, 615 lakes, and the 4,049-metre (13,000-ft) Bernina Massif, not to mention the glorious white winters and colourful summers.

A strange people: Their fellow Swiss tend to see the Bündner as direct descendants of the mountains, and thus endowed with all the lofty characteristics associated with such a heritage. Favourable clichés of this type are, of course, something the Bündner love to hear, and so often have they heard it that quite a few actually believe in the stereotype, considering themselves to be a happy hybrid of Gian Marchet Colani, the huntsman and "King of the Bernina", and a five-star hotel owner. The Swiss author, Conrad Ferdinand Meyer, attested to their combination of "Nordic maleness" and "southern litheness".

Switzerland's largest canton reacts sensitively to any opinions that differ from these. Spoiled by the lavish praise of visitors, the inhabitants quickly feel attacked when the slightest criticism is levelled at them. Thomas Mann's novel *The Magic Mountain* was considered by citizens of Davos to have "scorned the renowned health resort". Even now, they are only gradually coming to terms with what has ultimately been a beneficial effect that the great novel has had on their tourist industry.

No other word describes the people of Graubünden so well as *konservativ*. They reject nearly everything new out of hand. They were the last people in the civilised world still to forbid cars on their roads; right up until 1925 motorised traffic was banned in the canton. Graubünden was among the last Swiss cantons to continue to deny their women the vote. And when, just a few years ago, a standard, simplified ibex was designed for the canton's coat-of-arms, 22 municipalities fervently begged to be allowed to retain the more realistic animal they were used to.

Graubünden is even more conservative when it comes to language. There's a lot of variety here, too. In one and the same canton (and in Switzerland, too, which is polylingual anyway) there are three language groups: Rhaeto-Romanic, German and Italian. The most conservative group is the first one: Rhaeto-Romanic is derived from the vernacular Latin dating from the Roman occupation of 2,000 years ago. So far, so good. Unfortunately, the Latin that got mixed up with the Rhaetish spoken by the original inhabitants developed so differently in the various secluded valleys that today there are five different Rhaeto-Romanic styles of expression, all of which insist on their very own school-books, newspapers,

Preceding pages: winter on the Julier Pass. Left, peasant woman from the Schams. Right, a jeweller's shop in Davos.

and radio and television programmes.

All attempts to unite the various styles via a kind of Interromansch, *Rumantsch Grischun*, have so far failed. The language is not suited to this kind of fragmentation: even in the two bastions of Romansch, the Engadine and Surselva, which up to 10 years ago were 85 percent Romansch, only one in five people today says *bun di (*good day*)* and *buna saira* (good evening). Nor is it any help if a tourist in a restaurant assiduously raises his glass of Veltliner and calls out "*Viva!*", greets haymaking farmers with an "*Allegra!*", or christens his house *Chesa Romantica*. For deep inside, he is utterly convinced that Romansch is simply an invention of the local tourist board: after all, how much nicer to eat in an *Usteria*, *Stüva* or a *Chesa* than in a boring everyday restaurant.

Traces of the Roman legacy are evident everywhere in Graubünden . The people of the Engadine still hold their New Year's Day celebration on 1 March, just as the Roman occupiers used to do: on the *Chalanda Marz* (Kalends of March) the young people mark the end of winter by cracking whips, singing songs and ringing bells. Quite a few roads in Graubünden Alps still follow the old Roman routes.

Many and varied traffic routes: The Romans placed great importance on their roads and passes in the area. Their chief pass was, without a doubt, the Julier. Two Roman columns still stand at the top of it, their pupose to commemorate the triumphal procession of the legion under Drusus and Tiberius in 15 BC. Life in their nearby capital of Curia can't have been that bad, as the excavations in the **Welschdörfli** at **Chur** have revealed: finds from the site have even included oyster shells imported from Brittany.

The Graubünden Alps contain no fewer than 14 different passes, all very close to each other, but this was far more of a curse than a blessing for the inhabitants of Graubünden in the millennia that followed. Half of Europe fought over the most important through-routes across their territory, dividing the popu-

The nostalgic Rhätische Bahn railway crossing the Landwasser Viaduct.

lation's loyalties on several occasions. During the Thirty Years' War it found itself at the heart of bitter wranglings between the supporters of France and the Habsburgs. Even when calm finally descended on the European political scene, and Graubünden had joined the Confederation – albeit as late as 1803 – and begun their 100-year-long task of transforming the medieval gravel-covered mountain tracks into thousands of kilometres of navigable road, the region's luck failed to change: the new Austro-Italian Brenner railway and the Swiss St Gotthard railway snatched away the entire north-south traffic.

With this, the classic pass region of Graubünden was relegated to the status of a poor border region almost overnight. Whole valleys of people who had lived off the north-south traffic for centuries suddenly emigrated to California and Australia.

And it didn't stop there. When Graubünden picked itself up out of the dust by spending 26 years building its very own 375-km (235-mile) narrow-gauge railway network, the railway was used to transport not the wealthy nobility they had expected but World War I refugees instead. The first-class carriages went quietly rusty.

Today the **Rhätische Bahn** plays on people's nostalgia. The old trains are being made railworthy once again. They rock their passengers to and fro on velvet cushions, through 115 tunnels and across 485 bridges. A train such as the *Glacier-Express* takes seven-and-a-half hours to reach **Zermatt** in the Valais from **St Moritz**.

Most of the tourists on these trains are so preoccupied by their own enjoyment that they don't realise that the little red train and the delightful stations are not laid on by the tourist board but have a highly serious set of tasks to perform. No other railway in the world alternates between such extremes. Even when the champagne is bubbling and the caviare is being spread on the bread in the walnut-panelled, lavishly upholstered restaurant car with its shiny brass fittings, three carriages further down the farmers

In the Davos-Parsenn skiing area.

Etruscans, Celts or Semites?

Unterländer (the name the people of Graubünden reserve for anyone in Switzer land who does not live "up" in Graubünden) and foreign visitors who are seriously interested in the Romansch language – which is still spoken by around 50,000 people in Switzerland – are faced with a confusion of languages worthy of Babel.

You may already be aware that Romansch (the general term applied to the Rhaeto-Romanic dialects) is a mixture of the language spoken by the original Rhaetish inhabitants of Graubünden and the Latin spoken by the Roman conquerors, but the fact that five different versions of Romansch have developed over the centuries is often a surprise.

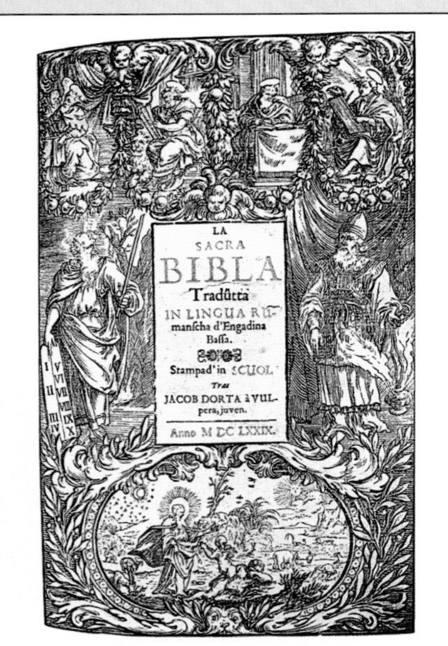
LA
SACRA
BIBLA
Tradûtta
IN LINGUA RUmanſcha d'Engadina
Baſſa.
Stampad' in SCUOL
Tras
JACOB DORTA à VULpera, juven.
Anno M DC LXXIX.

Because of the region's topography, five main dialects developed in what used to be Rhaetia: the *Bündner Oberländer*, the largest group, speak *Sursilvan* (from *Surselva,* meaning "above the wood"); in the Lower Engadine they speak *Vallader* and in the Upper Engadine *Puter* (the latter two are also known collectively as *Ladin*); and in the Oberhalbstein and Albula valleys, as well as in parts of the central Graubünden, *Surmiran*. In the rest of central Graubünden, *Sutsilvan* (from *Sutselva* , meaning "below the wood") is spoken.

All five dialects are considered standard Romansch languages; in addition to these five there are also dozens of local dialects which make the Romansch region an area of extreme linguistic confusion. In the Upper Engadine, for example, the inhabitants of a village only a few kilometres away can be recognised from the way they pronounce the letter "e". In Zuoz, the word for bread is *pem*, while in Samedan it is *päm* (and when written, *paun*). In the Lower Engadine, the word, both written and spoken, is *pan* – but that belongs to another dialect altogether, *Vallader*.

Those interested but also somewhat disconcerted by this might want to resort to basic research. Who were the original Rhaetian inhabitants, and which language was spoken by them? Unfortunately the origins of the *Räter* are still very much shrouded in mystery.

According to the latest research, the Rhaetians – who also include the early inhabitants of the South Tyrol and of Friuli, where Rhaeto-Romanic dialects also exist – are, in essence, not Indo-Germanic. One thing is certain: Etruscans living in the Po Valley influenced the Rhaetian language.

The Celts, too, an Indo-Germanic tribe from middle and western Europe, left their mark on pre-Roman Rhaetia. And new research based on Rhaetian inscriptions, field names and archaeological finds, indicates Semitic origins. That would mean that the mysterious original language was related to Arabic, Hebrew and Accadian.

But such speculations are of little use to the traveller. He or she might, however, be interested to know how things continued from Roman times onwards, and what today's situation is with regard to this one percent language minority.

To begin with, around the year 300, the Emperor Diocletian divided the province of Rhaetia into *Raetia prima* (with Chur as its capital) and *Raetia secunda* (Augsburg being its capital), both of which fell into the hands of the Teutons at some point during the 5th century.

When the bishopric of Chur switched from the archbishopric of Milan to the one in Mainz, it dissolved its connection with the Romansch south. German-speaking settlers from the Valais colonised the high valleys in Graubünden. And after Chur was completely destroyed by fire in the 15th century, the craftsmen entrusted with rebuilding it were predominantly from southern Germany. Later on, the economic problems of the mountain valleys forced many young Neo-Latins to emigrate. And then the tourists finally arrived.

Step by step, Romansch was pushed aside. The very first printing of a Bible translation into Lower Engadine Romansch between 1678 and 1679, which made Ladin a standard language and led to Bible translations in the other linguistic groups, wasn't a lot of help either. And the flowering of Rhaeto-Romanic literature, which began in the 19th century, was scarcely able to provoke a Romansch linguistic renaissance. Whether the standard language *Rumantsch grischun* developed by Romansch language scholar Heinrich Schmid will survive, or contribute to a new surge of interest, is doubtful.

are travelling to market, and the children to school. Indeed, between Christmas and the New Year every single seat is occupied, and even the most dilapidated-looking wooden carriages groan over the rails, transporting passengers to the skiing resorts. In May and November, on the other hand, the carriages are often almost empty.

The "showpiece" stretch of the Rhätische Bahn leads from **Chur**, through gorges and over the famous **Landwasser Viaduct** – 130 metres (420 ft) long, 65 metres (200 ft) high – to **Tirano** on the Italian border, which it reaches roughly four hours later. The most daring stretch of rail awaits the passenger at the **Bernina Pass**, where in winter and spring the locomotive, at a height of 2,257 metres (7,400 ft) above sea-level, and flanked on all sides by mountains over 4,000 metres (13,000 ft) high, ploughs its way through metre-high snow, before coming to a halt some time later among palm trees and magnolia. On the way is **Poschiavo**, where alongside several remarkable churches, the **quartiere spagnolo**, with its colourful and richly-ornamented facades, is certainly worth a visit: it was built around 1830 by emigrants returning from Spain. Near Thusis is another well decorated church, at **Zillis**. In November 1999, the Vereing railway tunnel opened. The new railway line goes from Landquart near Chur to the Under Engadine. It was built to allow travel to the Engadine all year round, as the Flünela pass between Davos and the Under Engadine was often closed in winter and a detour had to be made.

Railway enthusiasts will enjoy the stretch between **Bergün** and **Preda**. In order to gain height, the railway tunnels into the mountain via tight bends. For a more detailed look at the history of the railways, visit the **Rail History Footpath**; it can be covered in two-and-a-half hours, and detailed signboards provide all necessary information.

In winter, the trip can also be done by sledge. Then the 5-km (3-mile) stretch of road between Preda and Bergün is closed to cars, and turned into the most popular sledge run in the whole Graubünden Alps. Sledges can be hired from a shop at the station in Preda; a ride through the snow during a full moon is particularly recommended. The Rhätische Bahn ferries the sledge parties from Bergün back to their starting-point until 1.30 in the morning.

For the even more athletic, the Bahn also offers a very unbureaucratic bicycle service. Anyone who books two days in advance can pick up his hired bike from any station on the Rhätische Bahn, ride off on it, and hand it in at the station of his choice once his tour is over. There are cycles for rent – as well as mountain bikes – at the offices of the local tourist authority too.

Without doubt the finest cycle route is a 60-km (37-mile) stretch in the Upper Engadine, where every holiday resort is directly connected to the cycle route network. The way leads along the edge of the Oberengadiner See, through forests and across broad meadows.

A route less travelled, but just as comfortable, and almost as beautiful is the 42-km (26-mile) route from **Thusis**

Detail of the ceiling in the church at Zillis.

via **Chur** to **Fläsch**, which goes right to the heart of the **Bündner Herrschaft** wine region.

The canton's capital: Even though the capital of Graubünden, **Chur**, the *Curia* of *Raetia Prima*, seems rather jammed into one corner of the canton, it is the ideal starting-point for any Graubünden holiday because of its excellent road and rail network.

This town, the oldest in Switzerland, was already settled by the Celts 5,000 years ago. You can best see how conveniently situated it is, and thus how valuable strategically, from the cone-shaped **Pizokel**, part of the local mountain, the **Dreibündenstein**. Those only interested in the view should alight at the Mittelstation of the **Brambrüesch Cable Car** (its valley station is in Welschdörfli).

Anyone who proceeds to the end of the line will find himself inhaling superb Alpine air, surrounded by meadows and the tinkle of cow-bells – and all of it just a few minutes' cable ride from the bustle down on the Postplatz.

Seen from up here, the concrete wedges driven into the medieval town centre by profit-conscious property developers are all too painfully obvious. There again, all is well for anyone who follows the red and blue markings the tourist office has painted on the streets. They do not lead, as malicious rumour has it, from pub to pub, but from highlight to highlight, and at breathtaking speed. One passes the Gothic **Town Hall** and the **Obertor**; the **Arcas**, the town's loveliest square; the **Bishop's Palace**, and the rather squat-looking Romanesque **Cathedral**, once referred to by a well-meaning man of letters as a "*symphonie sur un air montagnard*"; it contains a magnificent late Gothic carved **High Altar**.

The way leads past some very imposing-looking mansions – most of them financed by soldiers' pay from foreign wars; massive grey blocks with whitewashed vaults and spacious stairways. Two in particular are worth a visit: one of them, situated on Reichsgasse, houses the government, and the other, on Poststrasse, the law-courts.

Left, national riflemen's festival in Chur. Right, the cathedral in Chur.

Chur cannot really be described as a charming town but the old part of it is exceptionally beautiful when snow lies on its mighty roofs, and the grey squared-stone masonry of the houses seems more intense and powerful than ever. It is at this time of year that one can find the renowned *Beinwurst*, or bone sausage, in the town's restaurants. This round-shaped sausage comes as quite a shock to many people, since it accurately lives up to its name. As well as pork, it also contains bone.

In the autumn, by way of contrast, when the *Föhn* wind whips down and colours the sky between **Calanda** and the Pizokel Prussian blue, and the smell of new wine forces its way out of the few remaining wine-presses in **Lürlibad**, every restaurant in town serves venison from the hunt.

Anyone visiting Chur in the summertime will hear voices echoing through the archways of the old town late into the evenings, just as they do in more southern climes. On mild summer evenings people sit out of doors enjoying

the warmth of the day radiating from the walls of the houses. On nights like these, Chur becomes the most Italian town north of the Alps.

Be that as it may, most people treat Chur as nothing more than the final obstacle on the way to their destination resort; red lights, narrow bends, and a troublesome transition from normal to narrow-gauge rail travel. Here is a mini-programme for people in a hurry; it can be covered in just the time it takes to change trains.

First, take a leisurely stroll up the old Reichsgasse to the **Hofkellerei**, a convivial inn, inside the **Gate Tower**, before carrying on to the so-called **Hof**, the heart of the old town of Chur, where you will find the Romanesque and Gothic cathedral, the Gothic bishop's palace, the priests' seminary and the former monastery church of St Luzius with its round Carolingian crypt.

The speciality of the Hofkellerei is *capuns*: noodles wrapped in beet leaves and boiled in stock, a traditional and very filling Graubünden dish and one which it would be a pity not to sample. It is also a good idea to take a seat at the wood-panelled, Gothic bar and order a glass of *Schiller* wine from the episcopal vineyards just below the Hof. It looks harmless, and one experiences its potent effects only when attempting to stand up, which few of the guests are in much of a hurry to do.

Or how about following the people of Chur on one of their typical outings? In autumn, take the route leading into the **Bündner Herrschaft**, to **Maienfeld**, 15 minutes away from Chur by rail. There's a tranquil walk to **Malans** on the itinerary too. This hiking route – which is completely flat – is also called *kistenpass*, because quite a few people end up in a *kiste* (the Swiss word for drunken stupor) while walking along it. This walk is ideal for those interested in enjoying a quick tipple. Without stops, it takes an hour, but temptations are there every step of the way and few people manage it in less than two-and-a-half hours.

Anyone more interested in culture

Looking up to the Albula Pass.

and literature than in Blauburgunder wine can take a look at the massive mansions in Maienfeld – the third town on the Rhine – and then hike, following the red markers, to **Unterrofels** from the Städtliplatz, and to the **Heidi-Dörfli** and the *Heidi-Hüsli*, where the heroine of Johanna Spyri's famous novel *Heidi* is said to have lived. Since 1998 the house has been a museum with an area outside set aside for farm animals.

Magnificent passes: Everyone who wants to cross the passes in Graubünden these days has to take the route used 2,000 years ago: through the narrow gap formed by the Bündner Herrschaft and Chur. For real pass enthusiasts, here are two particularly attractive routes.

The first is ideal for motorists with relatively little pass experience: it leads from Chur (via **Lenzerheide** and **Tiefencastel** or via **Landquart** and **Klosters**) to **Davos**, and then on over the **Flüela Pass** – which has a primeval-looking landscape of stone and water – to **Susch im Engadin**.

Those after more gentle scenery choose the variant – beyond Tiefencastel – that goes via **Bergün** and the **Albula Pass** (open to cars only in the summer). It features exceptionally attractive vegetation – and less stony desolation – but the road is very narrow, and so driving carefully is a good idea. Then again, there's a lot less traffic as a result. Taking this route, one ends up in **La Punt**, where there is the impressive Engadine memorial, the **Chesa Mereda**, which has a striking battlemented gable, built in 1642.

The way continues past **Zernez** and over the **Ofen Pass**, some of which forms part of the **Swiss National Park**, and into the **Münster Valley**. An absolute must, even for those in a real hurry, is a visit to the **Carolingian Convent** in **Müstair**; it contains the best-preserved and most extensive collection of Carolingian wall-paintings in all the Alps. Then finally the way leads on over the **Umbrail Pass** (open only between June and October) and the sinuous **Stilfser Joch** into the Vintschgau in the South Tyrol.

The village of Splügen in the Hinterrhein Valley.

Another trip into the southern part of Graubünden provides the possibility of going over a pass on the journey there and travelling back via a road tunnel. The pass in question is the **San Bernardino**, the alternative to the St Gotthard for road traffic travelling through Switzerland.

It's worth taking this route if only to make a reconnaissance of the **Misox Valley** (or Val Mesolcina as it appears on most maps): the way leads from Chur through the valley of the Hinterrhein, then up over the pass (which is dotted with Alpine roses in the summertime) to **Mesocco**, where the **Castello di Mesocco** dominates the valley from the heights of its rocky ridge. Anyone choosing a route through the villages in preference to the *autobahn* will see the picturesque stables built from rubble masonry dotting the fields outside the villages, and they won't miss **Roveredo** either, where the road branches off in the direction of the **Calanca Valley** high in the mountains. The entry to it is guarded by a 13th-century pentagonal **Tower** and the lavishly decorated **Church of Santa Maria Assunta** (17th century) in **Santa Maria di Calanca**.

Then there is a whole series of tiny villages nestling in a delightful landscape. Many of these look almost deserted, and not without reason: people have emigrated from this high valley since the 16th century. The able-bodied men have traditionally gone off to seek their fortunes in Italian cities, first as master builders and as artists, then later as chimney-sweeps.

Anyone who finds these pass routes a little too tame should definitely take another, third variation, which has been known to send a shiver up the spine of even pass-hardened travellers. This particular tour starts in Chur, then continues via **Thusis** on to **Splügen**, then over that classic north-south pass, the **Splügen**, and down several wildly romantic hairpins into the Italian border town of **Chiavenna**. Then back into Switzerland via the **Bergell**; the mountains surrounding it are so high that some villages remain without

Davos by night.

sunshine for months at a time. Over the **Maloja Pass** into the Engadine and then back to Chur via the **Julier**; and the Julier, a route once used by the Romans, is child's play compared with the route covered so far. By the way, anybody who would rather let others do the driving can do the whole round trip on comfortable post buses (with changes in Splügen, Chiavenna and Silvaplana).

Into the abyss: Let us spend a while longer on the first, and most delightful, part of this round trip. Along with **Via Mala Gorge** and the church at **Zillis**, it merits a special trip on its own. It's important, though, not to make the mistake of driving through the Via Mala along the uninspiring N13, which passes through long concrete tunnels and galleries for around 6 km (4 miles) on its way southwards. Unless you have an interest in engineering, you are unlikely to find much of attraction on this route; there is almost nothing to be seen, and almost nothing to be heard: the traffic is far louder than the **Hinterrhein**, hemmed in between the rocks. To travellers along this marvel of modern engineering, the very idea that people once used to shudder at the thought of this place and that countless people once died here is hard to grasp.

For a real sense of the place, it is better to take your foot off the accelerator in Thusis, resist being sucked down into the new, multi-lane motorway and choose the old road instead. This winds its way along the mountainside, leading through tunnels that are still crudely hewn. The sensation is similar to being on a particularly scary ghost train; you can even feel the moist coolness from down below on your cheeks. Black and forbidding, the crumpled-looking layers of slate, 300 metres (985 ft) high, tower to left and right.

But the real shock, the ultimate shiver down the spine, hits even the most inveterate thrill-seeker at the point where the gorge is at its most terrifying: at the foot of the 321 steps leading from the kiosk down into the depths. Anyone who dares do so (and after a long car trip it's not a bad idea if only to stretch the legs) is greeted by the thundering, foaming, hellish depths below. And anyone who can manage to make it all the way down to the railing – forgetting his sandwich-munching fellow tourists and the concrete, zig-zag path behind him as best he can – takes a small trip back into the past. Over on the sheer rock face on the opposite side it is possible to make out what looks like a kind of picture gallery, complete with holes for hanging up the thick planks and the nails that once supported the old Via Mala road as it hung, balcony-like, above the abyss below.

This was where travellers used to hang in the old days, literally between heaven and earth: the smooth mountain above them, and below, nothing but yawning emptiness and the rushing sound of the water. In winter, people of a nervous disposition would be lashed to the sacks of straw on the sledges, and have a bottle of schnapps pressed into their hands to keep out the cold. Women would keep the leather curtains on their sedan chairs tightly drawn until the worst was past. All too often, frightened horses

Painting by Ernst Ludwig Kirchner.

unfamiliar with the place would stumble or shy and, complete with their rider and luggage, leap into the yawning depths below.

Anyone who dares raise his head can see the famous **Via Mala Bridge** high above him, looking exactly as it did when Goethe sketched it in 1788. It also appears in several novels and plays. The most famous is John Knittel's book *Via Mala*, which has been filmed several times, and which the local inhabitants still haven't forgiven him for writing: he turned them into a group of drunkards and rowdies. He may also have drawn inspiration from the fact that the Romansch language contains more expressions for fighting and brawling than any other in the world.

Lingering idyll: The valley beyond the dreaded ravine, the **Schams Valley**, greets the traveller as delightfully as a ray of sunshine after a thunderstorm. Out here, the sun still sets behind mountains rather than *Aparthotels*. Not a single ski-lift mars the slopes, and the gardens in the village have not yet been asphalted over. No other Protestant area contains so many churches serving so few inhabitants as Schams. They are not situated, as many are, in the middle of the villages, but instead are perched on projecting sections of mountainside or wall, facing down into the valley below in a cheerful, friendly manner, rather like children on tiptoe.

Anyone who feels like leaving his car or post bus in Zillis should wander up to the ruined castle of **Cagliatscha**, then across the old wooden bridge to **Andeer**, and then go back to Zillis either on foot or by post bus again. He will be rewarded by church interiors of touching simplicity (the one at **Clugin**, for example, is particularly moving) and by villages which, thanks to strict building laws, still look the same as they did 100 years ago, unspoilt by clusters of holiday homes.

The finest church of all, however, lies practically on the main road: the Romanesque **Church** in Zillis, which contains the oldest completely painted and preserved wooden ceiling in the west,

The cattle market in Andeer.

constructed around 1150. No-one knows who the artist was, but it is thought that the masterpiece was probably intended to commemmorate a successful crossing of the Via Mala. It clearly shows the influence of book illuminations in Bavaria and Northern Italy. The life of Jesus Christ and several scenes from the life of St Martin are depicted on 153 painted panels. With the help of the hand-mirrors provided these can easily be inspected. The border panels depict mysterious monsters and strange, nightmarish-looking sea-creatures.

Anybody looking for a quiet idyll in overrun, over-visited Europe will certainly want to spend some time in Schams. The valley even tried to turn its back on the road: citizens of **Andeer** were not interested in a plan for an approach road linking the area with the N13 motorway. Finally, they had to give in.

Tourists with time on their hands will probably want to spend a night in this quiet backwater. The obvious place is the old Hotel Fravi, where various crowned heads, as well as Karl Marx, have stayed. They can take a leisurely look at the **Haus Pedrun**, covered in *sgraffito* decoration from the last quarter of the 16th century.

Few of the other valleys in Graubünden are able to offer their guests as much tranquillity and originality as the Schams, mainly because of a mistaken sense of tourism's requirements. The dung-heaps have been cleared from the municipalities all too swiftly, the cows have had their bells removed and the old Arolla-pine parlours have been transformed into slick-looking bars with stylish counters.

The Bündner Oberland: Much originality – alongside a few concessions to modernity – is provided by the **Surselva**, which was discovered by tourism only a short while ago. It is here that one can find those white-bearded individuals so loved by photographers, and houses burned dark by the sun. And yes, bread is actually still baked in some of the public ovens in the village squares. A particularly fine example can be found

Rafting down the Vorderrhein.

in **Luven** above **Ilanz**, decorated with the rather apt saying: *Nies paun da mintg gi* (our daily bread).

In fact, here it is only the entrance to the Surselva and the **Vorderrhein Valley** – above all at **Flims** and **Laax** – that is in the least touristic. In the summertime white-water enthusiasts go river-rafting here, down into the ravine of the wildly foaming Rhine. However, the Rhine is developing into more of a thin and miserable-looking trickle than a torrent since Graubünden allowed itself to be done out of its water rights – for a pittance – by lowland power stations. River-rafters on the **River Inn** in the Lower Engadine are also familiar with this problem.

In fact, Flims and Laax have long since turned their attention to wooing skiers: within the so-called "White Arena", the brainchild of a master butcher from Flims, which covers an area of 140 sq. km (85 sq. miles), even the most energetic skier cannot hope to cover all the descents in a single day. Unfortunately, the ski-lift reaching the summer ski resort on the glacier is no longer in regular operation.

At the very top of the valley, too, near the source of the Rhine at the **Tomasee** (incidentally, there is a very attractive walk which can be taken along its banks), the locals are trying to attract as many tourists as possible. In **Sedrun** on the **Oberalp Pass** (which leads on to Andermatt in the canton of Uri), snowfall is reliable, even when other health spa managers are wringing their hands in despair. And **Disentis** (in Romansch: Mustér), at least as far as a certain clientele is concerned, has long stopped being famous for its **Benedictine Monastery**, the finest baroque edifice in Graubünden: its reputation now rests on its six lawn tennis courts, facilities which have labelled it the "Wimbledon of the Alps" – some exaggeration, of course, but not as far as the tourist office is concerned.

It is also worth pointing out that no other valley in Switzerland contains quite so many baroque churches and chapels. Many of them were built at the time of the ravages of the Plague, when people were frightened of being infected in the bigger churches. The finest examples – some of them Gothic – can be found in **Falera** (the Church of St Remigius), **Sevgein**, **Ilanz** (St Margarethen), and **Waltensburg** (the Reformed church).

For art and nature lovers, **Ilanz** is the best base to choose: everywhere is within easy reach – by car, on foot, or by post bus. In the lateral valleys of the Surselva, far from the through-routes and their filling stations, it is possible to take a journey back 100 years into the past.

The wild **Safien Valley**, which because of the legendary intelligence of its inhabitants has become known as "Schulmeistertal" (schoolmasters' valley), can only be reached via 365 hairpin bends; in the **Valser Valley** one can drink the mineral water of the same name and actually swim in it too; as for the exceptionally delightful **Lugnez** – it prides itself on having successfully avoided tourism.

The village of **Tersnaus** is one of the five villages in Graubünden that do not

Lakeland scene in the Bündner Oberland.

provide overnight accommodation for a single one of the six million tourists who visit here every year. The other four? **Santa Domenica** and **Buseno** in the wild Calanca Valley, **Leggia** in the Val Mesolcina and **Pratval** on the Hinterrhein.

The church and politics: In no part of Graubünden is politics so closely tied to the church as it is in the Surselva. When votes are taken on Sundays, the ballot boxes stand in front of church doorways. The priests' sermons also tend to be far more political than they are in other parts of the country. And it is not only ethical issues, such as refugee problems or abortion, which concern them; such secular matters as nuclear power stations and highway construction are also likely to come under fire from the pulpit.

Centuries of religious apartheid have certainly left their traces in this region. The differences are already evident in the language itself. In the Romansch-speaking Surselva, one confession writes "*de*" (*of*) while the other uses "*da*" in preferen ce – this is still a consequence of the Reformation, when anything that had been written or printed in the heretical neigbouring valleys was totally ignored. It was only very gradually that the barriers between the Catholic and Protestant areas crumbled. In fact today, things have progressed so far that, when the expression "mixed marriage" is mentioned in conversation, the first thing that crosses most people's minds is not their religion but the language that the couple speak: every second Neo-Latin is married to a partner who speaks a different language.

Away from the bustle: Alongside the two brightest stars in the Graubünden holiday firmament, St Moritz and Davos (*see pages 194 and 199*), the less dazzling resorts have quite a hard time of it. **Lenzerheide**, situated on the **Julier Route**, prides itself on being a family resort, while **Parpan** and **Churwalden** are said to have introduced Graubünden *Bindenfleisch*, air-dried beef which, because it is low in calories, has become an integral part of slimming diets. The

Nursery slopes near Laax.

dish is known all over Switzerland by its local name, *Bündnerfleisch*. Gourmets, and people who are in search of some peace and quiet, are liable to feel a lot more at home in such places than avid downhill skiers and celebrity-spotters.

Another place completely isolated from the noisy outside world is **Arosa**, another classic Graubünden holiday resort, which now boasts the largest indoor golf course in Switzerland. The resort can be reached from Chur in an hour, via narrow-gauge railway; it is a romantic trip which is at its most attractive in the summer. In good weather, the **Arosa train** also has a special observation car. With no roof overhead and the wind in their hair, passengers travel over deep ravines, through quiet forests and finally over the famed viaduct at **Langwies**.

A must for all tourists when they've reached the end of the line is a hike up to the famous **Inner-Arosa church**, with its wood-planked tower. Visitors from the US who look at its two bells are in for a surprise: according to the inscription the bells were cast in 1492, the year Christopher Columbus reached America.

Magic Mountain: The **Prättigau** shares the same fate as many other valleys with famous spa resorts lurking at the end of them, in this case **Klosters** and **Davos**: it is treated as merely an access route and most visitors drive through it quickly, sparing no time for a closer look. In the autumn, though, the unexpected magnificence of the huge beech woods here can be quite captivating.

Whatever, something about the Prättigau certainly attracted the people of the Valais. When German-speaking Valaisans emigrated to Graubünden in the 13th and 14th centuries they had to make do with what the Romansch peoples, who were already in the process of settling here, left for them: for the most part, steep slopes and remote mountain terraces. But this actually suited the Valaisan character perfectly: Valaisans don't like having close neighbours, they keep their distance. They are the exact opposite of the Romansch. The latter build their stone houses in close-knit village communities. Valaisans tend to prefer remote wooden houses. Differences in sociability are reflected in other characteristics, too. For example, the Romansch peoples have always had more splendid festivals; it is hard to find a Romansch village without its own music or theatre society. The Valaisans, on the other hand, consider such goings-on as almost irresponsible. The Romansch peoples are mostly solid Catholics, while the Protestant Valaisans – much to the despair of their priests – are prone to all kinds of superstition. Almost every village in the Prättigau has its own local healer or clairvoyant.

It was through the Prättigau in 1889 that the Rhätische Bahn (Rhaetian Railway) transported the very first tuberculosis patients to the sanatoria of Davos, which today publicises itself with the slogan "Davos – famos". The mountain air was thought to be particularly beneficial to people with lung complaints. The forbidding buildings of former days have long since become five-star hotels, one example being to-

Fresco depicting St Christopher on the church at Waltensburg.

day's Steigenberger Hotel Belvedere, on which Thomas Mann based his *Magic Mountain* sanatorium.

Instead of looking around Davos (in vain) for old ruins, it's a better idea to take a leisurely walk into the two valleys next door, **Sertig** and **Dischma**. The German expressionist painter Ernst Ludwig Kirchner used these landscapes in many of his works. The artist lived here from 1917 to 1938. His house in Davos-Frauenkirch is privately-owned and so cannot be visited, but there is the **Kirchner Museum**, containing oil-paintings, sketches and assorted documents, in the old post-office building.

But it is the **Parsenn** rather than Kirchner that has made Davos famous: 200 km (125 miles) of the Davos' 320 km (200 miles) of piste lead down from it into the valley below.

The slopes here are so gentle and predictable that they don't even worry big-city beginners. Anyone keen on avoiding waiting-time at the crowded ski-lifts on weekends and public holidays should do as the natives do and take the **Schatzalp-Strelabahn** to the top of the slopes.

Davos, with a population of over 10,000, is a town that pulsates with life year round. Other towns in Graubünden that rely just as much on tourism become deserted ghost towns 40 weeks out of the year, with the wind howling eerily down their concrete walkways; **Savognin** in the Oberhalbstein, for instance, which compensates for the sins visited on its architecture by having the biggest snow-cannons in Switzerland.

The Engadine: The insensitive development of some villages has resulted in municipalities becoming all the more concerned about their appearance: no-one wants to imitate places that have been criticised for ugliness. The **Lower Engadine** is particularly conscious of its ancestral heritage. **Ardez**, for instance, was chosen as a model municipality in Europe's year of preservation; the "Fall" depicted on the double-oriel facade of the **Haus Claglüna**, the most richly decorated house in the whole of the Engadine, is worth stopping to ad-

The monastery village of Disentis.

mire. From Ardez a small road, which is also good for hiking, leads up to **Guarda**, which clings dramatically to the sunny slope; it has been painstakingly renovated with the help of national funds. In 1975 it was awarded the Wakker Prize for its architecture. The village's houses and inns are typical of a style prevalent in the Lower Engadine since the 14th century, combining living quarters and stables under one roof. The window openings slope inwards and many of the houses feature the elaborate *sgraffito* decoration which originated Italy.

The traveller will discover a way of life that is still largely unspoilt in the neighbouring municipality of **Sent**, with its cheerfully vivacious gables, as well as on the **Panorama High Path**, lying on the former route through the Lower Engadine. The hamlet of **Ftan** has recently gained a reputation as a centre for excellent food.

The best starting-point in the Engadine is **Bad Scuol**, down in the valley below, whic has a romantic atmosphere and old bakery ovens. Bad Scuol's mineral water, known as the "champagne of the Alps", can be drunk from the village fountain. Note the ubiquitous *balcun tort*, the oriel window from which the street can be observed from both sides. Oriel windows of this type are not found anywhere else in Switzerland; they were a means by which the community kept a careful eye on its members.

Such close supervision has made life in Graubünden too claustrophobic for many of its inhabitants and the village has witnessed a steady stream of emigration over the centuries. It was often the brightest who upped and left; philosophers and idealists never really felt much at home under the watchful gaze of their neighbours in Graubünden.

Architects who had build such castles as **Schloss Tarasp**, were also attracted abroad. The Bavarian castles of Nymphenburg and Schleissheim were built by Graubünden architects from Roveredo. Powerful Graubünden merchants traded in Italy, Russia and Spain, and ran the most famous cake shops in Venice. Meanwhile, the vacancies they left at home were filled by foreigners: the German Hennings and the Dutchman Holsboer planned the most difficult stretches of the Rhätische Bahn; the German doctor Alexander Spengler turned the Davos area into the international health spa that it is today. The end-of-year ice hockey game known as the "Spengler Cup" is named after him.

The **Swiss National Park** is best reached from Zernez. Here, in a rugged mountainous area covering 1,700 sq km (650 sq miles), nature has been left to itself since the park was founded in 1914. Visitor information is provioded at the **Nationalparkhaus** in Zernez, where an slide-show exhibition prepares them for the experience ahead. It is cut through by the Müstair Valley which leads to **Müstair** on the border, which has a fine monastery church, St John.

Travellers can find more room to move and as much wild and romantic natural scenery in the **S-charl Valley**, which can be reached easily from Scuol either on foot, by car or by post bus. It is also a favourite haunt of hunters.

A world apart: The Lower Engadine

Left, Schloss Tarasp in the Lower Engadine. Right, inside the monastery church of St John in Müstair.

BEAR ESSENTIALS

The fauna and flora of Graubünden is incredibly rich. But as in many other places world-wide, numerous species of animals, birds and plants are already extinct or are in danger of dying out, and one such is the brown bear. In Ulrich Campbell's *Topography of the Grisons*, published in 1570, we read: "This part of the Alps is filled with large quantities of bears."

This bear, predominantly vegetarian and only carnivorous when it cannot find enough plant food, has appealed to mankind's imagination, as well as to his hunting instincts, from time immemorial. Numerous legends and just as many hunters' tall stories have been handed down over the years.

The fact remains, though, that as late as the 19th century, above all in the Surselva and the Engadine as well as in the southern valleys of Mesolcina, Bregaglia and Poschiavo, many bears still roamed the land, and many were thus duly hunted down and killed. The last bear in Graubünden, and in all of Switzerland, was shot by two hunters from Scuol in 1904 in the Val Mingèr, which forms part of today's National Park.

As far as chamois, stag and deer were concerned, another hunter had those in his sights: Gian Marchet Colani (1772–1837), hero of J.C. Heer's *King of the Bernina*. He is reputed to have killed thousands of wild animals, though the list only includes two bears and one wolf. Vilified these days as an unscrupulous poacher, Colani was, in the eyes of his contemporaries, an exceptionally prudent man, who pursued his hunting activities in harmony with nature.

Hunters of former days were a lot less cautious in their attitude to the ibex, the heraldic animal of Graubünden. By the middle of the 17th century the ibex had already died out, a victim of superstition: apparently, its body was meant to possess miraculous powers, and this led to its every morsel being used for all kinds of necromancy.

The Swiss National Park, founded by the wildlife protection organisation, dates back to 1914. Stags in particular – not a single one of which could be found in the park when it first opened – have meanwhile become so numerous that the natural balance has begun to show signs of wavering. And what about the ibex? They were placed in the park several times during the 1920s, but most of them wandered off and formed the foundations of today's ibex colony on the Albris peak, above Pontresina.

Visitors to the National Park are not allowed to stray from the marked paths. This is not to everyone's taste, and tends to disappoint many visitors.

Spoiled by their experiences on safari in Kenya or in the national parks in America, many tourists want to see the animals close up. Here, one needs a pair of binoculars to be able even to make out a group of stags or chamois up on the scree slopes. But those responsible for the park are at pains to point out that it is *not* a zoo, but a wildlife reserve, in which nature should be left to itself. They have a point: nowhere else in Switzerland is the landscape so unspoilt and beautiful.

and the **Upper Engadine** are not divided by any visible border, but are worlds apart when it comes to their attitudes. In the Lower Engadine, extremely valuable Romansch artefacts still stand in parlours; in the Upper Engadine, they are more likely to be found in chic establishments such as the *Chesa Veglia* in St Moritz, where the finest examples of Romansch artefacts are lined up one after the other. By and large, they are far more valuable than the exhibits displayed in the various museums of local history in the area.

In the Lower Engadine, tradition is still considered very much a private, local affair; in the Upper Engadine, on the other hand, it has been blatantly adapted to meet the demands of tourism. For example, in the Upper Engadine the *Schlitteda*, the traditional sledge outing of the village youth, is happily adapted in the summertime – horse-drawn buggies instead of sledges – to oblige the foreign visitors.

St Moritz.

In recent years, the resort of St Moritz has been compelled to hold its village festival on the roof of its multi-storey car park, because all the other open areas have now been built up.

But here, in **St Moritz**, is the winter resort *par excellence*. It all began in 1864, when Johannes Badrutt, who built St Moritz's Kulm Hotel, invited some English summer guests to spend the winter here, promising that they would be able to sit outside in their shirt-sleeves in December. Various other St Moritz premières followed: in 1880, Europe's first curling tournament took place in the town, and in 1884 the first toboggan-run was built here. In the case of the latter, the daring participants plunged down the run, reaching speeds of up to 140 kph (85 mph). It was also in St Moritz that the bob-sleigh was "invented" in 1891. Occasionally, a visitor to St Moritz will pluck up the courage to go down the famous bob-run – albeit usually in the passenger seat.

The Upper Engadine lives up to every cliché one hears about it. Here we see the jet-set stepping out of Rolls-Royces, and members of Europe's aristocracy at

play. There is always something astonishing going on – beautiful women wearing coats made from Siberian wildcat and being transported in a sledge pulled by dogs the size of calves are reality, not fantasy. Up on the sun terrace on **Corviglia**, St Moritz's local mountain, which can be comfortably reached via cable railway, VIPs and would-be VIPs greet one another like castaways who've just been rescued. After several *Kaffee Grischas* in the "Alpina" the welcoming kisses tend to be aimed rather less accurately: the four different kinds of schnapps in the solid-looking Arolla pine bowl being passed around have a pretty powerful kick.

This is when the fun really starts. Bolstered by schnapps and feeling positively foolhardy, revellers are suddenly willing to participate in the most dangerous sports. One of the most popular activities is hang-gliding down to the **St Moritzer See**, where the range of sports on offer seems to multiply every year: golf and polo in the snow (using red balls), or skijoring are all popular. In the evening, the bars are full of people sporting injuries: tobogganists with plaster casts and skijoring gladiators whose chests are covered in livid bruises (caused by the lumps of ice flying off the horses' hooves). As Art Buchwald said of St Moritz in *I Chose Caviar*, it is "the heart of the broken-limb country, where a man must prove himself first on skis and then on a stretcher."

No one can dodge the bustle in St Moritz, no one can avoid all the frantic activity. That's why there should be somewhere in the resort where one can retire. Luckily, the Upper Engadine is just like all other "in" places frequented by the rich and fashionable: one needs to take only a few steps off the beaten track and the roar of Ferrari exhausts and the cloying scent of perfumes and aftershaves fade away.

Only then can the visitor get a glimpse of the Upper Engadine as the Austrian poet, Rainer Maria Rilke, described it in 1919: "How demanding these lakes and mountains are, there is a strange abundance about them, the moments they

Dog-sledding near St Moritz.

provide are far from simple. The astonishment of our grandfathers and great-grandfathers seems to have had much to do with this place: they travelled here from their own countries which apparently had 'nothing', while here there was 'everything' in plenty. Nature with its ups and downs, full of abundance, full of increase, its outlines starkly emphasised. One mountain? Heaven forbid – a dozen on either side, one after the other; a lake, yes, but a fine one, of the highest quality, with mirror-images of the purest water, with a whole gallery of mirror-images, and Lord God himself as the custodian explaining one thing after another, that is if he's not already too busy in his role as director, levelling the searchlight of the sunset at the mountains where the snow can be seen all day, even in summer."

If you want to experience the region in the same way, skip the route around the St Moritzer See. The route from St Moritz to **Pontresina** on another lake, the picturesque **Stazersee**, may be very easy to cover, and it does pass two seductively situated restaurants, but you are unlikely to be able to enjoy the beauty of the area alone. Hikers abound in these parts.

Luckily there are ways of avoiding them. The route down the right-hand side of the valley from St Moritz up to **Maloja**, for example, is much less busy. It leads across wooded, sheltered slopes, past bog lakes and special stands containing food for the deer, through an idyllic landscape with wonderful views over Lake Silvaplana below; continue past the foot of the **Corvatsch**, considered by many to be the best mountain for skiing in the world. It is shady and cool here in the summer, and in winter the cross-country skiing routes are prepared and freshened up every day. These are particularly recommended for people wishing to avoid the thick columns of cross-country skiers on the frozen lakes and who want a bit more excitement and exercise.

The hamlet of **Grevasalvas**, situated high above the **Silser See**, can be reached on foot only in summer months, from either Maloja or **Plaun da Lej**. Thanks to the enterprising spa director of St Moritz, who also invented the slogan "St Moritz Top of the World" and "champagne air", large numbers of tourists have been making the pilgrimage to this still unspoilt Alpine hamlet for some years now. Impressed by the number of foreign tourists visiting St Moritz who asked about Heidi, heroine of Johanna Spyri's children's book (who inconveniently had her home in Maienfeld), he took advantage of the fact that one of the innumerable Heidi films had been shot in Grevasalvas and without further ado declared the whole of the Engadine "Heidiland". Today, he describes this act of child-snatching rather ruefully as "one of the sins of his youth".

Reaching Maloja is like reaching the edge of the world: the pass road plunges 300 metres (1,000 ft) into the depths, in 12 steep curves. The villages in Val Bregaglia are agreeably intact; the Valley is mainly attractive to mountaineers (who particularly like the Sciora and Bondasca groups), and hikers, too. The Giacometti family came from **Stampa**:

At the start of the Engadine ski marathon.

glass-painter Augusto, his cousin Giovanni, the Impressionist, and last but not least Giovanni's son Alberto, whose sculptures can be found in the world's top museums.

In **Bondo**, visit the **Valley Museum** inside the *Ciäsa Granda*, built in 1581. Further south, on a terrace above the valley lies **Soglio**, which can be reached via a journey through the largest chestnut forest in Europe, which extends as far as the Italian border at **Castasegna**. Here, the three **palaces** belonging to the renowned patrician family of *Salis-Soglio* dominate the scenery; one of them is now a hotel.

Back to the Engadine: Equally pretty in summer or winter are the two valleys of **Val Roseg** (accessible from the station in **Pontresina**, where horse-drawn sledges can be hired) and **Val Morteratsch** (which can be reached from the rail station of the same name). The footpaths here are not steep, and if you walk quietly enough you might just see some young and fearless ibex on the mountain slopes, or a few chamois rooting about in the snow for grass; and in summer, maybe even a herd of deer. If you are lucky, the wind might part the clouds suddenly and – for a few glorious minutes only – reveal the **Morteratsch Glacier** lying ahead, covered in fresh snow and bathed in sunlight, and the **Bernina Massif,** towering more than 4,000 metres (13,000 ft).

The Morteratsch Glacier, by the way, provides skiers with pretty demanding and varied downhill runs from the **Diavolezza**, and can be reached from the Bernina Pass road via cable car; through binoculars from here, one can see the mountaineers on the **Piz Palü**, the **Bianco Ridge** or the **Bernina**, whatever the time of year.

The twilight hours: After an expedition to the wild and romantic valleys, the hiker or cross-country skier may be in need of a fortifying meal. However hungry you are, don't plunge into the first, rough-plastered vault you come across. Folklore knick-knacks and an international menu should be taken as warning signs. Instead keep an eye out for the

The chain of lakes in the Upper Engadine.

generally unassuming little places that really take the trouble to prepare food in the traditional manner. Entrecôte steak and spaghetti Bolognese can be eaten elsewhere, after all.

Evening delights: And what about evenings in the Engadine? Shortly before dinner is the best time in the day to catch a glimpse of the rich and famous. However, you are more likely to see them by accident than design and it's rarely worth hanging around in the hope of sightings, because anybody who is anybody tends to prefer cocktail hour in the privacy of his or her own villa on the **Suvrettahang**. This area sloping to the west of St Moritz is the most exclusive part of the town. A tabloid newspaper once insisted that it contained some 50 multimillionaires. This is an exaggeration: for one thing, most of the celebrities are only in town over Christmas and the New Year.

A more rewarding way of spending the twilight hours is to travel via cable car from Punt Muragl (between Pontresina and Samedan) to **Muottas Muragl**: from no other observation point is the sheer breadth of the Upper Engadine lake landscape so impressive as when the silvery light starts to build up on the mountainside towards evening. Anyone who has experienced it once is always drawn back to this spot: it permeates the broad expanse of the plateau until both earth and heaven become a single supernatural shimmer – and then, suddenly, dusk falls.

Another spectacular place to be when evening falls is the **Silser See**, the final link in the Ice-age chain of lakes: Nietzsche wrote his *Zarathustra* in **Sils Maria**, in 1888. Plagued by almost unbearable migraines (probably caused by the Föhn), his eyes aching, and totally exhausted, he felt transported by nature on this plateau, "which has piled itself up fearlessly close to the terrors of the eternal snows, here, where Italy and Finland form a pact with one another and seem to play host to every silvery colour nature possesses – happy is he who can say: 'Nature certainly has bigger and better things to offer, but this is something truly close to my heart'." The house he used to live in here is now a museum, and may be visited.

In the village square of **Sils Maria** one can climb aboard a horse-drawn sledge and travel into the **Val Fex**, free of cars, overhead wires and pylons; all the lighting and telephone connections here were transferred to cable as early as 1954. With luck, there may be just enough daylight left to visit the pretty little church in **Crasta** and admire its wall paintings, dating from 1500. They have only recently been uncovered, but they look almost as good as new.

The warm, wood-panelled restaurant right at the very end of the valley is an excellent place to stop and have dinner. Emerging into the cold afterwards, you will hear the drowsy splash of the fountain, and see the horses standing in the cold, their sweat turning to steam. The journey home by sledge through the Christmas-card landscape is truly magical. Wrapped snugly in thick animal skins and with nothing to disturb them save the soft jingle of sleigh bells, passengers often drift off to sleep.

The chestnut harvest in Bregaglia Valley.

The Ticino

In Göschenen, the steady climb up the Reuss Valley comes to an end; the train accelerates – and disappears almost immediately into a tunnel which, since 1882, has provided the fastest and most reliable link between German-speaking Switzerland and the **Ticino**, the Italian-speaking part. After exactly 10 minutes of darkness the train emerges into dazzling light and the Ticino, the sunniest part of Switzerland, the long-awaited South.

It is not as warm as all that, though. In fact, it can get pretty cold and foggy up here in **Airolo**, 1,142 metres (3,747 ft) above sea-level; the winters are harsh, and even in summer the weather in the valleys in the northern part of the Ticino never gets as hot as it does in the south. This was actually an advantage in the days when people went to mountain health resorts for the summer rather than to the Adriatic: the first hotels in **Faido** and in the **Blenio Valley** were built around the turn of the century for wealthy visitors from Milan and Lugano, who came here looking for an opportunity to cool down and see the thundering waterfalls, a common natural feature in the Ticino: from time to time, one or two major thunderstorms travel across this landscape, generally considered so pastoral, and fill the **Ticino River** with floodwater, boulders, debris and fallen wood, tearing away parts of roads and bridges and, more often than not, flooding the Magadino Plain.

Preceding pages: summer evening near Ascona. **Left**, a shower in Maggia Valley near Locarno.

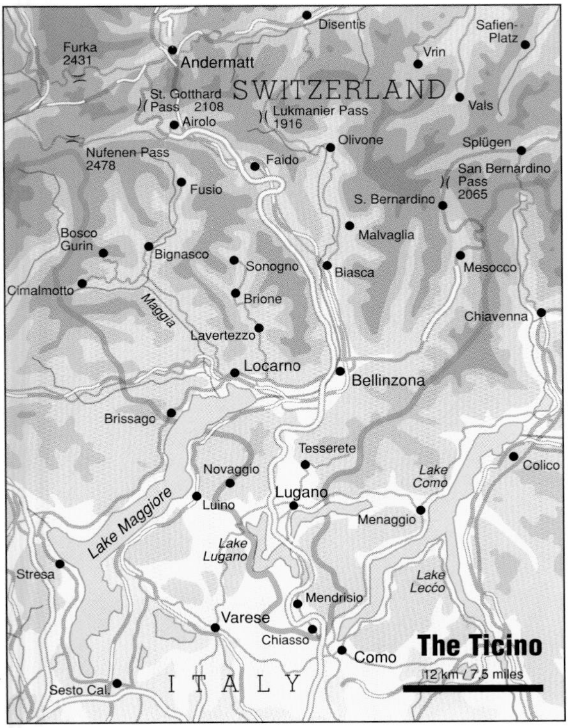

No wonder, therefore, that the old traditional settlements and villages, the Romanesque churches and the many small baroque chapels are located so high up the mountain slopes. They seem to cling to the sides of the valley in fear. The former tobacco-growing areas in the Mendrisiotto, and the Magadino Plain, which used to be swampland before it was drained, are the main areas of flat land that are fertile and agriculturally cultivable in the canton.

The Ticino is, first and foremost, a mountainous canton. It is fortunate to have been blessed with a number of attractive features as far as its geology and natural history are concerned. Among these are the two lakes at the foot of the Alps where the Ticino borders on Italy: **Lake Maggiore**, broad and majestic, nestling among the last of the Alpine foothills, and the contorted and somewhat confusing **Lake Lugano**, which lies between the majestic peaks of Monte Brè, San Salvatore, San Giorgio and Monte Generoso. Incidentally, in the Ticino it is still possible to find seemingly endless and wonderfully quiet valleys filled with sunshine and sub-Alpine vegetation, crossed by extensive, if semi-overgrown, footpaths, and these can be just a few kilometres from noisy motorways, railways and all the other intrusive accoutrements of Western civilisation.

Here, the gentle hills of the Mendrisiotto already mark the transition to the fertile plain of the Po, as you cross into northern Italy. Then, of course, there's the local climate, too: the annual average temperature here is some 3°C higher than in the north of the country, and spring often begins as early as March; the autumn lasts longer, too, with the warm days often extending into November – all of which is very good for Merlot, the most commonly found wine in the Ticino.

A land of emigrants: Of course, man has never lived by balmy air and lush-green slopes alone, and that includes the people of the Ticino. The aspects of the local way of life that foreigners and German-Swiss have consistently idealised – the contented simplicity, the *busecca* (entrail-and-vegetable soup) and the goat's cheese which goes so well with bread for supper – have often been nothing more than characteristics of a life of great poverty and hardship lived out with dignity and decency. In fact, for centuries the history of the Ticino has been predominantly one of continuous emigration.

An initial phase of industrialisation from the mid-19th century onwards, which made German and French-speaking Switzerland relatively prosperous, bypassed the valleys of the Ticino, and when a comparatively modest tobacco and silk industry was established towards the end of the 19th century it was mainly because the area had such a large pool of cheap labour. Even the construction of the St Gotthard railway tunnel in 1882 did little to change things in the early years (though it did gradually turn Lugano and Locarno into tourist resorts).

For the large majority of the population, nothing really changed for the better: between 1881 and 1930 alone, a total of 25,300 inhabitants emigrated abroad. Right up until the 1950s, a trip to the Ticino was still considered to be a trip back into a different era and a much simpler way of life.

Now all that has radically changed. The villages in the valleys are all still there – romantic and sleepy – but many of their former inhabitants have emigrated – not to Australia this time, but to the overcrowded industrial areas around Lugano, Locarno, Bellinzona and Mendrisio-Chiasso. Four-fifths of

***Risotto* and *Luganighe* are part of the Ticino village carnevale.**

the population of 300,000 and 90 per cent of the available jobs are crammed into approximately 14 per cent of the canton, within easy reach of the main traffic arteries.

Meanwhile Swiss-Germans, Germans and other strangers to the area are venturing into the mountain villages and *rustici* in the valleys, and are having the deserted houses and former stables converted into smart new holiday homes – which, of course, are only ever used for a few weeks in the year. If one includes the new buildings constructed since the 1970s, then every fourth house in the Ticino turns out to be a holiday home. As a result, locals are having increasing difficulty finding inexpensive places in which to live because of the massive rise in the cost of land.

Other changes have also affected the area, and not all of them depressive. Many factors have transformed the Ticino into a centre of finance and services: radically improved transport facilities, such as the international airport at **Lugano** and the direct motorway connection with the rest of Switzerland and Milan; the fact that manpower in the canton is still relatively cheap; the fact that Italians willingly commute across the border to work here; Swiss reliability; the Ticino's long tradition of producing the bulk of the country's lawyers; the social unrest of the 1960s, and the flood of capital into Switzerland associated with it.

Thus, in only 15 years, the city of Lugano has seen its very own banking quarter spring up, and flanking the motorway through Mendrisiotto and beyond Lugano are a string of warehouses. Meanwhile, storehouses, lawyers' offices, banks, insurance companies and an ever growing number of filling stations (the Ticino comes second only to Geneva in the number of cars it contains) employ some 56 per cent of the canton's workforce, half of which is made up of frontier commuters and foreigners who reside here.

This rapid development, combined with a vague feeling of becoming more and more dependent on Milan and Zu-

View from Monte Brè towards Lugano and San Salvatore.

rich, and being delivered up helplessly to outside influences, has led to renewed and frequent disputes about the Ticino's actual identity. One response to this threatening cultural monotony and uniformity – and the most visible one, too – is the new Ticino architecture, which has developed into something of an export commodity.

But there are some beautiful traditional buildings, too, like the spectacular Villa Favorita, home of Baron Thyssen-Bornemisza just outside Lugano (*see page 218*).

Rugged mountain town: The town of **Airolo**, once the staging-post where travellers took a rest and changed horses after the rigours of crossing the St Gotthard, and today the place where drivers emerge into the fresh air after 17 km (10 miles) inside the St Gotthard road tunnel, is an example of the rugged side of the Ticino, and of the tough living conditions still faced by many of its inhabitants even today. One can also reach Airolo by taking the rewarding route over the pass, along well-surfaced roads (and also pay the **St Gotthard Museum** at the top of the pass a visit in the process).

A monument by Ticino sculptor Vincenzo Vela erected near the railway station in Airolo is a reminder of the 177 people who lost their lives while the rail tunnel was being built. In winter the snow here can be as deep as a metre or more; the devastating winter of 1951–52, when avalanches caused death and destruction, is still remembered today.

To guard against damage by storms and floods the villages are built high up on the slopes of the valley of the Ticino river, or huddled against the mountainside: **Quinto**, **Rodi Fiesso**, **Ambri** and **Piotta** and, further down, **Faido** and **Bodio** are all examples of villages deliberately built away from the threat of natural disasters. One level higher up are the farming villages, often consisting of only a handful of houses and a church, some free from ornamentation, and some richly decorated like the one at **Rossura**.

Today, all these villages are connected

Baron Thyssen with his wife at Villa Favorita.

by the **Strada Alta**, a hiking trail (with modest overnight accommodation) that leads from Airolo high above the valley to **Biasca**. Unfortunately some of the mountain trails and paths along it have been asphalted over. A somewhat more attractive prospect here is the path that runs along the top of the right-hand side of the valley (one can be transported to exactly the right height via cable car from Airolo). The route has no real gradients, passes through extensive woods, and takes in the unspoilt villages of **Prato**, **Dalpe** and also **Chironico**, with its remarkable church.

Steeped in history: The centre of the **Leventina**, the second highest valley in the Ticino (the **Bedretto Valley** which connects the Ticino with the Valais via the Nufenen Pass is the highest accessible pass in all Switzerland) is **Giornico**, and it is here that the canton's history is most comprehensively illustrated: here, among the ruins of a Milanese castle that was destroyed in 1518, stands the 12th-century church of **Santa Maria di Castello**, with its frescoes dating from 1448. Only a few steps away lies what is probably the most important – and moreover practically unaltered – Romanesque building in the Ticino: the church of **San Nicolao**, built in the first half of the 12th century, with a baptismal font dating from the same period and an impressive series of frescoes from 1478. It was in Giornico that the Swiss gained their first decisive victory over the Milanese, and thus began to establish a lasting grip on the Ticino.

Up until the capture of Bellinzona in 1503, the *balivo* (lord) of the Leventina used to have his seat here, in the **Casa Stanga** (museum); the coats-of-arms on the outer wall remind us of the famous visitors who stopped here on their way over the St Gotthard.

Even older and just as important as the churches of Giornico from the point of view of art history is the **Collegiate Church of San Pietro e Paolo in Biasca**, which was built between the 11th and 12th centuries at a safe height above the village, and for a long period was the mother church of the whole of Upper

Siesta at a motorway service station in the Ticino.

Ticino. The **wall paintings** here (12th–17th centuries) are particularly fine. Anyone who wants to visit the church has to get the key from a house nearby – check at the parsonage in the village.

Biasca is positioned defensively at the entrance to the **Blenio Valley**, and thus also to the **Lukmanier Pass**, which along with the St Gotthard is one of the most important north-south routes across the Alps. A reminder of the strategic importance of this traffic route are the ruins of the once-mighty **Castello di Serravalle** at **Semione**; in **Lottigna**, the Swiss showed the right instincts when they erected their lords' seat high above the valley. The building, richly decorated with coats-of-arms, houses a museum of local history and an important weapon collection.

In fact, a whole series of fine churches more than justifies an extended stopover in the Blenio Valley: **San Martino** in **Malvaglia**, **San Remigio** near **Dongio**, **San Martino** in **Olivone**, and above all the remote Romanesque church of **San Carlo in Negrentino** near **Prugiasco**, with its extraordinary and very well-preserved frescoes and wall paintings dating from the 11th to the 16th centuries.

Today, the valley is a popular holiday, recreation and skiing area. The mighty heap of rubble at the entrance to the valley is the only reminder of the enormous landslide in 1512 which dammed up the **Biaschina**, creating a lake that, forcing an outlet for itself the following year, caused a flood that extended as far as Lake Maggiore.

A medieval barrier: The town of **Bellinzona** has been the canton's official capital only since 1878; before then, Bellinzona, Lugano and Locarno used to take the job in turns. Bellinzona is not only the ideal capital because of its geographical position (important Alpine passes near here include the St Gotthard, the Lukmanier, the San Bernadino and the Nufenen); the town has been a centre of authority for centuries, and was the starting-point for settlement of the Ticino's Alpine valleys.

There is proof that the castle mound

The well-tended Switzerland-in-miniature at Melide.

known as the **Castelgrande** (in the 14th century known as Castel Magnum; in the 17th century as Burg Uri; and in the early 19th century as San Michele) was settled as early as 5200 BC by small groups of farmers – at a time, in other words, when only hunters and gatherers were roaming the forests of German-speaking Switzerland. From then on, it is assumed, more neolithic settlers, followed by Celts, Romans, Lombards, Franks and native chieftains, occupied the safe position.

This strategically important site was then furnished with a fortress extending right across the marshy valley – and secured by several extra fortifications of generous dimensions (the castles of **Montebello** and **Sasso Corbaro**, alongside Castelgrande). Milanese dukes, Visconti and Sforza, who in the 13th century extended their dominion over the whole of the Ticino, were responsible for the construction. The Castello di Montebello, originally based on a keep, is a particularly interesting example of the art of fortification. In the long run, however, the fortress could not stand up to the repeated attacks from the Swiss, and in 1503 they succeeded in capturing Bellinzona; the three inner provinces of Uri, Schwyz and Unterwalden set up their lords' seats in each of its three castles, thereby ensuring that this most impressive example of medieval fortifications has remained largely intact.

Further edifices of note, both inside and outside what has since become a rather sleepy and sober-looking town full of civil servants, include the remarkable churches of **San Biagio** in **Ravecchia**; the church of **San Bernardo** on **Monte Carasso**, which can only be reached on foot; and, in Bellinzona itself, the former Franciscan church of **Santa Maria delle Grazie**, with its noteworthy Renaissance paintings – including a picture of the Crucifixion – and one of the few rood screens still in existence in the country making it one of the most valuable churches in south Switzerland.

As far as proceeding further south is concerned, travellers have a choice be-

The *cantina* (wine cellar) in Mendrisio.

tween the **Locarnese** on the one side of Bellinzona and the **Luganese** on the other; for **Monte Ceneri** divides the southern part of the canton into two sections. Their inhabitants live in two different worlds that are not just separated from one another in the geographical sense.

In the Luganese, they prefer to read the *Corriere della Sera* in addition to the local papers, and are culturally oriented towards Milan and Lombardy; in Locarnese, *La Stampa* from Turin is the most widely-read Italian newspaper, and here one feels a great deal closer to Piedmont, Novara and Turin. One explanation for this cultural division could be the historic transport route across Lake Maggiore: the narrow-gauge railway leads from **Locarno** through the **Centovalli** to **Domodossola** and then into Piedmont.

Locarno, Ascona and the numerous small villages on the banks of **Lake Maggiore** can claim to enjoy the mildest climate in the Ticino. This has encouraged tourism, and led to large numbers of Germans and Swiss-Germans coming to build second homes or retirement homes here, in many cases renovating *rustici*.

It has also led to the campsite at Locarno being booked solid throughout the summer months and a perpetual coming and going, year in, year out, around the lake area. The consequences of this increase in traffic have become almost unbearable: a whole series of housing estates blighting the slopes by the lake, second homes standing empty through the winter months, closed hotels, and the fact that it is now almost impossible to come across any real natives with whom one can exchange even a few words in Italian.

The few sights the area has to offer need to be looked for quite carefully among all the new buildings. One or two narrow alleyways in the old part of the town still hint that **Ascona** is one of the most ancient settlements on Lake Maggiore, and the houses along the promenade, too, are a reminder – from afar, at least – that fishermen once lived there. The church of **Santa Maria della Misericordia** (1399–1442) contains one of the most extensive late Gothic fresco cycles in Switzerland; the **Collegio Papio** surrounds Switzerland's finest Renaissance courtyard; and the **Casa Serodine** features the most richly decorated **stucco** facade on a secular building that Switzerland has to offer.

Finally, **Monte Verità** used to be a place of pilgrimage for vegetarians and nudists. From 1901 to 1920 it attracted a steady stream of people interested in alternative lifestyles and became a centre for natural healing. It was also a meeting-place for artists and writers (Hans Arp and Hermann Hesse among them) and later became an oasis of tranquillity for those in search of rest. Recently, however, the hotel was taken over by the Swiss Technical College.

Should you be looking for sights in **Locarno**, you are sure to be sent in search of the remains of the 14th-century **Castello,** which belonged to the Visconti Dukes of Milan and was largely destroyed in 1518. The Castello is still intact and houses the **Museo Civico** and

Harvesting grapes near Lake Maggiore.

an archaeological museum. Perched on a crag above Locarno is the pilgrimage **Church of the Madonna del Sasso** and its attendant Capuchin monastery. Founded in 1480, it was rebuilt in the early 17th century and renovated in both the 19th and 20th centuries. It contains Bramantino's *Flight into Egypt* (1536) and an Entombment by Ciseri (1865).

Other church buildings of merit in the region include the former **Monastery** and **Church of San Francesco** (1528–72), which serves the German-speaking Catholics of the town, and the **Collegiate Church of San Vittore** in nearby **Muralto** which, along with San Nicolao in Giornico, numbers among the most important Romanesque churches in the whole of the Ticino. Ecclesiastical splendour apart, Locarno's main claim to fame is its international Film Festival.

If you are looking for a refreshing change of scene your best bet is to visit the town's open-air swimming pool. It is one of the best laid-out swimming complexes in the whole of the canton.

A trip into the valleys: As well as being a thriving tourist centre Locarno is one of the most lively and active post-bus terminals in all the Ticino. From here, travellers can reach the three main valleys and some 12 lateral valleys, which make up a third of the canton. For many people these valleys epitomise the Ticino: stone-roofed houses huddled closely together in narrow village streets; picturesque slopes populated by goats and haystacks; forests of chestnut trees; and narrow little bridges spanning wild mountain streams of crystal-clear water. All these aspects contribute to the popular image of the Ticino.

Of course, the locals in the **Verzasca**, **Maggia**, **Onsernone**, **Vergeletto Valleys** and all the villages have seen things very differently over the centuries: poverty, need and, not infrequently, natural catastrophe forced the menfolk to work in Milan, Venice and Turin where they would hire themselves out on a seasonal basis as chimney-sweeps or builders, often not coming home again for years at a time. And the people of these val-

The Castello di Montebello in Bellinzona.

leys – including the Blenio Valley – comprised the bulk of emigrants to Australia and California. The few rich people living in the valleys capitalised on this trend. Accepting land as security, they lent the migrants money for their journeys; very few emigrants were able to repay the loans, and invariably their houses and estates fell into the hands of the moneylenders sooner or later.

This – and the fact that some natives who managed to make their fortunes abroad eventually returned to their villages and valleys – explains why even in the smallest, most remote and most godforsaken villages there are buildings that are large and even majestic, and why churches are often of a size and splendour quite unexpected in this region. This is certainly the case in the group of 17th-century **Franzoni Houses** in **Cevio**, and the **Casa Respini,** which used to be the seat of the Swiss lords in the Valle Maggia, in the same village. It also applies to the fine **Parish Church of San Maurizio** in **Maggia** itself and to the chapel of **Santa Maria delle Grazie** in **Campagna**, to the church at **Intragna**, the church in **Brione/ Verzasca** and to the baroque **Castello Marcacci**, also in Brione/Verzasca.

Among the distant ramifications of the valleys beyond Locarno, at the end of a lateral valley of the Valle Maggia, lies the small village of **Bosco-Gurin**. Here, unlike in the rest of the Ticino, German has been spoken for centuries. Its unusual and very traditional form is explained by the fact that the inhabitants of Bosco (Italian) and Gurin (German) moved here in the 14th century from the German-speaking Upper Valais, probably after taking a roundabout route via the Livinen Valley, and settled in the Ticino much in the same way that other Valaisans settled in various valleys of Graubünden.

The Luganese was sucked into the whirlpool of development a lot later than the Locarnese. For a long time, the region between Monte Ceneri and the Italian border at **Chiasso** was a kind of appendage of Switzerland.

As late as the 19th century it was quite

On Monte Verità near Ascona.

possible for travellers to be attacked and robbed by brigands on the heights of the Ceneri; the southernmost part of the canton, the **Mendrisiotto**, was vaguely considered to be a part of Italy anyway, even though its inhabitants had made their allegiance to Switzerland quite clear in 1803 with the slogan "*Liberi e Svizzeri*" (Free and Swiss).

The political developments under way in neighbouring Italy were frequently felt by Mendrisiotto's inhabitants. The local liberals and conservatives fought each other so fiercely that on a number of occasions they nearly resorted to using arms – methods which, even then, as far as the rest of Switzerland was concerned, were considered Italian rather than Swiss. It was only when the railway was built between Melide and Bissone that the Mendrisiotto was brought closer to the canton, and a long-lasting bond was established.

Since the St Gotthard railway tunnel was opened in 1882, **Lugano**, frequently described as "the pearl of Lake Lugano" has been deluged with tourists from all over the world. Unlike the flat and rather unexciting landscape to be found around Locarno, the bay of Lugano, between the two mountains of **Monte Brè** and **Monte San Salvatore**, can almost compete with Rio de Janeiro and its famous Sugar Loaf in terms of grandeur. Both Monte Brè and Monte San Salvatore can be scaled by funicular. From their tops, in fine weather, one can see the plain of the Po all the way to Milan in one direction, while enjoying a panoramic view of the whole of the Bernese and Valais Alps in the other.

Understandably, this has been at some sort of crossroads and traces of the Etruscans and Gauls as well as the Romans, Franks and Lombards have all been found around Lake Lugano.

Modern Lugano has been greatly influenced by the many big banks based in the city. The imposing-looking buildings housing the financial institutions seem to compete with one another in terms of splendour. Ticino architect Mario Botta has set the pace with two buildings, the **Banca del**

Tough terrain for the trains.

Gottardo and the **Palazzo Ransila**.

The rapid construction in the town has spared a few arcaded alleyways. Two traditional restaurants, the Bianchi and l'Orologio, have also bravely resisted development. Another building to survive is the **Cathedral of San Lorenzo**, situated on a steep slope between the railway station and the lower part of the town. Originally Romanesque, it was enlarged in the 14th century and renovated in the 17th and 18th centuries. A notable feature is its facade, a masterpiece of the Lombardy Renaissance.

The church of a former Franciscan monastery, **Santa Maria degli Angioli**, built in 1499 and jammed between two houses on the lake promenade, not only possesses a rood screen that is still intact, but also contains the most famous Renaissance wall-painting in the whole of Switzerland: the grandiose depiction of the **Passion of Christ** by Bernardino Luini (1529).

The **Piazza della Riforma** next to the Municipio, a generously-proportioned square right beside the lake, offers outstanding views. This is the place to laze in the sun or relax in one of the very convivial cafés.

With its **Museo d'Arte Moderna** and its **Museo cantonale d'arte** (where modern art exhibitions can be seen) in the Villa Malpensata, Lugano has made a name for itself as a city of the arts.

One of its chief attractions in this respect, the **Villa Favorita**, contains paintings from the collection of Baron Heinrich Thyssen-Bornemisza. Since 1993, when a large part of the magnificent old-master collection went to Madrid's Palacio de Villa Hermosa, works of American and European artists from the 19th and 20th centuries have been on show at the Favorita.

Another place that is worth visiting is the delightful little **Customs Museum** in **Gandria**, which can be reached only by boat, and which documents the ingenious schemes of whole generations of smugglers. Gandria itself is a delightful village clinging to a steep slope rising from the lake. With its baroque church, narrow alleyways and terraced vineyards, the village is a joy to visit for the day.

Away from the city centres: Anyone keen to venture out of the cities and towns and get to know a genuine piece of the Ticino at first hand is sure to appreciate the **Val Colla**, with its villages of **Tesserete, Bigorio, Cimadera, Sonvico** and **Dino**; and **also Malcantone**, where picturesque villages such as **Bedigliora, Astano** or **Breno** nestle in the hilly landscape.

Undoubtedly, the most popular mountain in the Ticino as far as tourists are concerned is **Monte Generoso**, which can be reached from **Capolago** via a rack railway. It affords magnificent views far across the plain of the Po. And the narrow, deep **Valle di Muggio** is a wonderful place for hiking.

The villages among the gentle hills of the Mendrisiotto, including **Meride**, where the San Silvestro church and the Casa Oldelli are official national monuments, have the motorway to thank for the fact that they have been left largely undisturbed by the modern world.

Left, Swiss precision engineering is on sale in Lugano. **Right**, tropical garden on Brissago Island, Lake Maggiore.

BOOK - SHOP

SWISS - WATCHES

THE VALAIS

"Individualists" is the word usually used to describe the people of the Valais, the area lying between the Rhône Glacier and Lake Geneva. At least that's what they are called when the speaker is being kind. The French-speaking part can't be treated as a subdivision of Western Switzerland, and the German-speaking people of the Upper Valais – who form one-quarter of the 255,000 people registered as living in the canton – are very different from German-speaking Swiss in general.

Most Valaisans stress their own identity and, in some cases, they actually rather like being thought of as bad-tempered, shameless and reliant on welfare. At the very least, they enjoy deriding the mania for standardisation and self-reliance that the Swiss nation in general seems to possess.

At one time the region was known for its unusual attitude towards idiots and the mentally deficient which, popular wisdom had it, were more numerous in the Valais. One 19th-century traveller noted how "the common people esteem them as blessings. They call them 'Souls of God, without Sin' and many parents prefer these idiot children to those whose understandings are perfect."

Historically, the relationship of the Valais to the Confederation has not been easy. While the south benefited from trade, the north and the west were attacked. The Counts of Savoy in league with their Confederate comrades-in-arms in the north repeatedly laid collective claim to the Valais.

The centuries-long dominion of the Upper Valais over the lower part of the canton came to an end when Napoleon's troops marched in at the end of the 18th century; then, in 1810, the Corsican annexed the land on the Rhône and gave it the status of "Département du Simplon". The region, impoverished, plundered and burned, could take only one course of action: joining the Swiss Confederation in 1815. All the same, it must be said that a lot of Valaisans have long cherished dreams of autonomy. Joining Switzerland was something to be tolerated rather than longed-for; the Swiss constitution is repeatedly rejected in referendums in the Valais.

Until recently many Valaisans were employed as seasonal workers on building sites or in hotels all over Switzerland. They also have a reputation for working as chauffeurs, cooks or gardeners in the homes of the wealthy. That may indeed be the reason for a certain arrogant attitude most inhabitants of the Lowlands seem to have towards this headstrong yet self-confident people. Because of their distinctive dialect, Valaisans can usually be recognised after saying only a few words; even today, among themselves, the Valaisans can distinguish which valley, and even which municipality, their fellow conversationalist comes from.

Stark contrasts: The Valais – the name comes from the Latin word for valley – really is one big valley, roughly 130 km (80 miles) long, nestling in the chain formed by the Valaisan and Bernese

Preceding pages: a goat jam in Zermatt. Left, the Matterhorn. Right, woman from Evolène in the Valais.

Alps, with their total of 51 mountains over 4,000 metres (13,000 ft) high. The particular attraction of this landscape lies in the stark contrasts on offer within a very confined area; the backdrop formed by the Alps is already immense, even claustrophobic. Nevertheless, the land up at the top of the Goms Valley seems to have an awe-inspiring breadth to it. Here, one of the lowest Alpine valleys – its lowest point is just 500 metres (1,600 ft) above sea level – is surrounded by the very highest peaks in all the Alps.

Rail links: No wonder that Albrecht von Haller spoke of the Valais as being "the Spain of Switzerland". The Valais lies on the Simplon rail line (Paris-Milan) and is connected to the north via the Lötschbergbahn (Berne-Brig). Narrow-gauge railways lead from Brig to St Moritz and to Zermatt (the trip on the "Glacier-Express" from Zermatt to St Moritz, or vice versa, is one of the most impressive stretches of railway in all the Alps), from Sierre to Montana and from Martigny across to Chamonix in France.

The N9 motorway takes you almost to Sierre and is being further improved; the cantonal roads in the main valley as well as those leading off into the side valleys are also in very good condition and make it easy to get around.

Travellers arriving from the direction of Lake Geneva make their first acquaintance with the Valais in **Saint-Maurice**. As well as visiting the abbey with its church treasures, it's worth spending some time in the centre of the town. But the real cultural and historical centre of the Lower Valais lies 10 km (6 miles) further up the valley in **Martigny**, where the narrow hollow formed by the lowest part of the Rhône Valley suddenly opens out. This ancient town has developed into an internationally celebrated cultural centre in recent years – in addition to its roles as an industrial centre and an important site of archaeological finds from Roman times.

The town has attracted travellers for centuries. Close to the Town Hall on the Place Central is the former inn La Grande Maison, once the town's leading hotel.

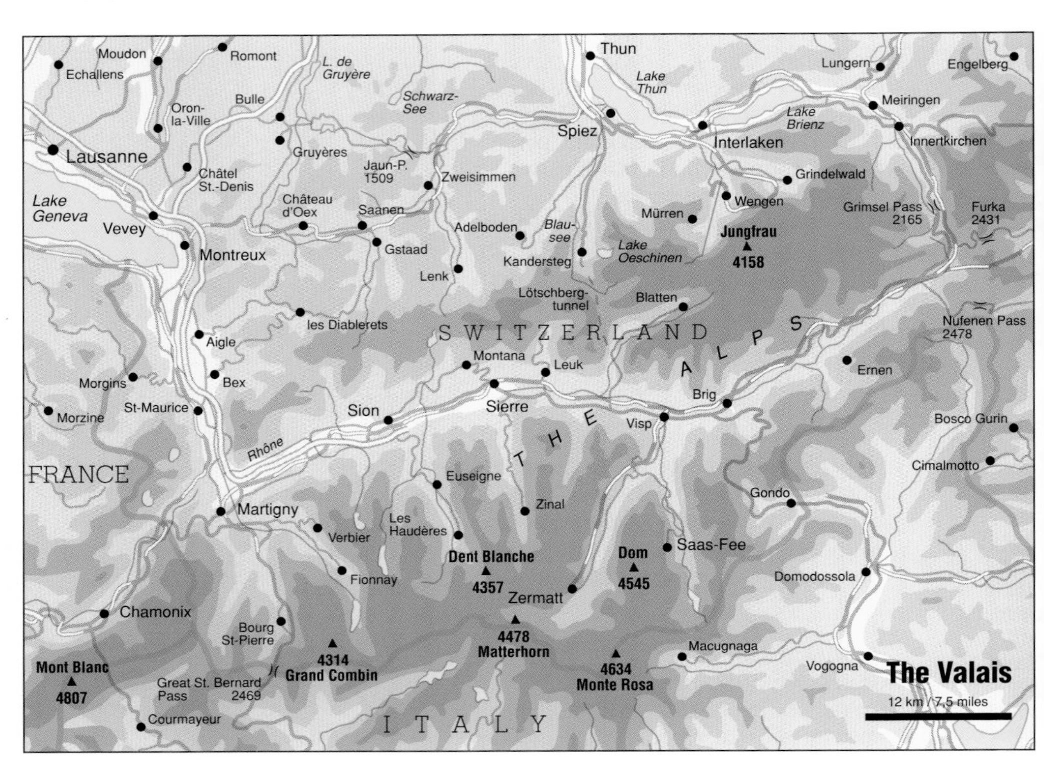

Both Goethe and Alexandre Dumas lodged here during their travels through the region.

The real hub of cultural activity, however, is the **Fondation Pierre Gianadda**. This was started by a member of the Gianadda family in memory of a brother who died in an accident. A modern **Cultural Centre** has been built here – it incorporates the ruins of a Roman amphitheatre – which has made a name for itself beyond Switzerland's borders. It has hosted exhibitions of works by such great artists as Rodin, Toulouse-Lautrec, Picasso and Giacometti, and the garden contains numerous works of sculpture.

The building also houses the **Gallo-Roman Museum**, containing finds from excavations at Martigny and bronze statues from Octodurus (discovered in 1883), as well as an **Automobile Museum**. The latter contains a display of some 50 vintage cars dating from 1897 to 1939 – most of them still roadworthy – including the first-generation vehicles of such prestigious names as Rolls-Royce, Mercedes and Bugatti.

Closely bound up with the fate of Martigny – Octodurus was the Roman name for this place which in the first century BC was developed into a fortified outpost by General Servius Galba under Julius Caesar's orders – is the **Great St Bernard Pass**. Since the road tunnel was opened, this route across the Alps, which was also used by Napoleon as a gate of entry into Italy for the decisive battle against Austria at Marengo, might have been all but forgotten – but ironically, its decline has saved the pass. The St Bernard dog – a close relative of the Pyrenean dog – used to save pilgrims and travellers who had lost their way from dying of exposure and exhaustion after sudden storms, and is today saving the pass itself from lapsing into insignificance.

The world-famous St Bernards, some 15 or 20 of them altogether, are housed in the **Hospice Museum**. Unconcerned by the stream of visitors who come to pay tribute to the famous canines, they doze all day long after their short morn-

A Swiss soldier talking with some Valaisans.

ing walk, and it's only when feeding time comes around that their 80 to 100-kilo (175 to 220-lb) frames show any further signs of movement.

A quick trip to **Aosta** and a visit to the **Val de Bagnes**, the **Val d'Entremont** and the **Val Ferret** makes a delightful detour at this juncture – but the route leads away from Martigny in an easterly direction. It's best not to use the four-lane autobahn here, but rather the small side-road which leads past the medieval castle-town of **Saillon**, the setting for many tales and legends.

The memory of the famous counterfeiter Farinet is kept very much alive here; challenging the state and its money monopoly, he was killed in a hail of police bullets, a fate which inspired the writer C.F. Ramuz to immortalise him in a novel.

Sion (German: Sitten), the canton's capital, has a reputation among Valaisans for being a boring town full of civil servants. In fact, the Planta Square area where the government building is situated, and the old part of the town reveal an astounding cultural and historical heritage.

A visit to the **Cathedral of Notre-Dame-du-Glarier**, the last medieval episcopal church in Switzerland and one of the most impressive religious edifices in the Valais, is highly recommended. Its carved 17th-century choir-stalls, magnificent St Barbara altar and 15th-century bishops' tombs are its most notable treasures. In 1988 the splendid 100-year-old organ, the work of the famous organ builder Carlen of Reckingen, was restored

At the foot of the two hills of **Valeria** and **Tourbillon** lie the **Town Hall**, the **Maison Supersaxo** and the cantonal museums which frequently hold interesting exhibitions of local history. The trip up the Valeria on foot, which takes a quarter of an hour, is worth doing if only to to take a look at the world's oldest functioning organ in the church on top – though this is a claim that some experts vehemently dispute. A few ruins consisting of hewn grey stone are all that remain of the

A mountaineer in Saas Fee.

Tourbillon fortress, erected in the Middle Ages by the once-mighty prince-bishops of the Valais.

Taking the **Val d'Hérémence** from Sion, one reaches another monument – but this time a more recent one: the concrete dam of **Grande Dixence**. Even now, 30 years after its construction – which took from 1951 to 1965 to complete – it is still the highest dam in Europe (285 metres/935 ft). There are 400 million cubic metres of water lurking behind this 700-metre (2,200-ft) long concrete construction. It is 200 metres (650 ft) wide at the bottom and only 15 metres (50 ft) wide at the top, and weighs 15 million tonnes. Construction of this dam – unlike the Mattmark dam in the Saas Valley where 88 people lost their lives in a glacier accident in 1965 – was largely disaster-free. In appreciation of this, the inhabitants of the main town in the area, **Hérémence**, built one of the most original churches in Switzerland. Like the huge dam rising behind it in the valley, the church is made of concrete.

Cow-fight canton: Golf is the main attraction for the fashionable visitors to **Crans-Montana**; the locals, however, are interested in something quite different: cow-fights, which take place every spring and autumn all over the canton. Around the middle of May, in **Aproz** near Sion, the great cantonal cow-fight takes place. It is a popular spectacle in which the most belligerent representatives of the *Eringer* breed – not large, but they can be suitably aggressive – are brought face to face. The fights developed from the natural sparring by which hierarchies were established within cowherds in the Alps, and they are something even a committed member of the RSPCA might condone – for the cows fight only when they feel like it, regally avoid chasing their rivals after they've beaten them, and scarcely ever injure one another.

The **Val d'Anniviers** near Sierre (Siders) is one of the valleys of the Central Valais in which a nomadic mountain people were still moving between the valley floor and the Alps with the seasons as recently as the middle of this century. The flat, rocky and chalky vineyards of **Sierre**, and above all **Salgesch** and **Varen** on the French to German linguistic border, reputedly produce the best red wine in Switzerland. The small vintners in Salgesch and Varen have readily adapted to tourists, and lay on wine-tastings. After a *dégustation*, visitors are invited to purchase any wine they particularly like. The prices aren't too expensive, and the red wines and specialities are remarkably good.

On the small, narrow road that leads from Salgesch in the direction of **Leukerbad**, the impressive-looking **Pfynwald** comes into view; it is the largest continuous forest of Arolla pine in Central Europe, and much of it is now protected. In the Leukerbad valley basin, surrounded by the rocky walls of the **Gemmi**, which impressed Goethe even more than the fleas in his tent, we reach the hot (50 degrees) healing springs of Leukerbad.

These springs not only nourish the expensively-furnished bath-houses here, but also keep the steep part of the street near the church completely free of snow

Sion, capital of the canton.

and ice in winter, thanks to a system of pipes laid under the road surface.

Anyone not too keen on a relatively long walk along the **Restipass** hiking trail into the Lötschen Valley can reach the Rhône Valley again via the medieval town of **Leuk**. A stroll through the old part of "Leuca fortis" (strong Leuk) is a sobering reminder of the rise and fall of small market towns.

Branching off to one side near **Gampel/Steg** is one of the most beautiful and unsophisticated lateral valleys in the whole Valais – the **Lötschental**. Bordered by a mighty circle of mountains, this valley has managed to preserve not only its villages, but also some pre-Christian customs, too, such as the winter tradition of the *Tschägättä*. With their frightening masks carved from Arolla pine and their shaggy sheepskins, the *Tschägättä* can send quite a shiver up the spine of visitors.

Generally more decently behaved are the *Herrgottsgrenadiere*, who, in their red and white uniforms and bearskin caps dating from mercenary days, escort churchgoers to the more important church festivals in spring and summertime. The mood at these processions is solemn rather than festive: the festivals reflect a deep and quite genuine religious faith.

A stay in the Lötschental would not be complete without a visit to the local history museum in **Kippel** and to the chapel in **Kühmatt**, a place of pilgrimage in **Blatten**, with its impressive votive offerings.

Further up the Rhône Valley, you can visit the grave of the Austrian poet Rainer Maria Rilke. It is next to the south wall of the impressive-looking church in **Raron**. The church was built between 1508 and 1517 at the request of cardinal Matthäus Schiner. One of its more interesting features is a fresco depicting the Day of Judgement in which the devils are dressed in the clothing of the notorious Swiss mercenaries of that time.

Secret rivals: At Visp, the Visp Valley branches off, and later separates into the Matter Valley and the Saas Valley at Stalden. **Zermatt** and **Saas-Fee** com-

"Les Violettes" skiing region near Crans-Montana.

pete for tourists' favours. Zermatt covers a large winter and summer skiing area with its Klein-Matterhorn cable railway, and Saas-Fee does much the same with its Metro Alpin. Indeed, if Zermatt didn't have the most original and thus most famous rock formation in all the Alps, the **Matterhorn**, up its sleeve, Saas-Fee would pose a far more serious competitive threat.

But the **Monte Rosa** with its **Dufour spitze** is no match for the Matterhorn. It is the highest peak in Switzerland, and in 1863, the government decided to name it after General Henri Dufour, who made a name for himself as a clever tactician and a far-sighted statesman in the Swiss Civil War of 1847 (between the old Catholic cantons and the reformed ones).

Brig, the capital of the German-speaking Valais, has one single person to thank for its fortunes: the greatest Valaisan merchant of all time, Kaspar Jodok von Stockalper. He established a dynamic and flourishing salt and silk trade between Milan and Lyons in the 17th century, sold snails and larch resin to the French, and was instrumental in organising the first postal service on horseback in his region. "The Great Stockalper" then went on to build his eight-storey **Palace**, with its three mighty towers topped with gilded spheres, as a lasting monument to himself. The **Stockalper Palace** is more generously proportioned and more imposing than any other building in the canton. It was purchased from the impoverished Stockalper family in 1948 by a foundation and the municipality of Brig-Glis, and restored at great expense.

For Stockalper, just as for the French some time later, the **Simplon Pass**, and the connection it provided with Italy, was vital to strategic planning. Under orders from Napoleon, forced-labour convicts had to raise it to the status of an army road within four years (between 1801 and 1805) in order, as the French Emperor once explained in a short despatch, "*faire passer le canon*" (let the cannon through).

Although a memorial plaque on a hotel situated on the southern side of the

The Renaissance courtyard of the Stockalper Palace in Brig.

Simplon insists that Napoleon had once enjoyed a glass of milk there and paid for it with a gold piece, it has been proved that, in fact, the Corsican never crossed the Simplon at all.

The first crossing of the Alps by aeroplane is also closely associated with the Simplon Pass. Geo Chavez, from Peru, won the competition in 1910 by flying his monoplane over the Alpine pass, which lies 2,005 metres (6,500 ft) above sea level. Unfortunately he crashed from a height of around 10 metres (30 ft) as he landed in Domodossola and was killed. Not far from Brig, on a terrace on the right-hand side of the valley, lies the mountain village of **Mund**. Anyone who wants to buy real Swiss saffron should come here, for Mund is the only place in the country left where this fragile plant is still cultivated.

Before the traveller continues his journey into the **Goms Valley**, he should take an appreciative look at the mighty **Aletsch Glacier** and the **Aletsch Forest** (by taking the cable car from **Mörel** to either the **Riederalp** or the **Bettmeralp**). This mighty river of ice, the largest (surface area: 118 sq. km/45 sq. miles) and the longest (nearly 24 km/15 miles) in Switzerland, which is nearly 800 metres (2,500 ft) thick in places, extends in an elegant arc from the Konkordiaplatz at the foot of the **Aletschhorn** to below the **Riederfurka**. On its northern slopes it has one of the finest forests of Arolla pine in the country, which has been strictly protected since the 1930s.

The nature conservation league has renovated the **Villa Kassel** on the Riederfurka. This building, in which Sir Winston Churchill used to spend his summers as a boy, now hosts courses in botany and conservation, under expert supervision.

In the Goms Valley: Three passes – the **Furka Pass** leading into Switzerland's interior and into Graubünden, the **Grimsel Pass** leading to Interlaken and Berne, and the **Nufenen** Pass leading to the Bedretto Valley in the Ticino – can all be reached by rail or road via the **Goms**. The breadth of this high valley

Shared food and drink in Törbel.

and the villages in the upper part of it – still intact, with their dark wooden houses and famous baroque churches – give the magnificent landscape its distinctive appearance.

Niederwald, one of the small villages in the Goms, was the home of the "King of hoteliers and hotelier to kings", César Ritz. The Valais is rich in ecclesiastical buildings, but the churches at **Ernen** and **Münster** are considered particular jewels.

Ernen is one of the prettiest villages to look at anywhere in Switzerland, and has been awarded several prizes. And nearby **Mühlebach** was the home village of Cardinal Matthäus Schiner, a politician of European dimensions, not just in his role as "Maker of Popes and Kings" but also as a wartime commander. The Goms has devoted itself to a gentler form of tourism than the other regions of the Valais.

Many visitors who dislike the hectic pace of life in the larger winter sports resorts are attracted to the uppermost parts of the canton. The carefully tended cross-country ski trail here, which is nearly 40 km (25 miles) long, is especially popular, while in summer the Goms is considered an absolute paradise for hikers.

The passes are open only in the summer. If you have time, driving along them is well worth the trouble, even though an efficient rail-car ferry through the Furka tunnel between **Oberwald** and **Realp** reduces travelling time between Central and Eastern Switzerland considerably. Since the Furka-Oberalp-Bahn cut its service, driving through the pass is the only way of getting to know the mighty **Rhône Glacier** – the source of the great river.

In the early Middle Ages, starting out from the Goms and Saas valleys, the people of the Valais colonised all the valleys lying to the south and the east. Traces of these emigrants, who managed to survive in the high valleys because of their simple mountain-farming way of life, can still be found today in Valsesia, Val d'Anza, Formazza, the Ticino, Graubünden and in Austria.

Harvesting apricots in the Rhône Valley.

6

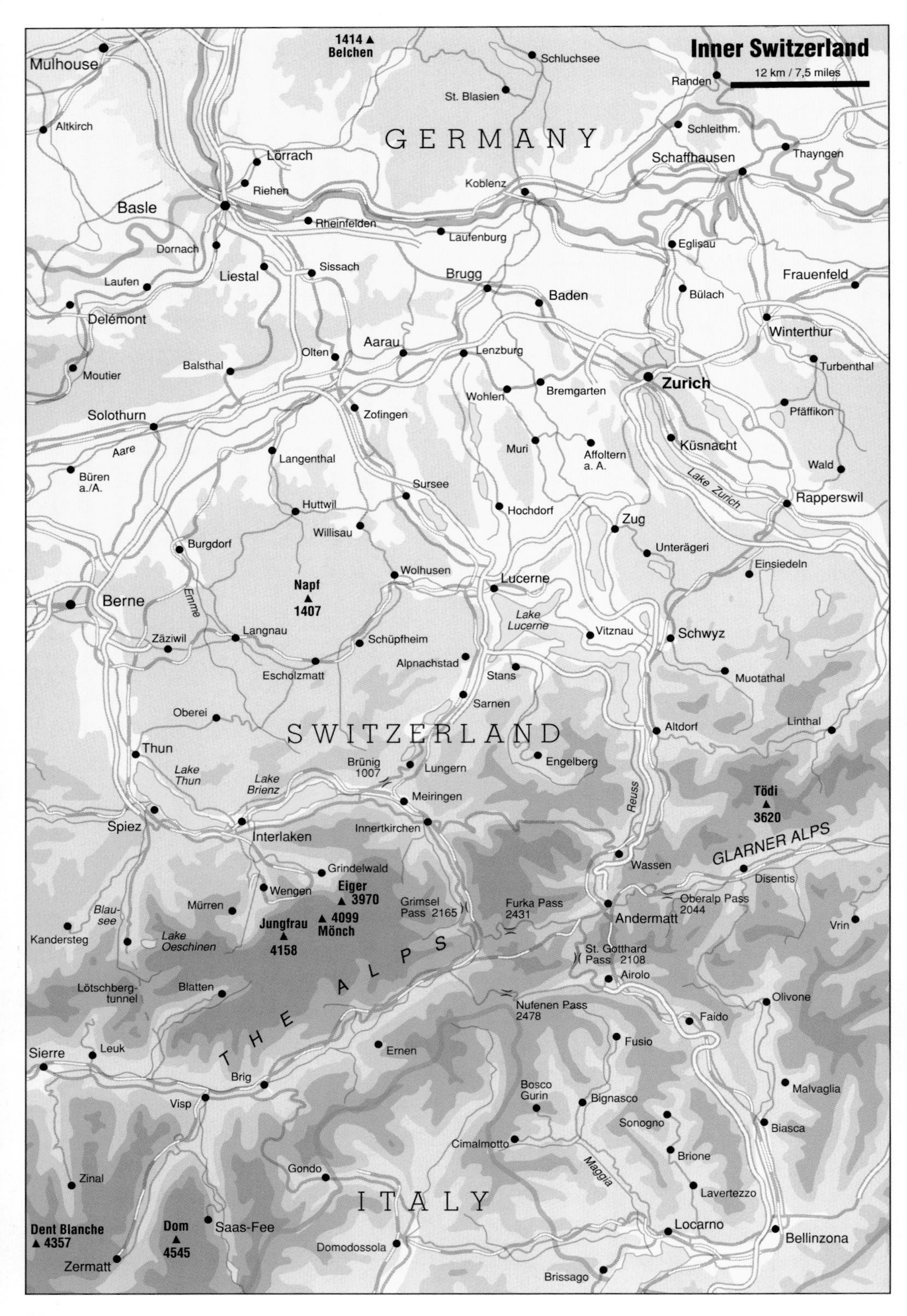

Inner Switzerland
12 km / 7,5 miles
GERMANY
SWITZERLAND
ITALY
THE ALPS
GLARNER ALPS
1414 ▲ Belchen
Mulhouse
Altkirch
Schluchsee
St. Blasien
Randen
Schleithm.
Schaffhausen
Thayngen
Lörrach
Riehen
Basle
Koblenz
Rheinfelden
Laufenburg
Eglisau
Dornach
Liestal
Sissach
Laufen
Brugg
Baden
Bülach
Frauenfeld
Delémont
Winterthur
Aarau
Olten
Lenzburg
Turbenthal
Moutier
Balsthal
Wohlen
Bremgarten
Zurich
Solothurn
Zofingen
Pfäffikon
Aare
Muri
Affoltern a. A.
Küsnacht
Langenthal
Büren a./A.
Sursee
Wald
Lake Zurich
Rapperswil
Huttwil
Hochdorf
Zug
Willisau
Unterägeri
Burgdorf
Einsiedeln
Wolhusen
Napf ▲ 1407
Lucerne
Berne
Emme
Lake Lucerne
Zäziwil
Langnau
Vitznau
Schwyz
Schüpfheim
Alpnachstad
Stans
Escholzmatt
Muotathal
Sarnen
Oberei
Altdorf
Linthal
Thun
Brünig 1007
Lungern
Engelberg
Lake Thun
Lake Brienz
Meiringen
Reuss
Tödi ▲ 3620
Spiez
Interlaken
Innertkirchen
Wassen
Disentis
Grindelwald
Eiger ▲ 3970
Wengen
Grimsel Pass 2165
Furka Pass 2431
Oberalp Pass 2044
Andermatt
Blau-see
Mürren
▲ 4099 Mönch
Jungfrau ▲ 4158
Vrin
Kandersteg
Lake Oeschinen
St. Gotthard Pass 2108
Airolo
Lötschberg-tunnel
Blatten
Nufenen Pass 2478
Olivone
Faido
Fusio
Sierre
Leuk
Ernen
Brig
Bosco Gurin
Bignasco
Malvaglia
Visp
Sonogno
Cimalmotto
Biasca
Brione
Maggia
Gondo
Zinal
Lavertezzo
Locarno
Dent Blanche ▲ 4357
Dom ▲ 4545
Saas-Fee
Bellinzona
Zermatt
Domodossola
Brissago

INNER SWITZERLAND

Historically speaking, a sensible starting-point for a journey through Inner Switzerland would be a small meadow at the northern end of **Lake Uri** known as the **Rütli**. Here, in 1291, three representatives of the regions of Uri, Schwyz and Unterwalden are said to have held a secret meeting at which they solemnly swore to uphold a mutual assistance pact (the content of this agreement is given in the history section on page 41).The Rütli meadow, at the centre of so-called Inner Switzerland, is where, according to legend, the liberation of the Confederation from those nasty, penny-pinching, bloodsucking Landvogts had its origins.

The usual way to reach it is via Lucerne, but a common misunderstanding needs to be cleared up before we go any further: Lucerne is not part of Inner Switzerland – indeed, the Inner Swiss themselves see Lucerne simply as an unavoidable geographical feature, a view which has a whole series of historical and psychological roots. The Inner Swiss themselves never seem to tire of telling the rest of the country who or what they are.

Cradle of the Confederation: However, it is not disparaging at all, nor is it felt to be, when the Western Swiss refer to the *Urschweizer* (the inhabitants of the original cantons) quite innocently as "*la Suisse primitive*". In this case, the word "primitive" evokes the germ, the root, or the cradle of the Confederation, indeed the region on which the rest of today's Switzerland is based. This "primitive" epithet also carries connotations of purity and originality.

The Inner Swiss react with some annoyance, however, when their fellow Swiss, and especially those close to them geographically, put the cantons of **Uri**, **Schwyz** and **Unterwalden** – and, if need be, **Zug** and **Lucerne** too – into the same historical picture. Only for convenience's sake should the town of Lucerne at the lower end of Lake Lucerne be thought of as part of the Alps, and thus, at least from a geographical point of view, part of the area known as Inner Switzerland. From the point of view of tourism, Zug, too, is often considered to belong to Inner Switzerland, but like the city of Lucerne, the largest part of it actually lies in the Lowlands.

The concept of "Inner Switzerland" conveys no sense of unity, or of any common economic, political or even geographical identity, and the idea of a kind of "Confederate unity" linking Uri, Schwyz, Obwalden and Nidwalden as well as Zug and Lucerne is something that will, at best, provoke a smile of sympathy from the Inner Swiss. Even nearby Nidwalden, not to mention the canton of Schwyz and the central part of Inner Switzerland, shares the same rather distant attitude to Lucerne.

For its part, Lucerne happily regards itself as the economic and cultural centre of Inner Switzerland. And more than anything else it is this assumed superiority – the relic of a pre-revolutionary, patrician way of thinking that has never completely died out – which now and

Preceding pages: wall-painting of Lake Uri and the Rütli meadow in the National Council Chamber. **Right**, amateur actors playing William Tell and his son Walter.

then gets on the nerves of the so-called "genuine" Inner Swiss.

Back to the beginnings: So what about Urschweiz, and the "little cantons", as 19th-century travellers called them: Uri, Schwyz, Obwalden and Nidwalden (the latter two known collectively as Unterwalden)? In the final years of the 13th century, they must have comprised an astonishingly lively body politic.

A glance at any map reveals that this rather enclosed area was by no means likely to achieve political and enonomic union. Nature, aided by Lake Lucerne, had arranged things so that the regions of *Urschweiz* were not forced to maintain harmonious and lasting relations with one another. The three regions have combined a policy of co-operation towards the other side of the lake – a policy they regard as expedient more than anything else – with a frequent and forthright pursuit of their own interests.

It was thus obvious that **Schwyz** would start trying to extend its influence, first against Arth, Zug and Küssnacht, then against Einsiedeln and out into the Linth plain. **Uri**, which, until the Axenstrasse was built in the 19th century, could only be reached by crossing the lake, was only able to extend its influence in the direction of the Urseren Valley, a short way into Glarus, and in the direction of the southern Alpine valleys.

So **Unterwalden**, stuck between the Seelisberg and the Bürgenstock, between the Urner Alps, the lake and the Brünig, never had any real chance to expand: instead, the Unterwaldner just argued amongst themselves and in this way created **Obwalden** and **Nidwalden**, which are separated by a high moor and a dark forest.

As the centuries progressed, the powerful leaders of Schwyz, the cosmopolitan cattle-drivers of Uri and the rather introverted Obwaldner and Nidwaldner, all situated in close proximity to each other in this small area, developed ways of life, economic patterns and political cultures that were distinctively different from each other. Today, the political dominance of the *Christliche Volkspartei* (Christian People's Party),

The daily trek.

the fond way in which traditions and old customs are upheld in all the *Urschweiz* cantons, the common religious persuasion (Catholicism), plus a certain consumer conformism combine to give an outsider the happy impression of Inner Switzerland as a rich but smooth stew with the odd hint of archaism. It is considered charming, but also a rather unimportant sort of place that tends to be neglected.

Whether this is true or not remains to be seen. What with the corridor for goods traffic, the future trans-Alpine rail link and everything else that Inner Switzerland is currently threatened by, they might feel like reaching for their halberds and poleaxes to defend themselves against a new wave of intruders.

Going in by the back way: So to avoid using Lucerne as a starting-point and to start a visit to Inner Switzerland at one of its outermost points, one should really enter **Obwalden** from the direction of Berne via the **Brünig Pass**. Today, there is a road as well as the **Brünig Railway** with panoramic carriages across the pass, making the journey easy; but in the Middle Ages a barrier blocked the way here (denying access to the lords of the Bernese Oberland who were eager to expand their territory) and the steep terrain falling away in the direction of **Lungern** provided the canton with extra protection against conquerors and invaders.

After **Giswil**, the landscape gets a lot broader and gentler and also provides enough room for the **Sarnersee**. **Sachseln**, nearby **Flüeli** and the **Ranft** form the centres of an important pilgrimage. Niklaus von Flüe, Switzerland's only saint, was born in Flüeli in 1417; after an active life in local politics he spent 20 years fasting and praying in the remoteness of the Ranft. His grave, visited by about a hundred thousand pilgrims each year, has been in the church in Sachseln since 1934. No wonder, then, that the area is full of guest houses and hotels. Indeed, Switzerland's first motel was built in Sachseln.

It's true that **Sarnen**, the capital of the canton of Obwalden, has no saints to

Föhn **weather on Lake Uri.**

speak of, but it does have a modern and architecturally remarkable **Monastery Church**, and its hill, the **Landenberg**, provided an attractive setting for the *Landsgemeinde* (vote), which from 1646 until 1998 was held outdoors annually on the last Sunday in April.

Of all the museums in Inner Switzerland, the **Obwalden Local History Museum** in Sarnen seems to be the most varied and well-endowed, and it provides a comprehensive overview of the culture and history of the region. Exhibits include a number of prehistoric items, Roman material from the settlement of Alpnach, weaponry from the Middle Ages, various examples of religious art and pictures and sculptures by local artists from the 17th century until the present day.

Sarnen's **Rathaus** (Town Hall) contains the so-called "White Book", which includes the earliest account of the history of the Confederation.

Near **Alpnach**, the traveller has already reached the lower end of the canton. On one of the oldest rack railways in Switzerland it takes 30 minutes to travel between **Alpnachstad** and **Mt Pilatus** (affording unparalleled views of the Alps and out across the entire Lowlands). On the shore of the lake, the remains of a Roman villa were unearthed some time ago – evidence that this part of the country has been inhabited for at least 2,000 years.

Anyone wanting to go to **Nidwalden** from Obwalden can do it via the road that runs along the shores of the **Alpnachersee** in the direction of **Stansstad**, but a more attractive route is via **Kerns**, through the dark **Kernwald** and across the practically flat Ice-age trough valley to **Stans**. This is the main village in Nidwalden, and it has a small aircraft industry,. The old town has been painstakingly restored and cleaned up over the last few years; the "**Höfli**" in its centre and the **Winkelriedhaus** slightly outside the village – both of them museums – reflect the wealth and power of the patricians who once lived here. The early **baroque church**, the old Romanesque tower and the Gothic **ossuary**

***Landsgemeinde* (open-air vote) in Sarnen, in the canton of Obwalden.**

dominate the broad village square, which also contains the **monument** to Arnold von Winkelried who, legend has it, helped a Confederate army out of trouble near Sempach in 1386 by throwing himself on to a flurry of enemy lances.

Although it belongs to Obwalden, **Engelberg** is simpler to reach via Stans. With its excellent walking country, hills and lakes, it is a popular winter and summer resort. Its **Benedictine Abbey** was founded in the 12th century and remodelled in the baroque style between 1730 and 1737; as well as containing an important library it also doubles as a boarding school.

High above the lake: Leaving Stans and taking another direction, via Stansstad, one arrives at the **Bürgenstock** mountain, which has an imposing group of late 19th-century hotels and an incomparable view of **Lake Lucerne**. A small path leads away from the hotels along a rock face to the **Hammet-schwandlift**, a panoramic lift that takes anyone with a head for heights up to the summit in breathtaking manner. Afterwards, you can go down into the valley by funicular from the hotels.

Going in another direction, northeast this time, you will reach Lake Lucerne, which looks almost Mediterranean; there the route disappears into the **Seelisberg tunnel**, emerging in the canton of Uri a few minutes later. Alternatively, you can board a ship in **Beckenried**, travel to **Treib**, take the funicular up to **Seelisberg**, and then hike along the "Swiss Path", which was constructed as part of Switerland's 700th-birthday celebrations, high above Lake Lucerne and the Rütli meadow. It goes past the little castle of **Beroldingen**, down to **Bauen** and along a passageway cut out of the rock to **Seedorf**, where you can rejoin the motorway.

The baroque **church**, the **tower** of the Lords of Seedorf, the small 16th-century **Castle of A Pro** and the nearby **convent** form a delightful ensemble. They also make it instantly clear that this place must once have been a very important shipment point for goods coming across Lake Uri. From here they

Assembling aeroplanes in Stans.

would have been transported throughout the canton via the St Gotthard Pass. Also on the old route to the St Gotthard, a little further inland, are the ruins of a **castle** that once belonged to the Lords of Attinghausen.

Altdorf, the capital of the canton of Uri, lies on another old route, the one leading from **Flüelen** via Altdorf into the **Schächen Valley**, and which also leads in the direction of the St Gotthard Pass. Reminders of the city's former importance and busy traffic are the **Fremdenspital**, a hospital which offered refuge to pilgrims and sick and impoverished travellers, the **Capuchin Monastery** high up on the mountainside, where the Counter Reformation in Switzerland had its origins, and the patrician houses which give one some idea of the wealth engendered by the brisk trade across the St Gotthard.

Moreover, the town of Altdorf and nearby **Bürglen** are particularly closely connected with the legendary origin of the Confederation. It was in Altdorf that William Tell defied the hated bailiff, Gessler, and as a result was forced to shoot an apple off his son Walter's head. Bürglen is said to have been where Tell's house stood and so the **Tell Museum** is there, but the archer is commemorated in Altdorf by a much photographed monument by Richard Kissling and by the Tell theatre, built in 1925, in which Schiller's *Wilhelm Tell* is regularly performed.

Traffic past and present: Over a period of roughly 600 years, travellers and goods would leave Flüelen and Altdorf and head in the direction of the St Gotthard Pass and Italy, past the **Von Silenen Residence Tower** in **Silenen**, the **Castle of Zwing Uri** near **Erstfeld** and, from the 18th century, the **church** in **Wassen**. In the early days the journey was done mostly on foot or, at best, on horseback; later, after a road had been constructed, people travelled by coach and wagon. From1882 onwards traffic used the rail tunnel and, since 1980, the St Gotthard road tunnel.

The valley, narrow and dignified, and for centuries dominated only by the

***Schwingen*, Swiss wrestling.**

thundering sound of the Reuss River, is now filled with the sound of heavy traffic 24 hours a day; even worse, the clear mountain air is being polluted by exhaust fumes. While it is still possible to ascend the wild Schöllenen ravine on foot along the old mountain trail and hike all the way to the St Gotthard, complete silence and really fine hiking can only be found high up in the lateral valleys: in the **Urseren Valley**, and in the **Göschener**, **Maderaner**, **Meien** and **Schächen** valleys.

In the 1940s there was a plan to flood the whole of the Urseren Valley in a massive hydro-electricity scheme. It was only when the locals ejected the gentlemen from the lowland electricity board out of their valley that the entire plan, which seems crazy today, was eventually dropped. Today the valley is one of the few skiing areas in Switzerland that can guarantee snow every winter.

In the Schächen Valley stories are still told about General Suvorov and his Cossack troops, who fought Napoleon and the French on Swiss soil; although he brought war, devastation and hunger to the country, the General's forced marches across the St Gotthard, Kinzig and Pragel passes earned him the respect and the admiration of the local inhabitants.

The canton of Schwyz had its own experience of Suvorov: the General, forced to retreat from the French via **Muotathal** in the direction of Glarus, incurred heavy losses. It is assumed that the **icon** which hangs in the **Parish Church** in Muotathal was left behind during this retreat. There again, nothing is known of the origins of the 8th-century **Merovingian Reliquary** that forms part of the church treasure, though Muotathal, **Illgau** and **Morschach** were populated as early as the 10th century, something quite astonishing for such a remote area.

Elegant edifices: The town of **Schwyz**, capital of the canton, has seen so much uncontrolled construction over the past 20 years or so that its original housing pattern can scarcely be discerned. The very centre of the town, however, re-

Mountain farmstead in the canton of Uri.

tains traces of its original character, notably the broad square and the richly-decorated baroque **Church of St Martin**. Originally, a dozen or so town houses, complete with imposing facades and extensive gardens, would have graced the square. Today, only a handful of traditional patrician houses (17th–18th century) remain and they have been interspersed with modern structures.

Particularly noticeable is the baroque-influenced **Ital-Reding-Haus**, with the 700-year-old **Haus Bethlehem** (today a museum) beside it. The Haus Bethlehem is the oldest wooden house in all of Switzerland. Still quite grand, and quite cool too because of its air-conditioning, is the **Bundesbriefarchiv**, the archives which as well as the **Bundesbrief** of 1291 (the original deed of confederation) contain other important documents and written alliances from Swiss and cantonal history, plus a collection of pennants, flags and banners.

Also of interest in Schwyz is the **Rathaus**, opposite the Church of St Martin. Its splendid facade is decorated with a series of frescoes illustrating different events in Swiss history. Inside the Great Council Chamber is a series of portraits of cantonal presidents.

Other places of interest historically are the ruins of the **Gesslerburg** in Küssnacht (seat of the Habsburg governor Gessler, killed by William Tell), the ruins on the island of **Schwanau**, the **Hohle Gasse** ("sunken lane", where Tell killed Gessler) near **Immensee** and the last remaining pieces of *Letzine* (barrages) at **Arth**, **Morgarten**, **Rothenturm** and **Brunnen**. They are all testimonies to the series of battles fought against the local nobility and the House of Habsburg at the beginning of the 14th century.

The municipality of Gersau has the warm *Föhn* wind, as well as its sheltered position by the lake, to thank for the fact that it can support both chestnut trees and palm trees; both grow in profusion. A further attraction is the well-constructed road that leads from Brunnen to Küssnacht via Gersau, which is full of bends and, along some stretches, almost

Ornate panelling in the Ital-Reding-Haus in Schwyz.

like the corniche at Monte Carlo. From Gersau it's about 20km (12 miles) to the **Astrid Chapel** at the exit of Küssnacht, where Queen Astrid of Belguim, who died in an accident here in the 1930s, is venerated almost as much as a saint.

Nearby **Merlischachen**, a small village containing a few dignified-looking farmhouses, is a good place to break your journey. The Swiss Chalet hotel, brightened by geraniums and small red lanterns, is a thoroughly romantic place to stay, and in the Schloss Hotel – popular with honeymooners – you can sleep in a gondola in a swimming pool.

Monastic community: The town of **Einsiedeln** is another focal point in the canton. In the 10th century, Eberhard, Dean of Strasbourg, founded a monastic community above the hermitage of a monk from Reichenau, Meinrad, who had been murdered in 861. Duke Hermann of Swabia gave the monastery a portion of land to farm.

For years the Habsburg-controlled abbey was involved in a long and bitter dispute with the people of Schwyz about rights to the cattle-grazing land between Schwyz and the monastery. In 1314 a band of Schwyz men attacked the abbey, took the sleeping monks prisoner, drank the abbey's wine and desecrated the religious relics.

The abbey, whose prince-abbots minted their own coins, lost much of its secular power in 1798 as a result of the revolution, but as a place of pilgrimage, and the next station on the pilgrim route after Santiago de Compostela, Einsiedeln has been a major centre of Catholic Christianity for centuries.

The heyday of the monastery, however, was during the 17th and 18th centuries. Then pilgrimages to the picture of the "BlackMadonna" in the Gnadenkapelle (Chapel of Grace) were at their height. This resulted in the construction, between 1674 and 1770, of the splendid baroque church and the spacious monastery area, both of which have been restored. The buildings are widely considered to be among the finest examples of baroque architecture in Switzerland.

The Benedictine Abbey of Einsiedeln.

Ze zyten do der Wynmärkt bas
Den Burgern ihr Theatrum was,
Do sach ich viel der Osterspill
Und ouch der Fastnacht kurzewill
Der am Grund, Blätz ouch CVSATVS
Agierredt als POETICVS
Dess freuwt ich mich der Wunnen,
Heiss derohalb "zer Sunnen"
Leinenweberei
Langenthal AG
Ganzer Platz

COUTELLERIE H. WEBER MESSERSCHMIED
weber
CAFE
TEA ROOM

THE REUSS AND THE AARE

The **Lucerne Lowlands**, which are made up of several valleys, extend from Lucerne in a northwesterly direction. All of these valleys have been given their distinctive relief by the ice masses and moraines of the Reuss glacier. Three lakes – the Baldeggersee, the Hallwilersee and the Sempachersee are the legacy of the last period of Ice-age glaciation more than 10,000 years ago.

These valleys, interspersed by ranges of gentle hills, are used predominantly for arable farming in the northern areas facing the canton of Aargau, and for dairy farming in the areas to the south, where there is more rain. Beromünster, Sempach and Willisau are all situated within this Lucerne Lowlands region, which leads on to the pre-Alpine and Alpine regions near Lucerne.

Tourist centre: Francs, dollars, yen, deutschmarks and gold may not change hands quite as quickly in **Lucerne** as they do in, say, Zurich or Basel, but one thing is for sure: the whole process takes place in a much more relaxed manner – through tourism. Although it is the largest town in Urschweiz (the collective name given to the country's original Forest Cantons), Lucerne has no stock exchange of its own, nor is it of much economic importance for financial Switzerland. It is not at the heart of a sophisticated transport network, it has no international airport and has no connections with Swiss chocolate. In spite of all this, it is nevertheless famous throughout the world.

Roughly 200 years ago, the poets discovered the beauty of the mountains here, and the verses they penned in celebration provided the first publicity material for promoting tourism in Inner Switzerland. Because of its geographical proximity to the Alps, the town of Lucerne developed into a convenient base for mountaineering expeditions. It lies 439 metres (1,400 ft) above sea level. Just 10 km (6 miles) away to the southwest is **Mt Pilatus**, 2,129 metres (7,000 ft) high.

Preceding pages: alpenhorn player, Lucerne. **Left**, a meadow in bloom. **Right**, water ballet on the Rotsee near Ebikon.

One gets an idea of the town's unique situation from an old mail coach timetable of 1850: on the three-day-long trip from Basle to Milan, the travellers actually spent only one night in a hotel – and that was in Lucerne.

The tourism of that time altered the town's appearance quite considerably. Because of its slow development, Lucerne managed to retain its medieval city walls right up until the 19th century, when most of them were razed to the ground. But 870 metres (2,800 ft) of the **Musegg Wall** (built in 1400), still stand, and it is still possible to walk along the wall iytself.

The city's first big hotel was built in 1845. Others soon followed, most of them on the right-hand side of the lake facing both the sun and the Alps. Then the quay was built, so that the local population as well as distinguished tourists could take their constitutionals along the bank of Lake Lucerne whenever they wished.

For centuries, Lucerne, sometimes officially and sometimes unofficially, has

been the capital of Switzerland. In the old Confederation, up until the Burgundian Wars (1474–77), Lucerne, which had joined in 1332, adopted a kind of "senior" role, and the emissaries of the individual towns often used to meet here. In the 16th century this role was gradually taken over by Zurich, but by then Lucerne was an undisputed centre of the Catholic towns. From 1798 to 1799, for a few months only, it became Switzerland's official capital.

When the Federal State was formed in 1848, Lucerne, which had suffered from the political and military disturbances prior to that, was not even considered as a potential capital. Not until 1917–18 did Lucerne become the headquarters of the Confederate authorities. It became the headquarters of the Swiss *Unfallversicherungsanstalt* (Accident Insurance Institute) and of the Federal *Versicherungsgericht* (claims court), a remarkable stroke of luck when one considers that the Swiss are among the most highly insured people in the world. Many people consider Lucerne to be the secret capital: if Berne is the head, and Zurich the hand, then Lucerne can certainly pride itself on being the heart of Switzerland.

As far as culture is concerned, this is certainly the case. There's not just a lot to see, but a lot to hear, too: the dull thud of footsteps crossing what was the oldest roofed wooden bridge in Europe, the **Kapellbrücke**, reconstructed after a fire in 1993 (the octagonal water tower was a bastion of the 13th-century fortifications and once used as the town treasury) and an interesting cycle of pictures in its roof truss; the overpowering din of the *Guggenmusik* bands during the time of the Fasnacht; the rattling sound of the old propeller-planes inside the **Swiss Transport Museum**, the largest museum of its kind in Europe; or the far more harmonious sounds (should one be lucky enough to get a ticket) of the **International Festival of Music**. The festival features orchestras such as the Berlin Philharmonic and takes place in the very modern **Culture and Congress Center** on the shore of the lake.

Fasnacht **in Lucerne.**

Opened in 1998, it has some of the best acoustics of any international concert hall. Lucerne offers sporting attractions, too; international rowing competitions, for example, are regularly held on the nearby **Rotsee**.

On even a short walk through this pedestrian-friendly town you can cover a fair number of interesting sights. Only a few steps from the quayside is the **Collegiate Church**, formerly part of a Benedictine monastery and later a secular canonical foundation. The arcaded churchyard, which is reminiscent of an Italian *Campo Santo*, commands a good view of the lake. After taking a short detour to see the **Löwendenkmal** (Lion Monument), commemorating the 786 officers and men of the Swiss guards who died defending Louis XIV and Marie-Antoinette during the attack on the Tuileries in 1792; and the **Gletschergarten** (Glacier Garden), with its unusual potholes and its museum, head back towards the Reuss.

The **Bourbaki-Panorama** in Löwenplatz also merits inspection: it is an enormous round painting by Edouard Castres, depicting the crossing of the Bourbaki army into Switzerland in 1871. Continue past **Hirschenplatz**, where several houses have richly painted facades (No. 12, the Göldlinhaus, has an interior courtyard in Renaissance style) and on to the **Town Hall**, built by Anton Isenmann of Prismell from 1602–6. Its facade was strongly influenced by the Florentine early Renaissance style, while the hipped saddleback roof reflects local traditions. Here, a second covered wooden bridge spans the river, the **Spreuerbrücke**. It contains a cycle of pictures on the theme of death, painted between 1626 and 1635 by Kaspar Meglinger.

The bridge leads to the **Historical Museum** and the **Naturmuseum**. Walking along the Reuss in the direction of the lake, you pass the **Jesuit Church of St Franz Xaver**, built between 1666 and 1677, Switzerland's first large baroque church. It contains the first examples of stucco by the Wessobrunn school. Anyone who now wishes to rest his

View of Lake Lucerne from Mt Pilatus.

weary feet is best advised to take a boat trip – and the possibilities are virtually limitless: they range from a short voyage to a six-hour round trip that takes you to the far end of the Lake.

The Reuss and Aare basins: From Lucerne, the Reuss flows in a northerly direction towards the Rhine. To the east of the city and the canton, also bearing traces of the Reuss glacier across its landscape, lies the canton of **Zug**. On the old road from **Küssnacht** to **Immensee**, which used to connect Lake Lucerne and the Zugersee, lies the **Hohle Gasse** (sunken lane) and the **William Tell Chapel**. It was here, in 1307, at the foot of the massif known as the **Rigi** (its rack railway was built in 1871) that Gessler, the Habsburg bailiff of Schwyz and Uri, who had forced Tell to shoot the apple from the head of his son, was killed by "Tell's shot".

Zug is one of the smallest towns in Switzerland, and the canton of Zug is one of the smallest cantons, but it still forms a notable economic centre. The considerable construction work going on in the town gives a clue to its new-found role as an international service centre. In the 1980s, a huge shopping, office and residential area emerged, forming quite a marked contrast to the late Gothic architecture of the old town. So far there have not been any controversial alterations to the structure of the town's historic centre.

The *Zuger Kirschtorte* is a local speciality. It has a very high alcohol content, so the best thing to do after eating it is to stay overnight and visit the old part of town. Founded in the 13th century, Zug has a wealth of interesting sites: from the **Castle** (once the residence of the Habsburg governors, today housing a cantonal museum) to the **Catholic Church of St Oswald**, with its fine choir stalls, and the **Zeitturm** (clock tower), with its blue and white painted tiles (the colours of the canton). Also of interest are the imposing mansions and richly decorated **Brandenberghaus**.

Tradition, cigars, birds and jazz: The fact that Lucerne and the canton of Lucerne are mainly Catholic is something

Office building in Zug.

that can be experienced at first hand in **Beromünster**, an old town that grew up around a monastery founded in 981 by Bero von Lenzburg. Each Ascension Day the impressive "**Ascension Ride**" takes place: over 100 riders, including the lay canons from the foundation, take part in this church procession on horseback. Beromünster is also famous for being where, in 1930, the first Swiss national radio station began broadcasting. Switzerland's older generation still talk of "Radio Beromünster" today, even though the station was moved to a new location long ago.

To the north of Beromünster lie the villages of **Pfäffikon** and **Burg**. These names mean very little to most Swiss, but smokers may recognise them straight away: both villages produce cigars and *stumpen* (cheroots). Many a schoolboy must have developed his first smoker's cough from a Villigerstumpen or a Burgerstumpen. In the big cities, cigarettes, cigars and pipes have long since eclipsed the traditional Swiss *stumpen*. But now that a member of the Villiger family is in the cabinet, the *stumpen* are enjoying something of a revival.

Sempach reflects an altogether more serious aspect of Swiss history. The battle of Sempach in 1386, when a small Swiss force managed to defeat Duke Leopold III of Austria, is described in every school textbook. More relevant these days, though, are the attempts that were made to restore the formerly heavily polluted **Sempachersee** (Sempach Lake) to health. Thanks to "artificial respiration" using oxygen, and much stricter water protection laws, this has largely succeeded – good news for the **Vogelwarte Sempach** birdwatching area, the centre of ornithology in Switzerland.

Willisau has established itself as the venue for a jazz festival famous far beyond the country's borders. Indeed, members of the local yodelling club have ventured into the realms of jazz improvisation as well.

The speciality from the local bakeries is the so-called *Willisauer Ringli* biscuit, which is as hard as stone.

A picnic on the the Reuss near Sins.

Here at Willisau we are already in the **Napf**. This region, full of deep valleys, thrusts its way between Berne and Lucerne far into the Lowlands. The valleys radiate out in a star pattern from the 1,411-metre (4,500-ft) peak of the Napf. Their waters collect in a valley that forms an almost perfect circle. The road as well as the railway makes use of this ring valley, but this mountainous region is not crossed by any major traffic routes. During the last Ice Age, the Napf was free of glacial activity, but Ice-Age glaciers formed the ring valley and the neighbouring landscapes. Their broad and rather flat appearance stands out starkly against the Napf.

Because of the high rainfall the Napf is suited to pastoral farming and some agriculture. The very deep valleys make it impossible for just a few centrally situated villages to look after the cultivation of the fields, and the Napf region thus contains the largest number of scattered settlements in Switzerland. The farmsteads are situated right in the middle of the land they have to till, and many of them are completely surrounded by forest.

These farmsteads, especially on the Bernese side, are prosperous. They comprise a whole series of different buildings and, from afar, they can often look like small hamlets. Each farm has a farmhouse, barn and a somewhat smaller, richly decorated wooden building, the storehouse, in which food supplies and valuable objects used to be kept. Keeping the buildings apart minimised the danger of spreading fire. Nowadays, the storehouse has lost its former significance, and quite often the farmers have built an additional small house some distance away, for their elderly parents.

Fortresses and castles: To the west of the Napf region, on Bernese soil, lies **Burgdorf**, a flourishing industrial town built on a hill above the Emme River. The oldest parts of its mighty **castle** go back to the 12th century, and like Lenzburg Castle in canton Aargau, it makes you think of all the old clichés: castle ghosts, dragging chains, dank dungeons. But one thing is certain: it is one of the earliest brick buildings in Switzerland. The teacher Heinrich Pestalozzi had an elementary school at Burgdorf before moving to Yverdon in 1805. Today the castle houses a **Museum of Local History** and will shortly house the first Gold Museum in Switzerland.

To the southeast of the Napf region, the **Kleine Emme River** flows in the direction of the **Reuss**, and eventually joins it below Lucerne. This valley is known as the **Entlebuch**, and leads to the mountainous Alpine dairy farming regions. The people here, like those from the nearby **Emmental**, were accurately portrayed by the novelist Jeremias Gotthelf (1797–1854), who was pastor at Lützelflüh. Even today they are well known for their unmistakably independent streak.

Most of the region downriver of the Reuss from Lucerne belongs to the German-speaking canton of **Aargau**, the least mountainous region of Switzerland. It is here that the Habsburg family had its origins. There are numerous castles and manor houses dotted

Commemoration of the famous battle in Sempach.

along the route here, reminding the traveller of the days of chivalry and the life of the landed gentry, or *Junkertum*, in the rococo period. But memories of the Habsburgs also evoke the old Catholicism – the canton of Aargau is now largely reformed – that still survives in the former **Benedictine Abbey** in **Muri**. Founded in 1027, and one of the great centres of religious art in Switzerland, the monastery was re-modelled in baroque style by Caspar Mosbrugger in 1695. The Loreto Chapel in the north walk of the former cloister has served as a family vault of the Habsburgs.

The delightful little town of **Bremgarten** has a covered wooden bridge across the River Reuss, and has retained an air of Catholic supremacy for which it was once renowned. It received its charter from Rudolf of Habsburg in 1256. Bremgarten has many medieval and baroque buildings, making a walk through the town particularly enjoyable. The fine facades conceal richly furnished rooms, and a collection of coaches, featuring original examples from many European manufacturers. Unfortunately these collections are privately owned and hidden from view.

Across the triangle formed by the Reuss and Aare rivers, which join up with Zurich's Limmat in the so-called Wassertor (water door) before all three of them humbly join the mighty Rhine, are found further seats of political and economic power. The castles and fortresses at **Hallwil** (a moated castle), **Lenzburg**, **Wildegg** and **Brunegg** are only the better known ones. The landscape, with its distinctive fields, forests and meadows nestling among rows of hills, is just the place for a real country outing similar to the one described in the 19th century by Zurich author Gottfried Keller in his novel *Der Landvogt von Greifensee* (The bailiff of Greifensee). Such scenes can also be found in many pastoral paintings.

The castles at Hallwil, Lenzburg and Wildegg (all of them museums as well) give the visitor a sense of history in more ways than one – they are often chosen as venues for the latest technol-

Evening falls on Lake Sempach.

ogy exhibitions. In some cases the proprietors stage their own attractions. Schloss Lenzburg, for example, has a *son et lumière* of the various wars that raged in the region. The exhibits include a realistic, fire-breathing dragon to scare off visitors. In accordance with the last will and testament of its last owner, Wildegg Castle does not allow alcohol to be served in its restaurant.

Wildegg is an offshoot of the Swiss National Museum and has a new garden landscaped in the baroque style. In the 3,300 sq metres (35,500 sq ft) of garden tomatoes in a star formation and blue potatoes grow alongside flowers.

Brunegg is not your average privately-owned Swiss castle (incidentally, more than two thirds of the Swiss are rent-payers). It was occupied by the renowned historian Jean-Rodolphe von Salis, who died in 1998. In World War II Salis kept the Swiss people informed about what was happening by broadcasting on Radio Beromünster. His castle has also provided lodgings for many dramatists, journalists and writers.

Habsburg Castle is the obvious starting-point for understanding the history of this region, and of Europe, come to that. The home of the dynasty of the same name, it has declined like its former owners – it has now become small and unassuming in aspect, and only the western half of it has survived. But you should not be disappointerd: the restaurant inside should make you glad you visited.

Following the Aare away from the castle one reaches **Aarau**. This town is the capital of the canton of Aargau. Right up until the present day, Aarau has had difficulty in being recognised as the centre of this heterogeneous "patchwork canton", which consists of almost a dozen small towns and several rural regions that were formerly of equal importance. However, Aarau's role as a seat of cantonal government, parliament and administration has definitely contributed greatly to the outward appearance of the town.

Aarau's situation does not reflect only the difficulties faced in the Swiss-Ger-

A reminder of the days of chivalry: the moated castle at Hallwil.

man Lowlands. Regional as well as local peculiarities make it almost impossible to define differing mentalities. Every valley can speak a slightly different dialect, and the character of the population is just as varied. Despite this, even these people cannot ignore the influences of the major cities and their internationalism. The younger generation is emigrating, and long-cherished traditions are in danger of vanishing altogether.

Indeed, the Aargau region and the land around it face the prospect of degenerating into a mere agglomeration as the cities of Berne and Zurich continue to expand. A lot of industry has been based along this main artery, as well as in Aarau itself. This is especially true of the small towns of Brugg and Baden, which lie northeast of Aarau, and are less than half-an-hour away from Zurich by car.

Windisch, near Brugg, which the Romans knew as Vindonissa, stands on the Aare close to its confluence with the river Reuss. Here there is a Roman amphitheatre that once had room for 10,000 people, and also a well-endowed Roman museum. Outside the city walls of Brugg lies the former 14th-century **Abbey of Königsfelden**, with its magnificent stained glass.

Baden, too, can pride itself on its Roman heritage: as *Aquae Helveticae* it appears in the work of Tacitus. Situated on the left bank of the Limmat above an abrupt bend, this ancient town and spa is now an industrial centre. In the 19th century, however, when spas were the height of fashion in Europe, the town boomed. Even today people come to cure their various complaints by taking the waters.

Visitors not in need of healing should take a stroll through the marvellously intact old town, the ruins of Stein Castle towering impressively above it. The Landvogtei-schloss, the bailiff's castle which dates from 1414 to 1712, houses a historical museum. Baden has also become associated with a major local firm, Brown Boveri, now taken over by the Swedish company Asea and known as ABB.

Another world-famous business has its headquarters only a few kilometres up the Aare in **Schönenwerd**. Apparently, Bally shoes are the preferred footwear of Saudi Arabian sheiks. Bally is now in charge of a worldwide distribution network for high-quality shoes and has extended its collection to include accessories. The **Museum of Footwear** in the former owners' villa provides an interesting history of the shoe and its various styles.

The last Aargau town before we return to the Lucerne Lowlands is **Zofingen**, a small industrial centre, dating back to the high Middle Ages. It was in Habsburg hands from 1251 and its ramparts were besieged by the Bernese in 1415. With its imposing-looking baroque buildings, it also provides a fine example of the numerous towns that were founded here in the high and late Middle Ages and which determined the entire pattern of settlement in Switzerland. Two mosaic floors from a large **Roman Villa** very close to the town are another reminder of earlier inhabitants of this area.

Portrayal of a drummer boy at Schloss Lenzburg.

BÄCKEREI

THE FOOT OF THE JURA

Historians would like to know more about the Raurici, the ancient warriors and heroes who once populated the forests and valleys of the Jura. Despite a lot of archaeological finds, no-one actually knows how large an area they covered. There is, however, very precise information about the prince-bishops of Basel who used to hold sway in the area until the arrival of the French revolutionary troops in 1792.

On the **Lac de Biaufond**, a lake created in recent times by artificially damming the Doubs on the border of the cantons of Neuchâtel and the Jura, a boundary stone has stood for more than 1,000 years. Hewn into it is a coat-of-arms depicting the three bishoprics of Lausanne, Basel and Besançon (in France). In its day the territory owned by the prince-bishops of Basel extended as far as Lake Biel. They managed to get the land as much by luck as anything else. King Rudolf III of Burgundy, terrified that the world was going to end on New Year's Day in the year 1000 and keen on securing a place in heaven, gave away large areas of the Jura to the Bishop of Basel.

But the first settlers were neither Raurici nor devout monks: around Lake Biel and in the valley of the Birs near Delémont alone, there are more than 30 (of a known total of 200 throughout Switzerland) lake dwellings. But when people from Solothurn talk about "their" Jura, they usually mean the **Southern Foot of the Jura**. Probably for various political, geographical and historical reasons, this region begins at the **Unterer Hauenstein**.

Olten, largest town in the canton of Solothurn, has some interesting features – the old town, with its wooden bridge built originally in the 13th century, and the splendid twin-towered St Martin's Church, dating from 1908. The Museum of Art (Kunstmuseum) has works by local artist Martin Disteli (1802–44). The History Museum covers local archaeological finds from 40,000 years ago as well as military uniforms, weapons, costumes and ceramics. It also shows the development of the railway, which brought industry to the town and made it an important junction of north-south traffic.

The mountain ridges of the Solothurn Jura go their separate ways at the Unterer Hauenstein, the nearest one being the **Weissensteinkette**. This ridge is interrupted by the mighty gorge at Oensingen, with **Neu-Bechburg Castle** towering above it. The ridge is called the **Weissenstein** because of its white chalk cliffs, and is the most-visited mountain in the area because of its views. The Weissenstein can be reached by chairlift from **Oberdorf**, or by car.

The people of Solothurn love the Weissenstein, both because of the fantastic view it provides of the Alps and for its spa, built in 1827, which has recently been painstakingly restored. Quite a few famous names have spent time here: Napoleon III, Alexandre Dumas, Romain Rolland, and Carl Spitteler, awarded the Nobel prize for

Preceding pages: vineyard near Ligerz on Lake Biel. Left, a typical village high street. Right, in the Taubenloch Gorge near Biel.

his verse composition *Olympic Spring,* in which he made the Weissenstein into a home for gods.

Anyone tackling the Weissenstein from the direction of **Gänsbrunnen**, the linguistic border, will have no trouble finding the typical Jura cavern of **Nidleloch**, 1.5 km (1 mile) of which has been explored; it was named after its cream-coloured (*nidle* means cream) chalk deposits.

Solothurn, town of ambassadors: The canton of **Solothurn** does not possess geographic unity, but is the result of a political development. The canton's history is mirrored by the history of the town, which possesses some of the best-preserved baroque and neoclassical buildings in all Switzerland.

The town is, unmistakably French in character. Although cut off from the rest of the Catholic federation by the powerful Protestant canton of Berne, Solothurn always remained loyal to the Catholic church and to France (the town used to maintain an office for recruiting Swiss mercenaries). This formerly rather insignificant town thus grew prosperous, a happy state which the citizens expressed in a particular appreciation of building. The supreme architectural achievement is the imposing-looking **Zeughaus** (arsenal), which today contains what is regarded as the most important collection of weaponry and uniforms in all Switzerland.

Another impressive site in the town is the **Jesuit Church** (1680). The backdrop of patricians' houses is dominated by the neoclassical **St Ursen Cathedral**, built in 1762 by the Pisonis of Ascona. Solothurn is also an excellent town for museums; most worthy of mention is the **Art Gallery**, containing works by Holbein, Buchser and Hodler, to name but a few of the artists represented here. In a wooded ravine up on the Weissenstein lies the **Hermitage of St Verena**, steeped in legend and set amid beautiful countryside.

Anyone following the ridgeway leading from the Weissenstein, where there is also a **Botanical Garden**, in the direction of **Grenchenberg**, finally ends

Solothurn's main street, with St Ursen cathedral in the background.

up in the second-largest town in Solothurn, **Grenchen**, which lies on the cantonal border with Berne. This is a rather haphazard collection of houses, dominated by the all-powerful Swiss watch industry.

Contrasts in a small area: In autumn, on the slopes of the **Chasseral**, the highest and southernmost ridge of the **Bernese Jura**, where it gradually falls towards Lake Biel, the Chasselas and Blauburgunder grapes slowly ripen in the sun (the vintners of Lake Biel produce a palatable sparkling wine). The Chasseral,* accessible from the south and the north via various roads, affords unique panoramic views of almost the whole of the Alps. On its southern flank lies the coomb of the **Tessenberg**, a huge sunny terrace. The Tessenberg can also be reached from **Ligerz** by cable car or on foot through Twannbach Ravine. Opposite is **St Peter's Island**, a paradise for birds and plants, where the philosopher Jean-Jacques Rousseau said he spent "the six happiest weeks of my life" in 1765.

Lake Biel is the most northerly of the three Jura lakes (Murtensee and Lake Neuchâtel are the other two), which had their water levels deliberately lowered in the 19th century. The reason for this was twofold: to reclaim land and to act as a preventive measure against malaria and other epidemics which struck 1868. At the bottom end of the lake lies the only bilingual town in Switzerland, **Biel** in German, or **Bienne** in French. Its older quarter is most definitely worth a visit. Nearby Magglingen is home to the Swiss Sports School, and their building was a trailblazing piece of architecture when it was unveiled in 1944.

The windy **Taubenloch Gorge**, a narrow defile that leads to the pass of Pierre Pertuis, was considered inaccessible until almost the end of the nineteenth century. Then, in 1890, a path was hewn out of the rock, and now nature-lovers visit in their hundreds. Today, a road connects Biel with the **Vallon de St-Imier**. Its inhabitants insist that they are born with an innate ability to make watches. They are cer-

Little and large: the Swiss and their Swatches.

tainly an active community and their talent appears to keep them busy.

The valley dominated by **Mont-Soleil** used to contain a Benedictine monastery given to the Bishop of Basel as a present in 999. All that is left of it now is the Romanesque **Collegiate Church**, but this is worth visiting. Apart from the church itself you will find wild daffodils, Alpine violets and gentians, which grow here in their thousands.

There are several ways in which to approach **La Chaux-de-Fonds**, a relatively modern town, situated around 1,000 metres (3,000 ft) above sea level, and metropolis of the Neuchâtel Jura. This watchmaking town, in which the great architect Le Corbusier and the poet Blaise Cendrars were born, was designed on a drawing-board and right-angles predominate.

The other relatively large town in this high valley is only 5 km (3 miles) further away: **Le Locle**. This is where the Swiss watchmaking industry is said to have begun. Most of the original watchmakers were farmers who needed to earn a bit of extra money in the cold winters. The main watch museum, **L'Homme et le Temps** (Man and Time), is situated in La Chaux-de-Fonds, but Le Locle has its own watch museum. Its other attraction is a 3-km (2-mile) long lake resembling a fjord, **Lac des Brenets**, beyond the cliffs known as the **Col des Roches**. The River Doubs, which enters Swiss territory for the first time here, was dammed up by a prehistoric landslide. The biggest attraction here is the waterfall, the **Saut du Doubs**.

The Neuchâtel Jura: The Haut Jura Neuchâtelois extends a long way, right up to **Les Verrières** where, during the Franco-German war in 1871, the troops under general Bourbaki, faced with a hopeless situation, crossed over into Swiss territory. **La Brévine** is also known as the Siberia of Switzerland because temperatures there can drop extremely low, sometimes even as far as -40°C (-40°F).

Nearby is the quiet **Lac de Taillères**. There are several ways to approach the Neuchâtel Jura, and one of them is from Neuchâtel itself, via the **Vue des Alpes Pass** to La Chaux-de-Fonds. The pass was not given its name in vain: the view really is magnificent, and extends for many miles.

Neuchâtel, at the bottom end of the largest lake lying wholly on Swiss territory, is a very old town at heart. It was founded in the 11th century by the Counts of Neuenburg, who turned the **castle** above the town into a mighty fortress. The **Collegiate Church** which Count Ulrich II built next to it in 1147 makes it clear how important this town – which has now developed into a very lively commercial centre – used to be in former days. More proof of this can be found in the town's fine museums. One of the best of these is the **Museum of Art and History** which has a large collection of old clocks and watches and other antiques.

But the moors of the Jura can also be reached via **Grandson**, where the Confederate army defeated Charles the Bold of Burgundy (*see page 265*). Grandson is famous above all for its mighty **castle**, which is today the repository for a col-

The watch-making centre of La Chaux-de-Fonds.

lection of old cars, motorcycles and bicycles. No less fascinating a building is the Romanesque church of **St John the Baptist**.

The Jura, a mighty system of mountains 780 km (500 miles) in length, should really be tackled in hiking boots. Those who are up to it should gain access to the heights of the Jura from Lake Neuchâtel by crossing the **Val de Travers**, a lateral valley that made quite a name for itself in the 19th century: on the slopes of the **Creux du Van**, the most impressive limestone cirque in Europe, 1,200 metres (4,000 ft) wide and 2,000 metres (6,500 ft) long, there grows a plant known as wormwood, from which absinthe is derived. In the 19th century the valley developed into quite a lucrative absinthe producer. Absinthe contains *thuja*, which is addictive, and the drink used to be referred to as "La Fée Verte" (the green fairy). Inevitably the authorities eventually stepped in to stop its manufacture.

The main town in the valley is **Môtiers**. There are several fine patrician houses to be found here, one of them containing a museum of local history; next door to it, the **Maison Rousseau** – also a small museum – is a reminder of the famous philosopher and writer, who lived and worked here from 1762 to 1765.

Also of interest are the nearby **asphalt mines**, in operation until about a decade ago and now open to visitors.

The heights of the Jura: It is very fashionable to speak French in the Jura. One hears German only in the Solothurn Jura, in the Laufen Valley and in Biel. Since no-one really knows how and what the Celts spoke, linguistic research is not very fruitful.

Food and drink are what really interest the people of the Jura. The *fondue*, which was recognised as the national dish of Switzerland many years ago, is taken very seriously in these parts. After all, this distinctive mixture of cheese, sparkling white wine and kirsch was invented by the people of Neuchâtel – though the people of Fribourg and the Vaud also claim it as their own.

Cross-country skiing in La Brévine.

One of the oldest and most important buildings in all Switzerland can be found at **Romainmôtier**, in the Vaud Jura: the **church** of the former 11th-century **Abbey of St Peter** and **St Paul**. **Sainte-Croix** lies on the border between the Neuchâtel and Vaud Jura. Romainmôtier was formerly the centre of the music-box and musical automata industries; nowadays only its small **museum** is a reminder of that time.

Vallorbe, a strategically important border town, is famous for its Confederate fortress, known today as the **fortress museum**. International rail traffic passes through here from Paris via Lausanne to the south of France or Italy (Simplon). The **River Orbe**, which once provided power for mills and sawmills, has its source at the top of La Dôle, the second-highest mountain in the Jura.

Beyond **Brassus**, which is very familiar to all those interested in Nordic skiing, the river forms the **Lac de Joux**; from there the water flows underground, not re-appearing until Vallorbe where it emerges as the **Source de l'Orbe** in a magnificent Jura cavern. Nearby is another cavern which is particularly famous for its stalactites: the **Grotte de l'Orbe**.

The Vaud Jura: The western part of the Jura is rich in natural beauty too; here, the highest mountain in the whole range, **Mont Tendre**, sloping up from the Lac de Joux, provides an impressive panoramic view. Some people think **Mont Risoux**, which has the largest forest in Switzerland (23 sq. km/9 sq. miles), is the true symbol of the Vaud Jura. But another contender is the **Mont d'Or**, after which Vacherin Mont d'Or, a cheese available only in the winter months, is named.

One of the cornerstone peaks of the Jura is the **Dôle**, where there is a weather station which serves all of western Switzerland. Tourists, however, tend to prefer the **Marchairuz**, over which a pass road leads from Lake Geneva into the Jura. Here, at the end of a long and tiring hike, one can relax in a natural paradise, the huge (40 sq. km/15 sq. miles) and many-faceted **Parc jurassien vaudois** (Vaud-Jura Park).

Archaeological excavations by Lake Neuchâtel.

WHERE CHARLES THE BOLD MET HIS MATCH

The slopes of the Jura above Concise are the scene of the first battle to take place in the Burgundian wars of 1476, which was named after the castle and town nearby: *Grandson*. After Berne had declared war on powerful Charles of Burgundy ("Charles the Bold"), the Confederates defeated his armies of knights at Grandson, then later at Murten and finally at Nancy, where Charles was killed. These events were summed up in a popular saying which states that "Charles lost his *Gut* (possessions) at Grandson, his *Mut* (courage) at Murten, and his *Blut* (blood) at Nancy". The main beneficiary of these victories was King Louis XI of France, a tyrant as resourceful as he was cruel.

But the Burgundian wars were important for Switzerland, too, above all because the way into Western Switzerland had been opened up, and a first step had been taken towards bringing Geneva and the Vaud into the Confederation.

"As far as armaments were concerned," wrote the military historian Hans Rudolf Kurz, "Grandson was the first battle to feature the successful tactical use of pikes; the long pike, which had become an increasingly common form of armament for the Confederate army – the square had given way to the customary wedge shape – made it almost impossible for the army on horseback to attack the Confederates. The former kept colliding bloodily with the latter's 'hedgehog' formation, protected by the pikes, and was not even able to break up the foot-soldiers in the open field."

The Confederates captured 400 tents, furnished with valuable tapestries as well as gold and silver tableware, 400 pieces of cannon, 10,000 horses, wagons by the hundred, 600 standards, 300 powder-kegs, 800 crossbows – altogether quite sizeable booty, which together with the war purse would have been worth several hundred million of today's Swiss francs. The chronicler Diebold Schilling has left a very accurate description of this booty in his Lucerne Chronicle, which he wrote in the last quarter of the 15th century.

However, Charles the Bold's defeat at Murten had even more serious consequences for him. When the peace treaty was concluded with Savoy, Berne was given parts of the Savoy Vaud and control over Aigle and Erlach; Murten, Grandson, Orbe and Echallens were all put under the joint administration of Berne and Fribourg. Berne also wanted to occupy the Franche-Comté region of France, but its fellow Confederates were against the idea. The Swiss settled for reparations in the form of cash.

With the Confederates' victory, the glorious history of the lords of Grandson came to an end. The line still lives on in England under the name of *Grandison*. A countess of Grandson, mistress of King Edward III, was the reason behind the creation of the highest decoration in Britain, the Order of the Garter: she lost her garter at a ball, whereupon the king picked it up, and as he did so, uttered the now historic phrase, *Honi soit qui mal y pense* (shamed be he who thinks evil of it).

LIBERAM
HERZOG
HAT
DIE

BERNE AND THE BERNESE OBERLAND

The region to the south of Switzerland's capital of Berne, extending up to those extremely Bernese high-altitude health resorts, is characterised by all three types of Swiss landscape: the Lowlands, the Alpine foothills and the Alpine massif. John Webster, commenting on this in his *Notes of a Journey from London to Constantinople* in 1836, said: "If here things were reduced to a small scale, you would have a step up from the river to the town, from the latter to the table land of the valley, and from this last a few steps up to the distant and surrounding mountains."

The Bernese Oberland also reflects, in swift succession, the economic bias of each of these regions. As one travels southwards, industry becomes less important, and agriculture and tourism more so. Further south even the ploughed fields disappear. Meadow areas indicate animal husbandry; Alpine dairy farming is a matter of course in the Oberland. The area owes its present-day appearance to the Aare glacier, which eroded the rock.

Preceding pages: The Swiss capital on the Aare. Left, a bear on a fountain at Zahringen, Berne.

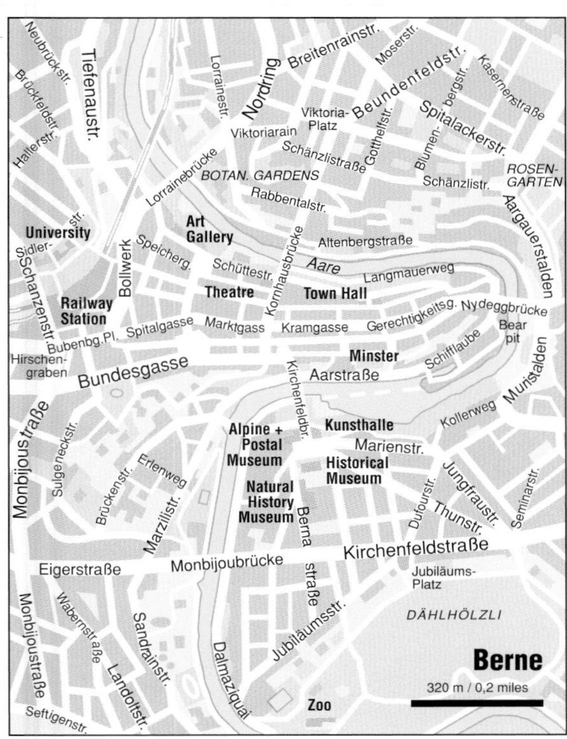

The federal capital: The city of **Berne**, in contrast to most other European capitals, is not obviously international in any way. Swiss history has not left any one centre where the "nation's greats" forged their destiny. There was never a unifying, inspiring personality around whom the upper echelons of society would gather, as there was, say, in the case of Europe's monarchies. Nevertheless, Berne is the result of the hegemony of a few patrician families who managed to retain their claim to a leading role for centuries. This social structure finds expression even today: Berne has a whiff of aristocracy, yet still remains provincial – rather Swiss, in other words.

The old town can be visited no matter what the weather and even in torrential rain you won't get too wet because the old streets are lined with covered arcades, 6 km (3½ miles) in length. The main streets run roughly parallel with the end of the rocky outcrop skirted by the **Aare River**. Outside these rows of buildings in the central part of the city, the land falls off steeply on three sides down to the Aare. This area beneath the town forms the "lower town" where the level of life was once lower socially as well as topographically. The view from the **Münster-Plattform** illustrates the point perfectly: deep below, at the foot of a mighty retaining wall, lies the area known as the **Matte**. Once a workers' and artisans' quarter, it is now particularly favoured by members of the creative professions.

Berne was founded in 1191 by Duke Berchtold V of Zähringen. When the Zähringen dynasty died out the town became free. Berne's compact structure is an accurate reflection of its single-minded spirit. Its victory over Burgundy and the ensuing policy of expansion transformed Berne into the largest city-state north of the Alps. Even internal unrest could not bring the absolutist rule of the patricians to an end. It was only in 1798 when the French army marched in that the old Bernese power structure finally collapsed.

This political consistency has left its mark on the enclosed, unified-looking streets of the old town. Medieval and baroque facades blend harmoniously. Today, the arcades are given over to rows of shops and visitors who are not keen on shopping will still enjoy the surprising views and perspectives afforded by the arcades; they might also cast a glance into the illuminated interiors of the houses in the evening – those that haven't yet been turned into office space, that is.

The English poet Dorothy Wordsworth, visiting Berne in 1820, was mightily impressed by the houses she saw: "There is a beautiful order, a solidity, a gravity, in this city, which strikes at first sight and never loses its effect. The houses are of one grey hue, and built of stone. They are large and sober, but not heavy, or barbarously elbowing each other."

The city contains numerous restaurants; note, though, that their doors are quite often "disguised" as cellar entrances, with steep flights of steps leading down from the street.

Bears everywhere: There is much to see in Berne, including plenty of bears, the city's and the canton's emblem. In the **Bear Pit**, live bears, small and large, can be seen rolling about, and worldwide concern about their continued health and happiness helps to ensure that they have as much care as possible. The bear emblem crops up all over town in many different guises, including a local teddy-bear shaped biscuit. The bears in the huge paintings inside the very traditional Hotel Bären are particularly handsome.

The bear emblem commemorates the founding of Berne by Duke Berchtold. Horace Walpole, English man of letters, explained the significance of the bear in a letter to a fellow countryman, George Montagu, in 1766: "The most faire City Berne hath the name of Beares in the Dutch tongue, because Berchtold Duke of Zeringen, being to build the Citie, and going forth to hunt, thought good to

The lake region near Berne, Switzerland's "vegetable garden".

give it the name of the first beast he should meete and kill."

The **Museum of Communications** shows the development of the Swiss postal service, a considerable feat in view of the former inaccessibility of many villages and towns. The **Museum of Fine Arts** (Kunstmuseum) includes an important collection of Swiss art, Italian works from the 14th–16th centuries, and a large collection of works by French artists of the 19th century. Its Paul Klee collection is the biggest in the world. Other museums of interest in Berne include the **Historical Museum**, the **Swiss Alpine Museum** and the **Natural History Museum**.

But you don't need to visit museums or art galleries to enjoy Berne. The streets themselves hold plenty to interest visitors, including 11 historical fountains from the mid-16th century, from which figures such as *Justitia* (Justice) and the dreaded *Kindlifresser* (child-devourer) peer down on the bustling streets below. Berne's most recent, and controversial, fountain (1983) was the creation of a famous woman artist, Meret Oppenheim.

The **Cathedral** (Münster) is the most important late Gothic edifice in Switzerland. This three-aisled pillared basilica, begun in 1421, was designed by Matthäus Ensinger of Ulm. The tower, however, was not completed until 1893. Inside, its most notable features include finely-carved choir stalls (1523), a Gothic font and the "Last Judgement" window in the Matter Chapel.

Another important symbol of the city that should be seen is the **Zeitglockenturm**, the clock tower. Its clock, on the east side, was built in 1530 and is also an astronomical clock. If you can, try to be there four minutes before the clock strikes the hour when its mechanical figures are set in motion.

If you are in Berne on the fourth Monday in November, the Zibelemärit (onion market), is well worth a visit. It is a magnificent sight: all the stands are covered with plaited onions.

The **Bundeshaus** (Parliament Building) forms the heart of Switzerland.

A Berne street with typical arcades.

Meetings of the National Council and cantonal assemblies take place here. However, the Federal administration has now grown so large that several external administrative agencies have been formed. There's even the odd call for decentralisation, and the shifting of these agencies to regions of low employment.

Diversified landscape: Hieronymus von Erlach, who commissioned the baroque **Erlacherhof** (begun in 1746), a horseshoe-shaped palace in the French style in Berne's **Junkerngasse**, also owned a country seat in **Hindelbank**, north-east of Berne. The whole Bernese-controlled region is full of castles that the gracious lords of Berne either had built or restored as country seats. Many are still in private hands, sometimes actually those of the original patrician families, but the one at Hindelbank was turned into a women's prison in 1896 and is still one today; its ancient fabric remains largely intact.

Not far away, near **Utzenstorf**, lies **Schloss Landshut**, the only moated castle in the canton of Berne. It houses the **Swiss Museum for Hunting and Protection of Wildlife**. Another interesting trip in the locality is into the **Seeland**, northwest of Berne and close to Lake Biel and the Murtensee; it is known as the "vegetable garden" of the canton of Berne.

Turning southwards and going via Burgdorf, we reach the **Emmental**. Emmentaler – the ultimate traditional Swiss cheese – is sold all over the world. Emmental, very hilly and mountainous, is a distinctly agricultural landscape. Not far from **Langnau**, the sedate regional capital with one of the most beautiful village squares in Berne, is Affoltern with its Emmental "show" dairy.

Everywhere one looks streams have cut their way into the sediment left by the glaciers. This means that few large areas of land can be cultivated from one centre alone, and so an area of individual farmsteads has developed, similar to the Lucerne Entlebuch.

To the west of the Aare, and separated only by a small range of hills, lies the

A Sunday stroll in the Emmental Valley.

Sherlock Holmes: the Final Drama

"It is, indeed, a fearful place. The torrent, swollen by the melting snow, plunges into a tremendous abyss, from which the spray rolls up like the smoke from a burning house. The shaft into which the river hurls itself is an immense chasm, lined by glistening coal-black rock, and narrowing into a creaming, boiling pit of incalculable depth, which brims over and shoots the stream onward over its jagged lip. The long sweep of green water roaring forever down, and the thick flickering curtain of spray hissing forever upward, turn a man giddy with their constant whirr and clamour..."

Thus Sir Arthur Conan Doyle, through the eyes of Dr Watson, recorded the scene of one of the most dramatic moments in English literature. Here, at Reichenbach Falls near Meiringen, Sherlock Holmes apparently met his end in a fatal fight with Professor James Moriarty, "The Napoleon of Crime".

The Final Problem, the story which should have been the last word on the world's greatest detective, appeared in *The Strand* magazine in 1893 an it was based on a trip Conan Doyle had just made to the falls. In the story, Dr Watson was not present, but had been sent away on a ruse to treat a consumptive woman in Davos. In real life Conan Doyle's wife, Louise, had been diagnosed as consumptive, and the author, who was also a doctor, blamed himself for not spotting her condition before they had embarked on what had been a gruelling journey. According to Conan Doyle's biographer, Charles Higham, the consumptive Louise brought about the death of Holmes, simply because she required Conan Doyle's attention, and the scene of his "death" was deliberate, as the visit to the Falls had aggrevated her illness and he had soon afterwards taken her to Davos.

Although Conan Doyle confessed he had had an "overdose" of his hero, as in the best soaps the hero was brought back to life by popular demand. But the sight of the fight is still rememberd by hundreds who pay a pilgrimage to it every year. A rack railway goes by the falls and a bronze plaque at the bottom of the chasm commemorates the desparate struggle.

In nearby Meiringen, meanwhile, a complete replica (*pictured above*) of the fictitious 221B Baker Street, London lodgings of Sherlock Holmes forms a museum to the illustrious detective. The museum, in the former English Church, was inaugurated in 1991 on the centenary of Holmes's "death" and the square outside has been named Conan Doyle Place.

There is also a statue of Sherlock Holmes in the town, by John Doubleday, which contains clues to each of the 60 Holmes stories, and gives visitors and members of the world-wide Sherlock Holmes Society, of whom there are more than 1,000, an opportunity to pit their sleuthing skills.

Gürbetal. The gateway, as it were, to this side valley is formed by **Kehrsatz**. The neoclassical **Lohn Country House**, now owned by the Confederation, is situated here. It is often used for official receptions, and for accommodating guests of the Swiss government. A little further up the valley, we reach **Rümligen**. This otherwise insignificant little village prides itself on having had a real Bernese patrician among its denizens. Rümligen Castle was inhabited by Elisabeth de Meuron (1882-1980), a famous Berne eccentric, who once locked a suspected thief up in a tower of her castle, claiming ancient legal rights to do so.

River landscape: It is via the valley of the Aare that the **Bernese Oberland** proper is finally entered. The course of the Aare between Berne and Thun, with its meadows, forests, reed grasses, sedge and backwaters, is one of Switzerland's most precious river landscapes. Much of it is a nature reserve.

The course of the Aare and its tributaries determined the regional layout of the Bernese Oberland. It can be broadly defined by the east-west course of the Aare with its two basins, **Lake Brienz** and **Lake Thun**. South of this line, the lateral valleys run almost parallel to each other, from north to south: the **Simmental**, **Frutigtal**, **Engstligental**, **Kandertal**, **Lauterbrunnental** and **Haslital** – far over to the east – where the Aare has its source.

But the real gateway to the Oberland is the town of **Thun**. Situated at the point where the Aare flows out of Lake Thun, it is dominated by its **castle** (now a history museum), perched up on a steep hill above the roofs of the town. The 12th-century keep, with its four corner towers, is reminiscent of a Norman castle.

Alongside the attractive old town, are military barracks and the **Wocher-Panorama**. This circular picture, painted between 1808 and 1814 by Marquard Wocher and then mounted on linen, is a lifelike representation of Thun in the Biedermeier period, and is situated in a round building in the park of **Schloss Schadau**.

The landscape of the southern side of Lake Thun is dominated by the 2,362 metre (7,700 ft) high **Niesen**. Legend has it that a dragon once lived here, and that the Niesen contained lost souls who haunted sleepers. The Niesen separates the entry to the Simmental from that to the Kandertal valley. It can thus be circumnavigated on three sides. From each of these three sides it looks like a pyramid and from the top there is a good view of the entire Lake Thun region. At the foot of it, right next to the lake, is **Spiez** with its **castle** (now a museum) and its castle Church of St Columba. They are more than 1,000 years old, and still retain many of their Romanesque features.

On the opposite side of the lake, the **Beatushöhlen** (caverns) are hidden beneath the sunny slopes of the **Beatenberg**. Visitors are allowed to venture inside, at least until about 1,000 metres (3,300 ft). About 8 or 9 km (5 miles) of caves have been explored so far, but this represents only a small fraction of the whole system. The moun-

Outdoor pursuits: left, "Hornussen", or "Swiss farmers' tennis"; right, mountain bikers.

tain itself is named after St Beatus who, legend has it, once drove a dragon out of its cave here. The saint probably belonged to a group of Irish monks who came and settled in Switzerland in the 6th century.

A region rich in tradition: The journey continues on up the River Aare. Only a very short section of this river connects Lake Thun with Lake Brienz. A far more important link is **Interlaken**. The town is noticeably full of splendid hotel buildings. They serve as a reminder of the health-spa-oriented, cosmopolitan lifestyle of the upper classes in both Europe and the rest of the world in the second half of the 19th century. Quite a few of these *fin de siècle* palaces are now used as old people's homes or congress centres.

The small town of **Brienz** at the other end of Lake Brienz is famous for its wood-carvings, which can be bought in every souvenir shop in the Oberland. It can be approached by bicycle, boat, train, car or even on foot, but tourists traditionally take the boat. A trip around this mountain lake, which is 14 km (9 miles) long, takes some two-and-a-half hours. The best means of transport to choose for this is the "Lötschberg", a paddle steamer every bit as good as its Mississippi counterparts, and the pride of the Brienz fleet.

Tourism in the old days: Elisabeth Grossmann, the "boatwoman of Lake Brienz" was immortalised in countless paintings. More than 150 years ago, she wept bitter tears over her unrequited love for a young professor. The grieving woman was immortalised by the painter Johann Emanuel Locher (1769–1820). His picture of *La belle Batelière* was one of the best-selling colour etchings of its time.

She was one of the young local girls who used to row the tourists to **Giessbach**, and who were always mentioned in any accounts of journeys. The German physicist and astronomer Johann Friedrich Benzenberg, who visited Giessbach in 1810 had this to say: "The maidens who acted as our guides were also skilled in the art of song, and did not

A pleasure-boat on Lake Thun.

take much prompting. The maidens here have the reputation of being the best singers of all the farm-girls in the Haslital."

The interest shown in the girls' rowing and singing – above all by the male visitors to the Bernese Oberland – grew, and the Swiss girls' moral soundness began to become the object of much speculation and supposition.

The real promoter of the Haslital valley turned out to be Hans Kehrli, a teacher from Brienz, at the beginning of the 19th century. In 1818 he had a footpath built to the **Giessbach Falls**, and erected a simple mountain hut there. On pleasant days the whole family would take up position and sing songs for the visitors, with father Kehrli himself playing along on an alphorn. The family became so famous that one of the many landscape painters of that time immortalised them in a picture entitled *The Giessbach and the Singing Family on its Alp*. In those days, landscape painting was a thriving industry, and there were studios in which employees would copy masterpieces or colour etchings, and these were the forerunners of today's picture-postcards.

The Giessbach Falls became one of the major attractions for 19th-century visitors to Switzerland. Inevitably many were inspired to capture the power of this natural phenomenon in verse or prose. Sir T. N. Talfourd, writing in 1844, said: "You are amazed at the power of so small a stream, which falls, as if of many tons weight, with a noise of thunder, and see the deep-coloured hills beyond the lake, and its dark-blue waters below them, through a crystal veil, where the water is unbroken, and through a brilliant drapery of drops where it is divided." The English poet Gerard Manley Hopkins used original imagery to describe the beauty of the Falls: "The Giessbach falls like heaps of snow or like laces of shining rice. The smaller falls in it shew gaily sprigged, fretted, and curled edges dancing down like the crispest endive."

Gradually the Giessbach began to be developed to accommodate tourists

The "Kulturmühle" in Lützelflüh, Emmental.

more comfortably. In 1840 a guest-house appeared, 1872 saw the opening of the first hotel, which was replaced by a larger, more lavishly furnished building after a fire in 1883. Franz Weber, the environmentalist, managed to save it from destruction in 1983 and had it restored to its former glory. It prospers under the motto "Giessbach belongs to the Swiss". From here the tourists can admire the Falls, which in 1854 were illuminated by Bengal lights. All the fuss made about the Falls irritated some travellers even in those days, for they complained about being "permanently yodelled and alphorned at" while trying to eat their dinner. The songs have now fallen silent, and people cross the lake in a steamer instead of in a barque with the beautiful boatwoman. The funicular, commissioned in 1879, still provides the tourists with a comfortable ride from the docking area to their hotel.

The 2,350-metre (7,700-ft) **Brienzer Rothorn** towers above the town of Brienz. The Brienz-Rothorn-Bahn, the only steam-operated rack railway in Switzerland, travels up to a height of 2,244 metres (7,300 ft). It was built at the end of the 19th century and copes with an average gradient of 22.5 percent. The railway operates only in the summer, but anyone who wants to enjoy the view from the Rothorn in winter can get there by cable car from the town of **Sörenberg** in canton Lucerne.

Following the course of the Aare: Before reaching the area where the Aare has its source, pay a visit to the **Swiss Open-Air Museum** of rural architecture and lifestyles, at **Ballenberg**. Original buildings have been brought to this 200-hectare (500-acre) site from all over Switzerland. They are dismantled, transported piecemeal and rebuilt, section by section, here. Many buildings hundreds of years old have thus been saved from demolition. The museum provides a picture of rural life throughout Switzerland, and also features demonstrations of rural crafts.

The **Haslital** valley, on the eastern edge of the Bernese Alps, is where the Aare has its source, and it ends at the

Lake on the Grimsel Pass.

catchment basin formed by the **Grimsel Pass**, the only adequately surfaced road between the Upper Valais and Northern Switzerland. The higher one goes in the valley, the rougher the landscape becomes, and it leads into the largest continuous glacier region of the Alps, covering a surface area of 300 sq. km (190 sq. miles); among the many glaciers here are the **Aare**, **Rhône** and **Aletsch**. They are all conservation areas. Their water does not only supply the surrounding region – it also flows into the Mediterranean via the Rhône and into the North Sea, too, via the Aare, in combination with the Rhine from the nearby Graubünden Alps.

Like everywhere else in the Swiss Alpine region, the water is put to good use by civilisation. Reservoirs and pressure pipes collect huge masses of seething mountain water with which to drive mighty turbines and generators, providing Switzerland with much of its hydroelectric power. The power stations themselves are situated inside the mountains and are an important source of employment in the mountain areas where they help to stem the emigration of the local population.

One of the best known holiday areas in the Haslital is the region around **Meiringen** and **Hasliberg**. High up here on the Hasliberg, on the **Mägisalp** and in the **Justistal** valley above Lake Thun, a special festival has developed: the *Chästeilet* (cheese-sharing). The cheese produced on an alp has to be divided up among the various farmers in relation to the "milk-efficiency" of the cows that grazed on the alp. In the old days this took place without any great ceremony, but the farmers of today have turned the whole thing into a small folk festival. Sales booths are set up on the alp and tourists and locals alike have the opportunity to buy the cheese directly.The food, drink and music add an extra dimension to the view of the mountain peaks around the alp.

Anyone visiting Meiringen should take a close look at the 200-metre (650-ft) deep **Aare Gorge**. Between **Innertkirchen** and **Meiringen** the river has to

The "Chästeilet" in the Justistal.

cut its way through a rocky ridge 1,600 metres (5,200 ft) in length. The footpath through the high and narrow rocky walls runs partly via suspended walkways and partly via galleries hewn out of the rock. Anyone who takes the path through the gorge in only one direction can be taken back to the car-park by bus.

If you follow the **Lütschine River** up stream from Interlaken, you will find that the valley divides after only 10 km (6 miles) or so, leading eastwards to **Grindelwald** and southwards to the **Lauterbrunnental**. The whole valley is separated from the Haslital by rocky massifs, some as high as 4,000 metres (13,000 ft) above sea level and they all form part of the glacier conservation area. The **Finsteraarhorn** (4,274 metres/14,000 ft), situated at the centre of this glacier region, is the highest point in the Bernese Alps.

The Alpine region: A whole series of mighty mountain peaks lie directly on the border separating the cantons of Berne and the Valais. Foremost among them are the **Eiger**, **Mönch** and **Jungfrau**; these are perhaps the most famous and are almost always thought of as a trio. Since 1912 there has been a railway line leading up to the **Jungfraujoch**. Information is provided in several languages during the journey and the train covers most of the distance inside the mountain itself, although intermediate stations with panoramic windows provide views of the mighty scene. A modern restaurant at the end of the line, 3,454 metres (11,333 ft) above sea level, provides food and drink.

The summit of the Jungfrau is 4,158 metres (13,500 ft) above sea level, and averages temperatures below zero even at the height of summer. The weather station up on the Jungfrau collects important data for meteorologists.

The Eiger, Mönch and Jungfrau have often been admired. In 1816 John Cam Hobhouse, who was later to become Lord Broughton and the British Minister of War, visited the region together with Lord Byron, the poet. That they had their own share of problems as a result of the popularity of the mountains

The classic trio: Eiger, Mönch and Jungfrau.

with visitors becomes evident from this extract from Hobhouse's contemporary diary: "We lay down for a moment, the better to observe that magnificent scenery, the purity of which was somewhat marred by the appearance of two females on horseback just as we were congratulating ourselves on the unsurpassable solitude..."

The cable-car ride up to the **Schilthorn** begins near the village of **Mürren** (closed to cars), below the Jungfrau group and at the upper end of the Lauterbrunnental. From the top of the Schilthorn there is a magnificent all-round view of the entire Alpine region.

This panorama can also be enjoyed during a meal. The revolving restaurant at the top takes an hour to do one complete revolution. The cable-car scenes and ski-chase sequences from the James Bond film *On Her Majesty's Secret Service* were filmed on the Schilthorn, and the tourist brochures still refer to it by its film name of "Piz Gloria".

One very unusual attraction in **Mürren** is the **Balloon Museum** of the International Spelterini Society. The name refers to the first-ever crossing of the Alps by gas balloon, undertaken by Spelterini (a native of Mürren) in 1910. The **International Alpine Balloon Festival** is held every summer in the Lauterbrunnental in memory of this pioneering achievement. Another spectacle is the **Staubbach Waterfall** in Lauterbrunnen. Goethe was inspired by this waterfall to write his poem "Song of the Spirits over the Water". The water crashes over a wall of rock 280 metres (900 ft) high, dissolving almost entirely into fine spray as it does so. When there is a lot of water, in the summer, this spray hangs in the air and can often be felt as far away as the village itself.

Wengen, another village without cars, hosts the annual international skiing contest on the **Lauberhorn**. Here we leave the valley of the White Lütschine River and arrive at **Grindelwald**, in the valley of the Black Lütschine River. (The "Black" river is so called because its water is the colour of slate from the Black Mountain.) Grindelwald's appear-

On the Schilthorn, the "Piz Gloria".

ance has been determined by tourism. After the village burned down in 1892 – the wooden houses provided the flames with more than enough fuel – the new buildings were adapted to suit economic factors, which had changed since the original settlement was built.

As was the case in most of the mountain regions, the first tourists were the English. They paid their first winter visits here in 1860, and in 1891 an Englishman amazed the people of Grindelwald by bringing a pair of skis along with him.

On the way back to Interlaken, a railway line leads up to the **Schynige Platte**, a rockshelf which is situated at the entrance to the Lütschinen Valley. An **Alpine Garden**, containing more than 500 species of plants which are native to the Swiss Alps, has been planted in this extensive hiking region and the Alpine flora can be admired across an area of over 8 hectares (20 acres). Anyone who doesn't feel like reading all the information provided should simply take advantage of the visual beauty of these plants, which should on no account be dug up or picked. They are protected by law.

The way to the Valais: Another key traffic junction in the Alps, alongside the St Gotthard, is the **Lötschberg Tunnel**. It provides a helpful connection with the Valais that is passable even in winter, which saves having to go the long way round the Alpine region via the Lower Valais. The chance to load their cars on to a train also provides motorists with a well-earned break on their exhausting journey towards the south. This stretch of railway was opened in 1913.

The route to the Lötschberg leads from **Spiez** and through the **Kandertal**, the third of the four huge valleys of the Bernese Oberland. (The others are the **Frutigtal**, **Kiental** and **Engstligental**).

The valleys are flanked to the west by the Niesen range. **Reichenbach** is a rather inconspicuous little village on the lower reaches of the **River Kander**, in the Frutigtal. Most of its houses were built in the 18th century, and are exam-

The winner's podium of the International Lauberhorn downhill race in Wengen.

ples of the fine carpentry that has been a feature of the Bernese Oberland for centuries. The village street is lined with solid-looking wooden houses with richly carved and painted facades.

Adelboden, a resort occupying a sunny position at the head of the Engstligental, can be reached via **Frutigen**, the main town in the area, where the River Kander and the **River Engstligenbach** flow into one another. The powerful torrents of water have cut deeply into the soft rock layers of the Niesen range. The strong erosion of the streams has given the valley its "V"-shape. This was not all that useful as far as road-building was concerned, for there was no suitable ridge for one to be built along. Despite this, bridges and flights of steps were constructed right next to the wild torrents, and here and there they provide spectacular views across the water. The numerous waterfalls of the region, and the rocks, worn smooth by the water, are a superb natural spectacle.

Adelboden is an exceptionally popular holiday resort and offers a broad range of winter and summer activities. Such buildings as the **church**, built in 1433, are consequently often disregarded, but they should not be overlooked. Its exterior wall has a late Gothic painting of the Last Judgement dating from 1471, and inside there is modern stained glass by Augusto Giacometti.

The church also bears witness to the legendary tenacity of the people of the Bernese Oberland. Apparently, Adelboden had to go without a church for a long time, because the lords and clergy of Frutigen did not consider one necessary. Thus many villagers, including new-born babies, died without receiving the holy sacrament of the Christian church. Eventually the people took their salvation into their own hands and erected this church by themselves.

Kandersteg, a beautifully situated resort and mountaineering centre of long standing, lies at the entrance to the Lötschberg Tunnel. In the 18th century considerable trading took place here between the north and the south. Cattle were sold and *chuchipulver* (spices) were purchased. The porters involved in this trading gradually diversified to meet the increasing needs of tourism, and whole dynasties of mountain guides arose. The **Blümlisalp** massif is an ideal destination for mountaineers. Water-sports are also possible: the **Öschinensee**, which lies 1,578 metres (5,000 ft) above sea level, is just the place for an Alpine swim. This lake was produced by a landslide in the latter part of the Ice Age. The water flows out underground, and is used to produce electricity.

The **Simmental** is the last of the large valley communities in the Bernese Oberland. It has belonged to Berne since 1386. At the end of the 14th century, the city-state of Berne took over political control of the region from the monastery at Interlaken. The inhabitants of the valley were, however, far from convinced by the Reformation in the 16th century and most of them remained loyal to their Catholic faith. Despite this, the Simmental did not become alienated from Berne. One conspicuous illustration of this is the Berne coat-of-arms

Gjessbach: falls and hotel, with the Lake of Brienz in the background.

that can be seen at **Schloss Wimmis**, marking the entrance to the Simmental.

The **Lower Simmental River** winds its way westwards through the mountain ranges and then describes a large bend before heading off southwards again as the **Upper Simmental**. The observant traveller – shortly after having entered the **Diemtigtal valley** (noted for its richly-decorated scissor work) – will have already noticed the typical Simmental houses in **Erlenbach** as well as in **Därstetten**. The **Knuttihaus**, built in 1756, is considered one of the finest farmhouses in Europe. With its whitened cellar and first storey and loft above it (built on what are known as the *Ständerbau* and *Blockbau* principles respectively), it is the archetypal Simmental house.

The village of **Bad Weissenburg**, beyond Därstetten, flourished thanks to a mineral spa. It was here, shortly before the outbreak of World War II, that Juliana, later to become Queen of the Netherlands, became engaged to Prince Bernhard. The water is still bottled and sold today, but the spa itself stopped operating long ago. Further up the valley, the road forks off, at **Boltigen**, into the **Jaun Pass**. This leads off into the French-speaking region of Gruyère. Further along the Simme, the valley changes from the Lower into the Upper Simmental.

A brief word about some beautiful females from the villages in the Lower Simmental. They're not boatwomen this time, but cows. Until a short time ago, the Simmentaler cow was the Swiss cow *par excellence*. Ideally, it weighs around 600 kilos (1,300 lbs). The breed is predominantly white, dappled with a reddish-beige colour, and horned. They are extremely attractive creatures and quite friendly.

But even the oxen of the region radiate extreme friendliness. Unfortunately, this reliable breed is disappearing in favour of the high-milk-yield cows. It has recently been cross-bred with the Red Holsteiner, which has altered its appearance somewhat but not diminished its good looks.

The impressive facade of the "Knuttihaus" in Därstetten.

Zweisimmen is, from the point of view of transport at least, the most important town in the Upper Simmental. From here one can either follow the Simme further up to the spa town of **Lenk**, or go off westwards into the Saanetal, the easternmost projection of the canton of Vaud. The **church** in Zweisimmen is all that remains of the old village, for Zweisimmen was destroyed by fire in 1862, just as Grindelwald was 30 years later. The 15th-century church, consecrated to the Virgin Mary, is decorated both inside and out with late Gothic frescoes which survived the conflagration. Lenk, like Zweisimmen, lives mainly from tourism, but it also has a sulphur spring that has been in commercial use since the 17th century.

The **Saanetal** has the town of **Gstaad** to thank for its fame. High society from all over the world meets up in the winter months. Cyril Connolly spotted the potential of Gstaad in 1946. In *Homage to Switzerland* he wrote: "Gstaad is an up and coming Kitzbühel, not too high, not too enclosed – a mountain village open to the sun, surrounded by fir-woods and fat pastures… The whole ambience has that exquisite stimulation of a mountain resort assured of a future."

Gstaad, as well as nearby **Gsteig**, is also a summer resort and, despite its snooty image, is as keen on receiving year-round visitors as any other town in Switzerland. For the Swiss tourist industry, despite satisfactory statistics as far as visitors to the country are concerned, is starting to become more and more aware of competition from abroad.

From **Saanen**, the **River Saane** continues as the Sarine (its French name) into the Pays d'Enhaut in the Vaud, later to flow into the Swiss-French Lowlands and eventually into the Aare. However, if, south of **Château d'Oex**, you cross one of two passes – the **Col des Mosses**, or the **Col du Pillon** – from **Gsteig**, you find yourself in the Rhône basin heading for the Mediterranean. If you leave the Pays d'Enhaut in a northerly direction and go up the Sarine you reach the canton of Fribourg.

Hot-air balloon racing in Château d'Oex.

URH
Le dit d'un vieil artisan:
«Savoir qu'un jour,
cela deviendra beau!»
En sa main pleine d'émerveillemen
tenant un morceau de bois, il jubilan
Outil de bois ou berceau,
fer rougi au feu et savamment forgé!
Il a fallu extraire de la matière
la part de beauté s'y trouvant enclose.
Le métal, par la cloche fondue,
sonne clair sur
les montagnes de Gruyère.

18
Pierre Joseph
Dumas, Maître
Sous le Nro 49
20

Western Switzerland

The cantons of **Vaud** and **Fribourg** divide into the Lowlands and the Alpine foothills of French-speaking Western Switzerland, with the valleys of the rivers Thielle, Broye and Sarine running almost parallel to one another. The strangely contorted borders in the **Broye Valley** and their many enclaves of Catholics are a reminder of the time when the city-republics of Berne and Fribourg captured the former Savoy Vaud (which extended from Lake Biel to Lake Geneva) in 1536.

At the time of the revolution, the areas captured by Fribourg – which had remained Catholic – did not want to be connected with the Protestant canton of Vaud for confessional reasons. This region, with its gentle hills and low mountains, its fields of waving corn, its green meadows and its spick and span towns has – if one discounts **Morat** (Murten in German) and **Gruyères** (Greyerz) – been spared may of the worst aspects of mass tourism.

The continental divide: The centre of the world for the ancient Greeks was Delphi; for the people of Western Switzerland, it is close to the small town of **La Sarraz**. If the streams leading from the nearby millpond were not barred off, the trout inside could choose which way they wanted to go: to the North Sea via the Rhine or to the Mediterranean via the Rhône. Local people have named the pond Le Milieu du Monde – the centre of the world. People here have dreamt for centuries of a trans-Helvetian and trans-European waterway. As we shall see, to an extent that dream was realised.

This continental divide between the Mediterranean and the North Sea is comparable to the St Gotthard. The railway here, however, has no northern and southern slope to climb and has few bends (it only twice enters a tunnel). According to the official railway timetable, **Eclépens**, on the La Sarraz watershed and 455 metres (1,500 ft) above sea level, is only 18 metres (60 ft) higher than the station in Biel. At the foot of the Jura, the train from German-speaking Switzerland, after passing Yverdon and the Orbe plateau, crosses the foothills of the Jura known as the **Mormont**, which forms a kind of barrier between the Rhine and Rhône river regions.

It is thought that the name of **La Sarraz** is based on the Latin *serrata* (saw-shaped): the road here squeezes its way between the Jura and the Mormont. On a rocky hill, nearly 1,000 years ago, the lords of Grandson built a **castle** from which they could supervise this access route. Near the castle there is a Gothic **Chapel**, containing the tomb of Franz of La Sarraz, on which his decaying corpse has been rendered in stone. It is a very graphic depiction of the transition from this world to the next: worms are crawling through the body and the face and the genitals are hidden by toads.

A descendant of the lords of La Sarraz turned the castle into a museum in 1911. On his death, his widow made it a centre where people working in the arts could

Preceding pages: inside the Gruyère Museum in Bulle. Left, Fribourg: the old town and the cathedral. Right, the tomb of Franz of La Sarraz.

meet and find inspiration: she invited the Russian film director Sergei Eisenstein, the German painter Max Ernst and the Swiss-French architect Le Corbusier to the castle, organised an architects' conference and, in 1929, hosted the first ever congress of independent film-makers. The castle stables house an interesting **Horse Museum**.

In the 17th century, La Sarraz Pass was chosen to become a major European traffic route, to be part of a canal linking the North Sea and the Mediterranean. The idea behind the scheme was to provide The Netherlands with an easy route to India, avoiding not only the straits of Gibraltar but also their Spanish enemies and the Moorish pirates who plagued the North African coast. Canals already led through Belgium and the County of Burgundy, both under Spanish domination. The Netherlands thus planned a trans-European connection through Switzerland.

Elie Gouret, a British Huguenot in the service of the Dutch, handed the council in Berne a memorandum with the plans of the ship canal and most of the capital he needed. He also brought with him technicians and carpenters to build the sluices and boats. The plan was to connect Yverdon, on Lake Neuchâtel, with Lake Geneva. After two years' labour, construction workers reached **Entreroches** on the Mormont. There, they built a harbour, along with a harbour-master's house which can still be seen today. Eight years later, they had got as far as **Cossonay**.

It was at this point that they ran out of money, and the dream of a trans-European canal was shelved. But the canal – or at least stretches of it – was used right up to the 19th century. Ships with wine, salt and grain (the Vaud trinity) travelled via the Canal d'Entreroches into Lake Neuchâtel, and then via the Zihl and the Aare up to **Solothurn**. Even today, it is easy to make out sections of the old canal. From the station at Eclépens a signpost points the way to the **Canal d'Entreroches**. In a forest full of beech and oak trees lies a ravine between some limestone rocks. The deep

The small town of Morat (Murten), seen from the lake.

trench between Cyclopean walls is the ship canal.

A landscape steeped in history: Most Swiss lakes were formed during the Ice Age; as it ended the glaciers gradually melted and their basins filled with water. After the Rhône glacier had receded, an area of water 100 km (62 miles) in length, covering the base of the Jura all the way to Solothurn, formed northeast of the continental divide of La Sarraz. This "Lake Solothurn" finally split up into three distinct parts: Murtensee, Biel and the lakes of Neuchâtel. After the large lake had receded, the Orbe plateau developed, and today this plateau provides fertile agricultural land.

Near the little town of **Orbe**, at **La Boscéaz**, there are some splendid mosaics to be seen which once decorated the floors of a Roman villa that was almost a palace. On the bank of Lake Neuchâtel beyond **Concise** (2.5 km/1¾ miles on foot from the railway station, and also accessible by car from the main road), lies the Roman quarry of **La Lance**. Wooden stakes were hammered into the unworked limestone and soaked with water until they cracked the rock: traces of this technique can be clearly seen in the stone today. Ships would then transport the stone across the lake to **Yverdon** (*Eburodunum*) or via the Broye over to the Helvetian capital of *Aventicum*, today's **Avenches**.

To the east of Orbe lies **Yverdon-les-Bains**, a small industrial town with its own thermal baths (sulphur springs). Between 1805 and 1823, the famous teacher Heinrich Pestalozzi ran his world-renowned education institute from the **château** here. Today it houses an **Ethnological Collection**.

In the Broye Valley (the main route through from Lausanne to Berne) lie the medieval towns of **Moudon**, which has a delightful old town; **Lucens**, which has a château and a Sherlock Holmes museum (*see page 273*); and **Payerne**, which has a Romanesque **Abbey Church**. The parish church in Payerne contains the tomb of the legendary Burgundian queen, Bertha.

Corpus Christi procession in Romont: "Les Pleureuses" (the Mourners).

In **Avenches**, the extensive and still well-preserved **Roman ruins** of the Helvetian capital of *Aventicum* can be visited. They contain an amphitheatre, temple, baths, theatre and museum. In **Morat**, there are well-preserved town walls. And in **Estavayer-le-Lac**, on the banks of Lake Neuchâtel, is a **château** with a museum containing, among other things, a collection of frogs preserved in glass jars. On a hill near the Broye Valley lies **Romont**; its château contains a **museum of stained glass**.

Fribourg, the bridge town: Within a loop described by the River Sarine lies the cantonal capital, **Fribourg**. The fine townscape is dominated by the tower of the **St Nicholas Cathedral**, which has the Last Judgement depicted on its western portal. The Sarine marks the linguistic border. Fribourg is – both literally and metaphorically – a bridge town; for nearly a millennium it has formed a bridge between German- and French-speaking Switzerland. Its setting is spectacular. At the end of the 18th century, William Coxe was so impressed by its aspect that he was driven to one of his not infrequent flights of fancy: "Many [of the buildings] overhang the edge of a precipice in such a manner that on looking down, a weak head would be apt to turn giddy; and an unfortunate lover, repulsed in his suit, might instantly put an end to his pains, by taking a leap from the parlour window."

Fribourg, founded as a *freie Burg* in 1157 by Berchtold IV of Zähringen, on a peninsula in the River Sarine, was bigger than both Berne and Zurich when it entered the Confederation, and in terms of prosperity it was easily on a par with Basel and Geneva. Trade and business flourished; the wool cloth and leather produced by the town were sought-after commodities.

After the Reformation – Fribourg stayed with the "old faith" – its economic power declined, even though the town managed to extend its dependencies, and it was not until the second half of the 20th century that Fribourg emerged from its somnolence and rapidly industrialised.

Monk at work in the Valsainte Carthusian monastery.

As an island of Catholicism in a Protestant land, the town went through a period of decline. The country was preparing to supply mercenaries to foreign princes (particularly to Their Most Christian Majesties of France), and the patrician upper classes became fossilised in class prejudice.

A contemplative life of solitude: Anyone who follows the River Sarine from Fribourg in the direction of Bulle can visit the Cistercian **Abbey of Hauterive** near **Posieux**. The 12th-century monastery is Switzerland's only remaining abbey belonging to Cistercian monks. Likewise unique is the **Monastery of La Valsainte** near **Charmey**, the only Carthusian monastery in Switzerland, inhabited today by members of this austere order who live as semi-recluses in rows of individual cells, each with its own little garden.

Despite industrialisation, Fribourg has remained the most markedly rural of Switzerland's cantons: 16.4 per cent of employed people work in agriculture (the figure was as high as 39.4 per cent in 1950), more than three times the number in Switzerland as a whole (5 percent).

Fribourg has its own breed of cattle, patriotically sporting the black-and-white colours of the canton, and two types of cheese: Gruyère and Vacherin, a fondue cheese. The language border is also a "cheese border": the French-Swiss part of Fribourg produces Gruyère, the Swiss-German part produces the large-holed Emmentaler.

The Gruyère region: The Valley of Gruyère, through which the River Sarine flows, is a microcosm of Switzerland: a plateau surrounded by mountain peaks, and right in the middle, in a commanding position, a small town with a château, whose lords have reigned over the region for centuries. The whole Gruyère region is steeped in history.

Every year over a million people visit the small town of **Gruyères** (Greyerz) and its château. Just outside the town is the **Cheese Dairy**, so spick and span that it looks more like a laboratory than the popular image of a rural dairy. The

Summer near Charmey.

town has only one street, so can be walked through quickly. The **château**, no longer in private hands, has been turned into a major tourist attraction complete with restaurants and souvenir shops. The corridors once walked by counts and their ladies are now packed with tourists from as far away as San Francisco and Tokyo.

The Song of Switzerland: As in German-speaking Switzerland, a rich cowherding culture has developed in the Alpine foothills. The cowherd's melody became known as the Song of the Swiss and – although much mocked (it was sometimes called the animals' *Marseillaise*) – became famous around the world. The song with the dialect refrain "*Lioba, lioba, por ario*" recalls the *Poya*, driving the cattle up to the Alpine pastures.

Folk artists immortalised the *Poya* (especially from the 18th century onwards) in colourful paintings which decorated crossbeams and barn doors: many depict the cows, along with a horse piled high with luggage, a pig and several goats, zig-zagging their way up the mountainside, accompanied by herdsmen with rucksacks and walking-sticks on their way to the Alpine hut. A fascinating collection of this farm art, so typical of the Gruyère region, can be found in the **Musée Gruérien** (Gruyère Museum) in **Bulle**, a rewarding place to visit; the architecture of the building and its layout are also interesting.

But back to the cowherd's melody (*ranz des vaches*). It is supposed to be so evocative of life on the Alps that in former days it provoked an uncontrollable feeling of homesickness in Swiss mercenaries. So strong was their feeling of nostalgia on hearing the song that they would burst into tears.

Rousseau wrote: "Some deserted or died; so strong was their yearning to see their homeland once again." In 1621, a minister of the king of France is said to have banned Swiss mercenaries serving in France from singing the cowherd's melody. But the melody proved so popular that it found its way into operas and operettas.

Production of Gruyère cheese in a Fribourg dairy.

In 1791 it was included in André Grétry's revolutionary opera *Wilhelm Tell* in Paris; in 1804 Friedrich Schiller made reference to the cowherd's melody several times in his *Wilhelm Tell*; Goethe had written to Schiller telling him that the cowherd's melody was found only in Switzerland.

Joseph Weigl's cowherd opera, *The Swiss Family,* joined the melody's long string of successes: after its première in Vienna in 1809 it was performed in the Château Saint-Cloud at the request of Empress Marie-Louise. In 1827 it was heard in the Odéon theatre in Paris, under the name *Emmeline ou la Famille Suisse*, and a year later, in London's Surrey Theatre, it was staged under the new name of *Home! Sweet Home! or the Ranz des Vaches.*

The opera described the fate of Swiss mercenaries who, plagued by homesickness, on singing the illicit cowherd's melody, deserted, and were subsequently condemned to death. Meanwhile the Royal Opera House in London's Covent Garden was performing a piece on the same theme: *Home! Sweet Home! or The Swiss Family.*

Giacomo Meyerbeer incorporated the melody, accompanied by "piano, harp or guitar" and sung by a shepherd from Brittany, in a comic opera. Adolphe Adam, in his opera *Le Chalet* (libretto by Eugène Scribe) made references to the homesick Swiss soldiers in the service of the French; three years later, at the end of the century, the opera was performed as *The Swiss Cottage* for Queen Victoria in Windsor Castle.

Then, in 1911, Wilhelm Kienzl, from Vienna, composed the opera *The Cow Dance* (containing the song *Zu Strassburg auf der Schanz*). It was performed in France and Chicago and again in Vienna after the end of World War I.

There are innumerable arrangements and piano reductions, libretti and arias containing the cowherd's melody. They all sing the praises of the rural Switzerland which the homesick mercenaries longed for, a way of life which in today's Switzerland is best summed up by the little town of Gruyères.

Cheese fondue brings people closer.

POLICE
GE
6695
CAMEL

POLICE
GE
5260.

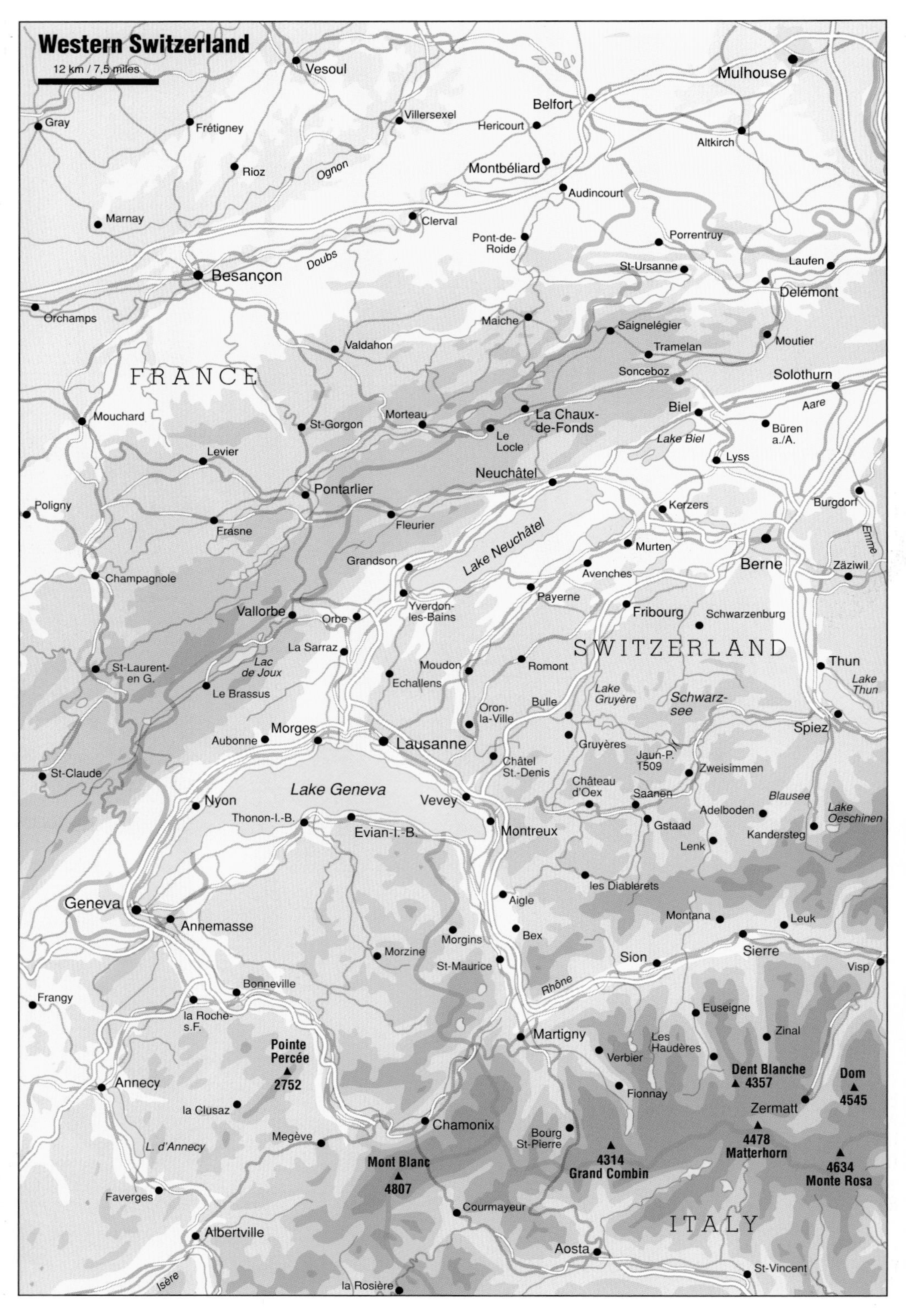
Western Switzerland
12 km / 7,5 miles
Vesoul
Mulhouse
Belfort
Gray
Frétigney
Villersexel
Hericourt
Altkirch
Rioz
Ognon
Montbéliard
Audincourt
Marnay
Clerval
Pont-de-Roide
Porrentruy
Doubs
Besançon
St-Ursanne
Laufen
Delémont
Orchamps
Maiche
Saignelégier
Valdahon
Moutier
Tramelan
FRANCE
Sonceboz
Solothurn
Mouchard
Morteau
La Chaux-de-Fonds
Biel
Aare
St-Gorgon
Le Locle
Büren a./A.
Lake Biel
Levier
Lyss
Neuchâtel
Pontarlier
Poligny
Kerzers
Burgdorf
Frasne
Fleurier
Lake Neuchâtel
Emme
Murten
Grandson
Berne
Zäziwil
Champagnole
Avenches
Payerne
Yverdon-les-Bains
Fribourg
Vallorbe
Orbe
Schwarzenburg
La Sarraz
SWITZERLAND
Lac de Joux
Thun
St-Laurent-en G.
Moudon
Romont
Lake Thun
Echallens
Le Brassus
Lake Gruyère
Schwarz-see
Bulle
Oron-la-Ville
Spiez
Morges
Aubonne
Lausanne
Gruyères
St-Claude
Châtel St.-Denis
Jaun-P. 1509
Zweisimmen
Lake Geneva
Château d'Oex
Nyon
Vevey
Saanen
Blausee
Thonon-l.-B.
Adelboden
Lake Oeschinen
Evian-l.-B.
Montreux
Gstaad
Kandersteg
Lenk
les Diablerets
Aigle
Geneva
Annemasse
Montana
Leuk
Bex
Morgins
Sierre
Morzine
Sion
St-Maurice
Visp
Rhône
Bonneville
Frangy
la Roche-s.F.
Euseigne
Martigny
Zinal
Les Haudères
Pointe Percée
2752
Verbier
Dent Blanche
4357
Dom
4545
Annecy
Fionnay
Zermatt
la Clusaz
Chamonix
Bourg St-Pierre
4478
Matterhorn
Megève
L. d'Annecy
4314
Grand Combin
Mont Blanc
4807
4634
Monte Rosa
Faverges
Courmayeur
ITALY
Albertville
Aosta
St-Vincent
Isère
la Rosière

AROUND GENEVA

If the traveller takes the train from Zurich and Berne in the direction of Lausanne and Geneva, he will be greeted – on emerging from a tunnel just before Lucerne – by a stunning view of the vast, light-blue expanse of **Lake Geneva**, and of the mountains surrounding it. The sloping vineyard next to the railway line here is jokingly referred to as the "Clos des Billets": Swiss Germans, overcome by the beauty of the landscape, are reputed to fling their return tickets (*billets*) out of the train windows.

Ever since the days when the poet Byron sang the praises of the region guests have been arriving *en masse*. Many never leave, including stars such as Charles Aznavour, Alain Delon and Peter Ustinov, and before them Charlie Chaplin, James Mason, David Niven, Richard Burton and Audrey Hepburn. Writers such as Georges Simenon, Han Suyin and Frédéric Dard have been similarly smitten by the place, as have untold numbers of artists, kings, oil sheiks and princesses. No wonder people jokingly refer to it as the Beverly Hills of Lake Geneva.

The French name for Lake Geneva – Lac Léman – refers to the legendary Lemanus who is supposed to have given the lake its name of *Lacus Lemanus*. He was a son of the Trojan prince Paris, who started the Trojan War by abducting the beautiful Helen.

The first record of the name Geneva was in the 1st-century BC *Commentaries* of Julius Caesar. The Romans introduced vines to the area, and later on Christian monks cultivated the slopes by the lake. The perfect spot for vines, **Geneva** is the third largest wine-growing canton in Switzerland after the Valais and the Vaud. It is said that the steep vineyards of **Lavaux** on Lake Geneva, between **Lausanne** and **Montreux**, benefit from the sun's rays three times: when it shines from the sky, when it reflects off the lake, and finally at night-time when its warmth, absorbed during the day, radiates from the vineyard walls. In the words of Vaud writer Jacques Chessex: "The wine draws its shrill and brazen fame from blazing heat from earth and stone." The vineyards slope rather more gently along the **Côte** between Lausanne and Geneva.

In the 16th century the Aare republic occupied the northern shore and sometimes the southern one, too. Later Berne established iys own navy – which included two galleys each with a crew of 500, as well as smaller ships. Its purpose was to protect trading vessels on their way to their ally, the republic of Geneva, which had no direct land access to the Confederation.

Western Europe's largest lake: The largest of the Swiss lakes, **Lake Geneva**, is shaped like a sickle, and is 72 km (45 miles) long, up to 13 km (8 miles) wide near the middle, and 310 metres (1,000 ft) deep; in other words, a miniature ocean. Like the sea, it is subject to tides, though they make only 5 millimetres or so of difference. Some 348 sq. km (134 sq. miles) of its total surface area of 582

Preceding pages: waiting for the "Tour de Romandie", western Switzerland's big cycle race. **Right**, Geneva Cathedral.

sq. km (225 sq. miles) belong to Switzerland, the rest, on the southern shore, belongs to France.

Such statistics make the following anecdote about Bernard, Abbot of Clairvaux in the 12th century, told by James Cotter Morison in his book about the abbot, all the more amusing: "'Do not the mountains drop sweetness? the hills run with milk and honey, and the valleys stand thick with corn?' wrote St Bernard of Clairvaux, but when travelling by the Lake of Geneva, after having passed a whole day in riding along its shore, in the evening, when his companions were speaking about 'the Lake', he enquired, 'What lake?'.

Lake Geneva, which contains 89 billion cubic metres of water, is the largest fresh-water reservoir in Europe. It contains twice as much water as Lake Constance, six times as much as Lake Neuchâtel and 22 times as much as Lake Zurich. Mathematicians have come to the conclusion that it contains enough water to drown all of humanity: the water level would rise by only 50 centimetres or so. They have also made it clear that the River Rhône would have to milk the Valais glaciers for 17 years before it could fill an empty lake basin of this size.

Two centuries ago water specialists were already predicting that the lake would be destroyed by pollution. Now, as a result mainly of pressure from conservationists, it is at long last making a recovery. On 1 July 1986 Switzerland banned the use of phosphates in washing powders: within only a short time the rarer species of fish, many of which were near extinction in the lake, started to thrive again. The number of water fowl has also risen substantially since a prolific species of mussel known as *Dreissena polymorpha* began to enrich the range of food available.

There is still some concern about the amount of nitrates in the fertiliser used by farmers in the region but, according to the Lake Geneva water protection commission, "over-fertilisation" with phosphates has been substantially reduced in recent years.

An advertisement for a cruise on Lake Geneva.

It was in 1823 that the steamer *William Tell* belonging to an American named Church first crossed the lake; to begin with, many of the locals thought it was an invention of the devil. For many years freighters with lateen sails were used to bring construction material for the two towns across the lake from Meillerie (Savoy). Unfortunately there are only two remaining examples of such vessels, the *Vaudoise* in Lausanne and the *Neptune* in Geneva, but it is still possible to experience something of the flavour of lake travel in the early days: paddle steamers take passengers over to the French side of the lake, to Evian-les-Bains (with its casino, olympic-size swimming pool and a mineral-water source) and Thonon-les-Bains. There are also regular sailings to the flower-bedecked French village of Yvoire and the Château (Castle) of Chillon, on the Swiss side, as well as a selection of half- or full-day round-trips.

Geneva (city pop. 180,000, canton pop. 410,000) has an international airport, from which it takes only 6 minutes to reach the centre of the city. But the city really needs to be approached from the lake (ideally on an old-fashioned steamer) to realise how magnificently situated it is: it nestles among hills and gardens, surrounded by mountain ranges and cradling its broad harbour, "La Rade". The superb fountain spounting heavenwards at the mouth of the harbour, the **Jet d'Eau**, can be regarded as symbolic as well as decorative: in its proud history this city-republic has not laid claim to any other regions, and has always maintained an interest in the things of the spirit.

That is not to say that gains of a different kind are not considered desirable. Money has enormous importance in the city. The British actor Robert Morley described Geneva as "this city of wealth by stealth" and there is no doubt about the pioneering role Geneva has played in the creation of the capitalist credit system. The Vaud writer C. F. Ramuz concluded: "Geneva based itself on abstract thinking quite early on; and trading and banking really are ab-

Geneva's suburbs seen from afar.

INTERNATIONAL GENEVA

International Geneva is a city or a state all to itself. The Palais des Nations (guided tours daily) has its own postal service as well as its own stamps – just like Monaco, Liechtenstein or the Vatican. It is larger than the Palais de Versailles, and is the daily place of work for 3,500 international civil servants; it is the most important congress centre in the world, with more than 5,000 meetings every year; and it is the most important centre of the economic and social-political UN capital of Geneva.

The international organisations provide 21,000 jobs; the diplomats and civil servants (numbering over 30,000 including their families) live tax-free, admittedly, but they also spend over 1.2 billion Swiss francs a year in Geneva, thus providing a catalyst for the city's prosperity. More than 100 countries, including Switzerland itself, have diplomatic missions in Geneva (compared with 74 in the captial, Berne); the Swiss embassy in Geneva represents the country in the various international organisations.

Geneva's rise to the world-famous conference centre it is today began in 1871: a court of arbitration was held in the Town Hall during the row about the sinking of the battle cruiser *Alabama* in the American Civil War. On the first centenary of American independence in 1876, in memory of the arbitration award, US officers handed in their swords, the metal of which was recast into the form of a ploughshare; it can be seen in the "Salle Alabama" in the Town Hall. Geneva's international mission, however, reaches right back to Calvin and his "Protestant Rome".

Geneva's big moment came in 1919, when it was chosen as the seat of the League of Nations. With the advent of World War II the International Labour Organisation moved to Montreal, New York was chosen as the seat of the United Nations, and it was only thanks to the efforts made by several diplomats that Geneva became the European seat of the UN. Then a whole series of organisations started moving to Geneva in an almost unstoppable stream: the UN possesses several special institutions, including 14 intergovernmental and 108 non-governmental organisations, and it is now considered very much the done thing for every organisation to be based in Geneva. Cardiologists, university chancellors, the World Council of Churches, the Women's League for Peace and Freedom, the World Wide Fund for Nature, as well as the YMCA and the Boy Scouts, all have their base here: it is difficult to imagine what the city would be without them.

Scarcely any other city in the world receives so many visits from foreign heads of state. Geneva has been the scene of many historically important conferences:

1954: The Indo-China conference ended France's intervention and decided, fatefully, on the division of Vietnam.

1955: The four-power summit: Eisenhower (USA), Bulganin (USSR), Eden (Britain) and Faure (France).

Since 1955: Meetings of The Conference for the Peaceful Use of Atomic Energy.

1983: Conference on the Palestine problem.

1985: Summit meeting between the world's most powerful presidents, Ronald Reagan (USA) and Mikhail Gorbachev (USSR), which paved the way for the arms reduction agreements and the beginning of the end of the cold war.

For this momentous event, four thousand journalists travelled to Geneva in 1985, and 3,000 soldiers and police were put on duty. The summit was the largest media event ever to take place in Switzerland. There was detailed TV coverage, including reports on the various outings undertaken by Nancy Reagan and the late Raisa Gorbachev. Both ladies jointly laid the foundation-stone for a new Red Cross Museum at the headquarters of the ICRI (International Committee of the Red Cross).

Also forming part of international Geneva is CERN, the European Laboratory for Particle Physics,where 3,000 full-time employees and some 6,000 visiting experts from all over the world conduct research into "what makes the planet tick". The annual budget of 940 million francs is shared by 19 states, Switzerland included. Since 1953, larger and larger particle accelerators have been built in order to allow scientists to explore the inner structure of matter. The largest ring-tunnel (LEP or Large Electron Positron Storage Ring), completed in 1989, is 27 km (17 miles) long.

stractions if one compares them to the concrete activity of farming." Nowhere else in Switzerland are arguments indulged in so eagerly, and words bandied about so assiduously as here in Geneva; nowhere else is there so much political discussion.

The fifth continent: Geneva is a city of great influence and famous personalities. In the 16th century the reformer Calvin turned Geneva into a "Protestant Rome", the effects of which were felt worldwide; in the 18th century, the city's "Golden Age", Jean-Jacques Rousseau paved the way for human rights and the French Revolution; engineer Henri Dufour, head of the army in the country's last civil war, became a confederate peacemaker, and the philanthropic businessman Henri Dunant turned his home city into the headquarters of his Red Cross organisation and elevated the Swiss flag – which has the colours reversed – into the international symbol of humanity.

For centuries, the tiny city-state was surrounded by regions controlled by enemy princes – Savoy and France – and completely cut off from the lands in the Confederation. The most important transport connection was across the lake. It was only at the Congress of Vienna of 1814–15 that the border came down and Geneva was finally provided with land access to Switzerland. But the umbilical cord is slender: today, the canton's border with France is 102 km (63 miles) long, while the boundary with the rest of Switzerland measures just 4 km (2 miles).

Princes and millionaires: The German magazine *Stern* recently came to the conclusion that Geneva contained "more millionaires than unemployed people": "for every 1,800 people out of work there are 2,767 people paying taxes on fortunes worth over a million". Even Voltaire, who lived in Geneva and nearby **Ferney** (where his house is now a museum), remarked derisively that the city had "very little else to do but earn money". It is said that the older inhabitants of Geneva grew rich by saving their money.

The old part of Geneva.

Geneva also has its poor, the victims of prosperity, but they don't make the headlines of the international press. And neither are they that visible, at least not in the places frequented by visitors. Geneva is so "breathtakingly elegant", as a certain type of visitor likes to say; French couturiers, Italian shoe firms and New York jewellers all have branches in the town, notably in the area around the Rue du Rhône.

It was thanks to a bridge that Geneva got its first mention in the history books. Julius Caesar "had the bridge at Geneva destroyed" in order to stop the Helveti from emigrating in 58 BC. He describes this in his *Gallic Wars*.

Around the year 450, Geneva became a bishop's see, and in the 11th century – after the kingdom of Burgundy had joined the Gallo-Roman empire – it became an imperial city, ruled by a prince-bishop. The Geneva coat-of-arms, with its Gallo-Roman imperial eagle and its bishop's key, is a reminder of the bishops' dual role as spiritual and secular lords. A less reverent interpretation is that the heraldic symbols represent "half a chicken" and the "key to the wine-cellar".

American links: Since the Reformation the coat-of-arms has borne the inscription *Post tenebras lux* (light after darkness). One can also find the words *Post tenebras lux* on the title pages of the English Bibles printed in Geneva that the Pilgrim Fathers took with them in the *Mayflower* (1620) to America. Calvin's teachings had a worldwide effect: American president Woodrow Wilson, who suggested Geneva as the seat of the League of Nations after World War I, was a Calvinist.

Geneva makes a great show of championing freedom. In December every year the city celebrates the "Escalade", commemorating the time, in 1602, when the duke of Savoy made a vain attempt to capture the city. His troops used ladders to climb the city walls but were repulsed by the population. More recently, in the 19th century, Geneva bankers financed the Greeks' struggle for freedom.

The Museum of the Swiss Abroad: French infantry (Swiss mercenaries are in red).

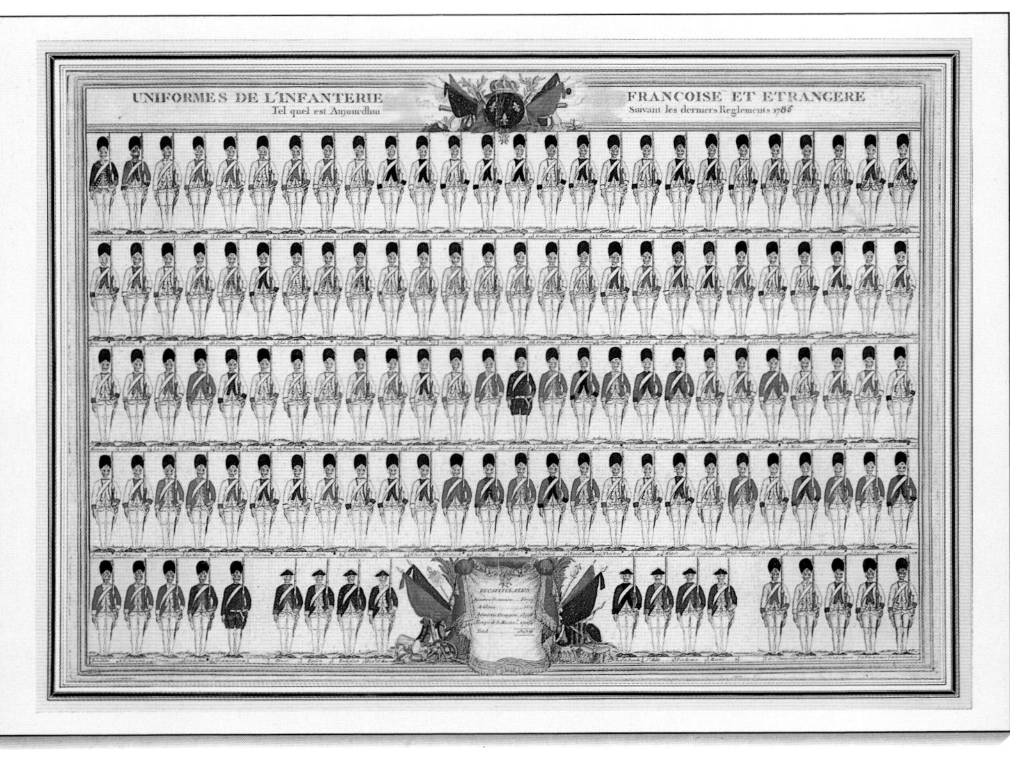

There are magnificent parks along the edge of the lake. The centre of the old town is situated on a small rise on the left bank of the Rhône, with the **Cathedral**, the **Town Hall**, shopping streets and excellent museums. International Geneva is on the right-hand bank, with the Palais des Nations, the offices of the International Labour Organisation, the International Committe of the Red Cross and other organisations.

The **Cathedral of St Pierre**, Protestant since 1536, dates from the 12th and 13th centuries. The 18th-century west facade is neoclassical. Describing the cathedral, a famous preacher, Pastor Henry Babel, said: "I have never entered the Cathedral St Pierre without the feeling that I was stepping into another world. The reverberating silence of its mighty walls, the shadow of its vaults and the brightness of its stained-glass windows have revealed to me that true greatness derives from a harmony in simplicity. The pillars support the vault towering above them, I told myself, just as science has to support belief."

In its 400 years of development the Protestant church of Geneva has learned not only to open its doors to those who believe themselves to be in possession of the truth, but also to those still seeking it. Its fundamental declaration, adopted at the beginning of the 20th century, expressly insists that it base its teachings on the Bible as explored in the light of Christian conscience and of science, and makes it the duty of each one of its members to take the time to form their own judgements.

The famous altar by Konrad Witz (1444) in the **Musée d'Art et d'Histoire** reminds the visitor of Geneva's patron saint, St Peter: it shows Christ walking on the water with the waterfront at Geneva in the background. As well as important collections of art, the museum also has a very interesting Egyptology section. The **Musée d'Histoire Naturelle** and the **Musée d'Éthnographie** are both very well laid out, and the **Musée de l'Horlogerie** is also worth visiting. The most important guild in medieval Geneva was that of the jewel-

The wine village of Féchy overlooking Lake Geneva.

lers. When Calvin set strict limitations on the use of gold and precious stones in 1566, they turned to clockmaking instead: the Geneva clockmakers' guild was the first in the world, and Swiss luxury clocks and watches still have a world-wide reputation.

The **Penthes Château**, situated in a magnificent park, houses the Museum of the Swiss Abroad, and brings to life the history of all those Swiss who left the country to find their fortune and sometimes their death too: "*Pas d'argent, pas de Suisses*" (no money, no Swiss), was a popular saying during the days when the Swiss fought as mercenaries. The Chateau is just one of some 30 museums, libraries, galleries and collections which can be seen on a visit to Geneva.

The villages on Lake Geneva: One of the highlights of the Côte is **Coppet** with its 18th-century château (open to visitors), originally the property of Jacques Necker, a Geneva banker. His daughter Germaine de Staël (1766–1817) was one of the most important figures in European intellectual life. Necker, the Baron of Coppet, was Louis XVI's Minister of Finance. He married off his daughter to Sweden's ambassador in Paris, the Baron of Staël-Holstein. First an admirer, then later a critic of Napoleon, she was exiled to Switzerland. The leading minds of the age used to meet in the Château de Coppet. Madame de Staël's autobiographical novels are as striking today as they were then in their advocacy of women's emancipation, and her political tracts such as *De l'Allemagne* are pleas for European reconciliation.

Another delightful little town is **Nyon**, originally a Helvetian settlement named *Noviodunum*, then a Roman fortified town founded by Julius Caesar (*Colonia Iulia Equestris*). Here, the **Roman Museum**, the **Lake Geneva Museum** (Musée du Léman) and the medieval **château** with its **Porcelain Museum** are well worth visiting.

The attractive little town of **Rolle**, situated on the lake itself, developed around the 13th-century **château** built

Château Vufflens, a private castle in the Morges countryside.

by Savoy count Amadeus V. On an island in the harbour there is an obelisk, a monument to Vaud freedom-fighter Frédéric César de Laharpe, who was also a tutor at the court of the Tsar. **Morges** also has a Savoyard château, which today houses the **Musée militaire vaudois**. The **Musée Forel** contains furniture and tapestries.

Cosmopolitan and rural mix: Anyone visiting **Lausanne** (pop. 130,000, 250,000 including suburbs), the capital of canton Vaud, can start at the harbour, at Château Vidy, the seat of the **International Olympic Committee**. After a tour of the ruins of the Roman harbour city of *Lousanna*, proceed to the medieval part of town.

A bishop of the Helvetians established a settlement on the easily-defendable hills above Lake Geneva when he was forced to give up his residence in Aventicum. He built a **château**, which still serves as a seat of government to this day. The **cathedral**, consecrated in 1275 in the presence of both the emperor and the pope, is considered one of the most beautiful early Gothic buildings anywhere in Switzerland.

But back to the lake. In the harbour of the former fishing village of **Ouchy** lies the brigantine *La Vaudoise*, a reminder of the time when hundreds of freighters with crossed lateen sails used to sail across the lake bringing rock from Meillerie on the opposite, Savoyard bank of the lake to use in the construction of Geneva and Lausanne.

At the *embarcadère* (quayside), where steamers have been mooring since 1823, a fountain decorated with stone asses' heads bears a mysterious inscription: "*En souvenir de l'Académie d'Ouchy*". Did this fishing village have its own academy? The answer is no: the "Académie d'Ouchy" was the name given to the columns of donkeys and pack mules that used to carry the construction material from the freighters up to Lausanne. As the caravan of animals made its way through the vineyards, students and townspeople, in a mocking reference to the professors who went in procession through Lausanne, would jeer: "*Voilà l'Académie d'Ouchy!*"

The rack railway is somewhat ambitiously referred to as the "Métro" (the former funicular is still popularly referred to as *la ficelle*, the string), but another way up to the **cathedral** in the old town is on foot. It is not for the faint-hearted and the people of Lausanne are kept fit by all the stair-climbing they are required to do.

From 10 in evening till two in the morning, just after the cathedral bell rings the hour, a rough male voice resounds through the vicinity: it is the watchman in the tower calling out the time, and calling for order. "*Il a sonné douze*," (it has struck 12) he shouts down from the tower; the long-drawn-out sound of each vowel echoes through the narrow streets.

Inside the cathedral, visitors can admire the stained glass of the rose window, whioch was built around 1240, the choir ambulatory, and the elegant pillars. The last king of Burgundy, Rudolf III, was crowned here. An Empire sarcophagus contains the mortal remains of Jean Abraham Davel, who tried to

The main portal of Lausanne Cathedral.

start a religious uprising against Berne in 1723 and was later executed.

In the autumn of every year, the national fair known as **Le Comptoir Suisse** is held. Visitors come to the exhibition from all over the world, elevating the occasion far above the purely commercial level. Bulls and cows are paraded in front of members of parliament and the government. Lausanne is as rural as it is olympic.

The best views over Lausanne are to be had from **Signal de Lausanne**, above the town; nearby is the **Ermitage Museum** (exhibitions change regularly). Other museums include: the **Musée de l'art brut**, a unique collection of works by fringe artists, the **Musée de L'Elysée** in Ouchy (photography), and the nearby **Olympic Museum**.

Beyond Lausanne, the wine region of **Lavaux** begins. The picturesque villages and small towns of the region nestle among vineyards on the terraced slopes or down by the lake itself. In fact, to get to **Vevey**, there is a choice of two routes: either along the lake, or further up, along the side of the valley. In the two large wine-growing regions of the Côte and Lavaux, carefully plotted vineyard routes and hiking trails lead to winegrowers' cellars (*caveaux*) and village inns (*pintes*).

In the *caveaux*, whether in **Mont-sur-Rolle**, **Aubonne**, **Epesses**, **St Saphorin**, **Chardonne** or elsewhere, winegrowers will offer wine accompanied by *saucisson* (sausage) with pickled onions and cheese. In the village inns one can find delicious ham, cabbage sausage (*saucisses aux choux*) and fresh trout from the lake or – in **Vinzel** – *Malakoffs*, a kind of cheese doughnut made to a recipe said to have been brought back by veterans from the Crimean War.

The journey continues to **Montreux**, the world-famous spa. The climate here is exceptionally mild, as the palm trees and camelias lining the lake's promenade testify. The town draws people from all over the world.The busiest times to be here are during the annual **Jazz Festival** and the TV competition for

The harbour at Lutry.

"the Golden Rose of Montreux". Mountain cable railways lead to **Caux**, and to the **Rochers de Naye**, where one gets a magnificent panoramic view of the whole of Lake Geneva.

The big attraction for most visitors, though, is probably the **Château de Chillon**, fortified by the counts of Savoy, and captured by Berne in 1536; beneath the château lies the underground dungeon of François Bonivard, a lay prior from Geneva who was set free when the Bernese came (Lord Byron wrote *The Prisoner of Chillon*, his romantic poem about him, in Lausanne, in 1817). This has made the château one of Switzerland's most popular tourist destinations.

The town of **Vevey**, founded in the Middle Ages, is the headquarters of the international firm Nestlé. The Nestlé **Alimentarium** is an attractively laid-out museum on the theme of food and nutrition, which helps their image and publicity. A visit to the **Musée du Vieux Vevey**, a charming town museum, is also highly recommended. The neighbouring town of **Corsier** contains the grave of Charlie Chaplin. Only four or five times a century (roughly every 25 years), Vevey celebrates its **wine festival**, the *Fête des Vignerons*, and it is famed far and wide.

La Fête des Vignerons: Annual grape-harvest festivals take place in **Lutry**, **Morges**, and **Russin** (Geneva) but Vevey's *Fête des Vignerons* leaves the rest standing. This unique wine festival was celebrated in the last century in 1905, 1927, 1955, 1977 and 1999. The date of the next festival has yet to be fixed. Its songs are sung by choral societies and its main personalities are treated like film stars. Charlie Chaplin, who settled in Corsier, near Vevey, after suffering political persecution in the US, said of the wine festival in 1955: "The finest thing I saw in Europe".

The roots of the festival go back to the Middle Ages, before the Bernese occupation. The winemakers' guild – known then as "the worshipful abbey of St Urban", and in revolutionary times by the somewhat more prosaic name of

Field of daffodils in Les Pléiades near Montreux.

"agricultural union" – supervised wine production and awarded prizes to the best workers in the vineyards. The prize-winning vintners were then led in a parade – known as "*pourminade*" (Promenade) – through the town of Vevey, annually first of all, and then at longer intervals.

In 1730 the event broadened into a celebration of Bacchus, the Roman god of wine, portrayed in the parade by a boy on a barrel. From then on the procession evolved into a performance reminiscent of Bacchanalian frolics mixewd with medieval Mysteries. The figure of Bacchus was followed by fauns and bacchants, then by a further deity, Ceres, the earth mother, then Noah from the Old Testament, and finally the shepherd goddess Pales.

Since 1905 the guard of honour has been led by the fifes and drums from musicianbs from Basel and from herdsmen from Gruyère. Haunting cowherd melodies have become just as much a part of everything as the Lauterbach waltz and *Allons danser sous les ormeaux* a song written by Jean-Jacques Rousseau.

Those people of Lake Geneva who witnessed the wine festival in 1999 will never forget it, and it will certainly give them something to look forward to when the next one is announced. First, the wine guild's banner with the monastic slogan *Ora et Labora* (pray and work) was carried down to the lake; then halberd and pike bearers marched in; and then came the banners of the cantons, at which point the vintners were awarded their prizes, just as in days gone by. When all this serious ceremonial was out of the way, the Festival King, a figure resplendent in gold, signalled the beginning of the merry-making.

Skiing and salt mines: The **Vaud Alps** contain a number of winter health spas, most notably **Villars-sur-Ollon** (an excellent hiking area in the summer), **Les Diablerets** (cable car leading up to the **Diablerets Glacier**, 2,940 metres/ 9,600 ft above sea level), and **Château d'Oex** (mountain cheese dairy). Less health-conscious visitors may prefer the

La Tour-de-Peilz, a countryside château .

winemaking centres along the Rhône Valley, such as **Aigle** (château with winemaking museum) and **Yvorne**. Most of the region – the town and dominions of Aigle (or Älen in German) – was captured by the city-republic of Berne in 1475 during the Burgundian wars and was the first French-speaking part of Switzerland.

Such towns became particularly valuable when salt was discovered in the region in the 16th century. The saltworks of Bex and Aigle are still in use today, contributing to the town' wealth. They provide the salt for the canton of Vaud and for the chemical industry in Monthey, in the Valais.

In the Middle Ages, salt was as important as oil is today. An imperial decree bestowed on princes the right to manufacture salt (the so-called *Salzregal*), and Switzerland's cantons have had a monopoly on the salt trade to this day. Before the salt deposits in Bex were discovered, the republic of Berne used to get its salt from Venice, and from saltworks in the Franche Comté region of Western France. Today, the **Bex Saltworks** are a tourist attraction: visitors travel on a railway through the tunnels, halls and corridors through which the brine (rock salt solution) is pumped out of the mountain. The salt deposits are estimated to amount to 10 million tons.

For six years, poet and all-round scholar Albrecht von Haller was director of the saltworks for Aigle, and for two years he was in charge of it. Haller's poems – particularly an early work of his called "The Alps" – heralded an interest in nature that reached its climax with Rousseau.

In **Aigle**, Haller wrote a scientific report on the saltworks, as well as a book of law for the government; he drained the Rhône Valley (which he describes in one of his works), in order to combat the diseases carried by the marsh mosquitoes; and he regulated deforestation in the region, a process which, because of the large quantities of wood used in salt production, urgently needed control.

A wine festival in Vevey.

B. Curiger. Sc.
Wilhelm Tell

INSIGHT GUIDES

TRAVEL TIPS

CONTENTS

Getting Acquainted

The Place

Area: 41,285 sq. km (15,935 sq. miles)
Maximum distance: North-south 220 km (135 miles), east-west 348 km (215 miles)
Length of the border: 1,882 km (1,170 miles)
Population: 7,082,000 million (with 19.5 percent foreigners)
Capital: Berne (pop. 126,000)
Largest cities: Zurich (pop. 342,000), Geneva (172,000), Basel (170,000), Lausanne (116,000)
Languages: Swiss-German (63.7 percent), French (19.2 percent), Italian (7.6 percent), Romansch (0.6 percent), Other languages, 8.9 percent
Religion: Catholic (46.1 percent) Protestant (40 percent)
Currency: Swiss franc (SFr)
Time Zone: Central European Time (GMT + 1 hour, + 2 hours in summer)
International dialling code: 41 then 31 (Berne), 61 (Basel), 22 (Geneva), 21 (Lausanne), 1 (Zurich)

Climate

Because of its geographical location, Switzerland has a share of the four main climatic regions of Europe: continental, Mediterranean, sub-tropical and marine. Therefore, when travelling here, you should be prepared equally for both warm and cold spells. Don't forget a warm sweater, raincoat and umbrella, even at the height of summer, and likewise, sunglasses and suntan lotion even in the dead of winter.

When in Switzerland, for an **up-to-date weather report** dial 162; the report will be delivered in the language of the region you are calling from. Weather reports are also intermittently broadcast on Swiss radio and television. Since the Alps function as a climatic divide, weather broadcasts distinguish between the north side of the Alps, Southern Switzerland and the Engadine.

Geographical Statistics

Highest mountains
(All in Valais)
Monte Rosa 4,634 m (15,203 ft)
Dom 4,545 m (14,911 ft)
Weisshorn 4,506 m (14,783 ft)
Matterhorn 4,478 m (14,692 ft)
Dent Blanche 4,357 m (14,295 ft)

Longest rivers
Rhine (in Switzerland) 375 km (235 miles)
Aare 295 km (185 miles)
Rhône (in Switzerland) 264 km (165 miles)

Longest glaciers
Aletsch Glacier (Valais) 24 km (15 miles)
Gorner Glacier (Valais) 15 km (9 miles)

Largest lakes
Geneva 581 sq. km (224 sq. miles)
Constance 541 sq. km (208 sq. miles)
Neuchâtel 218 sq. km (84 sq. miles)
Maggiore 212 sq. km (81 sq. miles)
Lucerne 114 sq. km (44 sq. miles)
Zurich 90 sq. km (34 sq. miles)

Oddest Fact
Although it is surrounded on all sides by land, Switzerland maintains a fleet of some 30 ocean-going freighters. Rhine shipping barges make their way between Basel and the sea. The Rhine ports in Basel are the only harbours of international trade in Switzerland.

Government

Switzerland is a jigsaw puzzle composed of 23 cantons, three of which are further divided into half-cantons. Each of these can be compared to a small, sovereign country with its own government, parliament, laws and courts. The cantons themselves are composed of approximately 3,000 municipalities which are to a large degree autonomous. All these taken together are referred to as the Confederation Helvetica, whereby the mystery of the "CH" seen on Swiss cars is finally explained: the Swiss Confederation.

The confederation was established in the year 1291. Farmers from the mountain cantons of Uri, Schwyz and Unterwalden met together and swore they would come to each other's aid to defend their traditional rights against the mighty House of Habsburg. The idea of states uniting without sacrificing their sovereignty began to germinate. But the very first federal state as it exists today was not formed until 1848. Federalism served to guarantee the people their rights on all levels. Each municipality has the authority to regulate its own affairs concerning education, taxes, building regulations, etc., as it deems fit. The cantons have relinquished only a clearly designated part of their authority to the confederation. This includes matters dealing with foreign policy, national defence, guidelines concerning economic policies, currency, civil and penal legislation, postal and customs regulations as well as certain public services, for example the railway system.

The Federal Parliament comprises the National Council, made up of 200 representatives, and the Upper Chamber, composed of 46 representatives from the various cantons. Together, both houses form the legislature, known as the Federal Assembly. The executive branch is made up of a group of officials, i.e. seven federal councillors. Each of these councillors administers a specific department which corresponds to a ministry. The chair of the Federal Council is rotated annually and the responsibilities of a federal president are then incumbent upon the current first among equals. Swiss citizens reach voting age at 18 and from then on are eligible both to run for office and cast their votes on all federal issues.

The four different languages spoken in Switzerland reflect how full of variety the country is. Depending on where you are, you hear Romansch, French, Italian or Swiss-German (the official language is German). But don't think that as a traveller you'll have to have a command of all these languages; many Swiss people speak or understand at least one foreign language, usually English.

Economy

The Swiss economy has had to come to terms with two hard facts: the country has extremely limited natural resources and a quarter of its surface area is unproductive. Nevertheless, indigenous agriculture is able to produce more than half of what the entire country requires in the way of food. Switzerland is exclusively dependent on the importation of raw materials which are then transformed into high-quality products for export. Swiss industrial concerns have representatives on all five continents of the world. Of all industries, engineering is perhaps the most advanced with plants specialising in the production of energy, appliances and machine tools. Following on its heels are the pharmaceutical, textile and watch industries. And, of course, let's not forget to mention the food; lovers of Swiss cheese and chocolate can be found everywhere, from New York to Tokyo.

The service sector in Switzerland is essential. Banks and insurance companies are internationally active. The tourist and hotel industries keep more than 200,000 people busy and constitute one of the most significant employers in the country. Around 3.6 million people – 54 percent of the total population – are gainfully employed. Of these 6 percent work in agriculture and forestry, 30 percent in industry and 64 percent in the service sector.

International Organisations

In 1863 Henri Dumant founded the Red Cross, an international symbol and agent for brotherly love. Even today the headquarters of the International Committee of the Red Cross (ICRC) and the International Federation of the Red Cross are in Geneva. Other world-wide organisations, for example the International Labour Exchange (BIT) and the European Representative of the United Nations, have also established head offices in Switzerland.

Switzerland is a member of the Council of Europe, the General Agreement on Tariff and Trade (GATT), the Organization for Economic Cooperation and Development (OECD), and the United Nations Committee for Trade and Development (UNCTAD).

Business Hours

Business hours cited here apply to the different service industries. Keep in mind that there are local and regional deviations from this general pattern.

Shops are open daily 8 or 8.30am–6.30pm and on Saturday until 4pm. In many cities you'll find that most stores are closed on Monday mornings. Once a week shops are allowed to open until 9pm (generally on Thursday or Friday).

In smaller towns and outside city centres businesses are usually closed for one to two hours during lunchtime. In most holiday areas shops have longer hours and are sometimes even open for a few hours on Sunday.

In large cities banks and bureaux de change are open 8.30am–4.30pm Monday–Friday and closed on Saturday. In the country hours are 8.30am–noon and 1.30pm–4.30 or 5.30pm Monday–Friday, closed Saturday.

Bureaux de change situated in airports and railway stations will exchange foreign cash, travellers' cheques and Eurocheques for you at the current rate. They are open 6am–9 or 11pm. There are also currency-exchange machines at the main airports.

Post offices are open 7.30am–6.30pm and are closed in smaller towns from 12 noon–1.30pm. On Saturday they close at 11am. In bigger towns the main post office is often open until 9pm and for some hours on Saturday and Sunday.

Government and other official offices: 8am–noon and 2pm–5 or 6pm Monday–Friday.

In general museums are open at the following times: 10am–12 noon and 2–5pm Tuesday–Sunday. Some larger museums have also started opening during the evenings, while smaller and regional museums are sometimes only open half-days or on weekends. In any case, to avoid disappointment, it's a good idea to find out exact opening hours prior to setting off.

Planning the Trip

Visas & Passports

Travellers from other Western European countries are required to have a valid passport. Visitors from most Eastern European countries are required to have a visa. Those from the US, Canada, Australia and New Zealand must be in possession of a valid passport but do not need a visa.

Customs

Tourists are allowed to take the following goods into Switzerland duty and tax free:

Personal belongings, for example clothes, sports equipment, cameras, amateur movie and video cameras (along with films), musical instruments, camping equipment, etc. Tourists can bring in two hunting or sporting guns as long as they are taken out of the country upon departure. Each canton is responsible for making its own policies regarding the bearing of firearms within its perimeters.

Food for the journey, not exceeding what can normally be consumed in a single day. This regulation also applies to food stipulated for special diets, babies and pets.

Alcoholic beverages: up to 2 litres of 15° proof wine, beer, etc., or up to 1 litre of spirits exceeding 15° proof (most liqueurs, schnapps, etc.)

Tobacco products: 200 cigarettes or 50 cigars or 250 grams of pipe tobacco. Members of non-European countries are allowed to bring double (400 cigarettes or 100 cigars or 500 grams of pipe tobacco).

Alcoholic beverages and tobacco products may be imported into the country duty-free only when transported by persons at least 17 years old.

Articles to be given away as gifts as long as their total value does not exceed SFr 100 (persons under the age of 17 may bring in gifts valuing no more than SFr 50 in total). Travellers entering the country are permitted no more than 500 grams of butter per person.

The following regulations apply to bringing in meat and meat products: each person is allowed to take in daily no more than 500 grams of fresh horse meat, beef, mutton, lamb, goat or pork; up to 1 kg of meat products (such as ham, sausage, dried and canned meats) produced from the aforementioned animals; and not more than 2.5 kg of meat and meat products from rabbits, fowl, game, frogs, fish, crustaceans, molluscs and sea urchins.

Important: the import of pork from southern countries is strictly prohibited.

For further information about customs and special permission contact:
Swiss Customs head office (Eidgenössische Oberzolldirektion), Sektion Zollverfahren
Monbijoustrasse 40
CH-3003 Berne
Tel: 031-322 6511
Fax: 031-322 7872
Internet: www.zoll.admin.ch; also
Zolldirektion Basel
Tel: 061-287 1111; and
Zolldirektion Schaffhausen
Tel: 052-633 1111.

ANIMAL QUARANTINE

Travellers bringing cats and dogs into Switzerland must be prepared to present a certificate issued by a vet stating that the animal has been vaccinated against rabies within the last 12 months. The vaccination has to be given at least 30 days before entry, unless it is a re-vaccination.

These regulations apply also to cats and dogs which are taken out of the country temporarily. It is not necessary to provide an official certificate if you take your pet through Switzerland by rail or plane without stopping off.

Owners without the required documents for pets will be turned back at the border.

Parrots, budgies and rabbits may be taken into Switzerland only after having been granted permission by the Veterinary Federal Office (Bundesamt für Veterinärwesen, CH-3003 Bern, tel: 031-323 8509).

It is possible to take hamsters, guinea pigs, canaries and ornamental fish into Switzerland without certificates issued by a vet.

Invertebrates are also allowed to be taken into the country – with the exception of those intended for consumption and those which are under the CITES reglementation.

Money Matters

There is no limit regarding the amount of foreign currency, as well as other means of payment, travellers are permitted to take with them upon either entering or leaving Switzerland. The unit of currency in Switzerland is the Swiss franc (Schweizer Franken, SFr), with 100 Rappen (Rp) to a franc. There are 5, 10, 20 and 50 Rappen coins, and 1, 2 and 5 Franken coins. Notes are issued in 10, 20, 50, 100, 200 and 1,000 francs.

Travellers' cheques, foreign currency and other means of payment can be changed into Swiss money at banks, bureaux de change, train stations, airports, travel agencies and hotels. Most Swiss banks accept Eurocheques. Travellers can often settle their bills in hotels, shops, department stores and restaurants with foreign money. Ask for the rate of exchange; in most cases it will be slightly worse than the current rate. It is best to carry Swiss Bankers Travellers' Cheques issued in Swiss francs. You can use these as cash, and in Switzerland they can be exchanged free of charge.

Holidays & Events

TRADITIONAL EVENTS

There are numerous festival traditions throughout the year. Among them are the **Vogel Gryff** in Basel (January), the New Year's Eve **Kläuse** in Urnäsch near Appenzell (New Year's Eve and 13 January), **Carnival** (**Fasnacht**) in Basel and Lucerne (February and March). In the Lötschen Valley there are the terrifying masks of "Dirty Thursday" and the "Good Lord's Grenadier" (the **Feast of Corpus Christi**); in the Engadine, **Chalanda Marz** with its ringing chimes (1 March); and in Mendrisio, the **Good Friday Procession**. The **Sechseläuten** in Zurich takes place in April and the **Swiss National Day** on 1 August. **Marché-Concours** is celebrated in Saignelégier, where every August hundreds of horses bred in the Franches-Montagnes are paraded through the streets. There are **grape-growing festivals** in Neuchâtel, Lutry, Morges, Lugano and many other lake villages, the **Claus Hunt** in Küssnacht on Rigi and in Arth (6 December), and the **Escalade** in Geneva (around 11 December).

Public Holidays

New Year's Day (1 January), **Good Friday**, **Easter Monday**, **Ascension Day**, **Whit Monday**, **National Day** (1 August), **Christmas Day** and **Boxing Day**. In addition to these there are many regional holidays.

TRADE FAIRS

The **Swiss Sample Trade Fair**, the art fair **Art** and the **European Watch and Jewellery Trade Fair**, held in Basel in March and April, are the biggest of the annual fairs. Contacts throughout the world are renewed and strengthened at these fairs. The **BEA** in Berne (at the end of April), the **Comptoir Suisse** in September in Lausanne and the **OLMA** in October in St Gallen are orientated towards trade and agriculture.

Swiss Tourism Offices Abroad

UK: Swiss Centre
Swiss Court
London W1V 8EE
Tel: (0)20-7734 1921
Fax: (0)20-7437 4577
Internet:
dino.dulio@switzerlandvacation.ch
US: Swiss Center
608 Fifth Avenue
New York 10020, NY
Tel: (0)212-757 5944
Fax: (0)212-262 6116
Internet:
joseph.buhler@switzerlandtourism.com
222 North Sepulveda Blvd
Suite 1570, El Segundo
Los Angeles CA 90245
Tel: (0)310-335 0125
Fax: (0)310-335 0131
Internet:
roland.ottiger@switzerlandtourism.com
CAN: 926 The East Mall
Etobicoke (Toronto) Ontario M9B 6K1
Tel: (0)416-695 2090
Fax: (0)416-695 2774
Internet.
fritz.lauber@switzerlandtourism.com
AUS: Brian Sinclair-Thompson
c/o Swissair, 33 Pitt Street
Level 8, NSW 2000 Sydney
Tel: (0)2-9231 3744
Fax: (0)2-9351 6531
Internet: swissair@tiasnet.com.au

Swiss Embassies Abroad

UK: 16–18 Montagu Place
London W1H 2BQ
Tel: 020-7616 6000
Fax: 020-7724-7001.
US: 2900 Cathedral Avenue N.W.
Washington, DC 20008-3499
Tel: 202-745 7900
Fax: 202-387 2564 (Embassy)
633 3th Avenue, 3th floor
New York NY 10017-6706
Tel: (0)212-599 5700
Fax: (0)212-599 4266 (General Consulate).
Canada: 5 Avenue Marlborough
Ottawa, Ontario K1N 8E6
Tel: (0)613-235 1837
Fax (0)613-563 1394.
Australia: 7 Merlbourne Avenue
Forest/Canberra A.C. T2603
Tel. (0)2-6273-3977
Fax: (0)2-6273-3428

Getting There

Because it is geographically in the very heart of the continent, Switzerland has always been a crossroads for the great European thoroughfares and it is easy to reach.

BY AIR

There are five international airports in Switzerland: in Zurich, Geneva, Basel, Lugano and Berne. Swissair and Crossair, the two main Swiss airlines, connect 163 cities with 78 countries. The airports in Zurich and Geneva have their own train stations which are part of the national fast-train network. In both these cities there are several trains each hour running between the airport and the main railway station. The Basel-Mulhouse airport is actually situated in France; the journey by bus from there to the Swiss train station in Basel takes about 25 minutes. There are regular connections between the Zurich, Basel and Geneva international airports. Regular and charter airlines as well as local air-taxi services fly in and out of the Berne-Belp, Lugano-Agno, Gstaad-Saanen, Sion and Samedan-St Moritz airfields.

With "Fly-Rail Baggage", train passengers don't have to lug their baggage around the airport any more. Instead, it is unloaded from the plane on to a train and forwarded directly to its destination point (in 117 train stations, mostly in cities and the larger holiday resort areas). The same service applies for the return trip: you can send your baggage – up to 24 hours in advance – directly through to your hometown airport from the town where you've been staying.

Travellers may also check in at 24 train stations (including Basel, Berne, Geneva, Lausanne, Lugano, Lucerne, Neuchâtel, St Gallen and Zurich) and obtain a boarding pass up to 24 hours prior to departure.

Further information regarding Fly-Rail services, plane and railway timetables can be found in the **Fly-Rail Brochure**, available at every train station in Switzerland.

The national carrier is **Swissair**. Its offices abroad include:
UK: Swiss Centre
3 New Coventry Street
London W1V 8EE
Reservations
Tel: 020-7434 7300
Fax: 020-7434 7219.
US: 628 Fifth Avenue
New York, NY 10020
Tel: 800-221 4750
Fax: 212-969 5747; and
222 Sepulveda Blvd
15th Floor El Segundo
California 90245
Tel: 800-221 6644
Fax: 310-335 5935.

Tour Operators

All local **Swiss Tourist Offices** (*see page 319*) are also tour operators. Other good tour operators can be contacted on 0900 55 2000 (**Switzerland Tourism Call Center**) and, in England, the **Switzerland Travel Centre**, tel: (0)20-7734-1921.

BY TRAIN

Comfortable Intercity trains connect Switzerland with all larger cities in the surrounding countries. These trains have comfortable first and second class compartments and leave every hour. For further information contact one of the Swiss Tourist Information Centres (ST), located in many European countries and overseas. From the ST you can also obtain the latest train schedules as well as the following travel tickets:

Discount **Gruppenfahrkarten** (group tickets), for groups with 10 or more members.

Swiss Pass: a personal network ticket issued for 4, 8 or 15 days, 1 month, or for 3 out of 15 days (referred to as a **Flexipass**) which enables its bearer unlimited mileage on railways, post buses and boats (and in 30 cities and towns on buses and trams too).

The **Swiss Card** is good for a round trip ticket from one of the Swiss borders or airports to a holiday resort area located in Switzerland. The Swiss Card – which is valid for a month – also gives 50 percent reduction on all other journeys you make.

The **Swiss Half Fare Card** offers 50 percent reduction on normal tariffs for trains, boats and mail buses throughout Switzerland.

BY CAR

Travellers can enter Switzerland by car from all neighbouring countries after passing through border customs, located on main thoroughfares (primarily along motorways). In addition to the major border customs, there are numerous, smaller borders which can be crossed, but keep in mind that these may not be open around the clock.

Motor vehicles weighing up to 3.5 tons (including trailers and caravans) are charged a flat tax of SFr 40 per year for what is commonly referred to as the "motorway vignette" (a sticker you place on your windscreen that permits you to drive on Swiss motorways). This is valid from 1 December to 31 January (14 months). They can be purchased at borders, post offices, petrol stations and garages in Switzerland and in other countries from automobile associations and Swiss Tourist Information Centres. The sticker should be fixed to the left edge of the vehicle's front windscreen. Hire cars come with a valid sticker.

Swiss Touring Club (TCS)
Chemin de Blandonnet 4
CH-1214 Genève-Vernier
Tel: 022-417 2727
Fax: 022-417 2020.
Swiss Automobile Club (ACS)
Wasserwerkgasse 39
CH-3000 Berne 13
Tel: 031-328 3111
Fax: 031-311 0310.
Oberzolldirektion
Monbijoustrasse 40
CH-3003 Berne
Tel: 031-322 6511
Fax: 031-322 6511.

SPECIAL DEALS

The brochure *Schweiz-Ferien für junge Leute* (Swiss Holidays for Young People) contains a comprehensive and indispensable wealth of information for all young people visiting Switzerland. You can pick up a copy at the tourist office along with other valuable information pertaining to special discount fares on public transport, in youth hostels, holiday camps, private schools, universities and language schools. Or visit the internet site at www.schweizferien.ch/youth

Swiss public transport services and various hotels offer price reductions to senior citizens. For more information, get a copy of the brochure *Saison für Senioren* (Season for Seniors) from the tourist office.

The *Swiss Museum Passport* enables visitors to gain free entry into more than 180 museums throughout Switzerland (*see Museums, page 331*).

Specialist Holidays

Adventure holidays

For canyoning, biking, skating, river-rafting, climbing, etc., contact:
Eurotrek
Freischützgasse 3
CH-8021 Zurich
Tel: 01-295 5555
Fax: 01/295 5640.
Adventure World
Rosshag
3812 Wilderswil bei Interlaken
Tel: 033-826 7711
Fax: 033/826 7715.

Skiing

Swiss Ski School Information
Tel: 081-854 0777.

Holidays with Children

The brochure *Ferienspass mit Kindern* (Holiday Fun with Children) is obtainable at the tourist office.

Farm Holidays

Holidays spent on the farm have been increasing in popularity. Such down-to-earth holidays offer the best opportunity to get to know the country and its inhabitants and are especially suitable for families with children. The brochure *Ferien auf dem Bauernhof* (Holiday on the Farm) is obtainable at the tourist office. Further information is also available from the following organisations:

Schweizerische Reisekasse (Reka)
Swiss Farm Holidays
Neuengasse 15, CH-3001 Berne
Tel: 031-329 6633
Fax: 031-329 6601.

Office du Tourisme Rural de Suisse Romande
CH-1530 Payerne
Tel: 026-662 6700
Fax: 026-660-7126 (in western Switzerland).

Pro Emmental
Schlossstrasse 3, CH-3550 Langnau
Tel: 034-402 4252
Fax: 034-402 4253 (in the wonderful farm region of Emmental near Berne).

Graubünden-Ferien (Graubünden Tourist Association)
Alexanderstrasse 24
CH-7001 Chur
Tel: 081-302 6100
Fax: 081-302 1414 (in the canton of Graubünden).

Holiday Courses

Courses are offered in practically every kind of sport. Those less interested in athletic endeavours can choose from a wide variety of courses focusing on practical, creative or cultural topics including theatre, dance, music, mime, art, crafts or cooking. For more information contact the tourist office.

Practical Tips

Media

TELEVISION AND RADIO

Television and radio in Switzerland are of a fairly high standard both technically and with regard to content, in particular the news. Swiss television has stations in German, French and Italian. There are also local television stations in some of the larger cities.

In all of the bigger cities and the major hotels and holiday resorts you can receive foreign television stations such as BBC World, CNN and others.

As well as the official Swiss radio stations there are many local stations, from which you may be able to glean information concerning your holiday destination. **Radio Switzerland International** has sections in many foreign languages, including English.

PRINT

The Swiss newspaper *Blick* can be found everywhere, from the largest city to the smallest village, as well as in most restaurants and bars. Daily newspapers of a superior quality include the *Neue Zürcher Zeitung*, which is held in high esteem abroad, the *Tagesanzeiger*, and many local and regional newspapers, such as *Luzerner Zeitung*, *Basler Zeitung*, and *Berner Zeitung*. In French-speaking Switzerland the most important daily newspaper is *Le Temps*.

In the cities and bigger holiday resorts you will find the usual selection of foreign newspapers and magazines.

Telecommunications

Telecommunications in Switzerland are very good. The dialling code from abroad into Switzerland is ++41. From Switzerland to other countries the dialling code is 0044 (England), 001 (US and Canada) and 0061 (Australia). Be careful when using hotel telephones: the charge, especially when you are calling abroad, is much higher than from elsewhere. Be aware also that some public telephones no longer accept small change. It is easier to use phone cards, which are available at post offices, train stations and some kiosks for 10 or 20 francs. The basic fee for using older public telephones is 60 Rappen. Generally, charges are much lower at the weekend and from 5–7pm and 9pm–8am on weekdays. Mobile phones – D1 and D2 – are widely used, although the reception is often bad in mountainous regions. While driving, you may use only hands-free mobile phones.

Some important telephone numbers:
Swiss Information Service: 111
Police Emergency: 117
Tourist Bulletin (summer)/Ski Report (winter): 120 (during the summer, tourist-related reports are issued on events of general interest as well as information on tours and excursions).
Road Aid: 140
Weather Report: 162
Road Conditions: 163
Avalanche Bulletin (winter)/Wind Predictions and Pollen Bulletin (summer): 187 (during winter an avalanche bulletin is announced by the Federal Institute for Snow and Avalanche Research, Weissfluhjoch-Davos).

Most hotels have fax machines and at every post office you can send and receive mail by fax.

Local Tourist Offices

Listed below are the local tourist offices responsible for cities, cantons and bigger regions. There are, in addition, local tourist offices in every holiday region and many

smaller villages, specialising in their own particular area.
Basel: Basel Tourismus, Schifflände 5, CH-4001 Basel, tel: 061-268 6868; fax: 061-268 6870.
Berne and Swiss Mittelland: Bern Tourismus, Railway Station, 3001 Berne, tel: 031-328 1228; fax: 031-311 1222.
Bernese Oberland: Berner Oberland Tourismus, Jungfraustrasse 38, 3800 Interlaken, tel: 033-823 0303; fax: 033-823 0330.
Bernese Jura: Office du Tourisme du Jura Bernois, 26 Avenue de la Liberté, 2740 Moutier, tel: 032-493 6466; fax: 032-493 6156.
Eastern Switzerland: Tourist Information St. Gallen, Bahnhofplatz 1a, 9001 St Gallen, tel: 071-227 3737; fax: 071-227 3767.
Fribourg: Info Pays de Fribourg, Restoroute de la Gruyère, 1644 Avry-devant-Pont, tel: 026-915 9292; fax: 026-915 9299.
Geneva: Genève Tourisme, World Trade Center, 1201 Geneva, tel: 022-929 7000; fax: 022-929 7011.
Graubünden: Graubünden Ferien, Alexanderstrasse 24, 7000 Chur, tel: 081-254 2424; fax: 081-254 2400.
Inner Switzerland: Tourist Information, Frankenstrasse 1, 6002 Lucerne, tel: 041-410 7171; fax: 041-410 7334.
Jura: Jura Tourisme, Rue de la Gruère 1, 2350 Saignelégier, tel: 032-952 1952; fax: 032-952 1955.
Lake Geneva Region: Office du Tourisme du Canton de Vaud, Case Postale 164, 1000 Lausanne, tel: 021-613 2626; fax: 021-613 2620.
Neuchâtel: Tourisme Neuchâtelois, Hôtel des Postes, 2001 Neuchâtel, tel: 032-889 6890; fax: 032-889 6296.
Northwestern Switzerland: Baden Tourismus, Bahnhofstrasse 50, 5400 Baden, tel: 056-22 53 18; fax: 056-222 5320.
Ticino: Ticino Tourismo, Casella Postale 1441, 6501 Bellinzona, tel: 091-825 7056; fax: 091-825 3614.
Valais: Wallis Tourismus, Rue Pré-Fleuri 6, 1951 Sion, tel: 027-327 3570; fax: 027-327 3571.
Zurich: Zürich Tourismus, Bahnhofbrücke 1, 8023 Zurich, tel: 01-215 4000; fax: 01-214 4044.
All local tourist offices are also tour operators.

Consulates and Embassies

UK: *Embassy/Consulate*, Thunstrasse 50, 3000 Berne 15, tel: 031-359 7741. *Consulate*, Rue de Vermont 37–39, 1202 Geneva, tel: 022-918 2422. *Consulate*, Via Sorengo 22, 6900 Lugano, tel: 091-950 0606.
US: *Embassy/Consulate*, Jubiläumsstrasse 93, 3001 Berne, tel: 031-357 7011. *Consulate*, Rout de Pré-Bois 29, 1216 Geneva-Cointrin, tel: 022-798 1615.
CAN: *Embassy/Consulate*, Kirchenfeldstrasse 88, 3000 Bern 6, tel: 031-357 3200. *Consulate*, Rue de l'Ariane 5, 1202 Geneva, tel. 022-919 9200.
AUS: *Embassy/Consulate*, Chemin de Fins 2, 1218 Geneva/Grand-Saconnex, tel: 022-799 9100. *Consulate*, Via Pretorio 7, 6900 Lugano, tel: 091-923 5681.

Travellers with Disabilities

Contact **Mobility International Schweiz** at Froburgstrasse 4, 4601 Olten, tel: 062-206 8835; fax: 062-206 8839. There are several tourist guides available for travellers with disabilities, including a useful guide to easy-access accommodation and restaurants (with 600 hotels and places to eat), and a hiking information brochure for those with mobility difficulties.
Natilus Reisen, Froburgstrasse 4, 4601 Olten, tel: 062-206 8830; fax: 062-206 8839 arranges holidays for the disabled from various tour operators and also organises travel tours.
Cato, Scheuchzerstrasse 14, 8006 Zurich, tel: 01-350 3175; fax: 01-350 3177 specialises in activty holidays and guided group tours for the disabled with or without able-bodied company.
Travelin' Talk, Wiesenstrasse 3, 8400 Winterthur, tel: 042-222 2288 is a self-help organisation covering Europe, with a travel network for the traveller with disabilities.

A brochure detailing wheelchair-friendly cable railways and other public transport to the mountains is available at the **Switzerland Tourism** tourist offices (*for addresses, see page 317*). A list of ski schools with professional company for the disabled is available at **Schweizerischer Zentralverein für das Blindenwesen**, Schützengasse 4, 9000 St. Galen, tel: 071-223 3636; fax: 071-222 7318.

Tipping

Officially in Switzerland all services are included in the price, but it is wide-spread practice to honour good service by tipping. In restaurants, the bill is normally rounded up to the next franc for snacks, and two or three francs extra is usual for a dinner.

Medical Treatment

The quality of medical treatment in Switzerland is very high. In case of emergency, go to the **nearest doctor** or to the **Emergency Station** in the nearest hospital. To call an ambulance, dial 144. Every city and the larger villages have a number for an emergency doctor. This can be found in local newspapers or on the general information number 111, which can also give you the addresses and phone numbers of the nearest 24-hour pharmacies.

Security and Crime

In comparison with other countries, Switzerland is very safe and there is very little crime. Nevertheless, it is better not to walk at night-time in some parts of the bigger cities. Ask for advice at your hotel or in the tourist office. Pickpocketing can happen in crowded places, such as on public transport and in supermarkets, so be attentive. The **police emergency number** everywhere is 117.

Getting Around

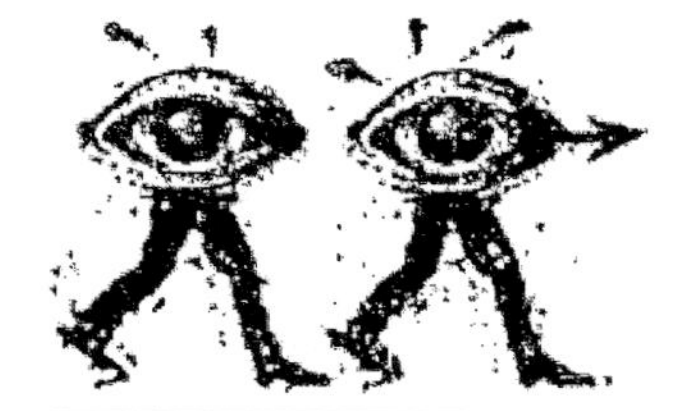

Public Transport

Switzerland maintains an extensive transportation network. Nearly every area can be reached comfortably by train, post bus or boat. Many mountains can be reached by rail (*see below*).

If you're travelling in Switzerland you can buy the **Offizielle Schweizer Kursbuch**, in which you will find timetables of all railways, post buses and boats. In addition to general information on up-to-date offers and railway services, it also contains guidance on the most important connections to foreign countries.

Where there are no rail services, hop on one of the yellow buses owned by the **Swiss Postal Service**. These vehicles not only serve the most remote areas (for example, Juf, the highest village in Europe that is inhabited year-round, located at 2,126 metres/7,087 ft), but will also make additional journeys.

Regularly scheduled **boats** cruise all the big lakes. There are also **steamships** to put you in a nostalgic mood on Lake Geneva, Lake Zurich, Lake Brienz and Lake Lucerne. It's also possible to take a trip along the Rhine, Rhône, Aare and Doubs rivers.

MOUNTAIN RAILWAYS

There are around 500 mountain railways that bring tourists quickly and comfortably into the mountain world. Included among these are **rack-railways**, **funicular railways**, **cable cars** and **chair-lifts**, as well as **alpine underground railways** (eg, the Metro-Alpin in Saas Fee). On these, you can travel inside the mountain to an elevation of almost 4,000 metres (13,333 ft). Timetables are available in railway stations and at local tourist information centres.

BY TRAIN

Thanks to regular departures, you won't have to wait very long for a train, even if you are travelling right into Switzerland. Intercity, rapid and regional trains have direct connections to all cities and most holiday resort regions; certain trains travel directly to Swiss holiday areas. **Die Züge** leave every hour, and sometimes every half-hour between the major cities such as Zurich-Berne, Zurich-Lucerne, Bern-Lausanne, Geneva-St-Gall.

There are approximately 86 trains with dining cars and 325 trains with mini-bars in operation every day. If you plan to travel in a large party or during mealtimes, you'd be wise to reserve a table in advance from the **Swiss Dining Car Association**, Zurich, tel: 01-444 5111; fax: 01-271 6456.

Private Transport

RULES OF THE ROAD

Speed Limits

On all country roads the maximum speed is 80 kph (50 mph); on motorways 120 kph (75 mph); within city limits 50 kph (30 mph).

Safety Regulations

Wearing a seat-belt is mandatory and children under the age of 12 must sit in the back seat. Motorcyclists are required by law to wear helmets. Driving while the alcohol level in your bloodstream exceeds 0.8 mg per millilitre is illegal.

Formalities

If you plan to enter Switzerland by car, you are required to be in possession of a passport, a motor vehicle registration and a valid national driver's licence.

Filling Stations

At many filling stations along the motorways as well as in cities you'll find machines which accept Swiss notes. These enable you to purchase petrol around the clock with 10 and 20 SFr notes. Prices vary depending on the international fuel market and the location of a particular petrol station. For instance, prices may be higher in mountainous regions.

Police

As their different uniforms and patrol cars indicate, Swiss police are organised regionally, by canton. Speed (by radar) and blood-alcohol-level controls are common .

Parking Places

It is becoming more common for motor vehicles to be banned from city centres, and the number of pedestrian zones is increasing. It's wise to leave your car somewhere on the city outskirts or in a car park. If you want to leave your car in the city centre, there are some short-stay parking areas (from half an hour to a few hours) with parking meters. These only accept small change, so it is useful to carry 20 Rappen (cents), 50 Rappen, and 1 Franc coins with you.

Road traffic queries can be answered by:

Swiss Touring Club (TCS)
Chemin de Blandonnet 4
CH-1214 Genève-Vernier
Tel: 022-417 2727
Fax: 022-417 2020.

Swiss Automobile Club (ACS)
Wasserwerkgasse 39
CH-3000 Berne 13
Tel: 031-328 3111
Fax: 031-311 0310.

Federal Traffic Police
Bundesamt für Polizeiwesen
Abt. Strassenverkehr
Bundesrain 20, 3003 Berne
Tel: 031-322 1111
Fax: 031-322 5380.

CAR RENTAL

There are car rental agencies in all cities of any size, so you'll have no trouble renting a vehicle. In the larger train stations tourists travelling by rail can take advantage of the automobile rental service operated by the Swiss Federal Railways.

Road Information

For information on road conditions in Switzerland (for instance whether or not a road is passable, whether or not ice is present, etc.), tel: 01-163 (German), 022-163 (French), 091-163 (Italian).

You can tune into Swiss radio traffic reports issued by the police after the regular news every half hour on the hour and at half past.

During winter, information on road conditions is read out daily at 5.30am, 6.30am, 7.30am and 12.15 pm Monday–Saturday, and forecasts for the coming night are broadcast daily after the 6pm and 10pm newscasts. Foreseeable traffic obstructions registered by the police (construction sites, detours, etc.) are announced after the news report at 5.30am, 6.30am, 7.30am and 12.15 pm.

BREAKDOWNS

Foreign car drivers can dial 140 (the same telephone number applies throughout Switzerland) for help in the case of a breakdown. One of the five action centres of the Swiss Touring Club (TCS) will answer your call and put you in touch with the closest repair shop or mobile help. If you are in possession of a letter of safe conduct, issued by your own automobile association, breakdown aid will be delivered free of charge by the TCS Road Patrol. There are emergency telephones positioned on the highways at 1.6-km (1-mile) intervals. You'll also find TCS and ACS (Swiss Automobile Club) emergency telephones along remote stretches on pass roads.

In the case of an accident resulting in injury, it is mandatory to inform the police. If there are no injuries but damage is done to a vehicle it is still advisable but not obligatory to call the police. Throughout Switzerland dialling 117 will connect you with the police.

SPECIAL REGULATIONS

Private vehicles with studded tyres are permitted on country roads only between 1 November and 31 March. Such vehicles are forbidden to drive on motorways and major thoroughfares (clearly designated as Autobahn or Autostrasse).

There are special regulations that apply specifically to trailers, caravans and boats. Further information is available from automobile associations or from the Swiss customs officials posted at the borders.

Emergency Numbers

In case of an accident, dial 144 to alert ambulances and other emergency vehicles.
TCS emergency centre: 140
Police: 117
Fire: 118
Swiss Helicopter Patrol: 1414

Tunnels & Passes

ROAD TUNNELS

The Great St Bernard Tunnel (5.8 km/3.6 miles) connects Valais to the Aosta Valley (in Italy). The price of the toll is contingent upon the type of vehicle you are driving and starts at SFr27. If the return trip is made within 30 days cars are awarded a 30 percent discount, buses 20 percent. It is also possible to purchase a booklet containing several toll tickets.

The Munt la Schera Tunnel (3.5 km/2.2 miles) between Zernez and Livigno (in Italy) is open 8am–8pm. One way tickets for private cars are SFr5, plus SFr2 for each occupant.

It is necessary to obtain a *motorway vignette* for passage through the St Gotthard Tunnel (connecting Inner Switzerland to the Ticino, 16.8 km/10.5 miles) and for the highway leading to the San Bernardino Tunnel (between Graubünden and Ticino, 6.6 km/4.2 miles). You will not have to pay additional fees inside the tunnel.

CARS ON TRAINS

Cars are transported through Alpine railway tunnels according to a timetable. Additional trains are employed during Christmas and Easter holidays.

Albula tunnel, Thusis-Samedan, up to 10 daily departures.

Furka tunnel, Oberwald-Realp, up to 16 daily departures.

Lötschberg tunnel, Kandersteg-Goppenstein, up to 31 daily departures.

Oberalp tunnel, Andermatt-Sedrun, up to 4 daily departures.

For Albula and Oberalp it is essential to call the embarkation train stations in advance and make a reservation for your car:
Albula: Thusis 081-651 1113 Samedan 081-852 5404
Oberalp: Andermatt 041-887 1220; Sedrun 081-949 1137
Furka: Realp 041-887 1446; Oberwald 027-973 1141
Lötschberg: Kandersteg 033-675 1253; Goppenstein 027-939 1702). At all other embarkation stations it is not possible to reserve in advance.

Further information on schedules and prices (including those applicable to buses, trailers, motorcyclists, etc.) can be obtained at Swiss Tourist Information centres or railway stations.

In order to spare car drivers a time-consuming journey to their holiday destination, European railways offer **Transport Trains for Cars**, with sleepers and/or couchettes.

MOUNTAIN PASSES

These are the months when the following mountain passes are passable:
Albula
(2,312 metres, 7,586ft)
Tiefencastel-La Punt, June–Oct.

Bernina
(2,328 metres, 7,638ft)
Pontresina-Poschiavo, all year (in winter mostly closed at night).
Brünig
(1,008 metres, 3,307ft)
Meiringen-Sachseln, all year.
Croix
(1,778 metres, 5,834ft)
Villars-Les Diablerets, May-Nov.
Flüela
(2,383 metres, 7,819ft)
Davos-Susch, April-Nov (in winter mostly closed at night).
Forclaz
(1,526 metres, 5,007ft)
Martigny-Le Châtelard, all year.
Furka
(2,431 metres, 7,976ft)
Gletsch-Andermatt, June-Oct.
Great St Bernard
(2,469 metres, 8,100ft)
Martigny-Aosta, June-Oct (tunnel passage open all year).
Grimsel
(2,165 metres, 7,103ft)
Meiringen-Gletsch, June-Oct.
Il Fuorn
(2,149 metres, 7,051ft)
Zernez-Santa Maria, all year.
Jaun
(1,509 metres, 4,951ft)
Boltigen-Bulle, all year.
Julier
(2,284 metres, 7,494ft)
Tiefencastel-Silvaplana, all year.
Klausen
(1,948 metres, 6,391)
Altdorf-Linthal, June-Oct.
Lukmanier
(1,914 metres, 6,280ft)
Disentis-Biasca, May-Nov.
Maloja
(1,815 metres, 5,955ft)
Chiavenna-Silvaplana, all year.
Mosses
(1,445 metres, 4,741ft)
Aigle-Château d'Oex, all year.
Nufenen
(2,478 metres, 8,130ft)
Ulrichen-Airolo, June-Oct.
Oberalp
(2,044 metres, 6,706ft)
Andermatt-Disentis, June-Oct.
Pillon
(1,546 metres, 5,072ft)
Aigle-Gsteig, all year.
San Bernardino
(2,065 metres, 6,775ft)
Thusis-Bellinzona, June-Oct (tunnel passage open all year).
St Gotthard
(2,108 metres, 6,916ft)
Andermatt-Airolo, June-Oct (tunnel passage open all year).
Simplon
(2,006 metres, 6,582ft)
Brig-Domodossola, all year.
Splügen
(2,113 metres, 6,933ft)
Thusis-Chiavenna, June-Oct.
Susten
(2,224 metres, 7,297ft)
Innertkirchen-Wassen, June-Oct.
Umbrail
(2,501 metres, 8,206ft)
Santa Maria-Stelvio, June-Oct.

Tours

BY TRAIN

The Glacier Express

St Moritz-Zermatt and back again (7hr 45min), or Davos-Zermatt or vice versa (7hr 15min).

This route provides the traveller with 291 km (182 miles) of varied scenery through the enchanting landscape of the Alps. On the slowest express train in the world, complete with a "panorama wagon", you'll make your way through 91 tunnels, over 291 bridges, across the 2,033-metre (6,777-ft) Oberalp Pass and through the longest metre-gauge railway tunnel in existence. The steepest parts of the stretch are accomplished by virtue of rack-railways. You can partake of a midday meal in the tastefully decorated dining car. For more information, pick up a copy of the brochure *Glacier Express* at the tourist office.

The Bernina Express

Chur-Tirano or vice versa (4hr 35min).

The highest crossing of the Alps by train is made on the Bernina Express; with a 7 percent gradient it is the steepest non-rack-railway in the world. During the 145-km (90-mile) ride the train first ascends to the Albula Line at 585 metres (2,860 ft) above sea level (Chur), before reaching Pontresina at 1,774 metres (5,913 ft). From here the express heads over the Bernina Pass (2,253 metres/7,510 ft) to descend twisting and turning all the way to Tirano (429 metres/1,430 ft). In just a short while passengers can experience the complete range of vegetation zones from the Piz Bernina Glacier (4,049 metres/13,497 ft) to the palm trees of Tirano in Italy. When the weather is good, some trains even offer open ìpanorama wagonsî – an unforgettable experience. Further information is available in the brochure *Bernina Express* at the tourist office. You can travel further on – to Lugano – by a connecting bus in Tirano

The Palm Express

St Moritz-Palmolino and back again (4hr 10min), from the end of May until the middle of October, and to Lugano only in summer and autumn.

The Palm Express, a recent connection between post bus and railway, travels from the snow and glaciers of the Alps to the palm fringed regions of Southern Switzerland and back again to the snow. This express connects the Engadine and Upper Valais with Ticino, St Moritz and Zermatt with Ascona (where passengers remain overnight), before continuing on to Locarno and Lugano. Additional information can be found in the brochure *Palm Express* at the tourist office, or call 081-833 3072.

The Golden Pass Route

Lucerne-Interlaken-Zweisimmen-Montreux or vice versa (5hr 6min).

This is one of the classic Swiss train journeys. It leads through charming scenery from the banks of Lake Lucerne to the Swiss Riviera. You travel on the narrow-gauge SSB Brünigbahn to Interlaken and continue on from there with the BLS to Zweisimmen. At Zweisimmen youìll change back to the narrower gauge MOB tracks all the way to Montreux – an especially pleasurable experience in the new panorama wagons with their enormous picture-windows.

The Centovalli Train

Locarno–Domodossola (1hr 30min).

This narrow-gauge track makes its way through romantic Centovalli and connects the two great European railway lines over the Simplon and Gotthard passes. The journey takes you 52 km (33 miles) over bridges, idyllic gorges and up inclines, some of which have a gradient of 6 percent, as well as through stretches of Italy. The round trip journey Zurich–Gotthard–Centovalli–Simplon–Lötschberg–Brig –Zurich is an extra-special treat which can be accomplished in a single day.

Wilhelm Tell Express

The Wilhelm Tell Express (6hr) runs daily from May to mid-October. This route, connecting inner Switzerland with Ticino, includes passage in a steamboat. You can sit back and enjoy the sights from the huge saloon or panorama wagons. During the ferry ride a delicious midday meal is served in the "Salon Belle Epoque".

This is a packed and varied day excursion from Lucerne to Locarno/ Lugano and back again.

SPECIAL STEAM TRAINS

A treat for train buffs takes place every spring when all railways issue a list of special steam train journeys, which gives information regarding timetables and prices, as well as the trains themselves.

BY POST BUS

Swiss post buses offer a comfortable and safe way of travelling through the Alps. Tours are offered throughout Switzerland. Examples include a triple-pass journey (over the Grimsel, Furka and Susten passes, starting from either Meiringen in the Bernese Oberland or from Andermatt in the canton of Uri), and a quadruple-pass trip (over the Grimsel, Nufenen, Gotthard and Susten passes, commencing in Meiringen) in Inner Switzerland.

During lengthy journeys with the post bus (for example from St Moritz to Lugano), a generous break is allowed to give travellers plenty of time for a bite to eat.

Car Tours

1. *270 km (170 miles)*
Basel – Biel – Neuchâtel – Murten – Fribourg – Berne – Basel
2. *445 km (275 miles)*
Basel – Zurich – Lake Lucerne – Wassen – Susten Pass – Meiringen – Brünig – Lucerne – Basel
3. *505 km (315 miles)*
Basel – Schaffhausen – Lake Constance – St Gallen – Toggenburg – Lake Zurich – Einsiedeln – Lake Lucerne – Lucerne – Basel
4. *775 km (480 miles)*
Basel – Swiss Jura – Lake Geneva – Valais – Furka – Oberalp – Graubünden – Inner Switzerland – Lucerne – Basel
5. *395 km (245 miles)*
Basel – Biel – Berne – Interlaken – Brünig – Lucerne – Emmental – Olten – Basel
6. *440 km (275 miles)*
Basel – Berne – Fribourg – Bulle – Gruyères – Château d'Oex – Col des Mosses – Les Diablerets – Col de la Croix – Villars – Aigle – Lausanne – Neuchâtel – Basel
7. *670 km (415 miles)*
Basel – Zurich – Landquart – Davos – Flüela Pass – St Moritz – Julier Pass – Chur – Zurich – Basel
8. *730 km (455 miles)*
Basel – Lucerne – Gotthard – Bellinzona – Lugano-Locarno – Centovalli – Domodossola – Simplon Pass – Brig – Martigny – Vevey – Basel
9. *950 km (590 miles)*
St Margrethen – St Gallen – Romanshorn – Schaffhausen – Zurich – Lucerne – Langnau – Berne – Fribourg – Vevey – Martigny – Sion – Brig – Ulrichen – Nufenen Pass – Airolo – Lugano – Chiavenna – Maloja – St Moritz – Scuol – Landeck
10. *490 km (305 miles)*
St Margrethen – Vaduz – Chur – Oberalp – Andermatt – Altdorf – Klausen Pass – Glarus – Ziegelbrücke – Wattwil – Urnäsch – Appenzell – St Gallen – St Margrethen
11. *360 km (225 miles)*
Schaffhausen – Zurich – Lucerne – Brünig – Interlaken – Berne – Olten - Basle
12. *745 km (465 miles)*
Schaffhausen – Rhine Falls – Zurzach – Baden – Olten – Biel – Neuchâtel – Fleurier – Sainte-Croix – Yverdon – Vallorbe – Le Brassus – La Cure – Nyon – Lausanne – Vevey – Bulle – Jaun Pass – Spiez – Thun – Berne – Lucerne – Zurich – Schaffhause

By Bicycle

If you are in possession of a valid ticket, you can have your bicycle transported by train or boat. It is also possible to get your bike aboard a post bus, but opportunities are quite limited and you must be sure to make arrangements in advance.

Bicycles can be rented at and returned to every medium to large railway station and at many smaller ones. Every station which is a starting-point in the large network of bike-hiking-routes has bicycles for rent, and these are modern and in top condition. It's no trouble to bring your own bike into Switzerland and a Swiss number plate is not required.

Bicycle Maps at 1:50,000 (complete with street categorisations, bicycle paths and road gradients) are available at:
Swiss Association for Transport and the Environment (VCS)
Lagerstrasse 18
3360 Herzogenbuchsee
Tel: 062-956 5656.

Taxis

Taking a taxi in Switzerland is relatively expensive; rates vary from place to place. There are fixed prices charged for extra services (luggage, etc.) which are posted in the taxi itself. The tip is included in the fare.

Where to Stay

Where to Stay

There are around 6,000 hotels, motels, pensions, mountain sanatoria and health resorts in Switzerland, amounting to more than 266,000 beds. There are 360,000 beds in chalets and holiday apartments and 7,300 youth hostel beds. Modest tourist resting-places have 226,000 couches and camp-sites have a further 238,000 places. For more information and brochures, contact the **National Tourist Office**, Tödistrasse 7, 8027 Zurich, tel: 01-288 11 11; fax: 01-288 1205 or one of the **Swiss Tourism Offices abroad** (*see page 317*).

Hotels

Information and prices can be found in free hotel listings, the hotel list for senior citizens, the index of country inns, the brochures *Fun for Family* and *Kids Hotels* (hotels specially suitable for families) and the comprehensive *Schweizer Hotelführer* (Swiss Hotel Guide), all available at travel agencies and Swiss tourist offices, including at its branch offices in other countries.

Swiss Hotel Association: **Schweizer Hotelier-Verein** (SHV), Monbijoustrasse 130, CH-3000 Berne, tel: 031-370 4111; fax: 031-370 4444.

BASEL

Basel City

Merian am Rhein
Rheingasse 2
Tel: 061/681 0000
Fax: 681 1101
Great view of river and Münster. **$$$–$$$$**

Kunsthotel Teufelhof
Leonhardsgraben 47
Tel: 061/261 1010
Fax: 261 1004
Eight rooms in which artists are given free rein to create a 'gallery', a great restaurant and a theatre. **$$$–$$$$**

Basel

Resslirytti
Theorodsgraben 42
Tel: 061-691 6641
Fax: 691 4590
Modern establishment near the Messe Basel. **$$$–$$$$**

Price Guide

Price for a double room for one night, including breakfast:
$$$$ expensive: more than 300 SFr
$$$ moderate: 200–300 SFr
$$ modest: 120–200 SFr
$ cheap: less than 120 SFr

BERNE AND BERNESE OBERLAND

Berne

Belle Epoque
Gerechtigkeitsgasse 18
Tel: 031-311 4336
Fax: 311 3936
Seventeen rooms in the picturesque old town, all uniquely furnished with beautiful antiques. **$$$**

Bellevue Palace
Kochergasse 3–5
Tel: 031-320 4545
Fax: 311 4743
The best hotel in town with a view over the Alps and with top cuisine. **$$$$**

Goldener Schlüssel
Rathausgasse 72
Tel: 031-311 0216
Fax: 311 5688
Near the clock tower in the old town, the restaurant serves international and Swiss cuisine. **$$**

Gstaad

Palace
Tel: 033-748 5000
Fax: 748 5001
Famous luxury hotel reminiscent of a castle on a hill above the village. **$$$$**

Posthotel Rössli
Tel: 033-744 3412
Fax: 744 6190
Cosy little hotel in an old wooden house in the centre, with modern rooms and Swiss cuisine. **$$$**

Interlaken

Victoria-Jungfrau
Höheweg 41
Tel: 033-828 2828
Fax: 828 2880
Very famous, old and luxurious grand hotel. **$$$$**

Sonne
Hauptstrasse 34
Tel: 033-822 7541
Fax: 823 2915
Family hotel with a big garden, toys, mountain-bikes – and a gourmet restaurant. **$$**

Ligerz

Kreuz
Hauptstrasse 17
Tel: 032-315 1115
Fax: 315 2814
Rural inn 13 km/7 miles from Biel on the northern shore of Lake Biel with a sauna and family-owned vineyard. **$$–$$$**

Wengen

Regina
Tel: 033-855 1512
Fax: 855 1574
Large traditional hotel established in 1894, overlooking the village. **$$$–$$$$**

Edelweiss
Tel: 033-855 2388
Fax: 855 4288
Cosy family hotel near the railway station, with sauna, no-smoking rooms, and special prices for children. **$$**

EASTERN SWITZERLAND

Neuhausen

Bellevue über dem Rheinfall
Bad. Bahnhofstrasse 17
Tel: 052-672 2121
Fax: 672 8350
Peacefully situated family hotel with

views of the Rheinfall near Schaffhausen. Large rooms, good fish restaurant. **$$–$$$**

Trogen

Krone
Tel: 071-343 6080
Fax: 344 4376
Magnificent Appenzeller house 10 km/6 miles from St. Gallen, built in 1727 with facade frescoes from 1767, and with excellent cooking. **$$**

ZURICH

Glockenhof
Sihlstrasse 31
Tel: 01-211 5650
Fax: 211 5660
Traditional, first-class establishment near the station with a garden restaurant. **$$$–$$$$**
Zürcherhof
Zähringerstrasse 21
Tel. 01-262 1040
Fax: 262 0484
Centrally located, popular with businessmen, with a famous restaurant. **$$–$$$**

GRAUBÜNDEN

Chur

Duc de Rohan
Masanser Strasse 44
Tel: 081-252 1022
Fax: 252 4537
Facilities in this luxury hotel include a fitness club and indoor pool. **$$–$$$**
Stern
Reichsgasse 11
Tel: 081-252 3555
Fax: 252 1915
Traditional hotel situated on the edge of the old town with a good restaurant. **$$–$$$**

Pontresina

Walther
Tel: 081-842 6471
Fax: 842 7922
This is an old hotel with modern features including swimming pool, fitness centre and tennis court. **$$$$**

Poschiavo

Suisse
Via da Mez
Tel: 081-844 0788
Fax: 844 1967
Pleasant hotel in the centre of town. **$$**

S-charl

Gasthaus Mayor
Tel: 081-864 1412
Fax: 864 9983
This delightful country inn is situated on the edge of the Swiss National Park near the Scuol holiday resort. **$$**

Scuol

Filli
Chantröven
Tel: 081-864 9927
Fax: 864 1336
A nice family hotel, very calm, friendly service and excellent cuisine. **$$$**

Silvaplana

Julier-Chesa Arsa
Tel: 081-828 9644
Fax: 828 8143
Comfortable, sensibly-priced, with good substantial food. **$$–$$$**

St. Moritz

Soldanella
Tel: 081-833 3651
Fax: 833 2337
Situated on a mountain slope. **$$$**

Zuoz

Crusch Alva
Huptstrasse 26
Tel: 081-854 1319
Fax: 854 2459
Stylish Engadine establishment with restaurant attached. **$$**

TICINO

Locarno

Arcadia al Lago
Via Orelli 5
Tel: 091-751 0282
Fax: 751 5308
Family hotel near Lake Maggiore with sauna, fitness centre and babysitting service. **$$–$$$**

Lugano

Villa Principe Leopoldo
Via Montalbano 5
Tel: 091-985 8855
Fax: 985 8825
Magnificently situated former residence of Prince Leopold of Hohenzollern, situated above the Collina d'Oro. **$$$$**
Ticino
Piazza Cioccaro 1
Tel: 091-922 7772
Fax: 923 6278
A small but very good hotel right in the heart of the old town. **$$**

Ponte Brolla

Centovalli
Tel: 091-796 3159
Fax: 796 3159
A small inn in a small village en-route to Val Maggia, 5 km/3 miles from Locarno, with fine cuisine. **$**

VALAIS

Ernen

Mühlebach
Tel: 027-971 1406
Fax: 971 3391
Family hotel in the upper Valais, idyllically situated. **$–$$**

Saas Fee

Etoile
Tel: 027-958 15 50
Fax: 958 1555.
Small hotel with mountain view, sauna and large garden. **$$$**
Feehof
Tel: 027-957 2308
Fax: 957 2309
Modest and charming, on the outskirts of the village. **$$**

Sion

Du Rhone
Scex 10
Tel: 027-322 8291
Fax: 323 1188
Peaceful hotel in the town centre, with fine cuisine. **$$**

Zermatt

Monte Rosa
Bahnhofstrasse
Tel: 027-967 3333
Fax: 967 1160

Mountain inn ambience since 1839, with beautiful dining room. **$$$$**

Romantica
Bahnhofstrasse
Tel: 027-966 2650
Fax: 966 2655
Small hotel in a cosy old house with beautiful garden. **$$–$$$**

INNER SWITZERLAND

Einsiedeln

Linde
Schmiedenstrasse 28
Tel: 055-418 4848
Fax: 418 4849
Very close to the abbey, with good rooms and an excellent restaurant. **$$–$$$**

Lucerne

Château Gütsch
Kanonenstrasse
Tel: 041-249 4100
Fax: 249 4191
First-class hotel on a hill with views over city and lake, reminiscent of a castle. **$$$–$$$$**

Waldhaus
Oberrüti
Tel: 041-349 1500
Fax: 349 1515
Magnificently situated in Horw, a Lucerne suburb, with swiming pool and excellent cuisine. **$$–$$$**

Rigi-Klösterli

Des Alpes
Tel: 041-855 0108
Fax: 855 0109
Small, quiet, family-run hotel right in the middle of the hiking region near the Rigi. **$–$$**

Zug

Ochsen
Kolinplatz 11
Tel: 041-729 3232
Fax: 729 3222
Traditional establishment in the town centre. **$$$**

SWISS MITTELLAND

Solothurn

Baseltor
Hauptgasse 49
Tel: 032-622 3422
Fax: 622 1879
Small, centrally-located hotel in the pretty old town, with good prices and a good menu. **$$–$$$**

WESTERN SWITZERLAND

Cortaillod

Vaisseau
Tel: 032-842 1942
Fax: 842 1092
Family hotel situated between a lake and vineyards. Beach and excellent cuisine. **$$–$$$**

Fribourg

Duc Bertold
Rue des Bochers 55
Tel: 026-350 8100
Fax: 350 8181
Right next to the cathedral in the old town, with a swimming pool and very good food. **$$–$$$**

De la Rose
Rue de Morat 1
Tel: 026-351 0101
Fax: 351 0100
Centrally-located hotel with good service. **$$–$$$**

Geneva

Angleterre
Quai du Mont-Blanc 17
Tel: 022-906 5555
Fax: 906 5556
Traditional luxury hotel established 1872 with views over the lake. **$$$$**

Balzac
Rue de l'ancien Port 14
Tel: 022-731 0160
Fax: 731 3847
Large rooms in the city centre, near lake and railway station. **$$**

Luserna
Avenue Luserna 12
Tel: 022-344 1600
Fax: 344 4936
Quiet little hotel situated in a park with ancient trees, between the railway station and airport. **$–$$**

Lausanne

Lausanne Palace
Grand-Chêne 7–9
Tel: 021-331 3131
Fax: 323 2571
Luxury hotel with a superb view of Lake Geneva, designed by Swiss artist Jean Tinguely. **$$$$**

Du Marché
Pré-du-marché 42
Tel: 021-647 9900
Fax: 647 4723
Little hotel in the centre of the old town, although quiet. **$$**

Montreux

Palace Hotel
Grand Rue 100
Tel: 021-962 1212
Fax: 962 1717
Plenty of Belle Epoque luxury. **$$$$**

Auberge de Chernex
Rue du Vieux Four, 1822 Chernex
Tel: 021-964 4191
Fax: 964 6857
Above Montreux with views of lake, good food. **$$**

Price Guide

Price for a double room for one night, including breakfast:
$$$$ expensive: more than 300 SFr
$$$ moderate: 200–300 SFr
$$ modest: 120–200 SFr
$ cheap: less than 120 SFr

Neuchâtel

La Maison du Prussien
Au Gor de Vauseyon
Tel: 032-730 5454
Fax: 730 2143
Historic hotel with old mill and menagerie, and views of the countryside. **$$–$$$**

Bargains

For travellers with tighter budgets, or for those who prefer simple lodgings, there are plenty of smaller hotels and inns. A listing of these can be found in the following brochures, available at the tourist office: *E+G Hotels*; *Preiswerte Unterkünfte in der Schweiz* (reasonably-priced accommodation in Switzerland); *Landgasthöfe* (reasonably-priced hotels in the countryside; and *Berggasthöfe in der Schweiz* (mountain inns in

Switzerland). You can also look for private rooms (ask at the tourist office) and even sleep on straw at various participating farms: the brochure *Schlaf im Stroh* is obtainable at the tourist office.

Holiday Apartments

To find out what's available, enquire at local tourist centres in Switzerland as well as at other Swiss and foreign agencies that serve as clearing-houses for holiday apartments.

Camping

There are more than 500 camp sites in Switzerland where you can pitch your tent. Of these, 90 are open in winter. You can obtain a listing of regional camp sites along with a map of Swiss camp sites from the tourist office.

Outside the boundaries of official campsites, caravans and trailers may only be parked with the permission of the property owner, the relevant local authority or from the police. Spending one night at a public car park is tolerated in many cantons. If you decide to do this, it's a good idea to inform the closest police station or the local authorities beforehand.

A list of Swiss camping and caravan sites is published annually by the following two associations:

Schweizerischer, Camping und Caravanning Verband, Habsburgerstrasse 35, CH-6003 Lucerne 4, tel: 041-210 4822; fax: 041-210 0002.

Verband Schweizerischer Campings (VSC/ASC), Seestrasse 119, CH-3800 Interlaken-Thunersee, tel: 033-823 3523; fax: 033-823 2991.

Youth Hostels

Swiss youth hostels (JH) are open to anyone in possession of a valid YH membership card. There is no age restriction. If, however, there are a limited number of beds available, guests under 25 years of age have priority. Families and leaders of schools or youth groups are required to have a special membership card which can be obtained from the **Schweizer Jugendherbergen** (SJH), 14 Schaffhauserstrasse, Postfach 8042 Zurich, tel: 01-360 1414; fax: 01-360 1460.

Student Accommodation

The **Schweizerische Studentenreisedienst SSR** (the Swiss Student Travel Service) offers reasonably priced overnight accommodation at the following places: Davos, Klosters, St Moritz, Scuol, Wengen and Lucerne.

Further information is available at the tourist office or at **SSR-Reisen** (SSR Holidays), 9 Falkenplatz, CH-3012 Berne, tel: 031-302 0312; fax: 031-302 3993.

The brochure *Studentenunterkünfte* (Student Lodgings) contains useful information about accommodation available in Switzerland's university towns.

The Swiss Alpine Club

There are more than 150 club huts in the Swiss region of the Alps. In spite of their magnificent locations, they are not meant to be used as holiday lodgings. The idea behind them is that they be used as starting-off points for mountain climbing expeditions or high Alpine ski tours. You can get an illustrated register of huts complete with a Swiss map and other important information from the **Schweizer Alpen-Club** (SAC), Zentralsekretariat, Monbijoustrasse 61, CH-3000 Berne 23, tel: 031-370 1818; fax: 031-370'1800; internet: www.sac-cas.ch

Where to Eat

Eating Out

Swiss cuisine has an excellent reputation internationally. The country's countless restaurants, inns and bistros are well known for the exciting variety of their cuisine. Depending on the region you are in, you can order, in addition to the various national specialities, food with a pronounced French, Italian or German influence.

Examples of distinctively Swiss dishes include *fondue*, *raclette* (melted sharp cheese served over potatoes or bread), *Bündnerfleisch* (cured, thinly-sliced meat produced in Graubünden), *Berner Platte* (sauerkraut or green beans with potatoes, bacon, sausage and ribs), *Zürcher Geschnetzeltes* (braised veal with a cream sauce) served with the popular *Rösti* (grated fried potatoes), *Luzerner Chügelipastete* (meat and mushroom pie), *Papet Vaudois* (sausage and leek with potatoes) and *risotto* (Italian-style rice).

Desserts include *Zuger Kirschtorte* (cake with butter cream and cherry schnapps) and a variety of meringues served with whipped cream.

Switzerland produces many different wines and has the highest vineyards in Europe. The best-known white wines are *Fendant*, *Dorin*, *Féchy*, *Dézaley* and *Twanner*. Well known red wines include *Dôle*, *Merlot*, *Gamay*, and *Pinot Noir*.

Some of the many different varieties of schnapps (said to be digestifs) are *Kirsch* (cherry), *Pflümli* (plum), *Williams* (pear) and *Bätzi* (a kind of mixed fruit cognac, consisting mostly of apple and pear).

Meal Times

Generally speaking, the midday meal is served from 11.30am, and dinner 6–9pm. Inns and restaurants usually stayopen until 11.30pm (later at weekends). In larger cities there are always a few places where you can order something to eat right up until 2am.

Restaurants & Inns

BASEL

Basel

Stucki
Bruderholzallee 42
Tel: 061-361 8222
Fax: 361 8203
The best gourmet restaurant in town, with a good-value midday menu. **$$$**

Goldener Stern
St-Alban-Rheinweg 70
Tel: 061-272 1666
Fax: 272 1667
Oldest inn in Basel (1412) with food served in the garden in summer. Good Swiss fare. **$$**

Gifthüttli
Schneidergasse 11
Tel: 061-261 1656
Fax: 261 1456
Nice old establishment in the old town, famed for its *Rösti*. **$**

BERNE AND BERNESE OBERLAND

Berne

Frohsinn
Münstergasse 54
Tel: 031-311 3767
Excellent, relatively inexpensive food. **$$**

Zimmermania
Brunngasse 19
Tel: 031-311 1542
This is a cosy Bernese restaurant with good food and excellent desserts. **$–$$$**

Brasserie Bärengraben
Muristalden 1
Tel: 031-311 4218
Little restaurant near the bear pit over the river, Bernese specialities, fish, and excellent desserts. **$–$$**

Biel

La Ciboulette
Zentralstrasse 26
Tel: 032-322 4746
Inexpensive on the ground floor with a large choice; more elegant and expensive on the first floor. Good regional wines. **$–$$$**

Grindelwald

Fiescherblick
Tel: 033-853 4453
Rustic ambience, excellent food, good wines at reasonable prices. **$–$$$**

Gstaad

Chesery
Lauenenstrasse
Tel: 033-744 2451
Old house with rustic ambience. The best gourmet local in town. **$$$**

Le Grand Restaurant
Wispilestrasse
Tel: 033-748 98 00
Nice old-fashioned restaurant with excellent classic and international food. **$$–$$$**

Interlaken

Im Gade
Höheweg 70
Tel: 033-822 2631
Very cosy, friendly restaurant in the hotel Du Nord, international cuisine, good wine at moderate prices. **$$**

Thun

Schloss Schadau
Seestrasse 45
Tel: 033-222 2500
Superb food served in the castle beside the gastronomy museum. **$$**

EASTERN SWITZERLAND

Appenzell

Säntis
Landsgemeindeplatz
Tel: 071-788 1111
Beautiful house, excellent regional and creative cuisine, good wine at reasonable prices. **$$–$$$**

Schaffhausen

Zur Gerberstube
Bachstrasse 8
Tel: 052-625 2155
Serving excellent Italian food, stylish decor. **$$**

St. Gallen

Zum Goldenen Schäfli
Metzgergasse 5
Tel: 071-223 3737
Favourite restaurant of the locals with a unique feature: the old house is lop-sided! **$$**

Jägerhof
Brühlbleichestrasse 11
Tel: 071-245 5022
Classic, creative and regional cuisine, excellent wine. **$–$$$**

Price Guide

Price for a meal for two people without drinks:
$$$ expensive: more than 80 SFr
$$ moderate: 40–80 SFr
$ inexpensive: up to 40 SFr

ZURICH

Kronenhalle
Rämistrasse 4
Tel: 01-256 6669
Traditional Zürich restaurant, French-style cuisine, delicious. **$$$**

Zunfthaus zur Saffran
Limmatquai 54
Tel: 01-261 6565
Local specialities, elegant dining on first floor of old guild house. **$$**

Bierhalle Kropf
In Gassen 16
Tel: 01-221 1805
Very filling food, attractive art nouveau decor. **$–$$**

GRAUBÜNDEN

Chur

Zum Kornplatz
Kornplatz 1
Tel: 081-252 2759
Popular with young and old, delicious food with a Grisons touch. **$$**

Obelisco
Vazerolgasse 12
Tel: 081-252 5858
Italian restaurant with a large choice of meals and good wines. **$$**

Pontresina

Saratz
Via Maistra
Tel: 081-839 4999
This is a friendly restaurant with an art nouveau hall, excellent regional cuisine. **$$**

Scuol

Crusch Alba
Hauptstrasse
Tel: 081-864 1155
Good regional specialities at reasonable prices, in the 400-year-old hall. Excellent gourmet cuisine rather more expensive. **$–$$$**

Sils

Marmotta
Tel: 081-826 5481
Good regional food, especially the Bündner Gerstensuppe. There is also a nice garden and view on the river inn. **$–$$**

St. Moritz

Monopol Grischuna
Via Maistra 17
Tel: 081-837 0404
Elegant restaurant, excellent Italian cuisine but also other specialities, lovely desserts. **$–$$$**

TICINO

Comano

Osteria Ronchetto
Tel: 091-941 1155
Pleasant Ticino restaurant 4 km/2 miles north of Lugano, local cuisine. **$**

Gudo

Osteria Brack
Tel: 091-859 1254
A perfect place for lovers of pasta and ravioli. Good wines. Located 13 km/7 miles from Bellinzona, **$$**

Locarno

Costa Azzurra
Via Bastoria 13
Tel: 091-751 3802
Typical Ticinese grotto with excellent grilled meat. **$$**
Trattoria da Luigi
Via Dogana Vecchia 1
Tel: 091-751 97 46
This is one of the most beautiful restaurants in the region, with a cosy area and an elegant area. Good food at reasonable prices. **$$**
Al Portone
Via Cassarate 3
Tel: 091-923 5511
Family restaurant not far from the lake, excellent Italian/French cuisine, especially the home made noodles. **$$$**

VALAIS

Brig

Schlosskeller
Alte Simplonstrasse 26
Tel: 027-923 3352
Excellent food with a French touch in the 16th-century Stockalper Palace. Large choice of cheese and wine. **$$**

Price Guide

Price for a meal for two people without drinks:
$$$ expensive: more than 80 SFr
$$ moderate: 40–80 SFr
$ inexpensive: up to 40 SFr

Saas Fee

Carl Zuckmayer-Stube
Tel: 027-957 2175
Good regional cuisine, meat-fondues and fish in a nice restaurant which takes its name from the famous German writer who lived in Saas Fee. **$$**

Savièse

Pont-du-Diable
Chandolin
Tel: 027-395 3030
On a sunny slope above Sion, with a varied menu, nice atmosphere and regional wines. **$$–$$$**

Zermatt

Portofino
Bahnhofstrasse
Tel: 027-967 1932
There are over 20 ingredients to choose from which you can add to your pizza. Also good pasta, meat, fish and seafood. **$$**

INNER SWITZERLAND

Lucerne

Old Suisse House
Löwenplatz 4
Tel: 041-410 6171
Excellent ambience and delicious food and wine, albeit rather expensive. **$$–$$$**
Rebstock
St. Leodegarstrasse 3
Tel: 041-410 3581
Nice French style bistro with shady terrace. **$$**
Galliker
Schützenstrasse 1
Tel: 041-420 1002
Traditional specialities since 1681, all very filling, such as pot-au-feu and leberli with *rösti*. **$**

Zug

Hecht am See
Fischmarkt 2
Right next to the lake, founded in 1435, famous for its seafood dishes, excellent wines. **$$**

SWISS MITTELLAND

Solothurn

Zum alten Stephan
Friedhofplatz 10
Tel: 032-622 1109
Famous restaurant with delicious food in its first-floor *Narrenstübli* and street café. **$$**

WESTERN SWITZERLAND

Fribourg

Buffet de la Gare CFF
Place de la Gare
Tel: 026-322 2816
Unbelievably good food, despite the fact that this is Fribourg's railway station. **$$**

Geneva

Parc des Eaux-Vives
Quai Gustave Ador 82
Tel: 022-735 4140
Fax: 786 8765
Great food, great wines, suberbly located, and therefore very expensive. **$$$**

Le Saint-Germain
Boulevard de Saint-Georges
Tel: 022-328 2624
Fax: 022-328 2624
The best seafood restaurant in town. **$$**

Café du Soleil
Place du Petit-Saconnex 6
Tel: 022-733 3417
Old-fashioned restaurant, excellent fondue and other cheese specialities, interesting mix of clientele. **$–$$**

Lausanne

Du Port
Place du Port 5
Tel: 021-616 4930
Popular restaurant with terrace on the lake, large choice of meals. **$$**

La Rotonde
Place du Port 17–19
Tel: 021-613 3333
Wonderful old-fashioned restaurant in the hotel Beau-Rivage Palace with excellent international cuisine, friendly service and lots of flowers. **$$**

Les Avants

Auberge de la Cergniaulaz-Orgevaux
Tel: 021-964 4276
Delicious substantial food, with only the best ingredients, 8 km/5 miles from Montreux. **$$**

Neuchâtel

Maison des Halles
Rue du trésor 4
Tel: 032-724 3141
Very good food served in a 400-year-old building, delicous desserts. **$$**

Attractions

Music & Theatre

Cultural opportunities in Switzerland run a lively gamut from yodelling clubs and village concerts to drama associations, from jazz and rock groups to literary or musical events and films.

All larger cities maintain at least one theatre and a symphony orchestra. There are performances by internationally acclaimed artists and even the smaller outlying communities put on dramatic and musical events.

In general, the **theatre and concert season** begins in September and ends in June. In summer, highly acclaimed **festivals** take place in which distinguished musicians and conductors entertain music lovers the world over. The best known of these take place at Lausanne, Zurich, Thun, Meiringen, Braunwald, in the Engadine, Sion, Gstaad, Interlaken, Lucerne, Ascona and Vevey.

Jazz and folk music festivals are organised in Berne, Nyon, Montreux, Willisau and Zurich. There are also regular points of rendezvous for the film and television industries: the competition for the **Golden Rose in Montreux**, **international film festivals** in Locarno, Nyon and Les Diablerets, and **film and literature days** in Solothurn.

In addition to all these offerings, **folklore** fans from all corners of the world congregate in Fribourg and at the Tell Games in Interlaken and Altdorf.

Art & Architecture

There are abundant patrician and farm houses, churches, castles and medieval town centres to discover in Switzerland. Traces of the **ancient Romans** have been found in Avenches, Orbe, Augst, Windisch and Martigny. The baptism chapel in Riva San Vitale dates from the **5th century** and the churches of Müstair and Mistail were built during the **Carolingian period**. The church of St Martin in Zillis contains the oldest preserved painted-wood ceiling in the Western World.

Well-preserved examples of **Romanesque** and **Gothic** historical monuments include the abbeys of Romainmôtier and Payerne, the cathedrals in Chur and Schaffhausen, the Minster in Zurich, the Collegiate Church in Neuchâtel and the cathedrals in the cities of Basel, Geneva and Lausanne.

The splendour of **baroque** architecture can be seen in the Einsiedeln, Engelberg and Disentis monasteries as well as in the abbey of St Gallen and the churches of Kreuzlingen and Arlesheim. There are other treasures well worth taking a look at in St Maurice, Beromünster and Chur.

Many Swiss artists of the **19th and 20th centuries** have won glowing international recognition. Names like Le Corbusier, Ferdinand Hodler, Paul Klee, Alberto Giacometti, Max Bill, Hans Arp, Meret Oppenheim, Bernard Luginbühl, Jean Tinguely and Mario Botta – to name a just few – should be sufficient to indicate the tremendous creativity alive today in Switzerland.

Museums, Gardens & Zoos

If you appreciate the unusual, you'll have no problem finding a museum in Switzerland (there are at least 180) which corresponds to your taste. Even little villages generally possess a small museum. Museums enjoying a world-wide reputation include the **art museums** in Basel, Berne, Zurich and Vaduz (Liechtenstein), the **Abegg Foundation Textile Collection** in

Riggisberg, the **Bodmer Foundation Manuscript Collection** in Cologny and the **Oskar Reinhart Painting Collection** in Winterthur. The **museums of natural history** in Geneva, Berne and Basel are also highly regarded.

In Basel, the relatively new **Jean Tiguely Museum**, dedicated to Jean Tinguely's lifework and designed specifically by architect Mario Botta, can be visited at Grenzacherstrasse/ Solitude Park, tel: 061-681 9320; fax: 061-681 9321. Opening hours are Wednesday–Sunday 11am–7pm. Another new museum in Basel is the **Foundation Beyeler**, Berowerpark, 17 Baselstrasse, Riehen, tel: 061-645 9700; fax: 061-645 9719. Designed by renowned architect Renzo Piano, and located in the Berower Park on the outskirts of the Basel suburb of Riehen, it contains a permanent home for the prestigious contemporary art collection of Hildy and Ernst Beyeler. Opening hours are daily 11am–5pm, closed Christmas Day, Boxing Day and New Year's Day.

If you're more interested in technical inventions, visit the **Verkehrshaus der Schweiz** (the Swiss Transport Museum) in Lucerne, the **Technorama** in Winterthur, or the **International Uhrenmuseum** (the International Watch Museum) in La Chaux-de-Fonds.

The **Schweizerisches Landesmuseum** (the Swiss National Museum) is primarily devoted to Swiss history; there are also excellent collections on this subject in Basel, Berne, Delémont, Fribourg and Geneva. You'll find the most unusual exhibitions displayed in the **Schweizerisches Freilichtmuseum** (the Swiss Open-Air Museum) for country architecture on the Ballenberg above Brienz and the **Rietberg Museum** in Zurich, as well as at the **anthropology museums** in Basle, Geneva, Neuchâtel and Zurich.

The **Swiss Museum Passport** enables visitors to have free entry to more than 180 museums throughout Switzerland. The passport may be purchased for one month or a year, and is obtainable, along with a planner/museum directory, from participating museums, the larger tourist offices in Switzerland and various "ticket corners". Adults Sfr 30/90. An *Adults Plus* card includes admission for children and costs Sfr 35/105; ahv, students Sfr 25/75.
There are also a number of zoos and botanical gardens.

Nature Reserves

Considering that Switzerland is a small country there are lots of nature reserves. The most important is the **Swiss National Park**. In Graubünden, a region at an altitude of 1,400–3,171 metres (4,593–10,413 ft) with a total area encompassing about 169 sq. km (65 sq. miles) has been turned into a wildlife and plant reserve. The park was established in 1914 and some 150,000 visitors come to walk along the 80 km (50 miles) of hiking trails every year. The single road threading its way through the reserve follows the Spöl, goes over the Ofen Pass (Fuorn) and into the Val Müstair before continuing into Italy. One-third of the park is made up of woods, one third of alpine meadows and one third of non-productive land. Chamois, marmots, roe and red deer, ibex, lynx and eagles are found here.

Persons under the age of 15 are allowed in the park only if accompanied by an adult; dogs and camping are prohibited. The National Park House Zernez and museum are open seven days a week June–October, 8.30am–6pm (Tuesdays 9pm).

Other beautiful nature reserves include the famous **Aletschwald** (Aletsch forest). At an altitude of 2,100 meters (6,900 feet) you reach the Valais by hiking across the Aletsch glacier, the largest ice stream in the alps. The forest has very old mountain fir-trees and many other plants, some of them relatively rare.

In the canton of Ticino there are wonderful flower gardens on the **Isole di Brissago** (islands of Brissago) on Lago Maggiore. You can reach them by boat from Brissago. As well as fabulous flora, there is Mediterranean vegetation, with the only lemon and orange trees in Switzerland.

From the boat which runs regularly between the cities of Biel and Solothurn on the **River Aare** you can see a wild and very green romantic bank landscape – home to many birds.

Bird-spotting is also possible in the **Untersee**, the western part of Lake Constance. Here you can observe and listen to many bird species which are rarely found elsewhere.

Important: in all nature reserves it is forbidden to disturb or to take away plants and animals, or to leave waste.

Nightclubs & Discos

Disregard the rumour that nightlife in Switzerland is pretty provincial. In larger cities you'll find a wide variety of bars, clubs, discos and other opportunities to dance. Some of the well-known holiday resort areas also offer attractive places to spend an evening, as well as world-class entertainment programmes. For further, up-to-date information enquire at a local tourist information centre, the hotel concierge, or just ask a likely-looking native.

Casinos

There are casinos in Arosa, Bad Ragaz, Baden, Berne, Brunnen, Courrendlin, Crans, Davos, Engelberg, Geneva, Interlaken, Locarno, Lugano, Lucerne, Montreux, Rheinfelden, St Moritz, Thun and Zurich.

In Swiss casinos – which are primarily found on the premises of health resorts and hotels – you can stake your money on *Jeu de la boule* (a game similar to roulette).

Sport

Winter

SKIING

Rack and funicular railways, ski and chairlifts take fans of winter sports to ski runs which, thanks to the high premium placed on safety, are well-marked and constantly maintained.

Some 200 ski schools employ about 4,000 instructors to teach at all levels. Instructors are also available for guided tours. You can rent ski equipment at all winter sport resort areas.

MONO-SKI

In numerous winter sport centres you can learn how to hotdog ski, do snow ballet and ski jump as well as how to manage on a mono-ski or snowboard.

CROSS-COUNTRY & SKI-HIKING

There are fully developed cross-country ski runs and ski-touring trails in all larger holiday areas of the Alps, Alp foothills and in Jura. You'll find cross-country ski schools everywhere.

SKI TOURS

Accomplished skiers can climb up mountain slopes with animal skins attached to their skis and roped to their fellow skiers for safety, then ski back down the slopes at a break-neck pace, accompanied by an experienced guide.

SKIBOBBING

Many areas have set up special skibob runs.

ICE SKATING, CURLING AND ICE HOCKEY

Over 300 natural and artificial ice-skating rinks, both indoors and outdoors, await ice sport aficionados.

SLEDDING

You'll find everything from the usual sledding slopes to especially prepared and marked runs.

SKIJORING

This is an extremely demanding sport in which a skier is pulled across a run by a galloping horse. The most famous area for skijoring is St. Moritz.

HORSEBACK RIDING AND SLEIGHS

You can hire horses in many places and most riding schools remain open in winter. If you prefer a more tranquil, contemplative excursion there are more than 70 holiday resort areas where you can sit back and relax in a horse-drawn sleigh.

HIKING

Hiking fans can also get their money's worth even in the snow season; there are about 3,000 km (1,875 miles) of hiking trails open during the winter.

Summer

HIKING

Hikers are spoiled for choice in Switzerland with approximately 50,000 km (31,000 miles) of marked hiking trails. In addition to these, there are innumerable other paths waiting to be discovered. Yellow signs keep walkers informed on destination points and estimated hiking times.

The detailed guides and hiking maps issued by the Bundesamt für Landestopographie (Federal Office of Regional Geography) and available in bookshops, kiosks and some local tourist offices are useful.

Numerous tourist information centres organise guided outings, from wildlife observation hikes to moonlight and sunrise tours. There are over 300 hiking holiday options, from botanical excursions to senior citizen hiking weeks, adventure trekking to long-distance tours.

The botanical and geological information-station nature trails which lead through nature reserves introduce you to the native flora and fauna of Switzerland.

MOUNTAIN CLIMBING

The Swiss Alps are full of peaks to tempt climbers, and glaciers can be crossed in the company of experienced mountain guides. More than 150 huts belonging to the Swiss Alpine Club (SAC) can be found listed. There are also schools which offer mountain-climbing instruction.

JOGGING

Around villages, towns and cities there are some 500 woodland paths, each 2–3-km (1–2-miles) long and punctuated by fitness stations where you can break your stride for a while.

GOLF

For those of you looking forward to a good game of golf, there are more than 30 beautifully situated golf courses to choose from as well as mini-golf.

TENNIS & SQUASH

In practically all cities and in most holiday resort areas there are indoor and outdoor tennis courts; many larger hotels have private courts at their disposal. You'll find squash facilities in about 40 different cities.

AEROSPORTS

It's possible to take a sightseeing tour by plane from many of the regional airfields. There are numerous air centres which regularly offer courses at beginning, intermediate and advanced levels for gliding, paragliding, delta and hang gliding.

WINTER SPORTS IN SUMMER

Various high-altitude ski areas have snow all year round and are in operation even during summer. You'll also find some curling, ice-skating and ice-hockey facilities open at this time.

RIDING

You can hire horses, either for indoor riding, or hacking through the countryside at around 90 horse-riding centres. Special trekking weeks are organised and riders can explore the Alps via old mule tracks.

COVERED WAGONS

If you have a yearning to journey through the Jura in the manner of pioneers and gypsies, climb aboard a horse-drawn wagon.

WATERSPORTS

Switzerland, with its many lakes and rivers, is suitable for just about every conceivable kind of watersport.

SAILING & WINDSURFING

There are sailing and windsurfing schools at most of the lakes in Graubünden and Inner Switzerland.

ROWING & CANOEING

Every year international rowing regattas take place on the Rotsee, near Lucerne. This lake is reputed to have some of the best rowing conditions in the world. Canoeists make for the Doubs in the Jura and the Muota in the canton of Schwyz.

RIVER RAFTING

Rafting trips along some of the turbulent rivers of the Alps (for example the Inn, Rhine, Rhône, Simme and Saane) and more leisurely journeys in canoes (along the Aare, Doubs, Reuss, Rhine, Rhône and Thur rivers) are offered during summer.

WATER-SKIING

It is possible to water-ski on most lakes in Switzerland. In the larger holiday resort areas you'll also find water-skiing schools.

SWIMMING

Swimmers have more than 350 natural bathing areas along lakes and rivers to choose from, in addition to hundreds of indoor and outdoor swimming pools and approximately 200 hotel pools. There are places to swim even in high-altitude holiday resort areas.

FISHING

There are roughly 32,000 km (20,000 miles) of running water and about 135,000 hectares (337,500 acres) of lakes available for fishing. Local tourist centres can provide you with information about permits.

Shopping

What to Buy

In Switzerland, as in all countries which beckon tourists, there is an enormous choice of mementos to take home. Interesting purchases from the region could include rock crystals, painted ceramic wares, utensils and vessels made out of wood, music boxes, dolls in folkloric costumes, carved wood, lace, embroidery, jewellery, chocolate, cheese, wine, schnapps, watches and Swiss-Army knives.

If you're searching for something typical and of good quality, look in one of the **Schweizerischer Heimatwerke** (Swiss Handicraft) shops, located in many cities and well-populated areas. They are staffed by competent sales assistants who can tell you anything you'd like to know. In smaller towns it's best to purchase articles directly from the source, in other words the company or artist.

Concerning food specialities here are some tips:

Chocolates

These can be found in any food store. Look out for real Swiss chocolate – recently there has been a glut of chocolate from Belgium and Germany. Home-made chocolates such as pralinés are sold in bakeries and confectioners in most villages. In Zurich you will find the best ones at **Sprüngli** and in the lovely old-fashioned **Café Schober**.

Cheese

Swiss cheese is for sale in every every grocers, but if you have the opportunity, buy regional cheese directly from village dairies or on mountain farms – they are authentic and taste especially fine.

Wine

In western Switzerland, Valais, Ticino and other wine regions, look out for wine farms. A lot of them sell directly to the customer.

Schnapps

There are a lot of local specialities such as kirsch (cherry schnapps) in Zug and Schwyz, and williams (pear) and apricot in the Valais.

Confectionery

Try – or take home – the famous *kirschtorte* (cherry schnapps tart) in Zug or the Engadiner *nusstorte* (nut tart) in Graubünden.

Shops are normally open daily 8 or 8.30am–6.30pm and on Saturday until 4pm. A lot of food shops close from 12 noon–2pm. Some confectioners in the larger towns and holiday resorts are open on Sunday.

Language

Language

About 64 percent of Swiss people speak **Schwyzerdütsch**, a variation of German, but don't be afraid to try out the more usual German on them. The three other official languages are French, which is used by about 19 percent of the population in the western part of Switzerland; Italian, used by roughly 7 percent of the Swiss in the southern part of Switzerland, especially in the canton Tessin; and Romansch, which is spoken by 0.6 percent of people in some regions of the canton Graubünden. All Romansch-speaking and a lot of Italian-speaking people also understand and speak German. But in the French-speaking part of Switzerland you would be more successful speaking English than German. Swiss people are in general friendly and patient, and will take the time to listen to foreigners who do not speak fluently in their language.

Since a lot of English vocabulary is related to German, travellers will often recognise many helpful cognates: words such as *hotel*, *kaffee*, *milch*, *markt* and *bett* hardly need to be translated. You should be aware, however, of some misleading "false friends" (*see panel on page 339*).

There is one rather puzzling characteristic of the Swiss: even if they are speaking real German, they use many words which they borrow from the French, such as *billet*, *lavabo* and *portemonnaie*; this is especially the case if they are speaking about eating.

The Alphabet

Learning the pronunciation of the German alphabet is a good idea. In particular, learn how to spell out your name.
a = ah, **b** = bay, **c** = tsay, **d** = day, **e** = ay, **f** = ef, **g** = gay, **h** = hah, **i** = ee, **j** = yot, **k** = kah, **l** = el, **m** = em, **n** = en, **o** = oh, **p** = pay, **q** = coo, **r** = ehr, **s** = ess, **t** = tay, **u** = oo, **v** = fou, **w** = vay, **x** = eex, **y** = eepseelon, **z** = tset.

Basic Rules

Even if you speak no German at all, it is worth trying to master a few simple phrases. The fact that you have made an effort is likely to get you a better response. More and more German-speaking people like practising their English on visitors, especially waiters in cafés and restaurants and the younger generation. Pronunciation is the key; they really will not understand if you get it very wrong. Remember to **emphasise each syllable**.

Whether to use **"Sie"** or **"Du"** is a vexed question; increasingly the familiar form of "Du" is used by many people. However it is better to be too formal, and use "Sie" if in doubt. You address people with "Sie" or, if you know their names, you address them **Herr** or **Frau,** and attach the relevant surname. To say Herr or Frau without surnames sounds in German rather ridiculous. If you say "Du" you attach, if you know the name, just the first name. When entering a shop always say, **"Guten Tag"**, and **"Danke, auf Wiedersehen"**, when leaving.

Words & Phrases

How much is it?
Wieviel kostet das?
What is your name?
Wie heissen Sie?
My name is... *Ich heisse...*
Do you speak English?
Sprechen Sie englisch?
I am English/American
Ich bin Engländer(in)/Amerikaner(in)
I don't understand
Ich verstehe nicht

Please speak more slowly
Sprechen Sie bitte langsamer
Can you help me?
Können Sie mir helfen?
I'm looking for... *Ich suche...*
Where is...? *Wo ist...?*
I'm sorry *Entschuldigung*
I don't know
Ich weiss es nicht
No problem *Kein Problem*
Have a good day!
Einen schönen Tag!
That is it *Das ist es*
Here it is *Hier ist es*
There it is *Dort ist es*
Let's go *Gehen wir*
See you tomorrow
Bis morgen
See you soon *Bis bald*
Show me the word in the book
Zeigen Sie mir das Wort im Buch
At what time?
Um wieviel Uhr?
When? *Wann?*
What time is it?
Wieviel Uhr ist es?
yes *ja*
no *nein*
please *bitte*
thank you (very much)
danke (vielmal)
you're welcome
bitte or gern geschehen
excuse me *Entschuldigung*
hello
Guten Tag or, more familiar, *Hallo*
OK *In Ordnung*
goodbye *Auf Wiedersehen*
good evening *Gute Nacht*
here *hier*
there *dort*
today *heute*
yesterday *gestern*
tomorrow *morgen*
now *jetzt*
later *später*
right away *sofort*
this morning *heute morgen*
this afternoon
heute nachmittag
this evening *heute abend*

On Arrival

I want to get off at...
Ich möchte in ... aussteigen
Does this bus go to...?
Fährt dieser Bus nach...?
What street is this?
In welcher Strasse sind wir?
Which line do I take for...?
Welche Linie muss ich nehmen nach...?
How far is ...? *Wie weit ist ...?*
Validate your ticket
Entwerten Sie Ihr Billet
airport *der Flughafen*
train station *der Bahnhof*
bus station *der Busbahnhof*
bus *der Bus*
bus stop *die Bushaltestelle*
platform *das Perron*
ticket *das Billet*
return ticket *das Retourbillet*
hitchkiking *Autostop*
toilets *die Toiletten*
This is the hotel address
Das ist die Adresse des Hotels
I'd like a room
Ich möchte ein Zimmer
single/double...
Einzelzimmer/Doppelzimmer
...with shower *...mit Dusche*
...with bath *mit Bad*
...with a view *...mit Aussicht*
Does that include breakfast?
Ist das Frühstück inbegriffen?
May I see the room?
Darf ich das Zimmer anschauen?
washbasin *das Lavabo*
bed *das Bett*
key *der Schlüssel*
elevator *der Lift, der Aufzug*
air conditioning
die Klimaanlage

Emergencies

Help! *Hilfe!*
Stop! *Halt!*
Call a doctor
Rufen Sie einen Arzt
Call an ambulance
Rufen Sie eine Ambulanz
Call the police
Rufen Sie die Polizei
Call the fire brigade
Rufen Sie die Feuerwehr
Where is the nearest telephone?
Wo ist das nächste Telefon?
Where is the nearest hospital?
Wo ist das nächste Spital?
I am sick *Ich bin krank*
I have lost my passport/purse
Ich habe meinen Pass / mein Portemonnaie verloren

On the Road

Where is the spare wheel?
Wo ist das Reserverad?
Where is the nearest garage?
Wo ist die nächste Garage?
Our car has broken down
Unser Auto hat eine Panne
I want to have my car repaired
Ich möchte mein Auto reparieren lassen
It's not your right of way
Sie müssen etwas warten
I think I must have put diesel in the car by mistake
Ich glaube, ich habe irrtümlicherweise mit Diesel getankt
the road to...
die Strasse nach...
left *links*
right *rechts*
straight on *geradeaus*
far *weit entfernt, weit weg*
near *nahe*
opposite *gegenüber*
beside *neben*
car park *der Parkplatz*
over there *dort drüben*
at the end *am Ende*
on foot *zu Fuss*
by car *mit dem Auto*
town map *der Stadtplan*
road map *die Strassenkarte*
street *die Strasse*
square *der Platz*
give way *den Vortritt lassen*
dead end *die Sackgasse*
no parking *Parkieren verboten*
motorway *die Autobahn*
toll *die Gebühr*
speed limit *die Tempolimite*
petrol *das Benzin*
unleaded *bleifrei*
diesel *der Diesel*
water/oil *das Wasser/das Oel*
puncture *die Reifenpanne*
bulb *die Batterie*
wipers *die Scheibenwischer*

On the Telephone

How do I make an outside call?
Wie telefoniere ich nach auswärts?
I want to make an international (local) call
Ich möchte eine internationale (lokale) Verbindung
What is the dialling code?
Wie lautet die Vorkennzahl?

I'd like an alarm call for 8 tomorrow morning
Ich möchte morgen früh um acht Uhr geweckt werden
Who's calling?
Wer ist am Apparat?
Hold on, please
Warten Sie bitte
The line is busy
Die Leitung ist besetzt
I must have dialled the wrong number
Ich bin falsch verbunden

Shopping

Where is the nearest bank (post office)?
Wo ist die nächste Bank (Post)?
I'd like to buy
Ich möchte etwas kaufen
How much is it?
Wieviel kostet das?
Do you take credit cards?
Nehmen Sie Kreditkarten?
I'm just looking
Ich schaue nur ein bisschen
Have you got...?
Haben Sie...?
I'll take it
Ich nehme es
I'll take this one/that one
Ich nehme das hier/das dort
What size is it?
Welche Grösse ist das?
Anything else? *Noch etwas?*
size *die Grösse*
cheap *billig*
expensive *teuer*
enough *genug*
too much *zu viel*
a piece... *ein Stück...*
each *das Stück*
(**eg bananas,** *4 Fr. das Stück)*
bill *die Rechnung*
chemist *die Apotheke*
bakery *die Bäckerei*
butcher *die Metzgerei*
bookshop *die Buchhandlung*
library *die Bibliothek*
department store
das Warenhaus
grocery
das Lebensmittelgeschäft
tobacconist
der Tabakladen, der Kiosk
market *der Markt*
supermarket *der Supermarkt*
junk shop *das Brockenhaus*

Market shopping

In a market all goods have to be marked with the price by law. This will be written 4.50 (*Rappen*). Prices are usually by the *Kilo* or by the *Stück*, that is, each item priced individually. Usually the stall holder (*Verkäufer*) will select the goods for you. Sometimes there is a self-service system – observe everyone else. If you are choosing cheese, for example, you may be offered a taste to try first: *Zum Versuchen.*
tasting *die Degustation*
organic *biologisch*
flavour *der Geschmack*
basket *der Korb*
bag *die Tasche*

Sightseeing

town *die Stadt*
old town *die Altstadt*
abbey *die Abtei, das Kloster*
cathedral
die Kathedrale, das Münster
church *die Kirche*
mansion *das Herrschaftshaus*
hospital *das Spital*
town hall *das Rathaus*
nave *das Kirchenschiff*
stained glass *das Glasfenster*
staircase *das Treppenhaus*
tower *der Turm*
walk *der Rundgang*
country house/castle *das Schloss*
Gothic *gothisch*
Roman *römisch*
Romanesque *romanisch*
museum *das Museum*
art gallery *die Kunstgalerie*
exhibition *die Ausstellung*
tourist information office
das Verkehrsbüro
free *gratis*
open *offen*
closed *geschlossen*
every day *täglich*
all year *das ganze Jahr über*
all day *den ganzen Tag*
swimming pool *das Schwimmbad*
to book *reservieren*

Dining out

breakfast *das Frühstück*
lunch *das Mittagessen*
dinner *das Abendessen*
meal *die Mahlzeit*
first course *die Vorspeise*
main course *die Hauptspeise*
made to order *auf Bestellung*
drink included *Getränk inbegriffen*
wine list *die Weinkarte*
the bill *die Rechnung*
fork *die Gabel*
knife *das Messer*
spoon *der Löffel*
plate *der Teller*
glass *das Glas*
napkin *die Serviette*
ashtray *der Aschenbecher*

Frühstück und Snacks/ Breakfast and Snacks

Brötchen *rolls*
Brot *bread*
Butter *butter*
Ei *egg*
... weiche Eier *boiled eggs*
... Eier mit Speck *bacon and eggs*
... Eier mit Schinken
ham and eggs
... Spiegeleier *fried eggs*
... Rührei *scrambled eggs*
Honig *honey*
Joghurt *yogurt*
Konfiture *jam*
Omelette *pancake*
Pfeffer *pepper*
Salz *salt*
Zucker *sugar*

Hauptgerichte/Main courses

Fleisch *Meat*
Blutwurst *black pudding*
Braten *roast*
Bündnerfleisch *dried meat*
Ente *duck*
Entrecôte *beef rib steak*
Fasan *pheasant*
Froschschenkel *frog's legs*
Gans *goose*
Gnagi, Schweinsfuss
pig's trotters
Huhn/Poulet *chicken*
Kalb *veal*
Kalbsleber *calf's liver*
Kaninchen/Hase *rabbit*
Lamm *lamb*
Leber *liver*
Leberwurst *liver sausage*
Nieren *kidneys*
Schinken *ham*
Schwein *pork*
Salami *salami*
Schnecken *snails*

Spiessli *kebab*
Steak *steak*
Voressen *stew of veal, lamb or chicken with creamy egg sauce*
Wildschwein *wild boar*
Wurst *sausage*
Zunge *tongue*
wenig gebraten, bleu *rare*
mittel gebraten, à point *medium*
gut gebraten, bien cuit *well done*
grilliert *grilled*
gefüllt *stuffed*

Fisch/Fish

Aal *eel*
Auster *oyster*
Egli *small regional fish*
Felchen *regional white fish*
Forelle *trout*
Hecht *pike*
Hummer *lobster*
Kabeljau, Dorsch *cod*
Krevetten *shrimp*
Lachs *salmon*
Langustine *large prawn*
Muscheln, Moule *mussel*
Meerfrüchte *seafood*
Sardellen *anchovies*
Schalentiere *shellfish*
Thunfisch/Thon *tuna*
Tintenfisch *squid*

Gemüse/Vegetables

Artischocke *artichoke*
Aubergine *eggplant/aubergine*
Blumenkohl *cauliflower*
Bohne *bean (green or dried)*
Chips *potato crisps*
Cornichon *gherkin*
Erbsen *peas*
Grüner Salat *green salad*
Haselnuss *hazelnut*
Kartoffel *potato*
Kefen *snow peas*
Knoblauch *garlic*
Kohl *cabbage*
Lauch *leek*
Linsen *lentils*
Mais *corn*
Nuss *nut, walnut*
Pastinake *parsnip*
Petersilie *parsley*
Pilze *mushrooms*
Pommes frites *French fries*
Radieschen *radis*
Reis *rice*
Salatgurke *cucumber*
Sellerie *celery*
Spargel *asparagus*
Spinat *spinach*
Steinpilz *boletus, mushrooms*
Trüffel *truffle*
weisse Rübe *turnip*
Zucchini *zucchini/courgette*
Zwiebel *onion*
roh *raw*

Obst/Fruit

Ananas *pineapple*
Apfel *apple*
Birne *pear*
Cassis *redcurrant*
Erdbeere *strawberry*
Feige *fig*
Grapefruit *grapefruit*
Himbeere *raspberry*
Kirsche *cherry*
Limone *lime*
Mango *mango*
Mirabelle *yellow plum*
Pfirsich *peach*
Pflaume *plum*
Traube *grape*
Zitrone *lemon*
Zwetschge *prune*

Desserts/Dessert

Glacé *ice cream*
Käse *cheese*
Kuchen *cake*
Schlagrahm *whipped cream*
Torte *tart*
Vermicelles
chestnut with whipped cream

Table talk

I am a vegetarian
Ich bin Vegetarier
I am on a diet *Ich bin auf Diät*
What do you recommend?
Was empfehlen Sie?
Do you have local specialities?
Haben Sie lokale Spezialitäten?
I'd like to order
Ich möchte bestellen
That is not what I ordered
Das ist nicht, was ich bestellt habe
Is service included?
Ist der Service inbegriffen?
May I have more wine?
Ich möchte noch Wein, bitte.
Enjoy your meal
Guten Appetit!

In the Café

drinks *Getränke*
alcoholic drinks *Drinks*
coffee *Kaffee*
... with milk or cream
... mit Milch oder Kaffeerahm
... decaffeinated *koffeinfrei*
... black espresso *Espresso*
... American filtered coffee *filtre*
tea *Tee*
... black tea *Schwarztee*
... herbal infusion *Kräutertee*
... peppermint *Pfefferminze*
... rosehip *Hagebutte*
... camomile *Kamille*
... vervain *Eisenkraut*
hot chocolate
heisse Schokolade
hot Ovaltine
heisse Ovomaltine (a common Swiss drink with chocolate and vitamins)
milk *Milch*
mineral water
Mineralwasser
fizzy *mit Kohlensäure*
non-fizzy
ohne Kohlensäure
fruit-flavoured carbonated water
Mineralwasser mit Aroma
freshly-squeezed orange juice
frisch gepresster Orangensaft
full (eg full cream milk) *voll*
fresh or cold *kalt*
beer *Bier*
... bottled *in der Flasche*
... on tap *offen*
pre-dinner drink *Aperitif*
with ice *mit Eis*
neat *trocken*
red *rot*
white *weiss*
rosé *rosé*
dry *herb*
sweet *süss*
sparkling wine *Schaumwein*
house wine *Hauswein*
local wine *Landwein*
Where is this wine from?
Woher kommt dieser Wein?
carafe/jug
Krug/Karaffe
... of water/wine
... Wasser/Wein
half litre
einen halben Liter
mixed *panaché (beer with lemon mineral water) or gespritzt (white wine with water)*
after dinner drink *Digestif*
cherry brandy *Kirsch*
pear brandy *Williams*

plum brandy *Pflümli*
cheers!
Gesundheit! or Zum Wohl!
I have a hangover
betrunken sein

In Switzerland wine, and sometimes also mineral water, is served in measures of 100cl (one decilitre). Usually you order *2 Dezi*, 3 *Dezi*, *einen halben Liter* or *einen Liter*. If it is a very good wine, you have to order a whole bottle.

Days and Months

Days of the week

Monday *Montag*
Tuesday *Dienstag*
Wednesday *Mittwoch*
Thursday *Donnerstag*
Friday *Freitag*
Saturday *Samstag*
Sunday *Sonntag*

Seasons

spring *der Frühling*
summer *der Sommer*
autumn *der Herbst*
winter *der Winter*

Months

January *Januar*
February *Februar*
March *März*
April *April*
May *Mai*
June *Juni*
July *Juli*
August *August*
September *September*
October *Oktober*
November *November*
December *Dezember*

Saying the date

20th October 2000 *der zwanzigste Oktober zweitausend.*

False Friends

False friends are words that look like English words but mean something different, for example
Der Car **coach car**
Der Kondukteur **train guard**
Es geht can sometimes mean walk, but is usually used to mean working (the TV, the car etc.) or going well

Numbers

0 *Null*
1 *Eins*
2 *Zwei*
3 *Drei*
4 *Vier*
5 *Fünf*
6 *Sechs*
7 *Sieben*
8 *Acht*
9 *Neun*
10 *Zehn*
11 *Elf*
12 *Zwölf*
13 *Dreizehn*
14 *Vierzehn*
15 *Fünfzehn*
16 *Sechzehn*
17 *Siebzehn*
18 *Achtzehn*
19 *Neunzehn*
20 *Zwanzig*
21 *Einundzwanzig*
30 *Dreissig*
40 *Vierzig*
50 *Fünfzig*
60 *Sechzig*
70 *Siebzig*
80 *Achtzig*
90 *Neunzig*
100 *Hundert*
1,000 *Tausend*
1,000,000 *Eine Million*

Further Reading

Background

The Music Guide to Belgium, Luxembourg, Holland and Switzerland: Brody, Elaine.
The Alps: Clark, Ronald W
Ideas and Places:Connolly, Cyril.
Switzerland: Hughes, Christopher S.
The Swiss and their Mountains: Lunn, Sir A.H.M.
La Place de la Concorde Suisse. McPhee, John.
Antiquities and Archaeology. Sauter, R.
The Eye of the Hurricane. Schwarz, Urs.
Why Switzerland?: Steinberg, Jonathan.
Switzerland Exposed. Ziegler, Jean:

Fiction

Hôtel Du Lac: Brookner, Anita
Prisoner of Chillon: Byron, Lord.
The Final Problem. Conan Doyle, Arthur.
A Pocketful of Rye. Cronin, A.J.
The Manticore. Davies, Robertson.
Sebastian. Durrell, Lawrence.
Man in the Holocene. Frisch, Max.
Peter Camenzind. Hesse, Hermann.
The Call Girls. Koestler, Arthur.
Lenin in Zurich. Solzhenitsyn, Alexander.
Not To Disturb. Spark, Muriel.
Heidi. Spyri, Johanna.

Other Insight Guides

Insight Guide: Austria gives the full picture of Switzerland's neighbour, from the ski resorts to the wine regions, with background on its music and cultural traditions.
Insight Pocket Guide: Bavaria is a personal guide to this romantic region of Germany.
Insight Compact Guide: Switzerland is a mini-encyclopaedia packed with concise information on the country's many attractions.

ART & PHOTO CREDITS

Emanuel Ammon 8/9, 14/15, 24, 84/85, 95, 97, 100/101, 108, 137, 158, 159, 165, 168, 173, 184, 191, 192, 194, 199, 203, 204/205, 206, 211, 220/221, 223, 226, 234, 235, 236, 237, 238, 239, 240, 241, 247, 248, 250, 251, 252, 256/257, 259, 283, 295, 312
Verkehrsverein Basel 117, 119
Edouard Curchod 311
Degonda 153
Herbert Distel 273
Lucia Elser 302
Philip Giegel 112/113, 193, 263, 279, 281
Michael von Graffenried 18/19, 79, 80/81, 122/123, 152, 169, 179, 188, 225, 272, 282
Robert Harding 2, 6/7
Walter Imbe 104/105, 124, 127, 130, 140, 148, 149,r 150, 180, 189, 196, 202, 209, 217, 222, 228, 231, 232/233, 249, 260, 262, 280, 285, 290, 309
Kunstmuseum St Gallen 22
Herbert Maeder 102/103
Meier 274
Jean Mohr 227, 299, 301, 305
Musée cantonal d'archéologie Neuchâtel: Photo Roland Stucky 29
Musée gruérien: Bulle 286/287
G. Poschung 143, 154
Ringier Dokumentationszentrum 198
H. Schwab 291
Schweizerisches Landesmuseum, Zurich 32R, 37, 64, 66, 67, 70
Schweizerische Verkehrszentrale: Hans R. Schaläpfer 121, 128, 183, 197, 200, 215, 289
Spectrum Colour Library 87, 88
Tony Stone 268
Storto 181
Swiss Tourist Office 115, 273
Topham Picture Source 39, 52, 54, 58, 59, 65, 74, 76, 77, 244/245
Alberto Venzago 16/17, 20/21, 106/107, 147, 156/157, 161, 164, 201, 212, 216, 261, 320, 336
B. Wassman 258
Eduard Widmer 34, 134, 135, 142, 154, 155, 162, 174, 219, 229, 242, 246, 254, 306
Zentralbibliothek Luzern 26/27, 30, 41, 43, 45

Map Production Berndtson & Berndtson

Cartographic Editor **Zoë Goodwin**
Production **Stuart A Everitt**
Design Consultant **Carlotta Junger**
Picture Research **Hilary Genin**

Index

"I was first drawn to the Insight Guides by the excellent "Nepal" volume. I can think of no book which so effectively captures the essence of a country. Out of these pages leaped the Nepal I know – the captivating charm of a people and their culture. I've since discovered and enjoyed the entire Insight Guide series. Each volume deals with a country in the same sensitive depth, which is nowhere more evident than in the superb photography."

Sir Edmund Hillary